PRIZEFIGHTING

# PRIZEFIGHTING

## An American History

Arne K. Lang

McFarland & Company, Inc., Publishers
*Jefferson, North Carolina, and London*

LIBRARY OF CONGRESS CATALOGUING-IN-PUBLICATION DATA

Lang, Arne K.
Prizefighting : an American history / Arne K. Lang.
p.    cm.
Includes bibliographical references and index.

ISBN 978-0-7864-3654-5
illustrated case binding : 50# alkaline paper ∞

1. Boxing — United States — History.  I. Title.
GV1125.L26  2008        796.830973 — dc22        2008010252

British Library cataloguing data are available

On the cover: (clockwise from left) Rocky Marciano (*Antiquities
of the Prize Ring*); Frank Klaus; and Jack Johnson (both from
the Library of Congress)

Manufactured in the United States of America

*McFarland & Company, Inc., Publishers
Box 611, Jefferson, North Carolina 28640
www.mcfarlandpub.com*

# Contents

# *Preface*

Putting together a history of something has a lot in common with an archaeological dig. One turns up artifacts that disabuse preconceptions. And when it's time to leave the excavation site, there's a sense of frustration knowing that a lot of good stuff remains buried.

This project wasn't born of a sudden flash of inspiration. However, there were two sparks that initiated the urge to tunnel deeper into the history of a sport that first captured my fancy as a young boy.

In 1992, I whiled away most of an afternoon listening to Marty Cohen edify a greenhorn boxing promoter, Alex Fried. Mr. Cohen's relaxed chalk talk, laden with peachy anecdotes, was delivered in the office of Mr. Fried's jewelry store in a rundown Las Vegas shopping center.

The late Mr. Cohen, a man with amazing recall, was well qualified to play the role of the mentor. He had soaked up a lot of knowledge in his 94 years. The late Mr. Fried was properly deferential, a concession to the age gap. "Kid Alex," as I whimsically called him, had only recently celebrated his 68th birthday.

Among the bromides that Mr. Cohen shared was that every boxing show, no matter the budgetary constraints, must include a title fight. As a gate-enhancer, the promise of lusty skirmishes was an insufficient enveiglement. The featured attraction had to be contrived into an event of importance, an event that someone would catalog for posterity.

This struck me as false-hearted. The cardboard container that Mr. Cohen brought with him housed a belt plated with the insignia of the International Boxing Council, a boutique organization. This oversized trinket would be bestowed upon the winner of the main go on Fried's forthcoming show at the Union Plaza Hotel. In return for a fee and other considerations, Cohen had authorized Fried to bill the match between Brian Lonon and Miguel Mercedes for the International Super Flyweight Championship.

As this project moved forward, it became obvious that the conventional wisdoms that Cohen espoused were deep-seated. The bare-knuckle era was saturated with title fights that lost their legitimacy when record-keepers cleaned up the clutter. One of the enduring myths is that there was a period when every weight class had an undisputed champion.

Somewhat later, my friend George Luckman gave me several boxes of magazines that he had accumulated. A hobbyist historian of boxing, recently widowed, George was downsizing as he prepared to take up residence in a smaller home in a neighboring state.

Far more interesting than the magazines were the IBRO newsletters scattered among them. They were chock-full of findings from dogged researchers who scrolled through old newspapers in search of lost fights.

Formed in 1982 with an initial cast of 15 members, IBRO, the International Boxing Research Organization, had been off my radar screen. I was aware that the records of many old fighters were incomplete and that some of their bouts were mislabeled, but the full extent of it was an eye-opener. Scouring the IBRO papers — simple mimeographed sheets, fastened with staples (we were still in the horse-and-buggy days of the Information Age) — aggravated a suspicion that many of the boxing books in my collection were splotched with half-truths or outright fabrications.

It soon became clear that most histories of boxing are bespattered with folklore. The good news is that there's been a distinct upgrade in the level of scholarship within just the last few years. Undoubtedly a large contributing factor is that it's become much easier to access primary sources. Even if a researcher finds it necessary to hunker down in the Library of Congress, he can do much of the preliminary work on the Internet, shortening his visit at a considerable savings in time and money.

Inevitably some falsehoods wormed their way into this book. Considering that the font of American boxing lore is literature veined with the elements of western dime novels, it would be arrogant to think otherwise. However, each time that I manicured this manuscript, I was alert to facts that I may have been too quick to swallow.

Every important fight is priced for betting purposes by the application of odds. The odds cut to the chase, eviscerating or reinforcing the hype and ultimately functioning as something of a shock meter when an upset occurs. Most boxing historians have treated the odds very loosely. Some writers have invented their own odds, imbuing upsets in storied fights with a higher shock quotient for dramatic effect.

In this book, there are frequent references to the odds. By and large, these have been culled from newspapers, a more trusted source than memoirs and other historical works. However, one should keep in mind that odds are fluid and vary somewhat from place to place. The odds cited in this book aren't necessarily more real than the odds cited elsewhere, save in the case of glaring discrepancies.

A number of individuals encouraged me in this venture. Top Rank matchmaker Bruce Trampler, a most interesting fellow, was a kindred soul. His colleague Lee Samuels lent a helping hand, as did Marc Ratner, Art Lurie, Harry Shaffer, Michael Ross, Larry Grossman, and Lisa Jacob. Shooting the breeze with Bill Graham transported me to a bygone era and gave me a greater appreciation of oral histories. Chris Wiatrowski and her associates on the second floor of the UNLV Lied Library were unfailingly polite and quick to guide me in the right direction whenever I was puzzled. Technical problems at my workstation were child's play for troubleshooter Shane Langvad.

I owe a big debt to those that contribute to boxing-related web sites, most notably BoxRec and Cyber Boxing Zone, the places that I visit most frequently. I know these individuals only by their names or signposts, but yet consider them my lodge brothers. I especially want to acknowledge those that have documented previously undocumented fights, a selfless labor with no payoff other than the satisfaction of setting the record straight. Whatever one's field of inquiry, I believe that setting the record straight is important.

The downside to writing a broad social history of boxing in a single volume is that one can't flesh out a full picture of any particular fighter, trainer, manager, organizer, policymaker, archivist, or image-maker. By necessity, many fighters of merit and men of influence don't even make the cut. Thankfully there are other writers giving these individuals their proper due. Like most books, this book is best understood as a companion piece.

I have a high regard for those that enter the squared circle and render an honest effort, no matter how brief or undistinguished their careers. One can rightfully snicker at the notion of an international title fight potted in a ballroom of an unfashionable hotel, but the match between Brian Lonon and Miguel Mercedes was a match between skilled boxers who were dedicated to their craft. It wasn't the cheesy belt that inspired them to fight to their limits to the full satisfaction of the thin crowd, but an innate integrity.

In the city of Las Vegas, where I have spent most of my adulthood, there are palookas that have enriched their lives through the vagary of luck. One may number me among this select few. I was very lucky to meet Kitt. The avouchment is hokey, but the sentiment is genuine: she is the undisputed champion of all the wives in the universe.

A.K.L.
Spring 2008

# CHAPTER 1

# Noblemen and Knockabouts

Scattered bands of men head out of London in the wee hours of the morning. Sharing a common destination, the travelers eventually close ranks. A fortunate few ride in horse-drawn carriages, but the majority are foot soldiers. It is a peculiar scene considering the hour, a surreptitious parade.

The congregants arrive at their destination shortly after dawn. They have come to a hollow on the outskirts of the city, a natural amphitheatre where the land tapers gradually to a clearing where the terrain is conveniently level. In the clearing, someone has strung thick strands of hemp between four corner posts, creating an enclosure that is perfectly square.

Under a shade tree, a man is filling wicker baskets with snacks for vendors. Under another tree, a steer is tethered to a stake. Elsewhere, crowds are forming around two men displaying their physiques. Attired in britches, they are naked above the waist save for the gaily-colored kerchiefs tied around their necks.

A shed sits at the intersection of well-worn footpaths. Men loiter about the shed and others gather in a queue at the counter. Inside the little plywood building, two men are transacting some sort of business. One takes money and issues a receipt, placing the money into a slot in a leather satchel, and the other makes a notation in a ledger.

In time, the bare-chested men and their aides are summoned to the roped enclosure. Those milling about surge forward, closing ranks again as they stake out patches of ground with unobstructed views. There is excitement in the air. The great prizefight is about to begin.

This is a book about the history of boxing. Sketches of great fighters and summaries of important ring battles are woven into the tapestry, but the emphasis is more on boxing as a marketplace and a representation of popular culture.

The marketplace includes those that bet on the outcome of fights. People of this disposition were there from the beginning. Indeed, the sport of prizefighting, in common with most spectator sports of old coinage, was conceived for the purpose of gambling. The earliest prizefights were supposedly held on feudal manors where Englishmen of noble lineage used pugilists as gambling pawns. The rules instituted to ensure that neither fighter had an unfair advantage were plumbed from the rules of cockfighting, an amusement inseparable from gambling. Bare-knuckle prizefighting reached its zenith at a time when gambling in England was a national obsession.

The promoters that founded sports leagues were pragmatic. Because betting was confined to adult males, they were quick to disassociate their product from gambling to draw a broader fan base. In time, many sports confederations adopted anti-gambling platforms. But boxing was a breed apart. In recent times, the sport has become more closely associated with gambling, turning back to its roots in a fashion. This is especially true in the United States, where the sport, to a large extent, derives its oxygen from the vaults of gambling casinos.

There are many reasons for this contravention. When boxing took the form of prizefighting, and for some years thereafter, the sport was held in contempt by ecclesiastic authorities. Early promoters made no attempt to recast the sport as a family amusement, as this would have provoked the abolitionists into greater spasms of outrage. At the professional level, the sport has never had an all-powerful overarching umbrella — a Vatican with the clout to bring about sweeping reforms. Then too, boxing predated mass leisure, and its roots were more firmly planted in the gambling subculture than the sports that arrived later. In merry old England, the folks that regularly attended prizefights were the same people one might encounter at a cockfight, a dogfight, or a horse race.

We began this chapter with a word painting meant to convey the impression of a sporting lithograph. There are clues in the "lithograph" that date the scene in the hollow to the early years of the nineteenth century.

Those in the cavalcade are traveling to an out-of-the-way venue under the cover of darkness. This suggests that they are participating in something unlawful, but that the chance of reprisal is minimal if they are discreet. The fight-goers are economically heterogeneous, consisting of men with the means to travel in carriages and others compelled to travel on foot. The presence of vendors and the display of livestock imbue the affair with a bit of a carnival atmosphere.

Gatherings of this sort were atypical during most of the bare-knuckle era, an era lasting roughly two hundred years, with the years 1690 and 1890 convenient, if imperfect, bookends. By and large, those entrusted with upholding the law took steps to prevent the formation of large gatherings, although exceptions were made for certain holidays and special occasions that came to be looked upon as safety valves for pent-up aggressions, and also for public hangings, which were viewed as educational. To circumvent police interference, prizefight organizers were frequently forced to play a cat-and-mouse game. A decoy fight might be arranged in hopes of tricking the authorities into following the wrong scent. A crowd unexpectedly large would worry the organizers, who might take the safe route and abort the match.

In the hollow, the *bruisers*, as they were commonly etymologized, are preparing to battle inside a roped enclosure. Up until roughly the midpoint of the eighteenth century, there was no such appurtenance. A line was scratched in the dirt with a sharp stick. The antagonists stood face-to-face on opposite sides of the scratch until commanded to begin or resume their affray. It was customary to draw a wide circle around the line to demarcate fair and foul territory. Spectators stood outside the circle, forming a *ring* around the fighters, a term that would remain part of the boxing lexicon. Rectangular "rings" made their first appearance in academies where sparring exhibitions were held. Sometimes organizers lugged these rings to an outdoor prizefight, but this was cumbersome, it required the services of set-up men, and the ring was liable to be reduced to rubble by an overzealous sheriff's posse.

In determining the age of the "lithograph," the betting shed is an artifact of enormous importance.

Prior to 1800, betting at prizefights, as at racetracks, was largely restricted to wealthy ringsiders who bet on credit with their peers or with the professional gamblers who were England's first bookmakers. Transactions between these "leviathans," commonly done with semaphores, are vividly described in the reports of early prizefights. But as crowds grew larger and more people escaped poverty, a separate market was established to accommodate the small bettor. This development coincided with the Regency Era of bare-knuckle prizefighting in England, so described because of the heavy patronage of aristocrats. A golden era, the Regency Era had a somewhat longer timeline than the interjacent Napoleonic Wars (1799–1815).

During this era, there were a tremendous number of fights in England, some of which could be fairly described as spectacles. An 1824 fight at the Worcester racecourse between Tom Spring and Irish Jack Langan purportedly attracted a crowd of 50,000. Half this number was probably closer to the true count, but this was still a remarkable turnout in a country where the total adult population was about nine million. Consider also that this was an outdoor fight in the chill of January at a venue a considerable distance from areas of dense population and that bad weather forced attendees to slough through mud several inches thick.

In this fight, the organizers hitched their promotion to a race meet, subletting a facility with an existing grandstand. This was brazen. Even during the Regency Era, venue-seekers were generally gypsylike, imbuing the sport with the flavor of a floating craps game. Leafing through the list of bare-knuckle battles, one is struck by the fact that locations were seldom re-employed. The major exception was Moulsey Hurst, a campground near the estate of the Duke of Clarence, later King William IV. An avid fight fan, the Duke attended many of the fights held there. In obeisance to him, the constabulary turned a blind eye.

Prizefighting in England had existed for more than a century before this great efflorescence. A seminal development was the opening of a School of Arms in London in 1719. Proprietor James Figg (1695–1734) came to be recognized as the foremost fighter in all of England, and his name would enter the history books as the first champion of boxing.

When he first started performing, James Figg was more of a juggler than a boxer. In his booth at the Southwark Fair — where he caught the attention of the Earl of Peterborough, who became his financial backer — Figg dazzled audiences with his dexterity, using swords, poles and cudgels (wooden clubs about the size of bowling pins) to candy-color his presentation. Remarkably nimble despite a thick torso, Figg had a natural talent for boxing and wrestling — prizefighting was a combination of both — and incorporated these crafts into the curriculum of his school.

To identify Figg as the original champion obscures a more salient fact about him — he spun prizefighting into a commercial amusement. A shrewd self-promoter, he derived his earnings from gate receipts rather than bets or a share of bets won by others. He reportedly never lost a fight, but it appears that most of his matches were with his students. An encounter with Ned Sutton on June 6, 1727, was a mixed competition on a stage with intermissions between the broadsword, bare-knuckle, and cudgeling segments. Although blood was drawn and Sutton reportedly had his knee broken, it's unclear whether Sutton went all out to win.

A 1733 show in the auditorium of Figg's academy featured a student named Bob Whitaker against an opponent identified as a Venetian gondolier. The mysterious stranger from Venice, described as a giant, was said to have left a trail of broken jaws on his journey to England.

Early in the bout, the gondolier heaved Whitaker completely off the stage, but Whitaker recovered and eventually forced his adversary to quit. The punch that turned the tide in favor of the house fighter was a blow to the pit of the stomach. It would be written that the punch "took all the conceit" out of the foreigner.

For this show, Figg reportedly jacked prices so high that the crowd consisted entirely of the well-born. Betting was reportedly heavy. However, while robust wagering is the best assurance that a fight will be contested on the level, a cynic can be forgiven for thinking that this set-to was nothing but a charade and that the story about it was warped through the prism of John Bull almightiness. Other competitions that Figg promoted were suspicious in their design. He sometimes spiced his shows with a battle royal featuring a man called Buckhorse, a brothel-born bruiser with a misshapen head.

The match between Whitaker and the big Venetian was a blueprint for matchmakers of later generations. The match had a defined hero and villain, a coloration it acquired by exploiting antagonisms rooted in ethnocentrism.

Figg's academy was an employment agency for fighters that toured the hinterland in traveling pugilistic shows. On these excursions, fighters had opportunities to earn side money by giving private lessons.

Fights packaged for fair-goers were usually bogus (more about that later), but a so-called booth fighter needed a strong constitution. Fairs were dangerous places, especially for outsiders. The Lansdowne Fair near the seaport city of Bristol was periodically shut down because of excessive hooliganism and too many complaints about swindles perpetrated by fairground workers. Lore has it that local toughs engaged in impromptu heats for the privilege of challenging booth fighters at the Donnybrook Fair near Dublin. This fair gave us the word "donnybrook," a term still used to describe a spirited melee.

James Figg has been called the Father of Pugilism, but one of his protégés, Jack Broughton, has a stronger claim to this honor because he popularized prizefighting as an art separate from fencing and related competitions. While Figg purportedly had nearly three hundred fights, there's no record that he ever participated in a fight to a finish, winner-take-all, for a big stake. Broughton had several encounters of this description. His pivotal fight was with George Taylor, who had assumed the day-to-day operations of Figg's academy. Broughton defeated Taylor in the ring and also in business. His establishment quickly superseded the Figg-Taylor archetype as the top school of its kind in London.

Broughton had built up his biceps as a "taxi driver" on the Thames. Fistfights were common among Thames watermen, a by-product of jostling for favorable locations. While still in his mid-teens, Broughton became the chief enforcer of the unwritten code that governed his chaotic workplace, a position automatically conferred on the toughest of the lot.

In February of 1741, Broughton accepted a challenge from a Yorkshire coachman named George Stevenson. After thirty-nine minutes of fierce fighting, Stevenson was so wasted that he subsequently died. Seized by great remorse, Broughton created a new set of rules to minimize the likelihood of another fatality. Drawn up in 1743, the rules were posted at the entrance to his academy.

Broughton's influence was so great his rules became the national model. Foremost was the prohibition against hitting a fighter when he was down. When a fighter fell or was knocked off his feet, he was entitled to a 30-second respite. The contest was terminated if he failed to beat the count, whereas previously a match lasted until one man surrendered or his aides made this decision for him. In the popular vernacular, a fighter unable to beat the count was "knocked out of time," an expression subsequently abbreviated to "knocked out."

The Duke of Cumberland was Broughton's benefactor. Unfortunately for him, he bought into the notion that his man was invincible. When Broughton's lengthy title reign was halted at the hands of Jack Slack, the Duke suffered a major financial reversal. Although Broughton was then 46 years of age, the Duke yet gave 10/1 odds. The turning point of the 14-minute fray was a punch that left Broughton temporarily blinded.

Slack had suffered a one-sided defeat in his previous bout. The more that he thought about it, the more the Duke of Cumberland became convinced that this bout was nothing more than a set-up. Deciding that he had been hornswoggled, he retaliated by closing down Broughton's academy and, for good measure, getting Parliament to pass an anti-prizefighting law. As for Broughton, his reputation remained solid. Upon his death, he was accorded his country's highest posthumous honor — burial in Westminster Abbey.

Jack Slack claimed to be the grandson of James Figg. Like his predecessors who claimed the championship of England, Slack was both a fighter and a fight organizer. Some of the matches he arranged were peculiar, notably a match between himself and a French giant imprinted with the name Monsieur Petit. Accounts of the 1754 tiff bear an uncanny

Jack Broughton and Jack Slack. *Collection of Pugilistica.com.*

resemblance to the fight at Figg's academy between Bob Whitaker and the Venetian gondolier. The seesaw struggle ended with a body punch that sent the mysterious foreigner running for the hills. England reigned supreme once again.

This match was staged near Slack's hometown of Norwich in a setting described as in the middle of nowhere. The anti-prizefighting law had caused bouts to be potted in more remote places. Concomitantly, dishonest fights became more frequent. The mere fact that prizefighting was illegal meant fewer reputable organizers and skewed the composition of fight crowds toward more of the lawless element. Disturbances outside the ring became more common.

The law had little impact on the fairgrounds boxing scene. If anything, it was a prod to more activity, swelling the number of boxing troupes. When there were few constraints to prizefighting, the community of booth fighters consisted mostly of up-and-comers, name fighters on the way down, and men of insufficient merit to attract sponsors. During periods when the sport was under siege, top-shelf fighters gravitated to the fair circuit.

Bare-knuckle fights had no time limit. A fight in a fairgrounds booth had a time ceiling. The timekeeper's clock moved fast or slow depending on the circumstance. Gloves were mandatory and challengers were customarily given gloves with more padding. All the subtle edges, which collectively amounted to a large advantage, were in favor of the booth fighter, consistent with the credo of the rascals that ran the games of chance at carnival midways: "Never give the sucker an even break." The fairgrounds boxing community — a subculture within a subculture — contributed almost nothing to the art or science of fighting but left a lasting legacy of guile. A large number of notable promoters paid their dues in the boondocks where chicanery was most rife.

The low point of prizefighting in England came in 1780 when an obscure Irish seaman named Duggan Fearns deposed title claimant Harry Sellers in a malodorous affair that was over in less than two minutes. Fearns vanished in the night, never to be heard from again. But there was a light at the end of the tunnel. Two charismatic fighters, Daniel Mendoza and John Jackson, would come to the fore by the end of the decade, revitalizing the sport.

Daniel Mendoza had a long and meritorious career. John Jackson had only three important bouts. However, Jackson was the superior fighter because of his greater strength and is a more important figure from a historical standpoint.

Most fighters worked at unskilled or semi-skilled trades. Butchers, coalheavers, and navvies (canal diggers) were overrepresented among the ranks of bare-knuckle pugilists. The son of a prominent building contractor, Jackson was cut from a more refined cloth. Reputedly a magnificent all-around athlete, he carried 200 pounds on a five-foot-eleven frame and was said to have the most perfectly formed physique in London.

While still in his early twenties, Jackson demonstrated his aptitude for business. Leasing a room in the fashionable Piccadilly district, he taught boxing to a wealthy clientele that included Lord Byron. According to Henry Miles, author of an 1863 treatise that covered 144 years of British boxing, Jackson's establishment became the "in spot" in London for aristocratic young men to work up a sweat. Like Jack Broughton before him, but on a much larger scale, John Jackson eliminated much of the stigma from pugilism. Attending prizefights again became a popular pastime of men high up in the social strata.

In his first prizefight, Jackson defeated a seasoned campaigner from Scotland, William Fewterell. He lost his second match when he slipped on wet grass and suffered a broken ankle. Six years later he returned to the ring to meet the celebrated Mendoza. Staged in a meadow near the town of Hornchurch on April 15, 1795, the fray lasted barely ten minutes but was full of goosebumps. Mendoza had the best of the early exchanges, but Jackson rallied and brought the fight to a swift conclusion after seizing Mendoza by the hair and pummeling him senseless with his free hand. This may not seem kosher, but it was perfectly legal (hair-pulling would not be outlawed until 1838). Other fighters shaved their heads bald to preclude this possibility. The vain Mendoza did not take this precaution and suffered the consequences.

Jackson quit the ring after defeating Mendoza to devote more time to his gym and related enterprises. He spearheaded the founding of the Pugilistic Club, an early attempt to regulate the sport under the jurisdiction of a central governing body. The men that competed in matches authorized by the Pugilistic Club were assured of compensation and reasonably assured of a fair shake. As the club's secretary, Jackson held the stakes, named the referee, and was the final arbiter in the event of a betting dispute. Jackson also came to be recognized as the "conscience" of the sport. He encouraged quicker stoppages of fights by cornermen, initiated the practice of collecting donations for a beaten fighter, and arranged numerous benefits for ex-prizefighters who had fallen on hard times or, as the case may be, for their widows.

Ten years after Jackson abdicated his title, John Gully got out of prison. Akin to Jackson, Gully would etch his name in British boxing lore, notwithstanding a defeat in one of the three important matches that summarized his brief career. And akin to Jackson, he became a very important person.

Gully was born in 1783 in a small inn near Bristol owned by his father. When his father died, he inherited the hostelry, which was bleeding money. Unable to pay his creditors, Gully was remanded to the King's Bench Prison, a minimum-security facility where detainees had opportunities to retire their debts.

As a boy working as an apprentice butcher, Gully had made the acquaintance of Henry Pearce, a prizefighter from Bristol known as the Game Chicken. On a trip to London, Pearce visited Gully and arranged a sparring match in the prison exercise yard. Gully acquitted himself remarkably well for a novice, landing several hard hits.

Fletcher Reid, an affluent sportsman with a keen eye for new talent, witnessed the encounter as a member of Pearce's traveling party. Reid arranged Gully's release and immediately put him into training. He then arranged a genuine prizefight between Gully and Pearce.

Gully had his moments after a slow start, but the Game Chicken was a glutton for punishment and prevailed in the end. Two months later, Pearce deposed title-holder Jem Belcher in a fight that turned Pearce's way when Belcher's vision became blurred in his one good eye. But Pearce was damaged too and vacated his newly won title, heeding the pleas of friends and relatives to leave the sport with his health intact.

With Pearce's retirement, Gully moved up in the pecking order. His next bout with Bob Gregson, the so-called Lancashire Giant, was billed for the championship. Standing six-foot-one and weighing 216 pounds, Gregson gave Gully a terrific battle before he succumbed from exhaustion. A second meeting was arranged, and this too was a hard fight for Gully, who came out on top after fifty-eight minutes.

A very active cornerman during the early years of his retirement, Gully was gradually drawn away from the world of the prize ring by an infatuation with horseracing. He became the foremost "penciler" in the betting ring and soon owned his own racing stable, a stable that produced two Epsom Derby winners. In time, he acquired substantial holdings in profitable coal mines and was elected to Parliament. His rags-to-riches saga personified the push toward democratization in a rigidly stratified society.

In 1820, twelve years after John Gully's last fight, eighteen of England's leading pugilists served as ushers at the coronation of George IV. Let's look closer at the forces that coalesced to bring prizefighting out of the closet (for a brief spell) to the point where bare-knuckle bruisers were even invited to a function at Westminster Hall, albeit with defined responsibilities.

Five years prior to the coronation of George IV, British and Prussian troops routed Napoleon's army at Waterloo in the last great battle of England's protracted war with France and her allies. Although prizefighting was unlawful, the professional fighting man, like the soldier, was admired because he objectified admired English virtues. Chief among these virtues was indomitableness. The most popular fighters were those that exhibited *bottom.* A fighter with bottom (the term was likely an abridgement of "bottomless courage") was capable of withstanding considerable punishment before gaining the upper hand. England's triumphs in war were attributed to this same steadfastness.

George IV developed an avid interest in the affairs of the ring. As the Prince of Wales, he helped arrange three fights at the Brighton racecourse in 1788, one of which ended in a fatality. His brothers the Duke of Clarence and Duke of York shared his passion. The Duke of York was such an ardent supporter that a fighter's fists came to be called "Dukes of York," a euphemism eventually shortened to Dukes and the derivation of the expression "put up your dukes."

The royal family was on the cutting edge of fashion. Their hobbies and peccadilloes were a topic of endless discussion and those that were affordable were copied by the masses. The allure of a prizefight was heightened by the patronage of royalty. Moreover, ordinary citizens could now attend these competitions with less fear of being accosted by magistrates or ruffians. A disturbance-free prizefight was still a rare event, but the appearance of royalty acted as a check on unruly behavior.

George IV ruled during a time of great social upheaval. The old order was crumbling in response to the redistribution of wealth. An associated development was a rise in literacy, with the consequence that newspapers gave more coverage to activities of interest to the common man. New periodicals were created expressly for people who thirsted to learn more about the athletes with whom they shared a similar background. Expanded coverage of sports in the popular press was also a stimulus to literacy. Sports were the leading topic of conversation at the pubs that were magnets to young men in the industrial labor force. A man who could read was better informed and his opinions commanded more respect.

The year 1793 saw the birth of *Sporting Magazine*, the first popular English periodical devoted entirely to sports. The inaugural issue contained reports of three recent prizefights and the first installment of a series of articles about the early days of the prize ring. The publication had a strong betting spin to it. Running competitions, equine and human, and blood sports — human, fowl, and mammal — were attracting a new breed of sportsman, the small-stakes punter.

Prizefighting was the most popular of the blood sports, but there was a great deal of overlap in their confraternities. Those caught up in one or more of these seductions came to be identified as members of *The Fancy*.[1]

The Fancy had no formal clubhouses. They gathered in pubs, especially those managed by ex-prizefighters. There they learned the latest gossip, debated the merits of those fated to meet in the next big match, and reminisced about great fighters and great fights of yesteryear. An evening of drinking and lively conversation would inevitably end with a "chaunt," a sing-song tribute to a fighting man, perhaps the evening's guest of honor, expressed in the form of a doggerel ballad.

During times when the upper class turned away from the prize ring, the ranks of the Fancy were swelled with proportionately more blacklegs. This element had seized control of the affairs of the ring after Jack Broughton left the scene and did so again near the end of George IV's reign when crowds at prizefights came to be bloated by petty thieves and bullies. It had seemed that an important precedent had been set with the Spring-Langan fight of 1824, perhaps the first big fight where gate-crashing was held to a minimum. However, five years later, a championship fight at Epsom Downs on the day following the Derby had to be postponed when the principals were arrested on the eve of the bout in a preemptive police raid. The Regency Era of bare-knuckle prizefighting ended not with a bang but a whimper.

Early in the reign of George IV, there was an organized effort to ban blood sports. The leader of this movement was Richard Martin, a Protestant Parliamentarian whose family controlled an immense estate in Ireland. In 1824, Martin, lampooned "Humanity Dick," founded the Society for the Prevention of Cruelty to Animals.

Chief among the goals of the nascent SPCA was the eradication of badger-baiting, bear-baiting, and dogfights. Prizefighting was vilified too because of the established link between it and blood sports in general. As the organization gained adherents, the counteroffensive against prizefighting picked up steam.[2]

Around this time, rural counties began to establish their own police forces and became less dependent on volunteer peacekeepers. With opposition to prizefighting more organized, the sport became more closely affiliated with the underworld. The tenor of the times was reflected in the adventures of William Thompson, an eccentric from Nottingham who adopted the ring name Bendigo.

Bendigo had three notable fights with Benjamin "Big Ben" Caunt. Each ended in a disqualification that precipitated a riot. By his own count, Bendigo was arrested twenty-eight times during his prizefighting career (1834–1850). During his last lock-up, he experienced an epiphany that led him to renounce prizefighting and embark on a new career as a Christian evangelist. He drew larger crowds to his revival tents than had witnessed all but a handful of his fights.

Although crowds thinned, occasionally a match was made that was so full of intrigue that the sporting crowd could talk of nothing else. Paramount in this regard was the April 17, 1860, bout between Tom Sayers and John C. Heenan.

An illiterate bricklayer who stood five-foot-eight and seldom weighed more than 150 pounds, Tom Sayers was exceedingly clever and full of bottom. He had an amazing knack for tapping into a reservoir of strength when it appeared that he was too arm-weary to strike a powerful blow. Sayers had lost an early fight against Nat Langham, a man of his own size, but had rebounded with several impressive wins, defeating such notables as "Slasher" Perry and Tom Paddock. Although Sayers built his reputation by defeating former champions past their prime, by the time the Heenan fight rolled around, he was being extolled as one of the best fighters in the history of his sport.

John C. Heenan was an inexperienced fighter with an unexceptional resume. Like John Gully before him, he had lost his first important engagement while impressing the cognoscenti with his toughness and gameness. When his conqueror retired rather than give him a second chance, Heenan became the top dog by default. But if Heenan was largely unproven, he was, in modern parlance, marketable. Carrying 195 pounds on a six-foot-two frame, he was an impressive physical specimen. His paramour, later his wife, was the voluptuous Adah Isaacs Menken, an internationally known performer who courted controversy with her scandalously immodest stage attire and libertine behavior. Foremost, Heenan was an American. It was a matter of considerable pride to the English that no one born outside the British Isles had ever toppled a native champion. Tom Sayers had the weight of England on his shoulders as he entered the ring against Heenan in the first fight extensively ballyhooed as a unification match between the champions of two continents.

After Queen Victoria ascended to the throne in 1837, there was a growing sentiment that working class leisure ought to be spiritually uplifting. Thomas Cook, a devoted Baptist, concurred in word and in deed. In 1841, Cook seized on the idea of chartering passenger trains to transport urban workers to Christian temperance rallies. In time, he became recognized as the man that invented the occupation of travel agent.

It no doubt pained Cook deeply when the railway companies with whom he had partnerships began accommodating prizefight promoters, an arrangement that girded the fugitive sport from sinking further into the abyss. It was difficult to herd people through an admission gate in a fight at an open field, but it was near impossible for would-be gatecrashers to cadge a free ride on a passenger train. Moreover, the gate money was more secure when collected by train agents. Trains were superior to river craft because they did not attract a flotilla of freeloaders and police were unable to give pursuit without commanding their own locomotive, an expense that could not be justified for a "victimless crime."

Two trains were chartered to take fight-goers to the Sayers-Heenan match. The two-and-a-half-hour excursion, destination unspecified, began at the London Bridge Station at 4:30 A.M. The trains chugged to a stop near the town of Farnborough, where advance men had pitched a ring near a remote section of rail. At 7:30 A.M., Sayers and Heenan made their entrance, prepared to do battle in what would ultimately be the last glorious bare-knuckle bout in England.

The fight was barely a minute old when Heenan was cut above his right eye. The first sight of blood always caused a buzz because "first blood" was a popular betting proposition. During Round 6, Sayers dislocated his right arm, but he continued to fight valiantly, turning

Heenan's face into a mask of blood with his unerring left jab. In Round 37, with both fighters a terrible mess and the outcome still in doubt, the American grabbed his British adversary in a chokehold and pinned his head over the top strand of ropes. In a matter of moments, Sayers' partisans stormed the ring, followed by a cordon of security guards who forced a cease-fire to prevent further trouble. The terrific battle — lasting two hours and twenty minutes — was declared a draw.

The promotion was successful on several fronts until things got out of hand. The aristocracy was present in droves. To find a crowd this elegant at a prizefight, one would have to go back more than thirty years. But the event also underscored the sorry state of pugilism. Although not intended as an amusement for the masses, the turnout was far below expectations and a far cry from the huge crowds during the Regency Era. Those old enough to remember rued the passing of the spectacles. As the Fancy feted the "co-champions" in an endless round of banquets, the clergy were denouncing the fight from their pulpits, demanding that the government put teeth in the anti-prizefighting statute. In 1868, Parliament approved a watered-down bill that forbade operators of railway companies from sharing in the proceeds of a prizefight.

The rules of prizefighting had not been significantly altered in more than a century. The backlash to the Sayers-Heenan fight sparked radical revisions. The reforms would modernize an ancient sport, but not without a hard struggle as the traditionalists balked at any attempt to "sissify" what they deemed to be England's manliest form of athletic endeavor. The fighter who might have benefited most from these revisions was Jem Mace, a brilliant ring technician. But Mace, the generally acknowledged champion of England from 1866 to 1882, was ahead of his time. To profit more fully from his fame, he went searching for greener pastures, exhibiting his know-how in the United States and Australia, where he schooled others with astonishing results.

Where Mace went, so shall we. England was the cradle of pugilism, but some of the best bare-knuckle fighters were baptized in her former colony, the emerging superpower of the Western Hemisphere known to her inhabitants as America.

# CHAPTER 2

# Diffusion to America

Immigrants and seamen introduced prizefighting to the United States. In the New World, the sport evolved along similar lines as in England. Depending on the social climate, prizefighting was tolerated or suppressed. Corruption and crowd control were constant problems. Of necessity, many matches were held at a secret rendezvous. American fight organizers, like their enterprising English counterparts, were quick to exploit new forms of transportation, chartering steamboats and trains for prizefight excursions, thereby making transit companies de facto partners in their promotions. Enthusiasm was fermented in the saloons, with saloon-keepers acting as stakes-holders and matchmakers. America would even produce its own John Gully, a man for whom bare-knuckle fighting was a doorway to politics and the bootstrap to becoming a giant of the turf. Although there were brief bursts of prosperity, bare-knuckle fighting in the U.S. never reached the giddy heights of England's Regency Era.

There is scattered evidence of prizefighting in the U.S. as early as the late eighteenth century, but it wasn't until 1824 that a prizefight was covered at length in a newspaper. On October 14, the *New York Emerald* sent a reporter to the southern tip of Brooklyn to cover the match between Dublin-born Ned Hammond and Liverpool-born George Kensett. The bout was deemed newsworthy because it played into a larger story — strife between rival ethnic groups. To an even greater extent than was true in England, this would become a recurrent theme in American prizefighting.

The Hammond-Kensett fight began at Coney Island, was interrupted by bayonet-wielding cavalrymen, and was then reconvened at Jamaica in the borough that came to be called Queens. The fight ended inconclusively and all bets were declared off.

The first prominent British fighter to have an important bout on American soil was James "Deaf" Burke. On May 6, 1836, Burke battled Samuel O'Rourke in a ring pitched at the convergence of two roads in a bayou swamp on the outskirts of New Orleans.

Called the "Deaf Un" because of a hearing impediment that affected his speech, Burke was recognized in many quarters as the champion of England. He had solidified that claim by outlasting an Irishman, Simon Byrne, in a long, drawn-out bout near Ascot in the spring of 1833. The contest was fatal for Byrne, who died two days afterward, and Burke thought it prudent to lay low in America until things cooled down. The first sight of him in the U.S. was in New York City, where he appeared on the stage in a series of "classical attitudes," essentially nothing more than poses inspired by statues of mythological gladiators.

Irish immigrants had a strong presence in New Orleans where they had been imported to build the levees and canals that made the Crescent City, however briefly, America's second-busiest shipping port. The fact that Burke had killed an Irishman in the ring was not lost on the Irish community of New Orleans. A former Thames waterman, the "Deaf Un" was also of Irish ancestry, but his speech impediment did not mask his thick Cockney accent. When he spoke disparagingly of O'Rourke, a former sparring partner, he may as well have been waving the Union Jack.

The match degenerated quickly into a riot. Partisans of the pugilists, fortified by cheap liquor, continued to battle long into the afternoon. Several pedestrians were attacked at random by roving bands, forcing the governor to call in the state militia.

Burke had one more fight in America before returning to England, where he died a penniless alcoholic at the age of thirty-four. In this bout, contested before an orderly crowd on Hart's Island, he defeated a fighter named Tom O'Donnell.

Until 1869, when it was put to use as a graveyard for the homeless and destitute (taking the name Potter's Field), Hart's Island in Long Island Sound was a lovers' hideaway and the preeminent venue for fight excursions that originated in New York City. It was there in 1842 that Yankee Sullivan defeated William Bell before an estimated six thousand onlookers.

Sullivan had a hazy background. Depending on the source, he was born James Ambrose in Ireland or Frank Murray in England. He reportedly served time in an Australian penal colony, arriving in New York as a stowaway. His choice of nickname broadened his appeal, and he is recognized in some boxing books as the first American bruiser to attract a following that extended beyond the pugilistic fraternity.

In Britain, renowned prizefighters invariably became saloonkeepers. With the money that he earned from prizefights and sparring exhibitions, Sullivan opened a saloon in the Bowery district of Manhattan that he named the Sawdust House. It was there that the articles were signed for the fateful fight between Christopher Lilly and Thomas McCoy.

Chris Lilly, an Englishman by birth, was twenty-three years of age and weighed 140 pounds fighting-trim. Thomas McCoy, born in Ireland, was three years younger and three pounds lighter. Old acquaintances whose relationship had soured, they had come to blows in a Bowery saloon. Their unpremeditated fight set the wheels in motion for a formal grudge match.

The bout was arranged for Tuesday, September 13, 1842.[1] The site chosen was an elevated clearing about a half-mile from the boat landing in the Hudson River town of Hastings, roughly twenty miles upstream from New York. An estimated two thousand people made the voyage, arriving in twelve separate vessels. The sum of their bets reportedly exceeded ten thousand dollars, a startling sum in an era when many unskilled laborers earned less than ten dollars a week.

The battle lasted 181 rounds spaced over two hours and 43 minutes. McCoy bled from the ear before the bout was two minutes old and his nose started bleeding shortly thereafter, but he continued to punch effectively. Slowly but surely, however, McCoy faded as Lilly's greater strength took its toll on him. After one hour, his face was disfigured. After two hours, he was conspicuously dragging. When he tottered to the scratch for the final time, helped along by a handler, his eyes were swollen shut and he was out on his feet — literally a walking dead man. By then, many in the crowd had turned away in disgust.

There was a firestorm of outrage when all the grisly details of the fatal fight surfaced in a round-by-round report that ran in the *Spirit of the Times*.[2] Lilly fled to England by way of Canada, returning after the furor subsided. Most of the accessories were eventually rounded up and brought to trial on charges ranging from disturbing the peace to manslaughter. Yankee Sullivan, who had seconded Lilly, was sentenced to two years in prison but served only a few months after cronies arranged a governor's pardon.

That prizefighting managed to survive at all in this hostile environment was partly due to "professors" who promoted the sport as a branch of gymnastics, imbuing fisticuffing with a veneer of respectability. William Fuller, a prizefighter with a high profile in his native England, opened a gym in New York City in 1820 and another in Charleston, South Carolina, in 1824. Modeled on John Jackson's school in London, Fuller's gyms catered mostly to men from the higher strata. He and others that opened boxing academies tended to shy away from taking the initiative in organizing prizefights, but often assisted in these promotions.

The anti-prizefighting movement might have ultimately succeeded if not for Ireland's potato famine. Between 1845 and 1850, the United States admitted almost one million immigrants, a disproportionate number from Ireland, where prizefighting had a strong tradition. Peasants in the old country, the immigrants swelled the slums of American cities, the men finding camaraderie in working-class saloons. In these establishments, a "bachelor subculture" emerged, characterized by a preoccupation with gambling and physical prowess. Elliott J. Gorn, a leading authority on nineteenth-century prizefighting in America, notes that unweddedness was so common in large cities at mid-century that 40 percent of males in the twenty-five to thirty-five year age group were single.[3] Unweddedness was especially pronounced among Irish immigrants, who would dominate pugilism in their new country well beyond the bare-knuckle era.

These forces exerted a powerful pull on Yankee Sullivan, who returned to the ring in 1847 after a five-year absence to meet Robert Caunt. He defeated Caunt in twelve minutes in a bout held near Harpers Ferry, Virginia, fueling interest in a bout between him and neighborhood rival Tom Hyer, a man touted as the most formidable fighter on either side of the Atlantic.

Roughly two years in the making, the Sullivan-Hyer bout was the first to transcend American working-class boundaries, commanding the attention of a wide spectrum of the population. To a larger extent than any preceding fight, it was a competition that exploited ethnic frictions. The nativist "Know-Nothing" movement was gaining steam. Adherents supported tighter restrictions on "aliens" (a Know-Nothing euphemism for Irish Catholics) by such measures as prohibiting foreign-born citizens from running for political office. Sympathizers were squarely behind Tom Hyer, a man of Dutch ancestry who was American by birth.

The buildup to the fight was terrific. After the Articles of Agreement were signed, each fighter raised five thousand dollars from the proceeds of sparring exhibitions, money placed in escrow for the winner. On the eve of the fight, the *Police Gazette* estimated the national wagering handle at three hundred thousand dollars. The *New York Sun* reported wagers as high as $40,000.

The site chosen was Poole's Island, a barren strip of marshland in Chesapeake Bay. In the days before the fight, contested on February 7, 1849, an estimated two thousand sportsmen arrived in Baltimore, the point of departure for the excursion boats. Law enforcement officials impressed a vessel to block the flotilla, forcing a last-minute change of plans. Many fight-goers were left in the lurch. Only several hundred succeeded in reaching the substitutional destination, a snow-covered bluff on the shores of Maryland's Kent County. Those that made it were unmolested, the pursuing police craft having run aground.

The buildup was far more exciting than the fight. Hyer was four inches taller, thirty pounds heavier, and almost six years younger. The long-simmering feud was resolved in his favor in less than seventeen minutes.

A brash young ruffian named John Morrisey pursued a match with Hyer, but Hyer refused to fight for less than a $10,000 stake and negotiations collapsed when it became obvious that Morrisey couldn't meet this demand. No one else could satisfy this stipulation either, which had the effect of sending Hyer off into retirement. Morrisey then set his sights on Yankee Sullivan. Although he was now forty years old and was coming off a poor effort, Sullivan was still judged to be a formidable entity.

Born in Tipperary County, Ireland, John Morrisey spent his formative years in hardscrabble Troy, New York, a city blighted by unemployment and labor strife during and after the completion of the Erie Canal. While still a young man, he acquired the nickname "Old Smoke." The origin was a bar brawl with a young tough named Tom McCann, a fracas that purportedly erupted over the affections of a prostitute. During the fight, Morrisey was badly burned by hot cinders from an overturned stove.

Morrisey succeeded in drawing Sullivan back into the ring. They met on September 1, 1853, in an abandoned brickyard in a place called Boston Corners. A hamlet on the Harlem Railroad line, Boston Corners was a natural destination for a prizefight because it was a no man's land where legal jurisdiction was unclear. Situated close to the borders of Connecticut, Massachusetts, and Vermont, the inhabitants eventually became citizens of New York.

Sullivan, the grizzled veteran, had the upper hand for most of the fight, but was disqualified for refusing to come up to scratch after the bout was interrupted by a free-for-all. Morrisey promptly declared himself the champion of America, a claim that acquired more legitimacy with each passing day, as Tom Hyer showed no inclination to contest it.

Morrisey soon cultivated an interest in politics, ingratiating himself to Fernando Wood, a rising star in Tammany Hall. In gratitude, Wood gave Morrisey the green light to run a faro bank free of police harassment. (A fast-moving card game that originated in France, faro was immensely popular in America in the decades before and after the Civil War, reaching its greatest popularity in the western states.) Operating a solitary faro bank was hardly a license to steal, but Morrisey was a sharp businessman.

Although he now had friends in high places, Morrisey was too truculent to roam far from the trenches where street gangs fought to establish a pecking order. In 1855, he was accused of masterminding the assassination of William Poole, a Know-Nothing bully who had left Morrisey in bad shape after an unceremonious fight on a pier. The charges were dropped for lack of evidence. Two years later, he was charged on three separate occasions with assault with intent to kill. Powerful friends interceded and he never spent a day in jail. Perhaps it was these incidents that prompted Morrisey to heed the challenge of John Camel Heenan and return to the ring. He needed a safe outlet for his volatile temper.

A raw but intuitive fighter, Heenan had worked in a steamship yard in Benecia, California, the derivation of his nickname "Benecia Boy." Stronger than Morrisey, he dominated the first few rounds, but "Old Smoke" eventually knocked him into a stupor. Contested on October 28, 1858, the bout was held on a spit of sand on the Canadian side of Lake Erie, a short boat ride from Erie, Pennsylvania, an important railroad hub.

The striking parallels between Morrisey and Heenan reveal a great deal about America's "culture of bruising." Born two years apart, both were sons of Irish immigrants. Both spent their boyhoods in Troy. Both ran off to California during the gold rush. Both became attached to Tammany Hall, serving the political machine as a shoulder-hitter (someone who intimidates people into voting for a specific candidate and disrupts the rallies of his opponents).

And both would go into the gambling business after quitting the ring, although Heenan, a great ladies' man, was less committed and would be involved on a far smaller scale.

By convention, when a champion retired the laurel passed to his most recent opponent, providing that the opponent had made a good show of it. Morrisey quit the ring after defeating Heenan, bumping the Benecia Boy up into his slot. In this particular case, there were few objections because Heenan could fairly attribute Morrisey's victory over him to the gods of fate. Heenan had drawn blood with the first serious punch that he threw and might have come out on top if not for a painful abscess on his leg that diminished his mobility. During the battle he broke his right hand on a ring post, a tide-turning mishap.

After his big bout in England with Tom Sayers, Heenan's career quickly fizzled. He hoped to resurrect it in a rematch with Morrisey, but "Old Smoke" was far too busy making money and networking with powerful politicians to entertain the thought of it.

Within five years after opening his faro bank, Morrisey had an interest in more than a dozen faro joints and was a major stockholder in the company that monopolized policy, the so-called numbers racket that provided the blueprint for state lotteries. He later built America's most opulent gambling emporium in Saratoga Springs, New York, and partnered in the opening of a thoroughbred racetrack there. Today it is the site of a flourishing summer meet and home to America's Horseracing Hall of Fame and Museum.

Morrisey entered the political arena in 1866, winning a seat in the U.S. House of Representatives, where he served two terms. At the time of his death, he was a New York state senator. He accomplished little as a public servant, but had an enormous impact on the

John "Old Smoke" Morrisey (left) and John C. Heenan square off at Long Point, Canada. *Antiquities of the Prize Ring.*

culture and presentation of casino gambling. Whereas most gamblers before him were grifters, Morrisey ran a clean operation that profited from the steadfast application of the law of large numbers. He donated heavily to local charities and municipal projects, and threw his weight behind political candidates favorably inclined toward gambling, or at least willing to condone it in return for a premium.

Morrisey's rags-to-riches saga was even more amazing than that of the British bruiser John Gully because he clawed his way up the ladder at a more furious clip. The pugnacious urchin from the streets of Troy was reportedly eighteen years of age when he learned to read and write, twenty-one when he engaged in his first prizefight in faraway California, twenty-two when he conquered Yankee Sullivan at Boston Corners, twenty-eight when he launched his faro operation, thirty-three when he built the Saratoga horseracing facility, and thirty-five when he was elected to Congress. A connoisseur of fine cigars, Morrisey died of an asthma attack in 1878 at the age of forty-seven and was buried in Troy.

After the Morrisey-Heenan match, boxing in America fell into a deeper rut. Concurrent with the situation in England, there were fewer fights but more disturbances, leading to harsher crackdowns. Sales of excursion tickets, a leading source of revenue, dwindled sharply because would-be fight-goers had no assurance that the promotion would come off at the appointed time and place. The major developments in the antebellum era were a westward drift and a reverse migration, with several prominent pugilists from the British Isles crossing the Atlantic in hopes of finding larger purses in America.

Although there was a westward drift after the Civil War, New York City remained the nerve center of prizefighting until the last decade of the century. No important bare-knuckle fight was ever held on the island of Manhattan, but it was there, in sparring matches, that unknown fighters built their reputations. New York was home to all the important sporting periodicals. A favorable mention in a magazine like the *Police Gazette* was a career-booster. With a fistful of favorable press clippings, a fighter was better able to find a sponsor and get to compete for higher stakes.

The fight crowd hung out in the Bowery, a district of lowbrow entertainment that reached its apex with the arrival of electric lights, a breakthrough in exterior ornamentation. The most popular gathering spot was Harry Hill's, a so-called concert saloon named for the proprietor. Akin to Yankee Sullivan's sawdust joint a generation earlier, Harry Hill's became America's leading pugilistic clearinghouse. Many important matches were hatched and hammered out here. Harry turned up at most of them, invariably in some official capacity.

Harry Hill's was the place where out-of-towners were most likely to be steered if they were in the mood for bawdy entertainment. On the stage, a Punch and Judy puppet show might be followed by a minstrel act and then a sparring exhibition. A small orchestra played dance music between sets. The ladies that sat at the bar were "working girls"—one purchased their companionship with overpriced and watered-down drinks—but Harry, a stickler for decorum, 86ed the most mercenary. A tourist traveling alone was relatively safe.

A horse trainer in his native England, Hill relished a good fight and was the equal of any of his bouncers, but he had a tender side. He fancied himself a poet and wrote odes to his mother. Harry was also deeply, if unconventionally, religious. On Sunday nights, his watering hole morphed into a temple of sacred music, an outrageous departure from the usual bill of fare. Harry Hill's was the site of the first revival service in the United States by the Salvation Army.

A section of Hill's establishment was reserved for friends of management, a kaleidoscope of politicians, entertainers, theatrical agents, bookmakers, songwriters, off-duty cops, and journalists. It was here in 1881 that a braggadocious up-and-comer named John L. Sullivan had his first brush with Richard K. Fox, the man that would make him a star.

John Lawrence Sullivan, born in 1858 to Irish immigrants in the Roxbury section of Boston, then had little recognition outside the pugilistic fraternity. Those that followed the sport closely knew him as an intriguing prospect with a few bright feathers in his cap. In a gloved exhibition in Boston with former middleweight champion Mike Donovan, Sullivan had clearly gotten the best of it. He had overpowered Professor John Donaldson, a respected name in the subculture. However, dozens of out-of-towners before Sullivan had hit the skids in Gotham.

Within days after arriving in New York, Sullivan secured an engagement at Harry Hill's with Steve Taylor, a mortician's helper who was expected to give him a good test. Sullivan demolished him in two rounds. Six weeks later, he was pitted against John Flood, a long-shoreman known to waterfront toughs as the Bull's Head Terror.

Sullivan vs. Flood was a prizefight in the classic sense, an outlaw match, winner-take-all, contested according to strict protocol in the glow of kerosene lamps on a barge in the Hudson River near Yonkers, outside the reach of the New York City Police Department. Sullivan won wire-to-wire in eight one-sided frames, dominating Flood so thoroughly that onlookers pronounced him a worthy opponent for Paddy Ryan, the man promoted by the apostolic *Police Gazette* as America's heavyweight champion. The Sullivan legend was born from this fight when an overstimulated reporter wrote that Flood's ankles swelled up from a punch that hit him in the neck.

Patrick "Paddy" Ryan was born in Ireland near the birthplace of John Morrisey. In common with Morrisey and John C. Heenan, he grew up in Troy, New York. Dubbed the Tro-jan Giant, Ryan stood six feet tall and weighed 190 pounds, about average for fighters of his era billed as giants; their numbers were legion.

Sullivan fought exhibitions in Chicago and Philadelphia to stir the pot for a bout with Ryan. Negotiations were slow because John L. had an aversion to fighting with bare knuckles, but he eventually gave in and agreed to fight without hand wrappings.

The organizers planted the match at Fort McComb, an abandoned Civil War fort on the outskirts of New Orleans, but Louisiana governor Samuel McEnery banned it, diverting it to Mississippi. On Tuesday, February 7, 1882, a ring was pitched on the expansive front lawn of a resort hotel in the seaside village of Pass Christian, where many Creole aristocrats had vacation homes. The turnout was easily the largest ever for a bare-knuckle fight on American soil, although nowhere near the reported twenty thousand. Many major metropolitan dailies assigned correspondents to cover the event, a milestone as most of these dailies had heretofore regarded a prizefight as news unfit to print. Among the correspondents was Jose Marti of the *New York Sun*, destined to become a martyr in his native Cuba.

An estimated $60,000 was wagered on the lawn in the hour preceding the start of the fight. The odds were tilted slightly toward Ryan, partly because he was more comfortable fighting without gloves. Ryan was expected to set a fast pace, skewing the odds on first blood and first knockdown somewhat more in his favor.

Ryan drew first blood, but John L. hurt him with the first punch that he threw, the effect of which Ryan likened to being speared by a telegraph pole. At the end of nine rounds, compressed into ten minutes and thirty seconds, Ryan's corner threw in the sponge. Sullivan's lusty triumph was an eye-opener that brought about a massive spike in his name recognition. The Boston Strong Boy (Sullivan's original nickname was the Highland Boy) immediately became the highest-paid fighter on the vaudeville circuit.[4]

Sullivan had only two pontific prizefights (meaning fights contested outdoors under London Prize Ring rules) during his decade-long title reign. On March 10, 1888, he opposed blustery British middleweight Charley Mitchell on the country estate of Baron Alphonse Rothschild in the parish of Chantilly on the outskirts of Paris. In their previous encounter at Madison Square Garden, ostensibly a sparring contest, Mitchell had scored a clean knockdown, but Sullivan knocked him silly before the police intervened. A second meeting was quickly arranged, but Sullivan showed up drunk complaining of an illness and the bout was canceled.

Sullivan was on a tour of England when the rematch was reborn, but fighting Mitchell there was impractical as both fighters were too recognizable. They were less conspicuous in France, but there were complications there too. The original venue was a small island in the Seine, but the fight was moved when it was learned that the gendarmes had been alerted.

On the day of the fight, the weather in Chantilly was miserable. An icy rain turned the turf into a quagmire. The fight was three hours and ten minutes of tedium. Mitchell stayed out of harm's way, constantly pivoting so that Sullivan's face was turned to the wind. The ground was slightly sloped, an advantage to the shiftier Englishman, who literally forced John L. to fight an uphill battle. Sullivan gave up the chase early on, standing like a fortress while imploring Mitchell to fight like a man. Finally everyone had had enough. Drawing the stakes was preferable to catching one's death of cold.

The semi-secret fight was fought under a canopy of chestnut trees behind a horse stable, an echo of early English prizefights on feudal manors. Perhaps forty people were in attendance, excluding those that worked on the estate and those that participated directly as cornermen or officials. They were the usual suspects — professional gamblers, wealthy sportsmen, and a smattering of journalists, one of whom, a cub reporter traveling with Sullivan on assignment for the *New York Tribune*, went on to become a legendary newspaperman. Arthur Brisbane covered this curio and later the first Dempsey-Tunney fight, an event that drew a somewhat larger turnout — approximately 120,000!

Sullivan's other outdoor prizefight was a less anachronistic promotion that pitted him against Jake Kilrain. Contested on a swelteringly hot July day in 1889, the match was held at a sawmill near Hattiesburg, Mississippi.

Born John Joseph Killion in the Greenpoint section of Brooklyn, Kilrain was said to have been a champion sculler before becoming a prizefighter. He wasn't in Sullivan's class, but many judged him to be a live underdog because he was a man of temperate habits who was constantly in training. The same could not be said of Sullivan, a bloated wreck of a man when he went into seclusion to train for the match. Incredibly, however, Sullivan showed up better prepared to survive a war of attrition, elevating his rejuvenator William Muldoon into a larger folk hero.

Muldoon was America's first celebrated Greco-Roman wrestler. A bodybuilder who looked every inch a gladiator, Muldoon had such an attractive physique that a publicity photo taken of him in 1887 was enlarged into a wall decoration to hang in the lobby of Madison Square Garden. Capitalizing on his growing fame, he opened "hygienic institutes" that were precursors of today's health and fitness centers. Iconic American musclemen of later vintage like Charles Atlas, Vic Tanny, Jack LaLanne, and Joe Gold all profited, at least indirectly, from his example.

Muldoon worked with a number of boxers and wrestlers, but usually in an adjunct capacity. He made an exception for Sullivan, putting all other obligations aside to give the fighter his full attention. In John L., he had the perfect guinea pig for testing his unconventional theories of physical conditioning.

Sullivan's health had deteriorated badly since his adventures in Europe. He listed his maladies as typhoid fever, gastric fever, inflamed bowels, heart trouble, liver disorder, and incipient paralysis (more than likely, all were manifestations of alcohol poisoning, magnified by hypochondria). Muldoon's prescription was rigorous exercise, abstention from cigars, healthy food, and proper sleep. To make certain that Sullivan was obedient, Muldoon took him to his vacation home in the upstate New York hamlet of Belfast and effectively placed him under house arrest.

Muldoon first had Sullivan walk the hills. Gradually the walks turned into jogs and then sprints. Whenever Sullivan would waver, Muldoon would speed up, goading his ward to keep pace. In the upstairs room that served as a gym, Sullivan shadowboxed, practiced his punches on light and heavy bags, and skipped rope, all the while wearing heavy woolens. Each session concluded with a friendly game of catch. The ball, filled with meal, weighed 20 pounds. A Muldoon invention, the contrivance came to be called a medicine ball.

Their relationship, cordial at best, became downright hostile as the fight drew near. Toward the end of his stay, Sullivan purportedly stopped talking to Muldoon altogether. Although they were literally inseparable, virtually Siamese twins, an entire day would pass with no verbal communication other than Muldoon's terse commands.

The trip to New Orleans, the gathering place for the final leg of the journey, consumed 54 hours. Worried that Sullivan would lose his edge, Muldoon arranged to have the train outfitted with an extra baggage car for punching bags and other apparatus so that Sullivan could continue his preparation. Muldoon also brought provisions so that Sullivan's dietary needs could be met without involving strangers. The only liquid that he allowed Sullivan to drink was bottled water from the well of his property in upstate New York. Right up to the day of the fight, Muldoon supervised every meal.

The Sullivan-Kilrain fight lasted two hours and 16 minutes. John L. had several anxious moments — at one point he began to vomit uncontrollably — but he somehow prevailed. The bout was inartistic and contested at a slow pace, but what Muldoon had accomplished was nothing short of miraculous.

Arrested for violating Mississippi's anti-prizefighting law, Muldoon wrangled a $250 settlement whereas Sullivan was fined $1000. The disparity fueled speculation that Muldoon had cut a deal with the prosecution to testify against Sullivan in the event that he was made to stand trial. Sullivan swallowed the scuttlebutt. Having acknowledged his gratitude to Muldoon, he now swore that he would beat him to a pulp when their paths crossed again. Muldoon replied in kind, drafting an open letter to Sullivan that appeared on the editorial page of the *New York World*. Translated into the vernacular, Muldoon's letter carried this message: "Come and get me, asshole."[5]

There was rampant speculation that they would settle their feud in the ring. Had it come to pass, it would have been a huge attraction. Sullivan had venom in his fists, but Muldoon was a boa constrictor who could squeeze a man limp with his arms or his legs. In untangling boxing and wrestling, the Queensberry revolution instigated a long-lasting barbershop debate of whether a champion boxer would beat a champion wrestler, a debate that raged especially fierce when Muldoon and Sullivan were exchanging brickbats. According to Muldoon biographer Edward Van Every, a prominent turf accountant seized the opportunity for free publicity by posting odds on the outcome. The unidentified pricemaker made Sullivan a 3/1 favorite.[6] (Their feud withered with the mellowing of age; Mulldoon was an honorary pallbearer at John L.'s funeral.)

No American trainer ever got as much mileage from a single fight as did Muldoon, who went on to chair the New York Boxing Commission. More than anyone since England's celebrated Captain Barclay Allardyce, Muldoon illustrated that boxing is a team sport.

Many large-circulation papers carried the result of the Sullivan-Kilrain fight on the front page. The battle was America's last great bare-knuckle prizefight.

Sullivan's next big fight was not merely another chapter in his career, but a watershed event. His September 7, 1892, title defense against James J. Corbett was in the broadest sense a ceremonial ribbon-cutting, a promotion that signified the completion of the reconstruction of pugilism, a project begun more than two decades earlier by reformers in England.

# CHAPTER 3

# The Queensberry Antiseptic

Prizefighting was in great disfavor in 1865, the year that former classmates John Graham Chambers and John Sholto Douglas founded an amateur boxing club in London. Skullduggery was rampant, bouts were frequently decided on technicalities, and disturbances outside the ring were commonplace. Some young men of high status were drawn to prizefights because of these factors. For them, a walk on the wild side was a rite of passage. But the allure of a prizefight diminished as the danger increased and one's lineage became less consequential in forestalling an arrest.

Outwardly the problem wasn't prizefighting per se, but extrinsic factors such as insufficient security at ringside. However, Chambers took the position that the malignancy originated inside the ropes. In his mind, expanding the rulebook to cover unexpected contingencies was as foolish as adding more stories to a tower built on a faulty foundation. It was time to implode the edifice and start from scratch.

Some prizefights were heart-pulsingly brutal. The 1791 bout between Tom Johnson and Benjamin Brain lasted only twenty minutes, but the battle was so ferocious that neither man fully recovered. Johnson never fought again, Brain only once more, and both were dead within four years. More often than not, however, prizefights were disappointingly dull, at least for long stretches. It was against the rules for a fighter to fall of his own volition, but few referees had the courage to enforce this rule stringently. Fighters would fall down to clear the cobwebs or simply to catch their breath. This was smart strategy and the spectators did not universally object.

By all indications, it was Chambers's idea to create a new template, but he readily deflected the credit to his partner because he knew that his innovations stood little chance of gaining a fast toehold without the backing of a man with the clout that accrued from a noble pedigree. His partner John Sholto Douglas was just such a man. Related collaterally to the Douglas clan of Scotland, noted for producing military leaders, Douglas was the Marquess of Queensberry.[1]

The new rules outlawed wrestling. The mediocre boxer with a mean cross-buttocks throw had no future in the Queensberry game. A round of boxing under Queensberry rules lasted three minutes, whereas previously rounds were of indeterminate length. The interim between rounds was elongated from a half-minute (perhaps with an eight-second grace period) to a full minute. And, most notably, padded gloves were mandatory. The weight wasn't specified, but it was stipulated that they had to be fresh out of the box to prevent tampering.

Previous amendments to Jack Broughton's rules were subtle. Many dealt with extraneous issues, such as the 1853 addendum that stipulated that bets were still on if a bout was interrupted and moved to a new location. The Queensberry revisions were radical, fomenting heated debates. The asphyxiation of antiquarian prizefighting was a slow and fitful process.

### LONDON PRIZE RING RULES vs. QUEENSBERRY RULES
### MAIN POINTS OF DEPARTURE

| | London Prize Ring | Queensberry |
|---|---|---|
| DURATION OF A ROUND | Indeterminate | Three minutes |
| INTERVAL BETWEEN ROUNDS | 30–38 seconds | 60 seconds |
| METHOD OF SCORING A KNOCKDOWN | Punch or wrestling throw | Punch only, throw abolished |
| MAXIMUM RECUPERATION TIME FOR A FIGHTER SUFFERING A KNOCKDOWN | 30–38 seconds | 10 seconds |
| HAND COVERING | None, bare knuckles | Padded gloves [2] |

The old guard resisted the reforms because they ruptured the sport's historical continuity, attenuating the thread from James Figg to champions not yet born. Devotees of bare-knuckle prizefighting were disquieted by the prospect of obsolescence. Some of them viewed the reforms as an emasculation of prizefighting that might lead to England's becoming less formidable in times of war. But the traditionalists were fighting an uphill battle. Pugilism was in dire straits and major reforms were needed to make the sport palatable to the masses, in particular the burgeoning middle class.

As the Queensberry rules became standard, organizers of bare-knuckle fights broadened their search for hospitable venues to include locales outside England. One of the last important bare-knuckle fights on the European continent was held on December 23, 1889, at a private estate in Bruges, Belgium. The principals, Jem Smith and Frank Slavin, were each allotted an equal number of admission-passes for their supporters, but a mob loyal to Smith invaded the premises and ignited a riot that spilled into the commercial district of the town. Smith's notoriously hot-tempered backer Squire Abingdon Baird was subsequently blackballed from the Pelican Club, the de facto sponsor of the event.

The bylaws of the Pelican Club were modeled on those of the Jockey Club, but the club was less exclusive and the members had a broader range of sporting interests.

The club was the progenitor of the National Sporting Club, which was formed in 1891 by Pelican Club defectors disassociating from the raffish element. In their eyes, the disturbance at Bruges demonstrated once again that the gatekeepers at boxing venues needed to be more vigilant in locking out the riffraff. The National Sporting Club succeeded where the Pelican Club had failed by restricting access to men schooled to behave like gentlemen.

Situated in London's fashionable Covent Garden district, the exclusive men's club was a venue for boxing, but also a seat of power where the Queensberry style of milling became firmly stamped. Members typically dined on the premises before going downstairs to the basement theater. Non-members were admitted by invitation only. Evening attire was required and spectators were discouraged from shouting. Initially no provision was made for the press, but eventually a section on the rear stage was blocked off for journalists. It was unthinkable that a sportswriter would get to sit up front where he might block the view of a dues-paying aristocrat.

A separate code of etiquette governed the boxers and their seconds, foremost strict obedience to the referee, who performed his duties in formal attire from a perch outside the ropes. Competitors were expected to accept winning or losing with stoic detachment and bow to the audience before leaving the ring. Fighters were allowed to watch other bouts on the program but were required to remain silent and were segregated in their own pen. Never was fisticuffing so dignified.

All matches at the National Sporting Club were scheduled for a specified number of rounds — 20 rounds maximum for championship fights. This innovation had important legal ramifications. Gloved fights did not always circumvent anti-prizefighting statutes, but the gray area was less gray when gloved matches were limited to a predetermined length, a characteristic of amateur boxing. In courtrooms on both sides of the Atlantic, sharp lawyers would successfully challenge anti-prizefighting ordinances on the technicality that such laws were aimed specifically at fights "to a finish." Initially a fight was declared a draw if it went the full distance, but pressure from bookmakers led to a change whereby the bout was awarded to the fighter who had subjectively scored the most points. The sole arbiter was the referee. His decision was final.

For a young British boxer, the club at 43 King Street was a temple. Established fighters commanded higher purses fighting elsewhere, but nothing matched the prestige of fighting for a British championship belt. (The NSC offered belts in seven weight classes, a number that increased to eight with the addition of a lightheavyweight category in 1914.) A champion who successfully defended the belt three times was entitled to a modest pension paid annually. For more than a decade, all British title fights were held at the National Sporting Club. The crowds were not large — the theatre held thirteen hundred people, including standees — but maintaining order was never a problem. And bit by bit, boxing distanced itself from its unsavory past and came to be referenced again as England's national sport.

Boxing at the National Sporting Club was never entirely free of reproach. There were four ring fatalities between 1897 and 1901, resulting in arrests, trials, and acquittals. These tragedies stimulated new reforms, notably a rule that empowered the referee to stop a contest whenever he saw fit. Knockouts now came in two varieties — *KOs,* where a boxer knocked off his feet failed to beat the ten-count, and *TKOs,* where a bout was halted to keep a fighter from taking more punishment.

Co-founder Arthur "Peggy" Bettinson ran the day-to-day affairs of the club and approved the matches. The autocratic Bettinson, a former amateur lightweight champion, personally recruited the original members, the list of which reportedly included every prominent bookmaker in London. Several respected British boxing historians have asserted that the primary purpose of the NSC was to provide a "curb" for bet-takers and their most prized clients, but this narrow viewpoint demeans the fabulous Earl of Lonsdale, the club's president and most charismatic personality. Lonsdale was not merely the face of the National Sporting Club, but the high priest of all the caretakers of England's sporting heritage.

Christened Hugh Cecil Lowther, the fifth Earl of Lonsdale was thirty-three years old when he was appointed the president of the National Sporting Club, a position he held for nearly four decades. At the time of his appointment, he was already famous for his athletic exploits and his extravagant lifestyle. A man of limitless energy and an inveterate joiner, Lowther — Lord Lonsdale to his contemporaries — initiated the Royal International Horse Show, and was chief steward of the Jockey Club and president of the Arsenal Football Association. He also belonged to the Scottish Naturalist Society, under whose auspices he led an expedition to the Arctic.

To suggest that the Earl of Lonsdale was rich is an understatement. He owned approximately one hundred thousand acres of land. From his coal mines, iron factories, and farms he derived an enormous income. He owned two castles, his own train, and two steam-powered yachts. Lowther Castle, his main abode, reportedly had 365 rooms.

Lonsdale wasn't expected to inherit the family estate, but those that outranked him in the line of succession predeceased him. Because the likelihood of this happenstance was so faint, he wasn't pressed to acquire the requisite grooming. He briefly attended Eton, but there is no evidence that he ever read a book. Nor was he embarrassed by his educational shortcomings. "I can tell everything I want to know about a man by the way he sits on his horse," he once said.[3]

The one thing that was not neglected was his physical education. As a boy, he took boxing lessons from Jem Mace. He reportedly had the tools to become a champion, but veered off into other areas of competition. He was an outstanding runner, courser, equestrian, and — with the advent of the automobile — car racer. According to his biographer, Donald Sutherland, one could have built a very strong case that the Earl of Lonsdale was the greatest hunter of all time.

What seized the public, however, was not the substance but the style. Because he had no children, Lonsdale saw no reason why he shouldn't live like an emperor. He maintained a large household staff and private orchestra, tipped generously, and spent a fortune on cigars customized to his specifications by the most expensive tobacconist in London. He dressed his servants in blue-trimmed yellow jackets, white beaver hats, and white buckskin trousers. His luxury cars had chrome made of genuine silver. Each was painted the brightest yellow, earning him the sobriquet "The Yellow Earl."

Ostentation invites ridicule, but Lord Lonsdale was immensely popular because he was yet considered a man of the people. His circle of friends included many commoners, toward whom he was sometimes belligerent, but without an air of condescension. "His passionate devotion to sport, his sure instinct for fair play, and his showman's love of the spectacular," says Sutherland, "earned him the adulation of the crowds.... As he drove down the course at Ascot behind the King, his yellow carriages and liveried postillions making the Royal carriages almost drab by comparison, the cheers for 'Lordy' were at least as loud and prolonged as they were for the Monarch."

(A revealing anecdote about Lonsdale appears in Gerald Walter's obscure biography of ring announcer Patsy Hagate. On fight nights at the National Sporting Club, the street outside would be jammed with a motley throng. One evening, Lonsdale had his wallet lifted as he alighted from his Rolls Royce. The product of a tough neighborhood, Hagate was sent out of the building to snoop around on the remote chance that he might be able to identify the pickpocket. Spying a man in the street that he knew to be a gang leader, Hagate begged him to assist in the recovery of the stolen item. "Don't do that to him, of all people," implored the ring announcer. "You know what he's done for boxing. There are plenty of other mugs to do without picking on a grand sportsman like him." As Hagate waited, the gang leader wandered off to retrieve the wallet. When he returned it, the contents were undisturbed.)[4]

Lonsdale was not a betting man in the conventional sense and his relationship with the club's bookmakers was often strained. In the boxing theatre, he forcefully discouraged indiscreet transactions. But Lonsdale was not averse to betting on himself. A famous carriage race with his rival Lord Shrewsberry was contested for the meager sum of one hundred pounds. Lonsdale invested more than sixty times his potential winnings in equipment and commemorated his triumph by commissioning an engraver to manufacture a set of expensive prints.

In his golden years, Lonsdale came to be regarded as something of a blowhard, but the public remained very fond of him. When the *Sporting Chronicle* conceived the idea of honoring him by building an old folks' home for former athletes, donations to the Lonsdale Convalescent Home for Incapacitated Sportsmen exceeded the target goal. When he finally consented to write his memoirs, they were serialized in a Sunday newspaper supplement and ran for twenty-eight weeks, boosting the paper's circulation to an all-time high. The royalties were useful in maintaining his facade. It was understood that Lonsdale had more money than he could ever possibly spend, but this understanding underestimated the man. Two years before his death at age eighty-six, he bottomed out and was compelled to vacate the impending ruin that was Lowther Castle.

The doors to the National Sporting Club were shuttered in 1928, sixteen years before Lonsdale's death. As a promotional group, the NSC had encountered early opposition. Legal concessions won by the club's attorneys were ironically most beneficial to wildcat promoters with access to larger sporting venues. The prestige value of NSC belts eroded as England became less rigidly stratified. In terms of dictating national pugilistic policy, however, the club remained supreme. Oligarchic rule of British boxing would continue without interruption as the torch was passed to the British Boxing Board of Control.

The National Sporting Club was a monument to the Queensberry revolution, a struggle in which many individuals played prominent roles. The contribution of John Graham Chambers was seminal, but his alterations would not have become sacrosanct without enforcers and popularizers. Lord Lonsdale, above all others, was the requisite enforcer. Foremost among the popularizers was John L. Sullivan. When he embraced the Queensberry anatomic, it was the best possible endorsement. As much as anyone, Sullivan was responsible for the eradication of bare-knuckle pugilism.

# CHAPTER 4

# The Watershed Fight

John L. Sullivan was a remarkably adaptable fighter. He fought bare-fisted and with an assortment of hand wrappings that ran the gamut from skin-tight riding gloves to heavily padded "pillows." He fought on wood, on canvas, on sod as hard as clay, and on damp sod matted with sawdust to improve traction. He fought matches restricted to four three-minute rounds, and bouts that lasted more than two hours. He fought before crowds that numbered a few dozen and he fought before large multitudes. He fought bouts where a quick knockout was prudent to hasten his getaway, and he fought bouts where prominent members of the judiciary sat in choice ringside seats. A few of Sullivan's opponents lasted the duration in bouts recorded as draws, but no man could honestly claim to have defeated him in his first 14 years in the prize ring.

Sullivan fought sporadically after 1886 — four significant bouts in six years — but he was constantly in the public eye. As would be true of the vainglorious Muhammad Ali, he inspired both adoration and loathing. And like Ali and other controversial athletes with long and productive careers, he gradually shifted public opinion in his favor so that, toward the end of his career, many of his most ardent fans were people that had bad-mouthed him.

Because he was larger than life, Sullivan held a special fascination for America's youth. Adolescent boys admired his anti-establishment spirit. Antipathy toward Sullivan by their elders was mitigated by his gregarious nature, his staunch patriotism, and his lack of pretense. When he bellowed: "I can lick any sonufabitch in the house," he did it with honest conviction. Like the future baseball icon Babe Ruth, his gluttony added to his mystique.

Some said that John L. was a throwback, a relentless fighting machine in the best tradition of the great bare-knuckle fighters of olden times. This was an oversentimentalized opinion. Sullivan sometimes fought with uncommon fury, but his style wasn't vastly different from that of the "textbook fighters" who were more deliberate in their approach. Because he was seldom in proper condition, it behooved him to dispatch his foes as quickly as possible. Moreover, the unnamed antiquarian prizefighters with whom he was compared were hardly the typhoons that they were depicted to be.

It was true, however, that Sullivan's style and temperament seemed better suited to the contumacious world of the London Prize Ring, where fighters could literally throw their weight around. When he turned his back on that world by embracing the Queensberry antiseptic, his behavior was incongruent with his persona. Jem Mace was the first prominent prizefighter to express a strong preference for the Queensberry alternative, but Mace was a much smaller man and his endorsement carried less weight because it was thought to be motivated by self-interest. Sullivan, much more than Mace, sold the traditionalists on the idea that the so-called Manly Art could survive — nay, thrive — with radical reforms.

While it was less obvious, Sullivan was also motivated by self-interest. Boxing with gloves reduced his legal expenses. Two days after his fight with Jake Kilrain, he was pinched in Nashville on a Mississippi bench warrant and briefly confined to a cell that he described as a rat pen. This indignity hardened his resolve to abandon the bare-knuckle style of prizefighting. This was no great sacrifice because his defeat of Kilrain gave him the leverage to dictate the terms of future engagements. When he decided that the time was ripe for another title defense, he issued a challenge to all the leading Caucasian fighters in a rambling letter to the Associated Press. The *defi*, which stipulated a purse of $25,000, winner-take-all, plus an additional $10,000 side bet, ran unedited and unabridged in dozens of newspapers.

It was speculated that Sullivan was bluffing; that he had lost his stomach for fighting and priced himself out of the market to deflect accusations that he was afraid to meet some of the young scrappers that coveted his title. But this was no bluff and all systems were "go" when Jim Corbett's booking agent, theatrical producer William A. Brady, raised the side stake and placed it in escrow.

In later years, Brady admitted that he had no great conviction that Corbett would win. He had commissioned a play for Corbett called *Gentleman Jack*. News of the impending fight would boost Corbett's box office appeal. If Corbett defeated Sullivan, that would be icing on the cake.

There wasn't much doubt about where the Sullivan-Corbett fight would be held. In March of 1890, chartered athletic clubs in New Orleans were granted permission to stage gloved matches. Keen competition between rival clubs resulted in higher purse offerings. Within a matter of months, the Crescent City leapfrogged San Francisco as the prime destination for important fights. The newly elected mayor, John Fitzpatrick, was closely aligned with prizefight organizers. This was the same John Fitzpatrick who had refereed the Sullivan-Kilrain match, thumbing his nose at the laws of neighboring Mississippi. That promotion had been kicked out of New Orleans, but it was a bare-knuckle event that pushed the envelope too far.

A well-rounded athlete, James J. Corbett might have had a nice baseball career.[1] He concentrated on boxing after winning an amateur tournament sponsored by San Francisco's Olympic Club. He was so impressive that he was given what amounted to a scholarship, having full run of the facility while continuing his lessons under the club's English immigrant boxing instructor, "Professor" William Watson. When Watson resigned, Corbett was tabbed to succeed him at a salary sufficiently large to enable him to quit his job as a bank teller. He was then only twenty-one years of age.

In 1889, Corbett was pitted against Joe Choynski, the leading light of the rival Golden Gate Athletic Club. Choynski, who acquired the nickname Chrysanthemum Joe, had a queer pedigree for a fighting man. His father, a rare book dealer who had taken some classes at Yale, was the West Coast correspondent of America's leading Yiddish newspaper. But Choynski was a rough customer who might have been champion if blessed with a larger physical frame. Although two years younger than Corbett and approximately 20 pounds lighter, the 165-pound Choynski was yet favored to defeat Corbett because of his greater experience.

Held in the loft of a barn in Fairfax, California, the fight was interrupted by the police after four torrid rounds. After a five-day recess, Corbett and Choynski went at it again on a barge anchored near the Benecia shipyards. Contested with two-ounce gloves under London

Prize Ring rules, the fight, which commenced shortly after daybreak, lasted one hour and 40 minutes before Corbett closed the curtain with a clean knockout punch. Six weeks later, there was yet a third meeting, a four-round contest under amateur rules. Fighting with a fractured left hand, Corbett outhustled Choynski and was declared the victor on points.

In 1890, Corbett enhanced his national profile by winning a lopsided decision over Jake Kilrain in New Orleans. The 6-round bout was contested for a winner-take-all purse of $3500. Eight weeks later, at a theater in Brooklyn, he won a 4-round decision over Dominick McCaffrey, one of the few men to last the distance with John L. Sullivan. By now, Corbett had Sullivan squarely in his sights, but the public remained largely indifferent. To make the match attractive, the San Francisco upstart would need to prove his mettle against another fighter of high repute in a match free of the scent of a sparring exhibition. No one was more qualified than Peter Jackson, an enormously gifted fighter who had added value because of his skin color. Jackson was black.

Sullivan had made it known that he would never risk his title against a man of color. This was rationalized as respect for social norms. Mixed matches were viewed, with some justification, as the stovewood of racial discord. The main drawback to drawing the color line was that one could not change his mind without being branded a hypocrite. But there were many who felt that John L. drew the line only because he wanted no part of Peter Jackson. It would be a great feather in Corbett's cap if he were able to defeat him.

Staged before an overflow crowd in the auditorium of San Francisco's California Athletic Club, Corbett vs. Jackson was a fight to the finish that turned into an inconclusive four-hour marathon. Corbett more than held his own in a performance that legitimated him as a worthy opponent for Sullivan.

After securing the match, the New Orleans Olympic Club built a 10,000-seat double-decked arena illuminated with electric lights. "Appetizer" fights were presented on each of the two days preceding the battle, creating a three-day pugilistic festival billed as the "Carnival of Champions." In the lid-lifter, lightweight titlist Jack McAuliffe scored a 15th round knockout over Billy Myer. The next night, George Dixon retained his featherweight belt, disposing of Jack Skelly in eight lopsided rounds. That set the stage for the grand finale, the biggest boxing match ever up to that time as measured by international curiosity.

An overflow crowd witnessed the sorry spectacle. One month removed from his thirty-fourth birthday, Sullivan was hardly ancient by modern standards, but he was a shell of the fighter he had been. After two uneventful rounds, Corbett broke his nose with the first clean punch of the

An undated publicity photograph of James J. Corbett. "Gentleman Jim" was credited with lifting prizefighting out of the gutter. *Antiquities of the Prize Ring.*

fight. The ensuing rounds were dreary. Sullivan pressed forward, but Corbett, a trim 178 pounds, easily dodged his punches. The end came in Round 21 when the predictably fresher Corbett landed a straight right hand that put John L. down for the count.

When his senses had cleared, Sullivan made a short speech, thanking the crowd for their support and saying that if he had to lose his title, he was thankful that it came at the hands of a fellow American. Many in the audience were visibly moved by his grace. Although Sullivan earned nothing for his labors, the sting would be cushioned by proceeds from numerous benefits, the first of which in New York City netted him six thousand dollars.

Sullivan was the sentimental favorite, save perhaps in San Francisco, where the telegraphed report of the fight drew a big crowd to the Orpheum Theatre. However, the tumbling odds bore witness that most big gamblers had their coin on Gentleman Jim.

Sullivan opened a 4/1 favorite. The action was light until two days before the fight when a trickle of money on the challenger opened the floodgates. Near post time, poolrooms in New Orleans and San Francisco were offering odds on Sullivan as low as 6/5. Fortunately for the bet-takers, Sullivan was the overwhelming choice of those that knotted the three title fights into a parlay.

The biggest winners were those with a financial stake in the future of the sport. The old guard derided "Pompadour Jim" as a dancing master, but the time was ripe for John L. to pass the torch to a better role model. A heavy layer of sugarcoating was required for Corbett to pass muster as a man of refinement, but a gullible public swallowed the confection and bought into the notion that Corbett's victory demonstrated the superiority of "science" over brute force.

The Olympic Club released figures showing a net profit of $42,650 for the three-day event. Equally impressive was the ancillary trickle-down, an eye-opener for movers and shakers in communities with foundering economies. The "conventioneers" created few problems for the police and, more importantly, they were big spenders.

# CHAPTER 5

# The Boomtown Boxing Phenomenon

The demise of New Orleans as a national boxing center was hastened by a ring fatality. In December of 1894, a new athletic club staged a three-day boxing carnival, a less extravagant parrotry of the great carnival of 1892. The middle bout pitted local hero Andy Bowen against George Lavigne in a bout billed for the American Lightweight Title. One of the most popular athletes in the city, Bowen had achieved national recognition the previous year for competing in a fight that lasted more than seven hours by some accounts, the longest gloved match on record.

Bowen fell into a coma after getting knocked out in the eighteenth round and was carted unconscious to his home, where he died the next day. The Attorney General of Louisiana promptly scuttled the big wind-up, a welterweight championship bout between Tommy Ryan and Nonpareil Jack Dempsey. Benefits for Bowen's widow were held in cities as far distant from New Orleans as Buffalo.

Protocol dictated that organizers lay low after a ring fatality. Prizefighting in the Crescent City did not cease completely during this dutiful cease-fire, but major promotional groups downgraded their presentations and imposed a longer moratorium after yet another ring fatality in 1897.

Barred from competing in New Orleans, Ryan and Dempsey were accommodated in Coney Island. The seaside retreat would enjoy a brief run of important fights, succeeding New Orleans as the top boxing venue east of San Francisco. The new welterweight division took root in Coney Island, the site of three championship matches between 1893 and 1895. On a sultry June night in 1899, the heavyweight championship changed hands as Jim Jeffries kayoed Bob Fitzsimmons. Jeffries successfully defended his title three times in the next eleven months, twice at the Coney Island velodrome where he defeated Fitzsimmons.

Boxing was a natural fit for Coney Island. A family amusement complex by day and an adult playground by night, commercial Coney Island was inspired partly by Manhattan's decadent Bowery and partly by English village fairs. The community had such a seamy underbelly that it was epithetized "Sodom by the Sea." A 1906 article in *Outing*, a popular travel magazine oriented around camping, warned readers that Coney Island was "the meeting place of the city's petty thieves, the touts from the neighboring racetracks and the lowest strata of the metropolis."

The spirit of Coney Island did not pervade the borough to which it had become politically attached. A city with a high concentration of Protestant churches, Brooklyn was a world apart. A highly organized campaign by Brooklyn clergymen was largely responsible for the passage of the Lewis Law, which made boxing a more shadowy industry by prohibiting private clubs from charging an admission fee. Promoters seeking freedom from these sorts of constraints found the fewest firewalls in emerging settlements that were magnets to adventurous young men.

Bare-knuckle bruisers like Yankee Sullivan and John Morrisey traveled by freighter to northern California during the great mid-century gold rush. The next generation came west by rail, utilizing new rail tributaries to find opportunities in emerging settlements that were off the main lines. Big-name fighters arrived with the advent of the mobile hotels named for the leading manufacturer, George W. Pullman. A detached Pullman car could sit stationary on a sidetrack, providing a place to sleep, relax, conduct business, and entertain guests, a boon to tourism in places with few accommodations for out-of-towners. Advances in the efficiency and comforts of land transportation were the main stimuli to the phase of American prizefighting that Barton W. Currie dubbed the "boomtown boxing phenomenon."

One of the first boomtown fights covered in rich detail was staged on January 2, 1865, in the territory of Montana in the mountain town of Virginia City. The setting was an auditorium built by James A. Nelson as an annex to his gambling saloon. The wooden structure boasted graded rows of seats for unobstructed viewing.

The fight pitted local saloonkeeper Con Orem against an Irish immigrant farmer named Hugh O'Neil. A stocky teetotaler from Ohio, Orem had fought newsworthy fights in eastern rings and was fairly regarded as the best pound-for-pound fighter in the vast inland empire of the Pacific Northwest. Although outweighed by nearly 50 pounds, he retained his unofficial diadem as the territorial champion in a brutal three-hour match punctuated by 91 falls.

The Orem-O'Neil fight is of passing interest because of the financial arrangement. The stake was $1000 in gold, winner-take-all, with both fighters sharing equally in the gate receipts. Nelson, who refereed the contest, absorbed the entire cost, gambling that the event would significantly inflate the *drop* at his faro tables. In this regard, he was almost a full century ahead of the Las Vegas casino operators that embraced boxing as a "loss leader."

A less fragile community than ephemeral Virginia City, nearby Butte boomed with the discovery of gold and copper deposits and became the epicenter of prizefighting in Montana. John L. Sullivan made two appearances in Butte during an 1883–84 tour. On the second stopover, a fighter in his troupe, middleweight title claimant Peter McCoy, arranged a winner-take-all match with a local sportsman named Duncan McDonald. Contested on the grounds of a quarter-horse track, the contest came to be hailed as the most thrilling prizefight ever waged in the area. The victorious McCoy delayed his leave-taking to attend the obligatory benefit for the man he defeated.

At its zenith, Butte was as important as Denver. More like Pittsburgh than a western frontier town, Butte at the turn of the century boasted a 12,000-seat outdoor stadium advertised as the largest amphitheatre in the country. It was the site of several fights and boxing carnivals with national significance. A bit later, Butte's 10,000-seat Holland Arena, an indoor, steam-heated facility, hosted fights on a semi-regular basis that featured some of the best-known boxers here and abroad.

With its large population, Butte produced a large pool of homegrown fighters. The 1903 Butte boxing carnival — three fights spaced across five days during the weeklong celebration of the Fourth of July — pitted local products against three reigning world champions, respectively Tommy Ryan (middleweight), Barbados Joe Walcott (welterweight) and Joe Gans (lightweight). The locals were overmatched and each contest ended quickly. Later that same year, Jack Munroe — the "Miner's Pride from Butte, Montana" — restored the prestige that was lost by upsetting Sailor Tom Sharkey. Munroe had enhanced his profile with a strong showing against barnstorming heavyweight champion James J. Jeffries in a four-round sparring exhibition that turned into a bloody slugfest. This bout occurred on December 30, 1902, at Butte's Broadway Opera House.

Munroe's popularity was fleeting — it evaporated following a dismal performance in a world title bout with Jeffries — but no fighter domiciled in Butte ever achieved the same degree of popularity among the locals, not even Stanley Ketchel.

A teenage runaway from a foster home in Grand Rapids, Michigan (his parents were reportedly murdered in separate incidents), Ketchel, born Stanislaus Kiecal, was working as a busboy in a Butte café when he had his first documented bout in 1904. After forging a 35–2–3 record in Montana rings, he headed off to California, where he came under the wing of well-connected Willus Britt and his sometimes partner in the management of prizefighters, the noted raconteur Wilson Mizner.

Billed as the "Fighting Hobo" in his first California fights, Ketchel shed the tag on the way to becoming a two-time middleweight champion. A hell-for-leather fighter, he was built into a big attraction by stories about him that played off fanciful images of life in western boomtowns. It was undoubtedly Mizner who cooked up the hokum that Ketchel put scores of roughnecks to sleep while taking on all comers as the house fighter at a Butte vaudeville palace. Mizner wrote Ketchel's epitaph with a quip that elevated the erstwhile Butte busboy into a legend following his murder at age 24 by a cuckolded farm hand at a ranch in Missouri. Informed that Ketchel was in the morgue, Mizner said, "Somebody start counting to ten; he'll get up."

Denver, a vacation getaway for miners from surrounding communities in the vein of San Francisco, was a lively fight town. In 1901, the aforementioned Sharkey established a boxers' cooperative in the Mile High City. At various times, his troupe included Jack Johnson, Young Corbett II, Abe Attell, and George Dixon, each a former, current, or future world champion. The unruly mining camps of Creede and Cripple Creek figured prominently in the itinerary of the ensemble.

During Sharkey's stay, Denver was home to two of America's most romanticized lawmen, Wyatt Earp and Bat Masterson. Restless men with chaotic work histories, they were already famous for their exploits as peace officers in Dodge City, Kansas, and Tombstone, Arizona. In Denver, Earp briefly resided in Masterson's boardinghouse while supporting himself as a faro dealer. We will encounter both again in this book, as both were connected to the world of the prize ring. A versatile fight functionary and later a newspaper correspondent, Masterson was deeply involved in the pugilistic subculture. Wyatt Earp's participation was haphazard, but five years prior to turning up in Denver he was at the center of a great ring controversy.

An earlier center of frontier pugilism was Virginia City in the territory of Nevada. The discovery of silver in 1859 in the spectacularly fertile Comstock Lode started a rush of immigration that echoed the California gold rush a decade earlier.

The first reported prizefight in the territory of Nevada was held at the Washoe Racetrack on September 22, 1863. Pitting Tom Daly and Billy McGrath, it ended in favor of McGrath when Daly was disqualified for hitting him while he was down. This ignited a gun battle between two individuals identified as professional gamblers, a fellow named Lazarus and a fellow named Maldonado. When the smoke cleared, Maldonado and two horses were dead. The story appeared in the local daily, the *Territorial Enterprise*, and was picked up by the *New York Graphic*, a paper that frequently titillated its readers with stories about woolly goings-on out west.[1]

While hardly indigenous to western boomtowns, gloved matches were frequently part of the bill at opera houses. Some of these matches were genuine, if only by accident, but the majority were choreographed as carefully as a dance routine. On April 23, 1864, the program at Sutliffe's Opera House in Virginia City consisted of a play written to commemorate the tercentenary of the birth of William Shakespeare, a gymnastic exhibition by a troupe of French acrobats, and a boxing contest — a most eclectic tripleheader indeed.

When the economy worsened in Virginia City, civic leaders were inspired to pursue prizefights of national importance. The celebrated Corbett-Fitzsimmons fight of 1897 landed in the general vicinity, ending a bizarre two-year odyssey for steadfast promoter Dan A. Stuart, who stayed the course through multiple postponements and an intervening promotion for Bob Fitzsimmons that brought new meaning to the term Murphy's Law.

## Dan Stuart's Wayward Merry-Go-Round

*Gentleman Jack*, the play crafted as a starring vehicle for James J. Corbett, was enormously successful. In the play, based loosely on his life, Corbett was transformed into a Princeton man. An elegant dresser off the stage, Corbett became more like his character and reporters took to calling him "Gentleman Jim." He had no financial need to continue fighting, but an occasional ring engagement was advantageous as the buildup kept his name in the news.

Sixteen months after defeating John L. Sullivan, Corbett defended his title against Charley Mitchell. Staged in Jacksonville, Florida, under the auspices of the Duval County Athletic Club, the promotion was beset by all sorts of legal complications. The governor of Florida attempted to suspend passenger train service to Jacksonville on the days preceding and following the agreed-upon date. His efforts were futile, and the same might be said of Mitchell. Gentleman Jim knocked him out in the third round and then sat on the title, content to make his living as a stage performer until the right offer materialized.

When Corbett defeated Sullivan, the reigning middleweight champion was Bob Fitzsimmons. While he too was a relatively inactive champion, his star grew brighter and he came to be seen as Corbett's most worthy challenger. A Cornishman by birth who spent his formative years in New Zealand and Australia, Fitzsimmons had come to prominence in Sydney when that city boasted the highest concentration of talented boxers in the world.

Part of his appeal was that he was an odd-looking specimen. Nicknamed Ruby Robert because of his reddish hair and complexion, Fitzsimmons was prematurely balding, knock-kneed, and covered with freckles. He had long, spindly legs and a slender waist, but his shoulders were broad and his upper torso was muscular. Some writers likened his appearance to that of a kangaroo on stilts. The public was also fascinated by his domestic situation. When he married contortionist Rose Julian in 1893, his former wife married his new brother-in-law, Martin Julian. Marrying into a family with a circus background was advantageous for a man in his profession. Martin Julian, his business agent, always made certain that the handsomely illustrated pamphlet that detailed Fitzsimmons' ring triumphs was widely distributed for sale in every community where he appeared.

Stuart conceived the Corbett-Fitzsimmons fight as the climax to a five-day fistic carnival to coincide with the 1895 Texas State Fair and Exposition. The 52,000-seat stadium he planned to build on the outskirts of Dallas would comfortably house the entire population of the city. He had the backing to pull it off and was in the process of clearing the land when the state legislature convened in a special session ordered by the governor for the purpose of passing a stricter anti-prizefighting law.

The impetus for the special session was a manifesto drafted by the Dallas Pastors' Association. The clergymen condemned prizefighting as inherently brutal and characterized prizefight patrons as the sorts of people that triggered epidemics of crime and debauchery. Frustrated by the abolitionists, Stuart switched the locale to Hot Springs, Arkansas, a city in need of an economic boost after a smallpox epidemic kept many regular visitors away the previous year. The local organizers were so bullish on the fight that they threatened to surround the town with vigilantes if the governor made good on his threat to call in the state militia, but they backed down when the anti-prizefighting lobby turned up the volume.

At this point, Corbett took his hat out of the ring, but Stuart was determined to have his prizefight. He matched Fitzsimmons with Peter Maher, slating the fight for February 15, 1896, in El Paso. As Corbett had been inactive for almost two years, Stuart billed the contest for the vacant heavyweight championship of the world.

Peter Maher, who first achieved notice in his native Ireland by winning a tournament sponsored by the Guinness brewery, was one of a long list of fighters that rose to prominence on the strength of a terrific left hook. In an earlier meeting with Fitzsimmons in New Orleans, he uncorked his signature punch moments before the end of the opening round. Virtually out on his feet, Fitzsimmons recovered and beat him to a pulp, but by some accounts the first frame ended prematurely, gypping the Irishman of his rightful due. Maher rebounded with a spate of quick knockouts, most notably a 63-second blowout of Steve O'Donnell, a fighter from Australia that Corbett considered his heir apparent.[2]

El Paso had fewer hotel rooms than Hot Springs, but the border city had a superior transportation network — America's second transcontinental railroad link was laid there in 1881— and there were more diversions for the sporting crowd. Bullfighting and quarter-horse racing were available in neighboring Juarez and cockfights were plentiful on both sides of the border.

In El Paso, however, the backlash was no less severe. The impending battle roused local clergymen into forming an alliance for the purpose of cleaning up the city. The El Paso Ministerial Alliance drafted a paper condemning the fight while calling for the enforcement of the Sunday closing law and a crackdown on wideopen gambling and prostitution.

Bob Fitzsimmons circa 1898. The first man to achieve recognition as a champion in three weight classes, Fitzsimmons had a punch that was likened to the kick of a mule. *Antiquities of the Prize Ring.*

In the face of this pressure, Stuart axed the preliminary bouts, reducing his fistic carnival to a one-act affair. The location of the fight was kept secret. One rumor that gained currency was that the fight would be held some 800 miles from El Paso on a barge off Galveston in the Gulf of Mexico. The promotion suffered another blow when Maher was stricken with an eye infection from blowing sand at his training camp, forcing a six-day postponement. Many would-be fight-goers left El Paso at this point, including a number of notables whose presence would have lent glamour to the event. Among the defectors were John L. Sullivan and his old rival Paddy Ryan, who were appearing in a play at an opera house.

Stuart eventually succeeded in pulling off the fight, frustrating a battalion of Texas Rangers mobilized to stop it. The battleground was a flat stretch of sand on the Mexico side of a narrow tributary of the Rio Grande, a short walk via a pontoon bridge from the isolated settlement of Langtry. A refueling stop on the Southern Pacific railroad line, Langtry was home to the Jersey Lilly, an establishment that was part saloon and part convenience store but better known as a courtroom, taking on that dimension whenever the proprietor, Judge Roy Bean, was of a mind to throw his weight around. Lore has it that Bean was responsible for rescuing the fight, working out some deal whereby the start of the contest would be delayed on some pretext so that fight-goers would spend more money in his clip joint.

Only a few hundred dogged fight fans made the journey. What unfolded was hardly worth the trouble. The odds (5/4 Fitzsimmons at El Paso's Oriental Turf Exchange) portended a highly competitive fight, but Fitz made short work of Maher, knocking him out before the bout was two minutes old. More unsettling from Stuart's standpoint, the skies darkened right before the onset of the bout and the camera crew was unable to capture a clear image of the combatants. It redounded well on Stuart, however, that Fitzsimmons' check in the amount of ten thousand dollars cleared the bank the next day, dispelling concerns that the novice promoter was a fly-by-night. Corbett came back to the fold and preparations began anew for the fight between him and Ruby Robert.

After his travails in Texas and Arkansas, Stuart must have been dumbfounded at the warm welcome he received in Nevada. With the state mired in a mining slump, Governor Reinhold Sadler was enthusiastically supportive. Nevada had an anti-prizefighting law, but Sadler promised to get it rescinded as soon as Corbett and Fitzsimmons were locked into iron-clad contracts.

Stuart was courted by delegations from Virginia City, Carson City, and Reno. The Virginia City contingent submitted the most meticulous proposal. It included a list of every lodging place, including private homes with extra beds. For good measure, the proposal denigrated the secondary accommodations in Reno and Carson City as consisting mostly of barns, sheds, and outhouses.[3] But the boosters in Carson City were more willing to defray the cost of building a stadium and the fight was ultimately staged there on St. Patrick's Day, March 17, 1897.

As the event drew near, a fusillade of vitriol was heaped on the denizens of Nevada, foretokening a greater storm of disapprobation when Reno hosted a more controversial fight thirteen years later. The *New Haven Register* published excerpts of "Nevada's Shame and Disgrace," a sermon written by the Reverend Levi Gilbert of the First Methodist Church of Cleveland:

> This state, this deserted mining camp, revives brutality by an exhibit that must make its Indians and Chinamen wonder at Christianity.... Such exhibitions promote criminality by feeding the bestial in man. They debauch the public ideal. Such men sell their bodies for merchandise as surely as the harlots in the street.[4]

Preparations for the fight included a roundup of hobos and vagrants. February 17 was a particularly fruitful day. Fourteen undesirables were exported to Reno in a boxcar of a train filled with hogs and cattle. But those coming to Carson City, in the estimation of *Gold Hill News* reporter Alf Doten, were low-lifes too. "Each train brings fresh cursedness ... pugs, gamblers, reporters, scrubs, whores, and sons of bitches in plenty," wrote Doten in an entry in his diary dated two days before the battle.[5]

Prominent among the early arrivals was Jim Corbett's brother Harry, who set up a faro game in an unused rear room of a saloon and opened a book on the fight. Harry established his sibling a 5/3 favorite, but was compelled to shorten the price to 5/4. It was surmised that much of the Fitz money was bet by transplanted Cornishmen who were well represented in the mining camps of the area.

As the day of reckoning approached, it became obvious that the crowd would fall far below expectations. Only in San Francisco was there sufficient demand for special rail excursions. Stuart had arranged "appetizer fights" for the two days preceding the battle, but changed his plans and ran all three bouts on the same day. The main bout went first, commencing shortly after 11 A.M. so that it would receive the most sunlight. The arena was then cleared so that a separate admission could be charged for the "post-liminaries." The first of the two matches, a featherweight contest between Dal Hawkins and Martin Flaherty, was over so quick that it was distorted into the shortest fight in history. Fifty-four seconds into the bout, Hawkins landed a sleeper.

The attendance was estimated at seven thousand. The medium-priced seats went largely unsold, leaving a naked swath in the middle of the 17,000-seat stadium. While the atmosphere was hardly electric, those in attendance witnessed an excellent fight. Corbett knocked Fitzsimmons down for a 9-count in the sixth round with a punch that split the bridge of the Cornishman's nose. The odds at ringside rose to 3/1 Corbett, an adjustment that would have been more severe if Fitzsimmons was not renowned for his powers of recuperation. From this point, Corbett's punches gradually lost steam but he was still ahead entering the 14th round when Fitzsimmons paralyzed him with a punch that landed in the pit of the stomach, slightly to the right of his heart. When Corbett came to his senses, he flew into a rage and had to be restrained. This lagniappe was quelled quickly, but not before Mrs. Fitzsimmons climbed through the ropes to join the fray. She was allowed to sit at ringside, unlike others of her gender, who were only admitted if in the company of a male escort and then remanded to a separate ladies-only section that reporters dubbed the Birds' Nest.

Old newspapers contain scant information about Dan A. Stuart the man, who fell quickly out of the public eye. It was said that he was born in Vermont and was a descendent of the Stuart clan of Scotland. It is known that he had an interest in poolrooms in Dallas and Fort Worth and that he was an accomplished poker player. He was clearly a wonderful salesman, but a poor judge of prevailing attitudes and the clout of special interest groups. This blind spot led to the Fitzsimmons-Maher catastrophe, and his reputation as a Pollyanna took another hit when Fitzsimmons vs. Corbett played to a sea of empty seats. However, there was a method to his madness and Stuart had the last laugh. The first independent promoter to make a big score from a prizefight film, Stuart profited so handsomely that Corbett sued him on the grounds that he didn't receive his fair share of the royalties.

The invention of the kinetoscope in 1894 gave birth to the motion picture industry. Within a few short years, kinetoscope parlors (peephole movie arcades) were all the rage. As film historian Charles Musser notes, exhibitors were quick to exploit a fascination with taboo subjects. Hoochie-coochie girls (go-go dancers) were a hot item. Prizefighters — also outside the pale of polite society — were likewise a natural kinetoscope "product."

Jim Corbett's mock prizefight with Peter Courtney, filmed in 1895 in Thomas Edison's studio, was the first boxing match to receive extensive viewing. In short order, the technology of filmmaking advanced to where it was possible to film a genuine prizefight without benefit of a black backdrop and adapt it for viewing on a larger screen. The novelty of motion pictures accounted in part for the popularity of the Corbett-Fitzsimmons fight film, but those that profited owed a huge debt to San Francisco physician John W. Gardner, who identified Fitzsimmons' paralyzing blow as a "solar plexus punch," a label that had a vaguely astrological connotation. The camera supposedly captured images that were not visible to the naked eye. People were curious to see the mysterious punch — even when it became known by word of mouth that the camera did not capture the moment clearly.

As for Stuart's collaborators in Carson City, they appear to have benefited also, despite the poor turnout. The fight-goers were free spenders, as evident by this entry in Alf Doten's diary: "Monte Carlo in full blast, more gambling games than anybody ever saw — like California in '49." The landmark fight did more than put Nevada on the international boxing map. It irrigated the soil, begetting other important prizefights in the so-called Battle-Born State.

Several important fighters, notably Philadelphia Jack O'Brien and Joe Choynski, braved the arduous journey to the Klondike. During the great gold rush, Dawson City emerged as the leading hive of prizefighting activity in the Yukon. The top fisticuffer among those with mining claims was globetrotter Frank Slavin, one of several Australian fighters to hutch in Alaska as their careers were winding down.

Slavin purportedly participated in several brutal mills, but his 1901 tiff with tyro Frank Gotch at a Dawson City opera house was likely more typical of his Klondike boxing phase. After tattooing Gotch with an assortment of punches, Slavin let down his guard, whereupon Gotch clamped him in a half nelson and tossed him out of the ring, ending the bout. Gotch would go on to become America's most celebrated wrestler.

Spurned in their bid to land the Corbett-Fitzsimmons fight, organizers in Reno gained a small measure of atonement by landing the 1905 heavyweight championship fight between Marvin Hart and Jack Root. The title had become vacant when Jim Jeffries retired. Jeffries refereed the contest, which ended in favor of Hart, who put Root down for the count in the 12th stanza.

Sportswriter Lou Houseman, Root's manager, told his readers that Reno was intoxicated with excitement. In truth, the promotion was a foreseeable flop. In the days leading up to the fight, reporters spent more time tailing Jeffries than harvesting information about the contestants, neither of whom was considered fit to inherit the mantle of heavyweight champion, in particular Root, who weighed only 170 pounds. According to a story in the *Reno Evening Gazette*, Big Jeff had a bad run during a dusk-to-dawn session at a craps table. He was reportedly five thousand dollars lighter when he returned to his Los Angeles alfalfa farm.

Jeffries' retirement stripped the sport of its most magnetic personality. Attention shifted to the lightweight division, home to a slew of talented and colorful fighters. The man with the strongest claim to the title was Joe Gans, an African American fighter from Baltimore with more than one hundred wins to his credit. Early into his career, Gans had picked up the nickname "Old Master." A bigger attraction was Battling Nelson, the Durable Dane. Born Oscar Nielsen in Copenhagen, Nelson, a southpaw, had captured the imagination of the public with his aggressive style, tremendous stamina, a well-deserved reputation for bending the rules, and attestations in stories about him that his head was as hard as concrete.

When it was announced that Gans and Nelson had agreed to fight on Labor Day, 1906, the most astonishing of the particulars was the destination — Goldfield, a town of about 14,000 near Death Valley in sun-parched, lunar-landscaped Esmeralda County, Nevada. To say that Goldfield emerged in the blink of an eye was almost literally true. Four years prior to the year of the big prizefight, the town had a population of 36!

An earlier fight in Goldfield was staged on September 16, 1905, as part of the shindig celebrating the arrival of passenger train service. Harry Tenny scored a 25th round knockout of Monte Attell in a bout billed for the American bantamweight title. According to a report in the *San Francisco Chronicle*, the little Jewish boxers fought like wild beasts to the great gratification of the crowd.

To land the Attell-Tenny fight, Goldfield businessmen subscribed a purse of two thousand dollars. The purse for Gans vs. Nelson ($33,500) was nearly a 17-fold increase and more than double the purse of any non-heavyweight fight on record.

The promotion would come to be seen as a tour de force for George W. "Tex" Rickard. A former cowboy and lawman, Rickard arrived in Goldfield in 1904, two years after the discovery of gold and silver deposits. With two partners, he opened the Northern, a gambling saloon that took the name of saloons he had managed in the Yukon. It was a queer name considering the locale — the Northern was named for the Northern Lights (aurora borealis) that were considered one of the great wonders of Alaska — but "Northern" was an established brand in western mining circles, identified with Southern-style hospitality and honest dealings. The Goldfield Northern, which reportedly opened with 80 bartenders on the payroll, was immediately the hub of social life in the business district. Many miners, distrustful of banks, harbored their life savings there in a safe deposit box, optimal liquidity as the place never closed.

Rickard would go on to become America's preeminent boxing promoter. When Madison Square Garden opened at a new location in November of 1925, it was dubbed "The House that Tex Built." But while Rickard was the driving force behind the big prizefight, he had plenty of help. Goldfield was full of energetic men who were civic-minded, and while they couldn't manufacture fresh gold, they could sustain the illusion of unbridled prosperity to raise fresh capital as the gold petered out. Sustaining the illusion was the whole purpose of holding the fight.

George Graham Rice, an ex-felon from the lower east side of New York who went on to earn notoriety as the Jackal of Wall Street, was indispensable to Rickard. A brilliant wordsmith, Rice had earned his first fortune as a racetrack tout, employing a novel direct-mail campaign that revolutionized his gambit. After running afoul of the U.S. Attorney General, he moved to Goldfield and entered the somewhat related enterprise of mining stock promotion. The glossy prospectuses that he designed depicted mines bursting with activity, some of which, it would be discovered, lacked the essential of a hole.

Rice had retained his sucker lists from his days as a horserace tipster. Those on the list received a postcard inviting them to the "Fight of the Century." Rice also helped in the preparation of daily updates for visiting reporters. Each release contained a startling new fact about Goldfield, the magnificent little city where fortunes were made overnight, enriching smart investors. Barton W. Currie's jaundiced retrospective in *Harper's Weekly* was a backhand tribute to Rice's promotional genius:

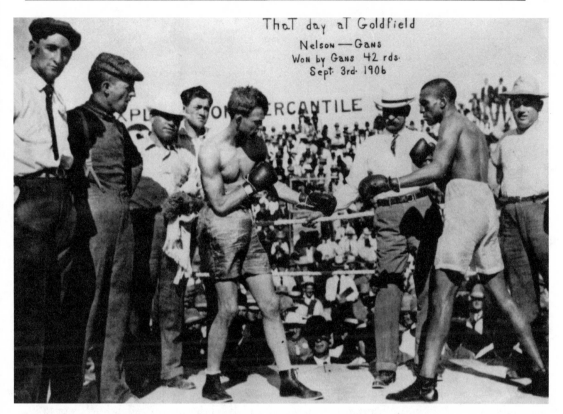

That day at Goldfield
Nelson — Gans
Won by Gans 42 rds.
Sept 3rd 1906

Battling Nelson and Joe Gans square off before their famous 1906 fight in Goldfield. *Pugilistica Boxing Memorabilia.*

Ten thousand sporting editors were wiring for copy. They got it, colored with every pigment in the literary prism-garish.... A paragraph about how many eggs the colored pugilist ate for breakfast would be followed by an account of how the Purple Fiddle was down to the one-hundred foot level, where the ore was so rich that free gold could be dug out with a shovel by the hundredweight.... One inspired correspondent wrote that Gans had wielded a pick in one of the deep drifts of a mine, dislodging a block of ore that contained his weight in gold.[6]

A fight to the finish, the Gans-Nelson fight lasted more than two hours before Nelson was disqualified for repeated fouls. There was hardly a whimper of protest, as Gans — forced to take the short end of the purse — had decisively outboxed the Durable Dane and won the sympathy of the crowd. (Gans and Nelson fought twice more in California. Nelson won both encounters by knockout. Within two years of their third meeting, Gans was dead of tuberculosis.)

Nearly eight thousand people attended the fight and thousands more turned up to bask in the excitement. The gate receipts totaled $69,715, topping the single-day box office record (Sullivan vs. Corbett) by almost nine thousand dollars. The event, noted historian Sally Zanjani, was Goldfield's penultimate happening, a temporal tidemark akin to the great Johnstown flood. Years later, residents and former residents would date their arrival in Goldfield as occurring either before or after the great battle.

The closest town to Goldfield was Tonopah, a mere 25 miles down the road. The two communities had a fierce rivalry. Not to be outdone, the citizens of Tonopah jumped on the bandwagon. Tonopah eventually surpassed Goldfield as the center of prizefighting activity in

Esmeralda County. The most notable fight staged there pitted Marvin Hart against Mike Schreck in a contest billed for the world heavyweight title. The May 30, 1907, bout was held in the massive dance hall of the aptly named Big Casino. The hall was rimmed with "luxury boxes," more exactly cribs for prostitutes. Schreck prevailed in a good action fight. Hart's corner threw in the sponge in the 21st round.

Nevada's entry into major prizefight promotions came during the period when San Francisco was the cynosure of pugilism. Forty-eight championship fights were held in or near San Francisco during the two decades that straddled the turn of the century, almost three times as many as in any other metropolis.

This development was almost inevitable. The city was relatively wide-open, a vestige of the gold rush days. The homegrown contingent of boxers was very strong, more so after Jim Corbett came to the fore. The city was the main port of entry for pugilists from Australia who were drawn to the U.S. when the fight game in America was infused with new money from the infant medium of motion pictures. Peter Jackson, Bob Fitzsimmons, and other prominent graduates of Larry Foley's academy in Sydney had their first American bouts in San Francisco rings.

With regard to interracial fights, no state was more progressive than California, where hostility toward blacks was tempered by a more intense hostility toward the Chinese. Jack Johnson had sixteen fights in California prior to winning the heavyweight title, three against top-tier Caucasian opponents. However, Johnson became so despised that he was ultimately unwelcome there too. His July 4, 1910, match with Jim Jeffries found a home in San Francisco, but was booted out of the Golden State by Governor James N. Gillett. Nineteen days before the match was scheduled to take place, Gillett commanded his attorney general to issue a restraining order on the grounds that the contest violated the anti-prizefighting law of 1850, a law that had been amended so often that it was considered obsolete. Gillett justified his action in a lengthy press release wherein he assailed prizefighting as demoralizing and corrupt, but he may have yielded to pressure from higher-ups in Washington. Rumor had it that federal support of San Francisco's forthcoming Panama Fair would be withdrawn if Gillett allowed the fight to go forward.

Gillett's edict was a harsh blow to promoters Tex Rickard and Jack Gleason. They had $130,000 in the till and had incurred $30,000 in expenses. But they salvaged the fight, spurning a rich offer from businessmen in Goldfield to stage the event on schedule in Reno, a city with a milder temperature and a more highly developed railroad grid. So it was that a battle that excited passions on four continents went to a remote community whose entire population would be outnumbered by visitors attending the fight. (Many fight-goers were forced to sleep on cots set up on the porches of private homes.)

Nevada's governor Denver Dickerson had no interest in prizefighting, but he trusted Rickard to pull the fight off without controversy and participated in the pre-fight hoopla, visiting both training camps in the company of reporters while singing the praises of the pugilists, extolling the beauty of the land, and touting Nevada's favorable business climate. Dickerson was especially impressed with Johnson. "I don't believe you could hit him with a handful of corn," he told Hearst correspondent Alfred Henry Lewis.[7]

Dickerson purportedly made a large wager on Johnson. He took the road less traveled. Although Jeffries had been idle for almost six years, he was bet up from a 10/7 to a 5/2 favorite. But he was mere child's play for Johnson, who was comfortably ahead when he brought down the curtain in the 15th round, knocking Jeffries to the canvas three times before his corner tossed in the towel.

An artistic flop, the Johnson-Jeffries fight was yet another masterpiece by Tex Rickard, who refereed the contest without incident. Although thousands of dollars had to be refunded when the venue was changed, the Memorial Day promotion drew 15,760 paying customers, producing a gate of $270,775. (Putting this in perspective, the gate receipts for that year's World Series between the Chicago Cubs and Philadelphia Athletics totaled $174,000 for all five games combined.)

Describing the scene in downtown Reno, a reporter with a vivid imagination said the gutters were littered with cheap watches discarded by pickpockets who tossed them away after determining they had little resale value. In truth, security was so tight that the criminal element was largely crippled. Deputized citizens, Pinkerton men, detectives from other cities, and Nevada Rangers assisted the local police force. Ticket-holders, with the exception of women, were frisked to prevent anyone from entering the arena with a weapon or hard object. As an extra precaution, Rickard had William Muldoon lecture the crowd on the importance of good sportsmanship. Muldoon paid homage to Nevada for "showing itself to the world as the one spot where all men were free and equal."

Elsewhere, writers were preparing editorials that presented a different image. The amorphous Nevadan would be accused of instigating the riots that erupted across the country in the aftermath of the fight. The *New York Times* estimated 5000 instances of disorderly conduct and pegged the national death toll at thirteen. Reno was riotous too, but in a manner consistent with fond expectations. The casinos were jammed until the wee hours of the morning with gamblers four-deep around every table.

Major prizefights in Nevada were destined to ebb away as the mines gave out, but two developments quickened this meltdown. In 1910, Nevada outlawed gambling. The law took effect three months after the Johnson-Jeffries fight, an embargo that lasted two decades. This dried up a major source of sponsorship money. In 1914, fights to a finish were outlawed. A new state law, subsequently liberalized, put the ceiling at 10 rounds. This stripped Nevada's prizefights of their relatively unique flavor, despoiling their value as a magnet for tourism. Coming up the ladder, Jack Dempsey had four fights in Nevada, appearing in Goldfield, Tonopah, Reno, and the copper mining town of Ely, but these were low-budget productions designed for locals.

Jack Johnson's 1912 title defense against Fireman Jim Flynn would come to be identified in some books with Las Vegas, Nevada, but the actual locale was Las Vegas, New Mexico, a railroad town once acclaimed as the murder-by-vigilante capital of the Wild West. The venue favored Flynn, the pride of Pueblo, Colorado, whose nickname accrued from having worked as a coal heaver on steam locomotives, but he was no match for Johnson, who had knocked him out five years earlier. Fewer than four thousand people witnessed the predictably one-sided skirmish in an arena built to accommodate 18,000. Fireman Jim was a bloody mess when he was rescued by the intercession of a state police captain.

Conceived with the vision of drawing a great influx of tourists, this promotion was a fine example of "chuckleheaded boosterism," a term coined by the great sportswriter John Lardner. In 1923, dunderheads in Montana manifested this syndrome to an even greater extent, manufacturing a boxing event that plunged the entire state into a fiscal crisis.

## Shelby — Boomtown Boxing Redux

The sleepy town of Shelby, Montana, was energized in 1922 by an oil strike on the outskirts of town. The population doubled in a matter of months, increasing to approximately one thousand people. Large landowners reaped a bonanza, as did the first wave of land speculators. Hoping to put their town on the map and drive up the price of oil leases, a group of local businessmen conceived the idea of holding a rodeo that would climax with a grand Memorial Day prizefight. Long-time residents were receptive. An event of this magnitude would be a kick in the pants to their more cosmopolitan cousins in places like Helena.

A boxing committee was formed. Canvassing the state, the members raised slightly more than a hundred thousand dollars, secured with vouchers to the best seats. With this money in hand, they sent a representative off to meet with Jack Dempsey's manager Doc Kearns. The idea was to get Dempsey to defend his heavyweight title against Tommy Gibbons. A veteran campaigner who had fought mostly as a middleweight, Gibbons hailed from St. Paul, Minnesota, and was perceived to have a strong regional following. The Great Northern Railroad connected Shelby to St. Paul and to Salt Lake City, Dempsey's hometown.

Loy J. Molumby, the state president of the American Legion, represented Shelby in the negotiations. He arranged to meet Kearns in Chicago, but Kearns did not keep the appointment. Doc had crisscrossed Montana many times but wasn't familiar with Shelby, which was situated in the least traversed part of the state near the Canadian border. He assumed that Molumby was some sort of crackpot, but Molumby was persistent and was granted an audience when he spoke the magic words: "Money is no object."

Kearns intuitively knew that the fight would be a hard sell — Shelby had no paved highways leading into town — and demanded a purse of three hundred thousand dollars, one-third up-front, with the remainder paid in two equal installments. Molumby was agreeable.

The organizers presumed that advance sales would generate enough money to meet their obligations and also cover the expense of building a stadium. To goose the gate, they hired a publicist to draft daily press releases. His dispatches made it appear that the entire country was converging on Shelby for the Fourth of July.

A release dated May 18 said that $350,000 was already in the till. The next day the figure was $380,000 and, on the day after that, a new release went out with the news that seven thousand seats had been sold in the ringside section, leaving only three thousand choice seats remaining. The figures were wild fabrications, invented to create the illusion of feverish excitement and induce a sense of urgency among fence-straddlers intrigued with the thought of attending the fight. The lies were yet printed in many newspapers.

The sales campaign was frustrated by doubts that Shelby could adequately provide for a large influx of visitors. The updates also addressed these concerns. It was asserted that side tracks had been laid to accommodate one thousand Pullman cars, two hundred of which had dining facilities, that the railroads were pitching in by making their refrigerated cars available for perishable foods, augmenting the town's cold storage facilities, that arrangements had been made to increase the capacity of the town's water tank sevenfold to 700,000 gallons, that the automobile camp had been expanded to where it was now the world's largest, that Shelby's two schools had been equipped with hotel furnishings, and that new lodging houses, restaurants and cabarets were opening daily, the latter providing satisfaction for every musical taste, from western music to jazz.

Some of the press releases were ill advised, containing tidbits that created unforeseen problems. A puff piece on Shelby's colorful sheriff divulged that the town's police force was a two-man operation. A retraction of sorts was quickly forthcoming: The sheriff had taken the precaution of enlarging his force by deputizing all of the ex-servicemen in the county, railroad detectives would be on the lookout for undesirables, a stockade had been built as an annex to the local jail, and the governor had authorized two National Guard regiments to stand by if needed. The assertion that Shelby was known for excellent beer sparked a visit from the superintendent of the Montana branch of the Anti-Saloon League and a crackdown on liquor sales by federal prohibition agents. Montana's Attorney General, Wellington D. Rankin, was infuriated to read that Shelby had abolished its 1 A.M. curfew for dance halls and threatened reprisals if Shelbyites did not clean up their act. The *Butte Daily-Miner* carried Rankin's ultimatum: "Shelby shall not be the rendezvous of thugs, yeggs, plug-uglies, pickpockets, gamblers, rum-runners, or any other class of anarchists who make their living by defying the law and the constitution."[8]

Many reporters suspected that the news coming out of Shelby was a lot of hooey. Their suspicions were confirmed when the second payment, due June 15, was late. Six days earlier, it had been reported that advance ticket sales had climbed to $450,000. A skeptical Associated Press reporter undertook a survey of railroad agents to get at the truth. He found that revenues from ticket sales outside Montana stood at $1600.

Kearns got his second $100,000 payment — most of it money supplied by the mayor of Shelby, a bank owner — but at this point the promotion was doomed to be a flop, if it came off at all. Although the bout was in limbo, many eastern sportswriters yet made plans to attend it, all the while castigating Kearns — "the Shylock of Shelby" — for drawing them into the wilderness on what shaped up as a snipe hunt.

The eager beavers in Shelby were inspired by the examples of Goldfield in 1906 and Reno in 1910. But those communities were more populous than Shelby in 1923, and their famous fights were one-of-a-kind, begetting many more that fell flat. Moreover, those promotions benefited from the "forbidden fruit" aspect. Boxing was now flourishing in places where it had until recently been outlawed.

As late as 48 hours before the scheduled start of the fight, some sportswriters were still speculating that the bout would be canceled. They implored Kearns to go ahead with the match, supplications that were likely unnecessary. Kearns was acutely aware of the importance of staying on the good side of sportswriters. It's a fair assumption that the impasse was broken with the first sighting in Shelby of a correspondent from an important paper. This took the promotion out of limbo, although Kearns wasn't yet ready to concede this fact.

The final payment was $96,000 short — there wasn't another nickel in the fight treasury — but Kearns was given full control of the box office. He steeply discounted ticket prices, scrapped the preliminaries, and delayed the start of the battle by one hour to hustle more people into the arena. At the scheduled starting time of the contest, the crowd inside the giant saucer-shaped stadium numbered seven thousand at the most. At least that many were milling outside, and most of them eventually found their way in. It was not the usual fight crowd. Most of the attendees were curiosity-seekers who lived within a three-hour drive of Shelby, and few bothered to spend the night. The fight was a snoozer. The defensively minded Gibbons, who received training expenses only, upset the odds by lasting the full 15 rounds.

The townsfolk had been instructed to dress in cowboy duds to give the event an authentic western feel. *New York World* correspondent Heywood Broun decided to amuse his colleagues by dressing in this fashion. He was living dangerously. As it became obvious that the promotion would be conspicuously unextravagant, the locals faulted eastern reporters for the embarrassment. In planting seeds of doubt that the event would ever take place, the press had encouraged would-be visitors to make other Fourth of July plans. Some of their pieces were peppered with observations about Shelby that were superciliously unflattering, slaps that were more irksome because the reporters had been indulged with free food and other amenities. The New York dailies, it was fairly alleged, had downgraded Shelby's promotion by giving more ink to a forthcoming fight in New Jersey between Luis Angel Firpo and Jess Willard.

Reporters from small papers were forced to bunk in the schoolhouse. Sensing the mood, they burrowed uninvited with their A-list brethren in the Pullman cars, where railroad detectives provided security from harassment. Doc Kearns had taken a similar precaution, chartering a locomotive and caboose for a quick getaway. Kearns and Dempsey were long gone by sunrise the next morning. Within six weeks, four of Montana's banks folded, including both banks in Shelby. The collapses were blamed on general economic conditions, but no one was fooled.

After bidding Dempsey goodbye, Kearns made a beeline to Broadway. But he had more on his mind than chorus girls. The Walker Law had invigorated boxing in the Empire State after two decades of stunted activity. New York City was ripe for a megafight and Kearns wasted little time seizing the moment. Ten weeks after the fiasco at Shelby, Dempsey risked his title against the aforementioned Firpo. The fight was staged at the Polo Grounds where Harlem abutted the Bronx, marking the first time that fight fans in North America's leading metropolis were treated to a dyed-in-the-wool heavyweight championship fight free of no-decision baggage or club-membership subterfuge.

Reportedly witnessed by 85,800, the savage slugfest lasted less than four minutes but left an indelible paw print on the Golden Era of Sports. The event was truly a "happening."

# CHAPTER 6

# The War and the Walker Law

From 1896 to 1900, the Horton Law governed boxing in New York. Fights were restricted to membership clubs, but otherwise promoters were largely unfettered. During these five years, fifty fights were staged at Empire State venues that would be certified by *The Ring* record book as world title fights. This feast was followed by a protracted famine. No authentic title fights were staged in New York in the first decade of the twentieth century, a scant seven in the decade that followed, when professional boxing worldwide was curtailed by strife in Europe.

Governor Theodore Roosevelt authorized the repeal of the Horton Law, effectively making boxing illegal. Ironically, Roosevelt — an intramural boxer at Harvard — was a vocal proponent of the "manly art." While serving as the chairman of the New York City Board of Police Commissioners (1895–97), he made a number of statements in defense of pugilism that caused quite a stir. By his reckoning, learning to box was a pathway to becoming a good citizen and a knockout received in a boxing match was no worse than a knockout received in a game of polo.[1]

When Roosevelt affixed his signature to the bill that abolished the Horton Law, it was not an about-face but an acknowledgment that the sport at the professional level had sunk too low to justify the expense of a makeover. Dishonest fights and pathetic mismatches had become endemic. In 1899, a particularly troublesome year, there were three ring fatalities at Manhattan fight clubs and several nasty disturbances. In one incident, a riot ensued after a fighter had his gloves doused with mustard oil, resulting in the temporary blindness of his opponent and also the referee. Even if Roosevelt's political ambitions had not propelled him to a national stage, he still had little choice but to disassociate himself from his friends in the pugilistic fraternity.

Repealing the Horton Law did not kill boxing in the Empire State. Many private clubs continued weekly "smokers." But the Horton Law killed ballyhoo, making it more difficult to run shows profitably. Formerly a magnet to champions, New York became a cradle of champions. Local stickouts like Brooklyn's Terry McGovern hit the road to find well-paying matches. The big money was in California.

It was impossible at a smoker to distinguish between club members in good standing and outsiders. Admission badges circulated freely and sometimes, when enforcement was lax, were issued for a one-time membership fee. This hypocrisy ended with the passage of the

Frawley Law in 1910, which permitted private clubs to charge admission to non-members. The Frawley Law also put a 10-round cap on competitions to reduce injuries resulting from dehydration and stipulated that no verdict would be rendered at the conclusion of the contest. This was meant to suppress gambling, fingered as the main cause of the corruption.

The no-decision rule, which originated in Pennsylvania, spread rapidly after New York came on line, diffusing even into parts of Canada. In certain places at certain times, the stricture was waived for important bouts, but this was rare. In some no-decision states, the law stipulated a 50–50 split of the purse money. The elimination of performance clauses discouraged the use of the term "prizefight," a word that came to have an antiquarian ring to it.

Ring fatalities declined under the Frawley Law, but bogus fights became more common. As no official decision was given, an uninspired fighter could lollygag through a match without concern that his record would be blemished. Top-tier American fighters during the no-decision era were extremely active relative to their counterparts in other eras. This owed partly to reduced purses, but also to the fact that no-decision bouts, by and large, were tame by early Queensberry (and modern) standards. The priority for a fighter with advance bookings was to avoid ring damage and be fresh to fight the following week, perhaps even the very next night. Barnstorming boxers pulled their punches against house fighters, stimulating interest in a do-over and resulting in a high incidence of rematches. Looking back, the most striking consequence was an extraordinarily low stoppage-to-decision ratio.

Memphis Pal Moore, a borderline Hall of Famer who competed from 1913 to 1930, was the uppermost pussycat, scoring only 10 knockouts in his 253 documented bouts. But the clever Moore would not have secured as many paydays if not for his reputation as a feather-fisted fighter, and he was content to leave inferior opponents upright so as to retain his "usefulness." In Pal Moore's day, champions preferred fighting in no-decision states where they could only lose their title by knockout, and they assiduously avoided fighters who packed a big punch.

Although referees were required to leave the ring without designating a winner, fights continued to attract betting. The outcome of wagers hinged on the opinion of one or more reporters. In many cases this was the referee, who rendered his verdict in print in his summary of the bout in the next day's newspaper. Sometimes a block of ringside reporters was surveyed to build a consensus, a practice largely limited to fights of national importance, but bookmakers weren't too keen on this alternative as polls were prone to be indecisive.

There was one heavyweight championship fight in New York in the no-decision era. On March 25, 1916, Jess Willard retained his title in a 10-round bout with Frank Moran at Madison Square Garden. The promotion earned a tidy profit for Tex Rickard. The gate receipts were $151,254, a figure surpassed only by the Johnson-Jeffries match at Reno in 1910. However, betting was extremely light. ("The lordly wagers of the old days were conspicuous by their absence," wrote the correspondent for the *New York Times*.) Private wagers at ringside rested on the verdict of Honest John Kelly, New York's leading referee during the Horton Law days. Although the bout was one-sided, many eyes were yet on Honest John as the final bell sounded. He stood erect from his front row seat, cocked his arm in the fashion of a shot putter, and wordlessly pointed to Willard.

Gambler-businessmen were logically in the forefront of the movement to abolish the no-decision rule. Some were affected on two fronts, as American bookmakers, like their counterparts in Great Britain, were well represented among the ranks of boxing promoters. Bookmaker-restaurateur Billy Gibson ran weekly shows at the Fairmont Athletic Club in the Bronx and managed a large stable of fighters that included the immensely popular Benny

Leonard. Leonard's popularity was bound to soar even higher if betting returned to previous levels, as those betting the fights were more inclined to attend the matches.

Pressure to abolish the no-decision law in New York gained momentum in 1914 when Californians voted in favor of a referendum that forced professionals to compete under amateur rules in bouts restricted to four rounds. This killed big-time boxing where it had been most lush, impelling Tex Rickard to try his luck in New York, where curbs were less shackling and offset by more favorable demographics. The departure of big-time boxing from California was a blessing in disguise to Rickard as it thinned the ranks of his competitors and acted as a check on spiraling purses. Rickard's chief rival, James W. "Sunny Jim" Coffroth, the kingpin of boxing in northern California, quit the fight game in disgust and turned to his second love, horseracing, becoming a highly prosperous track owner in Tijuana.

As had been true in New Orleans, opposition to prizefighting in California was intensified by ring fatalities. On April 29, 1910, British featherweight champion Owen Moran knocked out hometown favorite Tommy McCarthy in the sixteenth frame of a 20-round contest at San Francisco. Unconscious when he was carried out of the ring, McCarthy died that same night. At the inquest, Moran testified that he could have knocked out McCarthy quicker, but was intimidated by gamblers into letting the bout go 15 rounds, the dividing line of a betting proposition. The firestorm that followed a ring death raged especially hot in this instance, the indignation heightened by the concatenation of crooked gambling.

In 1913, the death of 21-year-old Luther McCarty caused a larger ripple. McCarty dropped dead in the second minute of his match with Arthur Pelkey in Calgary. His mysterious collapse was blamed on a pre-existing medical condition, but the mindset of the abolitionists was yet hardened by this tragedy. Hailing from Driftwood Creek, Nebraska (some sources say Sidney, Ohio), McCarty was rated the man with the best chance of defeating Jack Johnson, restoring the heavyweight throne to the Caucasian race. He had an especially strong following in California, where he had scored his most impressive wins. In his last outing in the Golden State, McCarty knocked out Al Palzer in a bout billed for the White Heavyweight Championship of the World.

Later that summer, anti-prizefighting sentiment was inflamed by the death of William "Bull" Young at the hands of Jess Willard in a bout at Vernon, California. A 26-year-old Wyoming rancher, Young was built like a block of granite, but he was unskilled and unschooled. He had no business in the same ring with the crude but more advanced Willard, although he had fought him twice before, losing both bouts by knockout (three of Young's four recorded fights were with Willard). Young's death suggested that boxing was becoming inherently more risky as humans grew larger in physical stature. There was talk of restricting competitions to men weighing less than 200 pounds. Several municipalities, notably Milwaukee, initiated measures along these lines.

The deconstruction of professional boxing in California, coupled with the devitalization of western mining towns and the drawing off of promising prospects by newly established military camps, had the sport sinking in quicksand. Punitive regulations were ubiquitous and promoters with grand visions had nowhere to go. No-decision fights, commonly restricted to four or six rounds, were a hard sell, even if the combatants had glowing reputations. The 4-round mains staged in California were fundamentally different, faster paced and often wildly entertaining, but patrons felt cheated because they were accustomed to larger portions.

The languor would be remedied in no time. The tonic was World War I. The American sporting scene was fallow during the war years. Most colleges discontinued football, baseball schedules were abbreviated, and annual events like the Indianapolis 500 and the PGA tournament were suspended. But this brief quiescence was the antecedent to America's Golden Era of Sports and boxing would reach dizzying heights.

It has been postulated that the war desensitized Americans to brutality, making prizefighting less controversial. It was certainly true that ring deaths commanded less and less newsprint as the list of fatal fights grew longer. However, opposition to prizefighting softened before the U.S. was drawn into the war (the dethroning of heavyweight champion Jack Johnson was likely a contributing factor) and it wasn't the war *per se* that turned the wasteland lush, but war-related developments.

In the summer of 1916, nearly 100,000 soldiers converged on Fort Bliss and two satellite camps on the eastern fringe of El Paso in anticipation of a protracted battle with the army of Mexican rebel insurgent Pancho Villa. Concurrent with the arrival of the soldiers — the largest mobilization of U.S. troops since the Civil War — there was an expansion of businesses catering to the caprices of unmarried men. To the embarrassment of the War Department, there were several instances where soldiers wrecked a whorehouse just for the sport of it.

Largely ignored by the mainstream press, these incidents did not escape the gaze of reformers. An article in the *New York Missionary Review*, quoted at length in the July 29, 1916, issue of the *Literary Digest*, assailed the Army for not chasing away "human vampires and vultures" from the Mexican border and advocated an extensive program of supervised recreation to relieve "the ennui and nervous desire for excitement and amusement [that] often lead [*sic*] the young soldiers into thoughtless excesses that involve awful consequences."[2]

The Army brass could scarcely ignore this behest, not with rumbles of imminent deployments overseas. In April of 1917, the War Department established the Training Camp Activities Commission. Under the direction of Raymond B. Fosdick, the commission instituted the most extensive intramural sports program in the history of mankind. The next month, in a related development, open prostitution within five miles of a military installation was outlawed under Section 17 of the Draft Act to "protect the doughboy." Gone in a blink were such landmark vice districts as Storyville in New Orleans, the birthplace of ragtime music and Dixieland jazz and the last urban enclave of legal prostitution in the United States.

At military camps, boxing was part of the daily curriculum. Dozens of active and retired fighters were pressed into duty as boxing instructors and tournament organizers. Serendipitously, it was discovered that many of these fighters were extraordinarily adroit with a bayonet and their role was broadened to include teaching this art. World War I would reveal that the bayonet had largely outlived its usefulness. However, it would be written that hundreds of American lives were saved because of the bayonet instruction provided by professional boxers, whose well-publicized contributions to the war effort uplifted their besotted profession.

Millions of Americans learned to box in the Army. Many developed a keen interest in the affairs of the ring. Competitions between regiments, arranged as morale-boosters, continued in Europe, where they were expanded to include teams from allied nations. An inter-allied boxing tournament in 1918 at Pershing Stadium in Joinville, France, attracted heads of state and received extensive newspaper coverage. Tournaments for servicemen continued after the Armistice was signed. An inter-allied tournament at London's Royal Albert Hall in December of 1918 had the flavor of an Olympiad, with King George V presenting medals to the winners.

The top fighters from these tournaments had established followings when the war ended. The most exalted American boxer, "Fighting" Bob Martin from St. Albans, West Virginia, was a headline attraction right out of the box. In his third postwar fight, he was pitted against Joe Bonds in a 15-rounder, the same Joe Bonds that had gone the distance with Jack Dempsey.

The career of Gene Tunney started with less fanfare, even though Tunney had won a decision over Martin in the finals of the Joinville tournament, saddling Fighting Bob with his only defeat in 40 recorded servicemen's bouts.

A caucus of the First American Expeditionary Forces at Paris in 1919 begat the American Legion. Literally within months of the Armistice, the Legion became the pre-eminent men's club in many American communities. Embracing athletic competitions as a chief source of fund-raising, the Legion in many locales acquired the exclusive rights to promote fights.

The American Legion, which actively supported the Boy Scouts, put a more respectable veneer on boxing than the athletic clubs of an earlier generation, many of which were loose neighborhood associations controlled by ward bosses and tied to a more narrow purpose like volunteer firefighting. When municipalities began to legalize boxing, they often confronted resistance from the Legion, which responded to the poaching by exacting concessions. Many postwar boxing bills contained provisions for veterans' homes and hospitals.

In 1919, as the last of the troops were returning home, three different bills were drafted to legalize boxing in New York. The winning bid — so to speak — was submitted by James J. "Jimmy" Walker, a member of the New York State Senate. In crafting the bill, Walker was careful to keep the military in the loop. The original draft put boxing under the supervision of the Army-Navy-Civilian Control Board, which conducted matches in armories. A key provision denied licenses to war slackers.

Walker steered the bill that bore his name through two rounds of contentious debates, overcoming the opposition of upstate Republicans. The general feeling was that he was wasting his time because Governor Al Smith was certain to kill the measure.

Smith was no fan of the flamboyant Walker, although both shared a common upbringing in lower Manhattan. A former Tin Pan Alley songwriter who went on to become New York City's most popular and most scandal-plagued mayor (1926–33), Walker was chummy with the racetrack and speakeasy crowds and had butted heads with the Protestant clergy while spearheading the successful fight to allow baseball games on Sundays. Governor Smith was highly sensitive to the Protestant point of view because he aspired to make history as America's first Roman Catholic president.

Walker found an unlikely ally in Anthony J. Drexel Biddle, the founder of an international Bible society with a purported 200,000 members. An eccentric millionaire of Quaker stock who could trace his ancestry to the Mayflower, Biddle, an ex-Marine, was an avid boxing enthusiast who frequently entertained guests at his Pennsylvania estate with demonstrations of his pugilistic skill. His foil in these recitals was usually his bosom buddy Philadelphia Jack O'Brien, the former lightheavyweight champion.

Biddle, so the story goes, contacted every member of his Bible society, requesting that they send Governor Smith a telegram indicating their support for Walker's proposal. Smith was flabbergasted by the response and changed his mind about vetoing the bill. In most versions of this story, the clergymen are portrayed as bottom-line pragmatists who acquiesced to Biddle out of fear that he would cut off their supply of free Bibles, but the "muscular Christianity" movement gained steam during World War I and many of the telegram-senders undoubtedly voted their conscience, having come to the conclusion that bootleg fights were ineradicable and that it made sense to regulate boxing under the supervision of conscientious citizens who would protect the combatants from harm and the public from fraud.

A unique feature of the Walker Law, which took effect on May 24, 1920, was that everyone deriving income from a boxing match — matchmakers, venue providers, managers, boxers, seconds, officials, ring doctors, etc.— had to be licensed and were accountable to the boxing commission, a panel appointed by the governor. The panel was empowered to approve matches, assign the officials, establish and collect fees, and levy fines and/or suspensions. The rules that governed the competitions were an amalgam of those used at the National Sporting Club in London and those used in the military. The Walker Law stipulated that two judges would score the bouts. The referee also kept score and his tally was used as the tiebreaker, if needed. Bouts were allowed up to 15 rounds.

The Walker Law legalized boxing in New York, but more precisely it legalized deliberate knockout punches. This was radical in that it exempted promoters, boxers, and accomplices from arrest in the event of a serious injury or fatality. No longer would bouts be stopped by peace officers on the grounds that they crossed the line of permissible brutality. A licensee — the referee, ring physician, or highest-ranking boxing official at ringside — would make this determination. A fighter could now fight full bore without worrying that he would be charged with a crime.

The national mood had changed and the dominoes were beginning to fall, but the passage of the Walker Law quickened the pace. By 1934, boxing was legal in every state in the union, although not legal in every county. The last major jurisdiction to come on line was Washington, D.C. Boxing remained a crazy quilt because each new pro-boxing law deviated in some respects from the Walker guidepost, but the patches in the quilt became less motley.

Of course, the Walker Law wasn't trendsetting because it cleansed professional boxing. It was trendsetting because it created spoils for political toadies and opened a new vein of tax money. Indeed, where legal boxing was put on the ballot, proponents pushed it as a sin tax.

During the first three months of Walker Law boxing in New York, the commission collected more money in license fees and taxes than had been appropriated to run the operation for the entire year. In 1924 alone, gate receipts in New York totaled more than five million dollars, a remarkable sum considering that only six recognized title fights were staged in New York that year, and that Jack Dempsey, the sport's biggest drawing card, was inactive.

Other spectator sports were also thriving, as were somewhat related forms of entertainment like burlesque. The Golden Era of Sports — the Age of Wonderful Nonsense — was in full bloom.

# CHAPTER 7

# The Golden Era

Born in 1895 in a one-room stucco house in the Mormon farming settlement of Manassa, Colorado, William Harrison "Jack" Dempsey towered above boxing like his contemporary Babe Ruth towered above baseball. His name, like that of Ruth, Red Grange, Bill Tilden, Bobby Jones, and the equine superstar Man o' War, would become synonymous with America's Golden Era of Sports. The era itself is synonymous with the decade of the 1920s, but one could fairly date the starting point to July 4, 1919, the day that Dempsey annihilated Jess Willard in Toledo.

Tex Rickard would have preferred staging the contest closer to New York City, but there were too many legal and political impediments. The advantages of Toledo were easy access — Toledo then ranked second only to Chicago in passenger train traffic — an enthusiastic business community, and a free-flowing supply of newly illegal booze — the good stuff smuggled across the lake from Canada. But the road to Toledo was bumpy too.

Ohio had no boxing law, but grandstanding Governor James Cox threatened to invent one to appease the Ohio Ministerial Association. To grease the skids, Rickard enlisted the aid of Walker Law facilitator Anthony J. Drexel Biddle, rewarding him for his help by naming him one of the judges and letting him choose the timekeeper, a prize he awarded to linen thread manufacturer W. Warren Barbour, a former amateur boxer and future United States senator. The brutally one-sided fight would likewise create controversy. The dispute centered on whether Willard had been saved by the bell in the opening round.

Dempsey smashed Willard to the canvas six times in the opening frame. Exhortations to stop the slaughter were muted in the great roar and referee Ollie Pecord, a local sportsman working his first title fight, let the carnage continue. The sixth knockdown, which knocked Willard into a sitting position, too stupefied to rise, came with three seconds remaining in the round, at least according to Barbour's stopwatch, which was running a tad fast. According to the rules in effect, the count could not continue after the bell, but the bell was inaudible.

The bout began in the middle of the afternoon on a wickedly hot day. During the preliminaries, the canvas gave off so much heat that a fresh tarpaulin was installed for the main event. During installation, a cord from the new apron got tangled with the gong. When Barbour hit the gong to signal that the round was over, it produced a sound too faint to be heard above the din. Seconds elapsed before he located his emergency apparatus, a military whistle that he blew with sufficient force to get Pecord's attention. Sizing up the situation — confusion and pandemonium — Doc Kearns hustled Dempsey out of the ring, but Dempsey, trapped in a surging wave of humanity, was summoned to return and the fight resumed, continuing for two more rounds before Willard's seconds threw in the towel.

Willard was so badly battered that he had no chance of reversing the momentum. Continuing the fight merely forestalled the inevitable. In subsequent years, so many individuals claimed to have bet Dempsey to win by knockout in the first round that the incident would come to be numbered among the great "bad beats" in gambling lore. Kearns and Damon Runyon, among others, claimed to have bet thousands taking 10/1 odds.[1]

The promotion turned a profit but far less than anticipated. The threat of a national rail strike, reports of price gouging by hotels and restaurants, and a wicked summer heat wave combined to depress attendance. As the challenger, Dempsey took the short end of the purse, earning a reported $19,000, a pebble after Kearns deducted his commission and expenses. The prestige that came with the title, however, coupled with a great surge of interest in Dempsey, gave Kearns enormous leverage in negotiating future purses. Within two years, a new phrase would be added to the sports lexicon: "million-dollar gate." This was an understatement in a sport built on overstatement. Dempsey's 1921 match with Georges Carpentier not only eclipsed the million-dollar plateau in gate receipts ($1,626,580), it also broke the existing record by more than a million dollars!

Dempsey was the lure in the first five million-dollar gates. Kearns was involved in only the first two, yet titled his fanciful autobiography (written with UPI sportswriter Oscar Fraley) *The Million Dollar Gate*, a direct slap at Rickard, then long deceased, who had continued to profit from Dempsey's popularity after Kearns was cut out of the partnership.

John Patrick Leo McKernan, alias Doc Kearns (a nickname likely acquired for his facility at closing cuts), was the uppermost wheeler-dealer in the world of hands-on fight managers. A pathological liar who knew every angle, Kearns was also a beguiling chap who came to be seen as a lovable scamp. In common with New York mayor Jimmy Walker, Kearns was a natty dresser who customarily changed clothes several times a day. A big tipper when he was flush, he could blow hundreds of dollars in a speakeasy with little recollection of it, but his recall was perfect on matters like how many inches of gauze his fighter had used up in training, an expense that would be deducted off the top before he took his commission. He was a wonderful storyteller, although the facts of an anecdote would change from one retelling to the next. In the October 1929 issue of *The Ring*, Nat Fleischer credited Kearns with inventing prizefight ballyhoo. He did no such thing, but he advanced the art.

Born in Waterloo, Michigan (some say Seattle), Kearns ran off to Nome, Alaska, at the age of fifteen, finding work as a gold-dust weigher in a saloon. In his off hours, he caroused with novelists Jack London and Rex Beach, or so he claimed. Recollecting his days as a prizefighter, Kearns claimed that he more than held his own with Dal Hawkins and Mysterious Billy Smith, men of considerable repute, and said that he once fought a bout in Cheyenne with Wyatt Earp in his corner ("a useless advice-giver, but a top-notch towel-swinger"). Documentation is lacking, but archivists have confirmed a 1906 bout for Kearns in Victor, Colorado. Fighting Maurice Thompson, a fighter that he managed, Kearns folded his tent in the third round. Somewhat later — before striking the mother lode with Dempsey — Doc worked as a matchmaker and scout for Sunny Jim Coffroth, arranged some fights for featherweight champion Abe Attell, and managed a troupe of boxers on a tour of Australia.

In his best version of the yarn, Kearns first encountered Dempsey in a seedy Oakland waterfront saloon. Attacked without provocation by a band of bullies, Kearns was rescued by

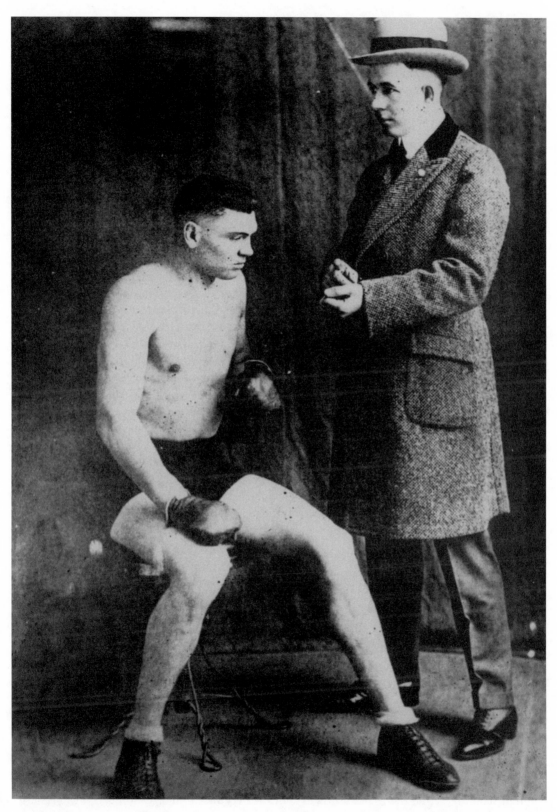

This photograph, circa 1917, is the earliest known photograph of Jack Dempsey with Doc Kearns. *Antiquities of the Prize Ring.*

a stranger who concussed the belligerents one-by-one with his spectacular left hook. The Good Samaritan was Dempsey, providently a down-on-his-luck prizefighter. Kearns repaid the favor with a home-cooked meal and then used his connections to revive Dempsey's moribund boxing career.

A more plausible conjecture is that Kearns first spied Dempsey in Ely, Nevada, on April 8, 1917. Dempsey's opponent Joe Bond(s) had been on Doc's Australia junket. Kearns was always on the lookout for a promising prospect and likely invited Dempsey to join his stable. One surmises that Dempsey declined because he valued his independence. A disillusioning trip to New York, where he fought three times in a three-week span but made barely enough to cover expenses, and a fluke loss to Fireman Jim Flynn were likely the prods that eventually led Dempsey into taking Kearns up on his offer.

Dempsey would become an engaging conversationalist, but in his early days was a wallflower content to let Kearns do all the talking. Doc liked to play up the fact that Dempsey had been a hobo — the rags-to-riches theme was good copy — even going so far as to assert that Dempsey's ruddy complexion resulted from cinders striking his face while he was riding the rods, the break beams under a freight car. As Dempsey began to acquire friends from high society, he became more self-conscious about his humble background and his relationship with Kearns became strained. "I was a hobo but never a bum," volunteered Dempsey whenever someone inquired about his railroad adventures. The distinction was that a hobo was too proud to panhandle and would insist on doing some chore in return for a meal.

In 1916, before his career took flight, the then 21-year-old Dempsey fell head over heels for Maxine Cates, a footloose woman in her mid-thirties then working as a pianist and extra-board whore in a Salt Lake City brothel. Their marriage was tempestuous and marked by long periods of separation, but that didn't stop Dempsey from naming her a dependent when he applied for a war deferment. In due course, Dempsey would be branded a slacker, meaning a draft dodger, a term that carried a very strong stain. He beat the rap in court, but his reputation took a terrible hit. When he was pitted against Georges Carpentier, who had fought on *our side* against the Germans, the confrontation was framed as a morality play. For good measure, Carpentier, the son of a coal miner, was fashioned into the urbane "Orchid Man," a Parisian boulevardier — the antithesis of the rough-hewn Dempsey, an alloy of the Wild West.

Carpentier had his first documented fight while working as a boy gymnast in a traveling circus. On the day of his fight with Dempsey, July 2, 1921, a wire service story about him reported that his record was 71–9–5 in a career spanning 15 years, a surprisingly close approximation of what one now finds in trustworthy compilations. He had one exposure in the United States before meeting Dempsey, winning the lightheavyweight title with a fourth-round stoppage of curiously uninspired Battling Levinsky in a Columbus Day promotion at a municipal park in Jersey City. In the trivia department, his match with Dempsey was his second engagement in a heavyweight title fight. In 1914, at the age of 20, he refereed Jack Johnson's match with Frank Moran.

European fighters with circus backgrounds are invariably fraudulent, but Carpentier was a breed apart. He had good technique and exceptional stamina, and had scored several legitimate one-punch knockouts over bigger men. However, although Carpentier was no fraud, he was unarguably fraudulent for Jack Dempsey. Generously listed at 175 pounds, he looked frail standing beside the Manassa Mauler. In the very first round, Dempsey split open his nose. In Round Four, Dempsey picked up the pace and decked him twice, first with a withering punch to the jaw and then a punch to the heart that put him down for the count.

The first of the postwar extravaganzas, Dempsey vs. Carpentier was contested in a mammoth wooden bowl built on a 30-acre parcel of land near the ferry landing in Jersey City. Sportswriters named the stadium Boyle's Thirty Acres. (Landowner John F. Boyle, a paper box manufacturer, was a crony of Jersey City political boss Frank "I Am The Law" Hague.) The Chamber of Commerce produced the souvenir program. Civic leaders were then campaigning to broaden the tax base by attracting more factories and warehouses to the community. In common with Tex Rickard's earlier promotions in Nevada, the local organizers conceptualized the event as something more than a convention of good spenders. It was hoped that the promotion would spur economic development. Among its distinctions, the fight was the first sporting event to be widely broadcast on radio. It reached an estimated audience of 300,000 spread over 125,000 square miles.

Rickard's publicists and their spear-carriers — the sportswriters — elevated ballyhoo to unprecedented heights. Their slick work was evidenced in the rush of Carpentier money two days before the bout. In New York, the odds favoring Dempsey dropped from 7/2 to 2/1.

Carpentier invited a cruel reappraisal of his merits with his lame performance, but by and large the scribes were kind to him, assessing his effort as gallant. The event was such a stirring spectacle that it was hard to cast stones. Americans had such fond feelings for their wartime collaborators that many spectators were stirred to tears when Carpentier was welcomed into the ring by a band playing *La Marseillaise*.

Carpentier was nothing more than a puffed-up middleweight, as was Dempsey's next opponent, Tommy Gibbons. The public clamored for Dempsey to take on a bigger man. Luis Angel Firpo, six-foot-three and 220 pounds, fit the bill, provided that he won his tune-up fight with 42-year-old Jess Willard, who had returned to the ring after a 46-month layoff. Contested on Boyle's battleground, the Firpo-Willard fight drew 75,712 paid at popular prices plus an estimated 20,000 gatecrashers, far and away the largest stadium crowd ever for a non-title fight. The aggressor throughout, Firpo wore Willard down and finished him with a barrage of head punches in the eighth round. With that victory, Firpo advanced his record to 26–0 for publicity purposes. Two early setbacks, in Uruguay and Chile, had been expunged from his ledger.

Firpo's buildup was another brilliant job by Tex Rickard's hoopla machine. Although raised in cosmopolitan Buenos Aires, Firpo, of Italian and Spanish descent, was packaged as the Wild Bull of the Pampas. "Propaganda," wrote Walter Davenport in the *New York Herald*, "made him a creature of instinct rather than habit [and] so far back in the ruck of civilization as to be just emerging from the dawn of things." A crude slugger, Firpo's fighting style was consistent with the atavistic greasepaint, but this wild bull was actually a supersharp businessman, a fellow who would go on to make a fortune in self-acquired endorsements and become one of the wealthiest cattle ranchers in South America.[2]

The betting was reportedly light — even the most ardent Dempsey boosters conceded that the big Argentine had a puncher's chance — but the promotion was a blockbuster and ultimately a clash of unbridled fury. The first round alone produced ten falls, mostly flash knockdowns, but Firpo was down for counts of eight and nine and he pitched Dempsey face-first out of the ring with a clubbing right hand. Dempsey retained his belt with a second round knockout, but Firpo returned home to a hero's welcome. Streets and schools across Argentina and even a professional soccer team in El Salvador would be named in his honor.

Dempsey did not fight again for three years, but his name was constantly in the news. In 1925, he married actress Estelle Taylor and officially severed his relationship with Kearns — related events, as it was widely understood that the new woman in Dempsey's life loathed his reprobate manager. The Dempsey-Kearns divorce was one of the most acrimonious uncouplings in the history of business partnerships, producing a flood of lawsuits and countersuits that continued even after Kearns was dead and buried.[3]

Dempsey had three official fights after Doc was reduced to an outsider. He wasn't the same fighter as before, but his matches with Gene Tunney were the grandest spectacles of the Golden Era.

Nicknamed Gene while still a toddler, John Joseph Tunney had been fighting professionally for two years when he joined the Marine Corps in 1917. While ripening into a 190-pound heavyweight, he had five fights with prominent middleweight Harry Greb. He won the last four after Greb saddled him with what would be his only defeat. In crossroads fights, Tunney outpointed Battling Levinsky in a match billed for the North American lightheavyweight title and scored a 15th-round stoppage of Georges Carpentier.

Tunney had a chilly relationship with sportswriters, with the consequence that the public never warmed to him. His match with Dempsey was intriguing because of their contrasting styles and because Dempsey might be rusty after a long layoff, but these were mundane come-hithers. Tex Rickard's publicists tried to frame the match as a bout between a patriot and a war slacker, but this contraposition no longer resonated. It wasn't as if Tunney was a war hero — he never served on the front lines — and Dempsey had shed the splotch of a slacker, a charge that hadn't held up in court. But no artificial coloring was necessary to boil this particular promotion into a roaring success, even in Pennsylvania, where the allure of a big fight was dampened by a 10-round ceiling. Anchored in Philadelphia's new municipal stadium abutting the exposition grounds for the sesquicentennial celebration of the signing of the Declaration of Independence, Dempsey vs. Tunney drew a paid crowd of 120,757, a mind-boggling turnout. An estimated 50,000 came from New York, where baseball games involving the Giants and Dodgers were postponed because of it.

Several days before the big shebang, the odds favoring Dempsey tumbled from 7/2 to 12/5 amidst reports that crooked gambler Arnold Rothstein had bet heavily against him. A provocative article by widely syndicated sportswriter Grantland Rice was more fodder for the notion that Tunney was a live underdog. Rice noted that Dempsey had never had his hands wrapped by anyone but Kearns since graduating from the tank towns. It was Doc's custom to wrap Dempsey's hands with several yards of hard black bicycle tape over a thick cushion of gauze and cotton. For this bout, the fighters were required to enter the ring bare-fisted and their hands would be dressed with inspectors looking on. Bicycle tape was prohibited, forcing Dempsey to fight with far less bandaging than was his custom.[4]

Bicycle tape would not have saved Dempsey. He was stale and never landed a meaningful punch. Referee Tommy Reilly, the lone arbiter, scored the bout 7–1–2, but many in the audience were of the opinion that Dempsey failed to win a single round.

Although Tunney out-boxed Dempsey at every turn, the bout was yet suspenseful. Dempsey's vaunted knockout punch was a thunderclap that could strike at any moment. From the standpoint of entertainment value, the restriction to 10 rounds was a blessing. The bout was over before it became crystal-clear that Dempsey had no fire in his furnace. Nor was Dempsey jeered when he left the ring. There was warm applause that seemed to say "Nice try, old chap." The fight had no indelible moments and was contested in a steady rain, but the audience yet seemed to enjoy the show. It was as if the meal was less relevant than the presentation.

Tunney was expected to make his first defense against Harry Wills, but Wills suffered a shocking upset at the hands of Jack Sharkey, a 24-year-old ex-sailor who fought out of Boston.

Sharkey was even more dominant in his next major fight, a fifth-round stoppage of Beantown rival Jim Maloney at Yankee Stadium. That led to an elimination bout between Sharkey and Dempsey to determine Tunney's next opponent.

A fighter of Lithuanian descent whose birth name was Joseph Cukoschay, Sharkey brought a 26–7 record into his match with the Manassa Mauler, but he was in excellent form and went off the favorite at odds of 17/10. Dempsey upset the odds in a manner that made him more legendary. In the seventh round, he collapsed Sharkey with a sneak punch as Sharkey was turning his head to the referee to complain of low blows. The so-called Boston Gob had gotten the best of it to this point and looked far fresher, but the short left hook that brought about the controversial ending was one of the most potent punches that Dempsey ever landed. The bout at Yankee Stadium attracted 80,000-plus and produced the first million-dollar gate for a non-title fight.

The Tunney-Dempsey sequel at Chicago's Soldier Field was even more fabulous than the first sortie in Philadelphia. There were fewer paid admissions, but the crowd appeared even larger, 150,000 in the view of some reporters. This would be Tex Rickard's crowning achievement, the first *two-million*-dollar gate, a staggering $2,658,660, almost beyond belief as the fight was aired coast-to-coast on 82 radio stations, an unprecedented number for a live sporting event, attracting an estimated 50 million listeners, roughly 45 percent of the U.S. population. The promotion attracted so many multimillionaires that every private car in the Pullman Company fleet was in service, the first time that this had happened since the company was incorporated in 1867.

Fanned by talk that the match was a set-up for an even more lucrative rubber match, Dempsey went to post a slight favorite, but support for the would-be avenger was hardly limited to those that swallowed the conspiracy line. A number of big gamblers that sided with Tunney in the first meeting switched sides, spurred by favorable reports from Dempsey's training camp. Arnold Rothstein remained steadfastly pro-Tunney, but others of his ilk took the opposite road. The *New York Times* reported that almost all of the underworld money was on the Manassa Mauler. Leading the charge was Al Capone, who was rumored to have clout with the regulators in selecting the referee.

The rumor impelled Chicago mayor William Thompson to call a secret meeting of the Illinois Athletic Commission. Thompson insisted on naming the judges. He chose oil magnate Sheldon Clark and department store owner George Lytton. Their great wealth supposedly made them immune to a bribe. As for the referee, it was decided that all of Chicago's referees would report to ringside and that the commission would not name the arbiter until both fighters had entered the ring. The nod would go to Dave Barry, the most experienced man in the pool.

In giving the fighters their instructions, Barry emphasized that a fighter scoring a knockdown must retreat to the farthest neutral corner before the count would begin. The rule, fairly new, was inspired by Dempsey's conduct in his bouts with Jess Willard and Luis Firpo. Dempsey would be slow to heed the rule after he belted Tunney to the canvas in the seventh frame, thereby affording Tunney more than ten seconds to clear his senses. The general consensus was a 14-second interlude. But aside from this moment — the famously controversial "long count" debated for years — the contest was pretty much a carbon of the first meeting. Tunney quickly regained the upper hand and went on to win a clear-cut decision.[5]

Dempsey retired after this bout. Tunney quit the next year after a soft title defense against Tom Heeney, a journeyman from New Zealand. The first heavyweight title fight held in

Yankee Stadium, Tunney vs. Heeney drew a crowd of more than 40,000 but was yet a financial bust. Tunney's $500,000 purse ate up more than 70 percent of the gate receipts.

Reporters were fond of writing that Rickard had the Midas touch, but his luck turned sour when Dempsey left the scene. The directors of the holding company that owned Madison Square Garden were none too happy with him after the Tunney-Heeney clinker. Rickard's lease to promote boxing at Madison Square Garden was close to expiration. There was speculation that it wouldn't be renewed.

Rickard pressed forward with a tournament to find Gene Tunney's successor. The invitees were Jack Sharkey, Young Stribling, Max Schmeling, and Paulino Uzcudun. In the first elimination bout, Sharkey opposed Stribling at Flamingo Park in Miami.

In Miami, Rickard forged an alliance with individuals hoping to build a gambling complex. The facility, as outlined to reporters, would include a hotel, casino, and racetracks for thoroughbred horses and greyhounds. It appeared as if the venerated gambler who had conquered New York after earning his spurs in western boomtowns was about to begin a new chapter in his life. But Rickard died in a Miami hospital on January 6, 1929, from complications of a ruptured appendix. The Sharkey-Stribling promotion went on without him but the show wasn't profitable. Reporters wondered whether Rickard's passing foretokened the end of the megafights.

The Roaring Twenties was the temporal analogue of a boomtown, by nature a boom-and-bust town. On Monday, October 28, 1929, the New York Stock Exchange suffered a record one-day loss. The next day, Black Tuesday, the market collapsed in a panic of frenzied trading. It was suddenly plain that Tex Rickard's death was inconsequential in the larger scheme of things. Boxing promoters chose to look on the bright side. At least they could count on the sportswriters to keep the cauldrons bubbling. Or could they?

# CHAPTER 8

# Fighters' Writers

From 1935 to 1974, Jack Dempsey's Restaurant was a prominent mid–Manhattan dining establishment. At its second location, across from Madison Square Garden, it acquired a new feature — a mural-sized painting by James Montgomery Flagg in the main dining room. It depicted Dempsey, bent low at the waist, poised to spring at a lunging Jess Willard.

Flagg's mural was a functional ornament, a conversational icebreaker. Among the front-row ringsiders in the painting were nationally known sportswriters Grantland Rice, Damon Runyon, Ring Lardner, and Rube Goldberg. Patrons would try to put names to faces. Disagreements invariably prompted a bet. An amiable host, Dempsey delighted in adjudicating these friendly wagers.

The reporters in Flagg's panorama were as symbolic of the Golden Era as was Dempsey. They kept the pot boiling, whetting and slaking the public's thirst for sports information at a time when a journalist, by definition, had a newspaper forum. The information they disseminated was often warped by highly subjective impressions and, in many cases, warped by quid pro quo. During his days at Madison Square Garden, Tex Rickard reportedly spent $160,000 entertaining sportswriters. He was repaid with news stories that often blurred the line between circus ballyhoo and straight reporting.

It's doubtful that any of the leading American sportswriters of the Golden Era had more than a cursory acquaintance with the work of Pierce Egan. His death in 1849 predated the Dempsey-Willard fight by seventy years and his publications were long out of print. But Egan is responsible for most of what is known about the sport's first Golden Era, when bare-knuckle prizefighting in England was all the rage. Egan's manner of gathering and reporting the news greatly influenced subsequent generations of sportswriters, even those unfamiliar with his work.

The son of a man who earned his living paving streets, Egan was a prolific writer who came to be enthralled by the world of the prize ring. He was in his mid-thirties when he founded *Boxiana*, a monthly newsletter in pamphlet form that was sold by subscription and widely circulated in taverns. At intervals, Egan would stitch a batch of his articles into a compendium. Five bound volumes were published between 1813 and 1828.

In addition to providing round-by-round descriptions of important bouts, *Boxiana* was full of gossip, anecdotal information about ring personalities, and tributes to stalwarts of earlier generations. Before Egan, most journeymen bruisers were deemed so insignificant that they have remained nameless, identified in record books only by their occupational trade or place of residence, or a combination of both. Egan humanized all the fighters that he came to know, outfitting his personal favorites with *noms de guerre* that enhanced their notoriety. He did this in a fresh style salted with colloquialisms and imagery that suggested a familiarity with Homer. His style was so fresh — and his writings so popular — that he would be injudiciously credited with inventing the genre of sportswriting.

In 1819, Egan collaborated with satirical cartoonists George and Robert Cruikshank on a project that spawned a fascinating artifact. Sold in a metal cylindrical box that could fit in one's pocket like a roll of film, it was a strip of drawings that depicted activity before, during, and after an imaginary prizefight. The panorama, titled *A Picture of the Fancy on The Road to Moulsey Hurst*, began with a scene in a London tavern, advanced to the meadow where the battle unfolded, and concluded with a scene at Tattersall's, the settling-up place, on the day after the event. A betting booth appears in one of the panels depicting the scene at the battleground, graphic evidence that sports betting in England had diffused beyond the higher social classes.

As a journalist, Egan was a hack. His sketches of pugilists were over ripe and he overdramatized the fights that he covered. However, he captured the milieu of prizefighting, plumbing an unexplored subculture with vivid insights.

In enumerating the exploits of pugilists that competed before his time, Egan drew heavily from a 1747 treatise by Captain John Godfrey. A patron of James Figg's academy and later a close friend of Jack Broughton, Captain Godfrey admired professional fighting men because they practiced a noble art that invigorated the national character. His treatise, dedicated to the Royal Highness (King George II), was something of a propagandistic tract. Egan was likewise a defender of pugilism, but his motives were suspect.

Besides the money that accrued from his writings, Egan profited from prizefighting in other ways. He made himself useful as a matchmaker and stakes-holder and supervised arena setups. The Fancy were constantly holding benefits and Egan was in steady demand as a toastmaster. "It is impossible to imagine boxing in its palmy days without Egan," says historian J.C. Reid. "Short of taking part in the bouts himself, he seems to have performed every function a devotee could, and to have been regarded by all and sundry as oil in the machine."[1]

The great essayist A.J. Leibling was more candid, acknowledging that Egan was probably a bit of a shakedown artist. The pugilist or promoter who wanted favorable attention undoubtedly had a better chance if he had a favor to exchange. Posthumously, however, Egan had no bigger fan than Leibling, who repeatedly cited passages from *Boxiana* in his wonderful musings about the fight game in *The New Yorker*. (The first collection of Leibling's articles would be titled *The Sweet Science*. The phrase first appears in Volume IV of *Boxiana*: "the sweet science of bruising.")

Egan's infatuation with prizefighting was not a lifelong infatuation. He rarely attended a fight after 1828. It has been theorized that he walked away in disgust after a spate of fixed fights. That may have been a contributing factor. Dishonest fights disquieted Egan because they challenged his assumptions about the virtues of pugilism. However, other reasons were more salient.

Egan was less attracted to prizefighting than to the *spectacle* of prizefights. When crowds became smaller and less heterogeneous, it was inevitable that his interest would wane. Then again, he probably felt he had nothing more to accomplish as a boxing scribe: nothing more to learn from the culture of bruising. Egan had spread his wings while still engaged in the production of his newsletter, shifting into fiction while continuing his collaboration with the

Cruikshank brothers. Their illustrations enhanced the popularity of Egan's book *Life in London*, a smashing best seller that begat long-running plays. The central characters, Corinthian Tom and his country cousin Jerry Hawthorne, are excitement-seekers flouting the norms of society while carousing about the London metropolis.[2]

Some of Egan's early work appeared in the sporting journal that came to be called *Bell's Life*. The leading periodical of its kind throughout most of the Victorian era, *Bell's Life* died in 1866, unable to sustain the circulation boost that accompanied its coverage of the Sayers-Heenan fight. That event was largely a co-promotion of *Bell's Life* and its American counterpart, *Spirit of the Times*. The editors were instrumental in making the match; the papers profited from special editions manufactured to commemorate the occasion. *Bell's Life* editor Frank Dowling refereed the contest.

Founded in 1831 by William T. Porter, *Spirit of the Times* provided readers with all the gory details of the fatal Lilly-McCoy fight. The account was bundled with a disclaimer that discountenanced prizefighting. After George T. Wilkes acquired the paper in 1856, the buildup to prizefights was accorded more ink, but there was a long lag before the discontinuation of the disclaimers. "Prizefighting has nothing about it in harmony with our institutions, it is here a mere gloss for the vilest kind of rowdyism," said the paper in false piety in an editorial sidebar to a story about the Sayers-Heenan match.

*Spirit of the Times* covered agrarian sports like hunting and fresh-water fishing. A rival paper founded in 1853, the *New York Clipper*, covered prizefights within the context of show business. Although publisher Frank Queen assisted promoters in arranging prizefights, his main contribution to the sport was that he built fighters into larger attractions on the vaudeville circuit. Heavyweight champions from Jem Mace through Jess Willard derived the bulk of their earnings as performers in variety shows.

Prior to acquiring the *Spirit of the Times*, George Wilkes owned a pulp magazine called the *National Police Gazette*. This weekly periodical became America's first Bible of boxing.

Begun as a muckraking publication, the *Police Gazette* gradually became more lurid, running stories about unsolved murders, marital infidelities, and organized vice. This drift accelerated in 1876 when the paper was sold to Richard Kyle Fox. A Presbyterian immigrant from Belfast, Fox changed the look of the paper by introducing graphics. Engravings of showgirls in provocative poses and drawings of bawdyhouse parlor scenes solidified its reputation as a scandal sheet. Circulation increased sharply and rose higher with expanded coverage of sports.

The post–Civil War era was a period of heightened masculinity reflected in a preoccupation with athletic prowess. The *Police Gazette* stimulated this preoccupation, covering all manner of sports — wrestling, weight lifting, foot racing, rowing, fencing, swimming, etc. — but none as extensively as prizefighting. The paper did not merely report the news but created it, arranging contests of strength and endurance and competitions for barbers, bartenders, oyster shuckers, and steeple climbers. Winners received cash prizes and commemorata — cups, ribbons, medals, trophies, etc. — adorned with an engraving of Richard K. Fox. With his distinctive moustache and foppish silk top hat, the self-aggrandizing Fox was one of America's most recognizable personalities.

Because the magazine was condemned as immoral, many newsstands refused to carry it. Fox overcame this impediment by going directly to his core readership, offering special rates to barbershops, saloons, billiard parlors, bowling alleys, and firehouses — the places where unmarried men congregated.

Fox had a peculiarly symbiotic relationship with John L. Sullivan. It was peculiar because they supposedly hated each other.

Their first encounter supposedly occurred at Harry Hill's on April 2, 1881. Sullivan, basking in the glow of his first New York fight, was drinking with his new friends. Fox invited him to his table, but was rebuffed. "Tell the son-of-a-bitch, if he wants to see me, he can come here," Sullivan reportedly told the waiter conveying the invite.

Fox was a powerful force in the world of prizefighting. Paddy Ryan was a complete unknown without a noteworthy victory to his credit until Fox manufactured a match for him with 42-year-old English bruiser Joe Goss. They fought in a ravine near Weirton, West Virginia, a literal stone's throw from the Pennsylvania line, with perhaps three hundred people in attendance. But six of those were *Police Gazette* correspondents and Fox fused their reports into a special edition that sold an astonishing 400,000 copies, boosting the triumphant Ryan into a position of eminence. Accustomed to deferential treatment in the company of pugilists, Fox was incensed at Sullivan's impertinence and resolved to humble him, or so it would be written.

Perhaps it was true that Fox actually loathed Sullivan, but that didn't stop him from making arrangements that made both men more rich and famous. Fox put Sullivan's likeness on souvenirs that bore the *Police Gazette* imprint. After Sullivan defeated Ryan, Fox promoted four 4-round bouts for him at Madison Square Garden against British Commonwealth opponents with little chance of defeating him. Clever British middleweight Charley Mitchell was legit, but the other "exotics" were badly overmatched, in particular Herbert "Maori Giant" Slade, a palooka from New Zealand who toured with Jem Mace (and later joined Sullivan's caravan). There is no record that Slade ever won a legitimate prizefight.

In 1888, the *Police Gazette* created a furor by stripping Sullivan of his title for inactivity and anointing Jake Kilrain his successor. Kilrain was deemed worthy because of his performance against English title claimant Jem Smith in their inconclusive bout held near Bonnaires, France. According to the *Gazette*'s report of the fight, Kilrain's face was a lumpy piece of raw beefsteak when the contest was halted on account of darkness, but Smith's appearance was even worse.

At a press conference in Baltimore, Fox presented Kilrain with an ornate championship belt layered with silver and gold and studded with diamonds. Wealthy Irish-American sportsmen commissioned a more elegant belt for Sullivan, presenting it to him at a rally in Boston. Fox likely orchestrated this rally too. It served his interest by stoking the fire for a "unification" match.

As his career wore on, Sullivan came to be portrayed as a quick-tempered, beer-soaked lout, a characterization with more than a kernel of truth. Fox's self-serving vendetta kept him in the public eye and built his forthcoming fights into larger attractions by imbuing them with elements of melodrama. His final fight with Jim Corbett was soaked with this flavoring.

Corbett was characterized as a man of good virtue, the opposite of the lowbred Sullivan. But beneath these antipodal veneers were two sons of working-class Irish Catholic immigrants who were pretty much cut from the same cloth. In his teenage years, Corbett was kicked out of two schools for fighting, with the consequence that he and Sullivan received about the same amount of formal schooling. Both had extramarital affairs with actresses. Sullivan was prone to bad behavior in public places, but Corbett was more prone to flights of bad sportsmanship. Sullivan was unquestionably the bigger drinker, but Corbett may have actually spent more time in saloons. His brother Harry ran a gin mill in San Francisco and he opened his own saloon in New York about the time that John L. became a teetotaler and spokesperson for the Women's Christian Temperance Union.

The *Police Gazette* sowed the seeds of its own demise. Circulation waned as established dailies introduced sports sections and theatrical gossip columns. The dailies delivered news in a timelier manner and the *Gazette* would eventually be out-sensationalized by the yellow journalism of the tabloids. Sportswriters became a more recognizable species within the newspaper kingdom during this flux, but they were initially at the bottom of the journalistic totem pole and were paid accordingly. To make ends meet, they found ways to derive income from the events that they covered, moonlighting as publicists, umpires, event coordinators, etc. This was a blatant conflict of interest but a well-established practice with roots in England. The archetype of the jack-of-all-trades boxing writer was Pierce Egan.

The most enterprising sportswriters became promoters. Otto Floto, the most influential sportswriter in Denver, owned a traveling circus and staged fights throughout the region. By far the most common avenue of extra income, however, was officiating.

Crisscrossed by the most passenger rail lines, Chicago produced a disproportionately large number of prominent boxing officials, the most notable of whom were George Siler of the *Chicago Tribune* and Ed W. Smith of the *Chicago American*. Siler refereed the bizarre Fitzsimmons-Maher fight on a Rio Grande sandbar, the Fitzsimmons-Corbett fight at Carson City, the Jeffries-Sharkey bout at Coney Island, and the first Gans-Nelson fight at Goldfield. Smith refereed the brutal rematch between Battling Nelson and Ad Wolgast at Richmond, California, the Johnson-Flynn heavyweight championship fight at Las Vegas, New Mexico, and the ill-fated McCarty-Pelkey bout at Calgary. *Chicago Inter-Ocean* sportswriter Lou Houseman officiated at many bouts before guiding Jack Root to the 175-pound title. Houseman is credited with inventing the lightheavyweight division, the only one of the eight standard weight classes to have originated in the United States.

A few turn-of-the-century boxing writers were fight functionaries first and then branched into journalism, most prominently Bat Masterson. The fabled western lawman spent the last eighteen years of his life in New York City writing for the *Morning Telegraph*, a paper devoted to sports, theatrical, and financial news with a heavy emphasis on horseracing.

The deputy marshal of Dodge City, Kansas, at the age of twenty-three, Masterson as a young man hopped from one wide-open town to another, managing gambling houses and burlesque troupes between stints as a peace officer, occupations that frequently overlapped. Lore has it that the first prizefight he witnessed was a private match inside Dodge City's Saratoga Saloon that started in the wee hours of the morning after the dancing girls had been shooed home. As prizefighting was illegal in the county, it was Masterson's sworn duty to arrest the principals, a conflict he supposedly resolved by the expedient of removing his badge. More than likely he insisted on a "sanctioning fee" to let the bout go forward.

Over a span of more than thirty years, Bat attended virtually every major American fight, usually in some official capacity. His specialty was fight security — hiring and superintending the guards and ushers — but he busied himself in other ways. He was Kilrain's timekeeper when Kilrain opposed Sullivan, and Mitchell's bottle-holder when Mitchell opposed Corbett five years later. Among the many fights that he refereed was the bout that came to be referred to as the first title fight in the lightheavyweight division. Masterson was also a big plunger whose action affected the odds.

Bat first dabbled in sportswriting in Denver, handicapping fights for a publication called *George's Weekly*. In 1903, shortly after settling in New York, he was arrested for bilking a Mormon church elder out of $16,000 in a crooked faro game. The charges were not only dropped, but Masterson was put on the federal payroll to keep him out of mischief. By order of President Theodore Roosevelt, he was appointed a United States deputy marshal for the southern district of New York. According to Jack DeMattos, "There is no evidence that he ever showed up for work except on payday — and on those occasions, just long enough to pick up his check."[3]

A walking tourist attraction on Broadway in his embroidered vest and spit-shined cowboy boots, Masterson was as synthetic as some of the popular fighters of his day. The handle of his six-shooter reportedly had twenty-eight notches, a figure he did not dispute, but this was unadulterated nonsense. Bat shot and killed at most three people *intentionally* (in a gun battle with a cavalryman in Sweetwater, Texas, an unfortunate saloon girl was caught in the crossfire). But this colorful gadabout would metamorphose into a rare bird among sportswriters of his generation: a scrupulously honest reporter.

After settling in New York, Masterson became less involved in the promotional side of boxing. Without conflicting agendas, he was freer to speak his mind and his viewpoints became more jaundiced. No other sportswriter was consistently more contemptuous of the White Hope craze. In Bat's estimation, it clogged the heavyweight division with men of inferior skill. His readers found his iconoclasm refreshing in an era when the sports pages were rife with sycophantic fluff.

Bat died at his typewriter in 1921. Prominent among the mourners at his wake was Damon Runyon. The son of a maverick frontier newspaperman, Runyon had traveled the same road to Broadway, inverting Horace Greeley's dictum that young men go west. Akin to Masterson, and perhaps inspired by his example, Runyon bet with both fists when he had a strong opinion. In the words of Broadway press agent Ed Weiner, "His bankroll fluctuated like the moods of an uncertain woman."

By all accounts, most sportswriters of this era bet on the fights that they covered. Those that didn't had more than ego invested in their prefight assessments. Boxing writers of the period, save the most talented wordsmiths and those employed by staid papers that downplayed sports, were expected to be proficient prognosticators. Bad selections obstructed career advancement.

The opposite side of the coin was that a sportswriter with a knack for picking winners had a better chance of moving up. George Barton, who chaired the Minnesota Athletic Commission and refereed thousands of fights while covering sports for Minneapolis papers, was a good illustration.

A stellar boxer in his teens who fought the great Terry McGovern (winning a hometown decision), Barton covered the Johnson-Jeffries fight for the *Minneapolis Daily News*, an arm of the Cloverleaf newspaper chain. In his final prefight dispatch, he came out strongly for Johnson, predicting that he would stop Jeffries between the tenth and fifteenth round. This didn't sit well with his publisher, who had requested to see Barton's column before it went to press. Concerned that Barton's assessment would get readers hot under the collar, he fired off a telegram imploring Barton to reconsider.

"I am standing pat on my pick," replied Barton defiantly. "If I am wrong, I will resign." When the young scribe returned to Minneapolis, he was informed that his stubbornness had induced his boss to switch his bet and that his salary was being hiked by ten dollars a week. In his 1957 autobiography, Barton numbered the incident the proudest moment of his fifty years in sports journalism.

No newspaperman got more mileage from a single sports selection than *San Francisco Bulletin* scribe Harry Grayson. On the eve of their first meeting, Grayson wrote that Gene Tunney would demolish Jack Dempsey: "This is the time to get well forever. This is the time to hock the family jewels. Gene Tunney will win every second of every round from Jack

Dempsey tonight. He may even cut up Dempsey and knock him out. But regardless of that, it won't be a contest."

In truth, Grayson believed that Dempsey was almost a lock. He touted Tunney in the most outlandish terms because he knew that his wild opinion, right or wrong, would get him noticed. His prescient prediction caught the eye of Joe Williams, sports editor of the *New York Telegram,* who hired Grayson to be his boxing writer. Six years later Grayson would be named sports editor of the Newspaper Enterprise Association, a position that afforded him the freedom to cover any sports event of his choosing. His calculated gamble paid off big.

The first Dempsey-Tunney fight was deemed to be almost as newsworthy as the signing of the armistice that ended World War I, the biggest news story as measured by column inches in newspapers up to that time. The *New York Times* devoted almost 1800 inches to the event in the two weeks leading up to the battle, roughly twelve and a half times the coverage it accorded the Sullivan-Corbett fight during the corresponding interval.

Among sportswriters with large readerships, only W.O. McGeehan of the *New York Herald Tribune* came out strongly for Tunney. Many of the others likely went against him because they did not like him. This was rather peculiar, as Tunney was a wholesome and courageous young man who, on the surface, had all the attributes necessary to become a pet of the sportswriters. More than that, in hindsight a strong case can be made that Gene Tunney was the finest role model to young boxers that the sport ever produced.

The son of a stevedore who had Tammany connections, assuring steady work, Tunney didn't rise up from poverty, but the cold-water apartment he shared with his parents and three siblings in Greenwich Village was barely adequate for their needs. At an early age, Gene resolved to better his station in life. He was partial to self-help books, but read extensively on a variety of topics, improving his vocabulary and his knowledge of world affairs. He even cultivated an interest in Shakespeare.

As a young fighter, Tunney was acutely aware of his shortcomings. He attended fights not as a fan, but in hopes of learning new techniques. He initiated conversations with old-timers, talking strategy with men like Jim Corbett, with whom he would ultimately be compared. His daily regimen included soaking his brittle hands in brine, squeezing a rubber ball until his wrists ached, and pushing with his fingertips against immovable objects, a novel exercise that others considered a waste of time. Every sparring session and every fight was approached with the idea of becoming more polished so that he would be at his very peak when he finally drew Jack Dempsey into his web. Preparing for any eventuality, Tunney even had the foresight to practice running backwards.

Tunney's ability to learn from his mistakes was never more apparent than in his five fights with Harry Greb, a famously dirty fighter who would come to be recognized as one of the all-time greats. Tunney was badly battered in the first encounter and fortunate to last the distance. The second fight was much closer. The nod went to Tunney after fifteen hard rounds, but the decision was unpopular. Tunney won the third meeting by a clear-cut margin, the fourth meeting by a wider margin, and the fifth meeting by such a decisive margin that the outcome was never in doubt. But it was not only his doggedness that set Tunney apart. Few fighters were as levelheaded.

During his career he had several managers, some of whom sold pieces of him to "facilitators," but Tunney basically called his own shots. Momentarily unhinged from his senses during one of his sparring sessions, he began to worry about the long-term effects. He resolved to quit boxing before his skills atrophied and stayed true to his resolution, becoming one of the few fighters in history to retire while still champion and never come back. He married an heiress to the Carnegie fortune, authored two autobiographies without ghostwriters, gave unstintingly of his time as an unpaid physical fitness consultant to the Army during World War II, served on the board of directors of two banks and eight corporations, and raised a son who became a United States congressman.

Not all of these facts of Tunney's life were foreshadowed as early as 1926, but it was obvious that he was no stereotypical pug. Perhaps no other athlete better exemplified the ideals of Horatio Alger, the Unitarian minister who authored books for young readers with rags-to-riches themes — books that were so popular that his name became synonymous with upward mobility achieved through honest toil and clean living. Bare-knuckle champions John Gully and John Morrisey had risen from humble beginnings to become rich and powerful, but they were forever typecast as bruisers. Tunney would be the first prominent fighter to be accepted by highly educated, socially prominent people as a co-equal. But many sportswriters were downright hostile toward him.

Tunney invited the hostility with an attitude that conveyed the impression that sportswriters were beneath him. He frequently cut interviews short, hinting that these conversations were insufficiently scholastic to hold his interest. The men that he professed to admire most were George Bernard Shaw, the Nobel Prize–winning playwright, and Chauncey Depew, a Yale-educated railroad magnate who lectured on the power of positive thinking.

The most spiteful of Tunney's detractors was *New York Daily News* sports editor Paul Gallico, a man of Tunney's age and temperament with stronger credentials as a Renaissance man. (The son of a concert pianist, Gallico eventually settled in Europe, married into royalty, authored critically acclaimed books for children, and wrote a best-selling novel, *The Poseidon Aventure*.) Gallico needled Tunney both privately and in print and his colleagues in the Fourth Estate came to his share his view that Tunney was an intellectual lightweight and a priggish parvenu.

For all his learnedness, Paul Gallico was a notoriously bad fight prognosticator. The same could not be said of his contemporary Damon Runyon, although Runyon's wrong picks attracted greater notice because he bet so big.

Runyon began the New York phase of his journalism career as a baseball beat writer. He was covering the Giants at their spring training camp in Texas when a telegram arrived directing him to go to Havana to cover the Johnson-Willard fight. From this point, Runyon took more interest in boxing than in baseball, a development that was inevitable as he was drawn to the sorts of characters that populated the fight game, the most colorful of whom came to be labeled Runyonesque. His fascination with boxing continued after he broadened his readership with accounts of sensational murder and divorce trials, accounts often garnished with droll sports imagery.

One of the first men that Runyon befriended in New York was Jimmy Johnston. Born in the Irish section of Liverpool, the sprightly, fast-talking Johnston then owned the lease to promote fights at Madison Square Garden. When Johnston tooled around Manhattan in his fancy Stutz automobile, Runyon often rode shotgun. It was Runyon that dubbed Johnston the "Boy Bandit," a nickname that somehow stuck although Runyon affixed it to a middle-aged man.

Elbowed out of Madison Square Garden by Tex Rickard, Johnston stayed active, promoting fights at smaller arenas and ultimately reclaiming his old desk after Rickard's passing. In 1933, Vanguard Press published his life story under the title *Wise Guy*. Runyon wrote the prologue, a paean that extolled Johnston for his "nerve, ingenuity, candor, gameness, perseverance, industry, and indomitable courage."

When the book was released, the title character was about to be fired again by his bosses at Madison Square Garden. The backstabbing Runyon knew that this was in the works, because he was one of the conspirators bringing about the palace coup. He and the sports editors of New York's two Hearst papers, Bill Farnsworth and Ed Frayne, were in cahoots with Broadway ticket broker Mike Jacobs, the mastermind of the takeover. They had demonstrated their usefulness to Jacobs through their involvement in Milk Fund fights.

The pet charity of Mrs. William Randolph Hearst, the Milk Fund provided free milk to babies whose parents were poor. The charity wrapped one of its annual benefits around a Madison Square Garden boxing show. Because Mrs. Hearst's husband was the nation's most powerful newspaper publisher, the arena was provided to her for a nominal fee. Runyon, Frayne, and Farnsworth coordinated the fund-raisers, ostensibly pro bono. In 1933, the Board of Directors of Madison Square Garden, miffed at what they considered a double standard — tremendous coverage in Hearst-owned dailies for the Milk Fund shows; inferior coverage of other events — informed Mrs. Hearst that they would be raising her rental fee. Jacobs and his minions seized the moment, forming the 20th Century Sporting Club under the pretense of saving the Milk Fund.

The first show by the new entity was a solid moneymaker. Jacobs' next move was to heed the advice of those in the know and sign an up-and-comer, Joe Louis, to an exclusive promotional contract. The Hearst papers built up Louis as the second coming of Dempsey. But Louis quickly justified the bouquets, prompting Jacobs to dissolve the partnership. This required only a simple declaration. All of the stock in the 20th Century Sporting Club was held in his name because the others could not publicly acknowledge their involvement.

Harry Grayson exposed the alliance in a column that ran in the *New York World-Telegram* on August 13, 1938. The careers of Frayne and Farnsworth were ruined, but Runyon, an untouchable in the eyes of the Hearst beancounters, was unaffected. Nor was he financially pained when Mike Jacobs cut the cord. The first collection of his short stories, published in 1931 under the title *Guys and Dolls*, sold briskly and streamed quickly into more money from screen adaptations. During the lean years of the Depression, Runyon purchased a vacation home on Hibiscus Island overlooking the Miami harbor, a short drive to Hialeah, his favorite racetrack.

Runyon was in many ways the reincarnation of Pierce Egan. A boxing scribe of the "gee whiz" school, he achieved his greatest success writing fiction. With an ear attuned to the patois of the Broadway underworld, he brought a fresh perspective to American humor. Unlike Egan, however, Runyon never abandoned journalism. Without the safety net of a newspaper affiliation, he once said, "I would be writing with scared money, which almost always loses."

After his breakup with Mike Jacobs, Runyon covered only the big outdoor fights, but he gravitated back to Madison Square Garden in his twilight years, attending the weekly fights on a regular basis. On September 27, 1945, he witnessed the battle between Rocky Graziano and Harold Green and then cranked out this sparkling rhapsody:

> I waited a long time to see another knock-down-drag-out ring fighter like Jack Dempsey. I mean a lunging, plunging, rip-snorter of a glove warrior with nothin' else on his mind but the immediate devastation of his opponent. I mean a savage, slam-bang slugger, all movement and action from head to toe, of fighting fury so intense as to cause him to forget about the rules, the officials, the bell; and everything but the business in hand. I was weary of back-pedaling, running, light hitting, grabbing, holding, polite and almost apologetic muggs. I wanted to see an old fashioned hell-for-leather bone-crusher like Dempsey. Then along came Rocky Graziano. Along came a

tousled haired, lean, loose-muscled, hard-featured, hard-fisted Italian from the lower east side of Manhattan to bring solace to my declining years and to restore my faith in the manly art of scrambling ears as thrill entertainment, such as it was in the days when "The Manassa Mauler" came roaring up out of obscurity to set the world of sport afire.

Overcharged sportswriting of this sort had fallen into disfavor. Perhaps Runyon felt that his readers needed something thrilling for breakfast, but one can't help but think that he was repaying a debt to Graziano's promoter. Regardless, he produced an epistle that turned back the clock, capturing the spirit of the Golden Era.

# CHAPTER 9

# Boxing and Jews

The first promotion of Mike Jacobs' 20th Century Sporting Club attracted an SRO crowd to the 12,000-seat Bronx Coliseum. The main event of the January 24, 1934, show was a non-title match between lightweight champion Barney Ross and Billy "Fargo Express" Petrolle.

Ross was one of six Jewish fighters on the five-bout card. Among the others were Al Roth and Davey Day, both of whom would go on to fight for world titles. While the Bronx was heavily Jewish, influencing the makeup of the cast of fighters, it would have been difficult to cobble a full fight card in New York during the Great Depression without a Jewish entry, even if the participants were drawn at random from the pool of licensed boxers.

The first prominent Jewish fighter came to the fore in the late 18th century. Daniel Mendoza inspired such ardor among his coreligionists that the Jewish community of London reportedly suffered a severe economic downturn from the aggregated sum of their lost wagers when he came up short in his first bout with Richard Humphries in 1788.

Jewish punters were drawn to Mendoza because he was a *landsman*, a proud Sephardic Jew with whom they could vicariously identify. But those that repeatedly bet on him were certainly not all blinded by tribal loyalty. Although he carried only 160 pounds on his five-foot-seven frame, Mendoza was a ring marvel. A party held in his honor at Windsor Castle in 1792 was a moment of great symbolism, marking the first time in modern English history that a Jew had an audience with His Majesty the King. Among other distinctions, Mendoza was one of the first fighters to publish an instructional manual on boxing and the first fighter to give exhibitions at respectable music halls.

Mendoza had his first prizefight at the age of eighteen and his last at age fifty-six. Had he continued fighting one more year, his career would have spanned parts of five decades. More than anyone, he was credited with alleviating prejudice against Jews in England.

There was undoubtedly some truth to this notion. Two years before Mendoza's first ring engagement, a German traveler, Pastor Moritz, noted that anti–Semitism was stronger in England than in other parts of Europe. It's doubtful that Moritz would have drawn this conclusion had his trip transpired during Mendoza's glory years. However, not everyone gave Mendoza his due. He won several seesaw fights in which he looked like a goner. Inevitably, there was talk that he feigned distress so that confederates at ringside could press their bets at more favorable odds. That Mendoza was a poor businessman, periodically in debt as he strived to provide for his growing family — his wife bore him 11 children — was grain for the mudslingers.

There were other Jewish prizefighters in Mendoza's day. There was a Yokel, a Youssop, a Lyons, and a fellow indecorously known as Ikey Pig. Some of Mendoza's contemporaries defeated men identified only as a Jew. A Jewish fighter named Elisha Crabbe was considered a rising star after defeating the formidable Steven "Death" Oliver, but his star faded quickly.

Dutch Sam Elias, a protégé of Mendoza, was outstanding despite the handicap of standing only five-foot-six-and-a-half. He twice defeated Tom Belcher, dispelling the widely held opinion that Tom would prove to be best of the three celebrated fighting Belcher brothers. The senior member of prizefighting's first notable father-son combination, Dutch Sam would be credited with inventing the uppercut, an attribution that invites an asterisk as he had an arm locked around his opponent's neck when he delivered his signature punch. Dutch Sam had a less enthusiastic Jewish following than Mendoza, perhaps partly because he advocated gin as a nutritional supplement, but was esteemed as a man of scrupulous honesty. According to Pierce Egan, Sam was once offered the magnificent sum of one thousand pounds to lose a battle, but spurned the bribe with "becoming spirit and indignation."

The son of Dutch immigrants, Elias was raised in the East London district of Whitechapel. Associated with the dregs of London's industrial work force and later infamous as the hunting ground of Jack the Ripper, Whitechapel would take on the trappings of a *shtetl* at the turn of the twentieth century as it ingested tens of thousands of Jewish refugees fleeing pogroms and famine in Eastern Europe. Many of the newcomers aspired to live in North America but were stuck in England because of insufficient funds to extend their journey. If anything, Jews newly arrived in Whitechapel were more impoverished than their brethren who crossed the Atlantic Ocean in steerage, finding shelter in the teeming Jewish ghettoes of the New World, places like New York's Lower East Side, the Maxwell Street section of Chicago, and the Kensington district of Toronto, all of which became hotbeds of boxing.

In the early years of the twentieth century, Jewish Whitechapel had London's highest concentration of boxing gyms. As John Harding points out, these gyms, although stripped to the essentials, were hives of social activity:

> These were converted lofts, garden sheds, and small back rooms equipped with punch-bags and dumb-bells, where young and not so young men sweated and pounded one another under the eye of a "trainer," an ex-boxer, perhaps, who would pass on the rudimentary skills. They were places where street bookies gathered with their runners, passed on gossip and tips, laid bets, handed over cash, wagers, and purses. Music-hall agents came and went, offering bookings, and old boxers lingered here and made themselves useful carrying the odd bucket or towel....[1]

The idea of Jewish boys trading punches, whether supervised or not, is sharply at odds with the image of Jews as a people who value brains over brawn. That young Jewish men did gravitate to boxing, often to the horror of their parents, was partly a rational adaptation to a hostile environment. A hard jab was a useful tool; one never knew when it would come in handy. The profit motive was a powerful incentive. A run-of-the-mill fighter at a neighborhood club could earn as much in one "recital" as a common laborer could earn in a week. Those with a special aptitude could earn more in a few years than most men earned in a lifetime. There were also religious proscriptions that diverted athletically inclined boys away from daytime sports oriented around Saturdays.

Barred from many spheres of employment, Jewish boxers in London circa 1900 had relatively less difficulty getting matches than their comparably talented non–Jewish cohorts. As was true of a wide variety of commercial amusements, Jews were overrepresented among the patrons at boxing shows, with the consequence that promising Jewish boxers were quick to develop a following. A contributing factor was that Jews were raised in a culture that valued sobriety and were therefore less likely to burn up discretionary income in saloons.

The Judaean Social Club of London, which opened in 1902, held boxing shows on Sunday mornings. Three-time English amateur lightweight champion Matt Wells, the first Jewish fighter to win a Lonsdale belt, had several of his early bouts here. At the professional level, the major nurseries for Jewish boxers were Wonderland and Premierland, boxing halls that attracted a broad cross-section of fight fans. Up-and-comer Ted "Kid" Lewis, a future world welterweight champion, was a big draw at Premierland. Opened in 1911 in a converted warehouse, the East London auditorium housed a number of important fights until it was shut down in 1930 as part of an urban renewal project.

Born Gershon Mendelhoff, Lewis was the first boxer from the East End of London to attract a significant American following. A veteran of more than one hundred fights on three continents before his twenty-first birthday, Lewis campaigned mostly in the U.S. in the years 1915 to 1919, fighting on average once every two weeks. His travels took him as far north as Montreal, as far south as New Orleans, and as far west as San Francisco, but demand for his services was greatest in New York City, home to legions of Jewish boxing fans and a burgeoning population of Jewish fighters.

"Kid" Lewis was actually the second Jewish fighter to arrive in New York bearing a world championship belt. Featherweight champion Abe Attell made his New York debut in 1908, but Attell's arrival wasn't greeted with much fanfare. Born to Russian immigrants in San Francisco, Attell's appeal was already blunted by his reputation for engaging in dishonest fights. In his first New York contest against a name opponent, Attell lost a newspaper decision to Jem Driscoll. His tame performance was consistent with his reputation as a finagler. In 1912, he was barred from fighting in New York for six months on the grounds that he tanked a fight with "Knockout" Brown while high on cocaine.

First-generation Jewish immigrants in New York City could more readily identify with a boxer from Whitechapel than a boxer from out west, but what the fans really wanted was a homegrown fighter who could lick any man his weight, a neighborhood son so skilled that he would awaken the echoes of Daniel Mendoza. Climbing the ladder, directly on the heels of Kid Lewis, was the fulfillment of their longing. Merely a lightweight, Benny Leonard never became a national celebrity on the scale of Jack Dempsey, but he energized the New York boxing scene like no one before him. His followers were not only loyal, but also exuberant. They rattled cowbells and yelled themselves hoarse.

Born Benjamin Leiner in 1896 in Manhattan's East Village to Yiddish-speaking immigrants from Russia, Leonard was inspired by the exploits of Leach Cross, an older boy from his neighborhood who was one of the top lightweights of his generation. One of several fighters credited with being the first to wear a Star of David on his trunks, the curious Cross, a licensed dentist born Lewis Wallach, was a crowd-pleaser who held his gloves high when pausing between his pell-mell flurries. Leonard patterned his style after Cross and borrowed Cross's practice of feigning grogginess to trick an opponent into letting his guard down.

Leonard had his first pro fight at the age of fifteen. He suffered a knockout at the hands of one Mickey Finnegan. In bouts sandwiched around his 16th birthday, he suffered two more knockouts, the second to Frankie Fleming, a young fighter recognized as the featherweight champion of Canada. But young Benny was soon holding his own with top-tier fighters like Johnny Dundee, a future world featherweight champion.

Leonard had most of his early fights at the Fairmont Athletic Club in the Bronx, run by his manager Billy Gibson, and at the Harlem Athletic Club, an establishment in which

Gibson had a financial interest. He wasn't an important name on the national scene until he TKOed "Swede" Hammer, a prominent fighter from Chicago. He fought Hammer in Kansas City. Prior to this bout, he had engaged in 95 fights without competing west of Buffalo.

Leonard's reluctance to leave home for an absence of more than one night was attributed to his devotion to his widowed mother, with whom he shared an apartment in the largely Jewish enclave of Harlem. Reporters came to describe him as a "mama's boy," but the reference wasn't meant to be derogatory and strengthened his appeal. Older Jewish men, cognizant of their responsibility as tribal elders, were skittish about glorifying a fighter, at least in their public pronouncements, but were inclined to make an exception for a clean-living young man from a close-knit family who gave every appearance of having the backbone to succeed without corrupting his standards.

In common with fighters of the no-decision era, Leonard went through long periods without forging a knockout. During one stretch, he fought 16 consecutive fights that went the full 10-round distance. But in contrast to the modern-day pattern, his knockout ratio improved as the competition got stronger.

In 1917, Leonard had arguably the greatest single year of any U.S. boxer in history, going undefeated in 28 fights with 17 wins inside the distance. His knockout victims included lightweight champion Freddie Welsh, future featherweight champion Johnny Kilbane, and Leo Johnson, the top African American fighter in his weight class. Neither Welsh — a brilliant defensive fighter approaching the end of the trail — nor Kilbane had ever been stopped, and both were veterans of more than 100 fights.

Leonard's performance in a lightweight title defense against Rocky Kansas in 1922 so enraptured Heywood Broun that he broke the bar for wild analogies. A Harvard-educated theatre critic who covered all the big fights, Broun likened Leonard's textbook style to Tennyson and likened the unorthodox style of Rocky Kansas to the formless prose of Gertrude Stein. The stumpy, ever-aggressive Kansas drew first blood and won the early rounds, but Leonard came on strong to win the decision, details omitted in Broun's flighty summation.[2]

Comparisons of this tint stamped Leonard a cerebral fighter and by extension something of an intellectual. Leonard heightened this perception by lending his name to several causes associated with arbiters of good taste. In 1924, he threw his weight behind the campaign to rescue the goddess Diana from the fate of the wrecking ball. A 13-foot copper sculpture by Augustus Saint-Gaudens, Diana ornamented the belfry of the soon-to-be-razed Madison Square Garden at 26th Street, the grandest of the four buildings that have taken this name. Several years later, during a break in his career when he was busy setting up his children's summer camp in the Catskill Mountains, he debated the noted philosopher Bertrand Russell. In rebuttal to Russell's claim that prizefighting pandered to man's primitive instincts, Benny replied, "[Boxing] has curbed the gang spirit; it has helped to refine countless boys." Excerpts from the debate ran in the *Literary Digest*.

Jewish writers that have drawn retrospectives of Leonard's career have accented his mental acuity. A more sober assessment finds that his chief asset was his fighting temperament, which he compartmentalized neatly so as not to clot his image. A wicked combination puncher, Benny had many gut-check fights where he threw caution to the wind.

Charley White had a frightful left hook, but his defense was so weak that Leonard was made an 8/1 favorite when they locked horns in a big Fourth of July weekend fight at Michigan's Benton Harbor lakefront resort in 1920. Electing to go *mano a mano,* Leonard was knocked completely through the ropes in the fifth round. He fought on instinct until the cobwebs disappeared and eventually knocked White into a cold sleep. In a fight with Richie Mitchell before a packed house at Madison Square Garden, Leonard came out winging. In a wild opening round, he smashed Mitchell to the canvas three times before getting clocked by a looping punch that had him almost out as the bell sounded. He went on to stop Mitchell in the sixth frame. A later fight in Chicago with Richie's able brother Pinkey Mitchell was also marked by reckless exchanges. The fight ended in a riot when Mitchell's clan of Irish hotheads rushed the ring. The referee escaped a beating when two of his brothers leaped into the fray.

Jewish boxers were well established when Benny Leonard arrived on the scene, but their ranks expanded sharply. At the onset of the Great Depression, Jews were the dominant ethnic group in boxing, at least east of the Mississippi River. In 1930 alone, sixteen men named Cohen had one or more fights in American rings. Virtually all the Jewish fighters that arrived on the scene during Leonard's heyday cited him as the ideal to which they aspired.

Some Jewish boxers before Leonard chose to banner their ethnicity. Harry Stone, a fighter from Whitechapel who competed on four continents, was known to enter the ring wearing a yarmulka. However, it was far more common for Jewish fighters to camouflage their identity by adopting an Irish or ethnically nebulous ring name. (A common rationale was to escape rebuke from disapproving parents.) Not only did this practice become less common after Leonard made his mark, but some Jewish boxers were inspired to adopt an alias that was conspicuously more Jewish than their birth name.

The Levinsky brothers, Battling Levinsky and King Levinsky, were not brothers at all, let alone Levinskys. John Dodick, an outstanding lightweight, competed as Jack Bernstein. Charles Green, briefly the bantamweight champion (he outgrew the division before he had a chance to defend the title), adopted the handle Charley Phil Rosenberg. There were several King Solomons, the most active of whom was exposed as a Gentile from Panama.

As a rule, Jewish boxers were matched against other Jews in the incubation stage of their careers. Jew vs. Jew in the feature attraction flouted conventional matchmaking wisdom. But in major East Coast cities, notably New York, and to a lesser extent elsewhere, this convention was frequently violated — inevitably so, as promoters were pressured to match champions and leading contenders against worthy adversaries. Nine times between 1920 and 1934, a world champion of Jewish descent risked his title against a Jewish challenger. Many other matches billed as title fights shared this distinction.

Some of these fights were huge attractions. A crowd estimated at 60,000 witnessed the 1922 bout between Benny Leonard and Lew Tendler at Boyle's Thirty Acres. The match was billed for the Jewish Lightweight Championship of the World. The rematch the next year at Yankee Stadium attracted a paid crowd of 58,522 and receipts of $452,648. Scalpers reportedly got as much as $70 for ringside tickets with a face value of $16.50.

A portion of the proceeds from the second Leonard-Tendler fight was earmarked for Catholic Charities, a common practice in New York when a Jewish boxer was matched against a fellow Jew in a big outdoor bout. Leonard's frequent involvement in charity fights enhanced his crossover appeal. Like Daniel Mendoza, he would be credited with improving "race relations." Arthur Brisbane wrote that Leonard garnered more respect for Jews from non–Jews than a thousand textbooks.

Leonard retired six months after his second fight with Tendler. In the months that followed, the most popular Jewish fighters in New York were the young Turks who showed promise of transmogrifying Leonard's lightweight diadem into a Jewish birthright. Foremost

Lew Tendler (left) and Benny Leonard shake hands before their 1923 fight at Yankee Stadium. Standing between them is referee Andy Griffin. The man over his right shoulder is legendary ring announcer Joe Humphries. *Pugilistica Boxing Memorabilia.*

was a baby-faced knockout artist from the Lower East Side named Ruby Goldstein, later one of New York's top referees.

Dubbed the "Jewel of the Ghetto," Goldstein was undefeated in twenty-four fights when he was pitted against Ace Hudkins, the Nebraska Wildcat, in a match at Coney Island in the summer of 1926. The fight was scheduled for six rounds, the new legal limit in New York for a fighter under 21 years of age, but rounds five and six were superfluous. The main unanswered question about Ruby was the substance of his jaw. Hudkins exposed it as consisting of china.

"What really hurt me," reminisced Goldstein in his 1959 autobiography, "was that I knew many of my friends had lost more than they could afford. Their names didn't get into the newspapers. They were the little people on the East Side and only their friends and their bookmakers knew their names."

Many big plungers took a big bath too. "$400,000 CHANGED HANDS" read the headline above Jack Conway's byline in the *New York Evening Journal,* an astounding figure for a 6-round fight.

> In the list of losers you'll find Waxie Gordon, part owner of Goldstein, who blew close to $45,000. Following the same hearse were Meyer and Sam Boston, well known Broadway characters. The two Boston "boys" are Arnold Rothstein's lieutenants. They are reported to have dropped $35,000 on Goldstein. Two more who "blew" were Jack Bluez, the Buffalo gambler, who went for $25,000, and Al Jolson, who dropped $5,000.... But for every sad face there was a smiling one. The biggest winners were Nick the Greek, who bet $10,000 and won approximately $80,000, and George McManus, who is reported to have beat the fight for $35,000.[3]

Goldstein's boosters were inclined to believe that he had been pushed too quickly into a bout with a top-shelf opponent. They turned out in force for his June 15, 1927, match at Yankee Stadium with Sid Terris, a tall, scrawny lightweight who was likewise a product of the Lower East Side. The bout between the Jewel of the Ghetto and the Galloping Ghost of the Ghetto attracted a crowd estimated at 40,000, generating more than $100,000 for the Boys and Girls Clubs of the Catholic Archdiocese of New York.

This show had a very strong undercard, but the bout between the East Side lads was the pièce de résistance, even though nothing more was at stake than neighborhood bragging rights. Goldstein vs. Terris was accorded top billing, marking the only time in Yankee Stadium history that a 6-round bout was framed as the feature attraction.

Terris was far more experienced and had fought stiffer opposition. He owned the distinction of winning the last main event staged in the old (i.e., second) Madison Square Garden, a gala event that concluded on a somber note when an Army sergeant bugled taps to mark the imminent destruction of the fabled landmark designed by the famous architect Stanford White. Cagey but feather-fisted, Terris was a 9/5 favorite to defeat his ghetto rival, but his jaw was also suspect and Goldstein could take a man out with one punch.

The bout was barely a minute old when young Ruby sent Terris crashing to the deck. Terris was dazed when he got to his feet, but as Goldstein moved in for the kill he was greeted with a punch that landed smack on his fragile jaw, knocking him down for the count. The showdown lasted only 107 seconds.

Terris went on to become *The Ring*'s top-rated lightweight contender, but was unable to scale the final hump to a title match. His most crushing setback was a first-round knockout at the hands of Jimmy McLarnin. Their bout at Madison Square Garden in 1928 was so compelling that the crowd spilled out into the street, where thousands milled about awaiting the result. (Terris retired in 1931, a washed-up fighter at the age of twenty-six. For many years, he was the headwaiter at Stampler's Restaurant, a popular hangout for Broadway bookmakers.)

The search to find a successor to Benny Leonard within the ranks of the Jewish fistic fraternity bore fruit in 1930 when Bronx-born Abraham "Al" Singer won the lightweight title with a first-round knockout over Sammy Mandell. (Born Salvador Mandala in Sicily, Mandell had purportedly altered his name with an eye toward enhancing his popularity among Jewish fight fans.) The scene at Yankee Stadium was one of joyous bedlam.

A dashingly handsome fellow, Singer was potentially a big gate attraction, but his career went south in a hurry. Within four months of winning the title, he suffered quick knockout losses at the hands of Jimmy McLarnin and Tony Canzoneri. But Jewish fight fans had another heartthrob in Jack "Kid" Berg, whose star was still rising.

Born Judah Bergman in Whitechapel, Berg had his first documented fight at the age of fourteen. By the time he reached his 18th birthday, he was a seasoned veteran with 53 fights under his belt. Twenty of these fights went 15 rounds.

Arriving in New York in 1929, Berg quickly became the most popular fighter in the city. In 1930, he upset former featherweight champion Tony Canzoneri, won six fights billed for the light welterweight title (a disputed weight class), and out-pointed Eligio "Kid Chocolate" Sardinias in a robust fight before a big crowd at the Polo Grounds. Sardinias, also known as the Havana Bon Bon, entered the bout undefeated (55–0–1) and was widely considered the most talented featherweight in the world.

Kid Berg wasn't a hard puncher, but he was a stylish fighter who commanded attention from his peers even during his gym workouts. But what drew many to him was not his ring generalship so much as the flamboyant manner in which he flaunted his Jewishness.

In an article that he penned for *The Ring*, Ben Sharav recreated the scene when Berg made his New York debut in a match at Madison Square Garden:

> [Berg] entered the ring wrapped in tallis, the prayer shawl worn in synagogues. Around his right arm and on his head he wore tefilin, the small leather box containing sacred Scripture, trailed by leather straps, which is put on by observant Jews for early morning prayers. Berg proceeded to go through an elaborate ritual of slowly unwinding the leather straps from around his body, tenderly kissing them, and placing the materials in a gold-embossed velvet bag, which he then carefully handed to his chief second, [Ray] Arcel. Berg's trunks, as always, were adorned with the Star of David.[4]

Undoubtedly many Jews were discomfited by Berg's ritual because of the setting. His presentation invited jeers and catcalls. However, by all accounts most of his coreligionists in the stands were exhilarated. In running the neighborhood gantlet, wrote George Walsh, Jewish boys were exposed to the fistic theology of Irish proselytizers.

In 1931, Berg twice came up short in rematches with Tony Canzoneri. The next year he returned to England. He campaigned mostly in the United Kingdom through 1937, returning to New York in 1938 in an abortive attempt to recapture his previous glory. By then, however, his popularity had been eclipsed by a lightweight from the Midwest, Beryl Rossofsy, known as Barney Ross.

The blood-soaked saga of Barney Ross is not for the squeamish. The third oldest of seven children, Ross was a boy of fourteen when he lost his father, a Talmudic scholar murdered during a holdup at the family's small grocery in the Maxwell Street district of Chicago.

In the wake of the tragedy, his two younger brothers were sent to orphanages and his mother was committed to a sanitarium. Left to fend on his own, young Barney made money organizing craps games in schoolyards and working as an errand boy for bootleggers. After winning an inter-city Golden Gloves tournament in 1929, he turned professional.

Ross was co-managed by Sam Pian and Art Winch. Their stable ranked with the best in the country. In 1933, they induced Tony Canzoneri to come to the Windy City to defend his lightweight title. Ross got the nod, but the verdict was roundly criticized as a hometown decision.

Ross was the sixth man to win the lightweight title since the retirement of Benny Leonard eight years earlier. The merry-go-round suggested that he was fated to be another one-trick pony like Al Singer. But Ross muted the cynics in a rematch with Canzoneri at the Polo

Jack "Kid" Berg walking the streets of Whitechapel with his niece and younger sister circa 1932. *Pugilistica Boxing Memorabilia.*

Grounds. Finishing strong in his New York debut and first 15-round fight, he retained the belt with a split decision that was well received. The victory advanced his record to 46–2–2.

Jews initially skeptical of Ross were quick to embrace the New York-born, Chicago-bred champion. Aside from being an excellent fighter, he was a great human-interest story. With his ring earnings, he was able to reunite his family. His biggest fan was his mother, who had made a miraculous recovery from her nervous breakdown. She reportedly walked five miles in cold weather to attend one of his fights, eschewing an automobile because that would have conflicted with her observance of the Sabbath. She was accompanied by children from her neighborhood, self-appointed bodyguards who allayed her concerns about her son's safety by touting Barney as a sure thing to passersby.

Ross was a busy fighter during the Depression, forging a 13–2–1 record in championship fights spread across the 135-, 140-, and 147-pound weight classes. His managers would have preferred that Ross take more time off to smell the roses, but he pressured them to keep the spigot flowing. Unbeknownst to Pian and Winch, Barney had become a big plunger at the racetrack and was blowing his money as fast as he made it.

He was not alone in this regard. Dozens of fighters became degenerate horseplayers, an occupational hazard in the days when the ring and the racetrack were socially intertwined. But Ross, introduced to the Sport of Kings by entertainer Al Jolson, probably surpassed them all in horse-betting futility. In one day at Santa Anita, he blew nearly $10,000, a princely sum in the Depression.

Ross had the good sense to retire after absorbing a terrific beating from Henry Armstrong in 1938. Despite his gambling misadventures, he had managed to save enough to purchase a cocktail lounge in Chicago's Loop. But the work did not sufficiently satisfy his craving for action. In 1942, at the age of thirty-three, he enlisted in the Marines.

Most of the name fighters who served in World War II were assigned to noncombat duties. Ross wouldn't allow it. During a bloody battle on Guadalcanal, he was credited with killing 22 enemy soldiers, earning both the Silver Star and the Distinguished Service Cross. But he paid the price in the form of shrapnel wounds, dysentery, and chronic malaria, conditions treated with massive doses of morphine. This led to a new and more powerful dependency. Ross was a full-fledged junkie when he voluntarily sought treatment at the U.S. Public Health Service Hospital in Lexington, Kentucky, in 1946. The story of his successful battle to resume a normal life was captured on film in the movie *Monkey On My Back* with Cameron Mitchell in the lead role.

Ross had three big fights with Jimmy McLarnin. These bouts were shamelessly packaged as Holy Wars.

A baby-faced assassin of Scotch-Irish ancestry who grew up in a strict Methodist home in Vancouver, McLarnin knocked out a long list of prominent Jewish fighters en route to his encounters with Ross. In chronological order, he stopped Jackie Fields, the youngest American fighter to win an Olympic gold medal, former featherweight champion Louis "Kid" Kaplan, Sid Terris in a sensational Big Apple debut, Ruby Goldstein, Al Singer, and then Benny Leonard, who had been forced back to the ring after a seven-year absence by the stock market crash. The Great Bennah was no match for the faster and heavier-hitting McLarnin, who retired him for good with a fourth-round stoppage at Madison Square Garden.[5]

An enterprising press agent dubbed McLarnin "The Scourge of Jewry." McLarnin was embarrassed by the cognomination, but the watermark paid big dividends. A crowd estimated at 60,000 filled the Madison Square Garden Bowl in Long Island City for the first McLarnin-Ross fight on May 28, 1934.

Ross won this bout by split decision. The rematch produced another split decision, with McLarnin reclaiming his welterweight title. The rubber match, decided in favor of Ross, was yet another nip-and-tuck affair. The high-volume trilogy shortened the careers of both men. McLarnin heeded the advice of his benevolent manager, Pop Foster, and retired the next year. Ross called it quits before his twenty-ninth birthday.

The heritage of Jews in boxing is deficient in one respect. The roster of heavyweight champions is bereft of Jews unless one includes Max Baer, who customarily fought with the Star of David on his trunks but was generally considered an imposter. However, several Jewish heavyweights accomplished noteworthy feats. Chrysanthemum Joe Choynski boxed Jim Jeffries to a 20-round draw and flattened young Jack Johnson. A little known fact is that a Jewish boxer upset Jack Dempsey in the last of Dempsey's bouts that had a betting line.

Dempsey's February 18, 1932, match with King Levinsky at Chicago Stadium was advertised as an exhibition, but the 4-round contest was strictly on the level. Dempsey came in trimmed down to 190 pounds, two pounds less than what he had carried in his second meeting with Gene Tunney.

Dempsey's match with Levinsky — his first appearance in Chicago since the famous "long count" — was one of the final legs of a well-plotted tour that had begun in Reno the previous summer. Dempsey was contemplating one last farewell fight — his quarry was Primo

Carnera — and used the tour as a method of getting back into shape and as a yardstick to determine the extent to which his reflexes had deteriorated. A week prior, he had manhandled fringe contender Meyer Christner during a stopover in Cleveland. Although not a hard puncher, the 21-year-old Levinsky was a step up in class. The son of a Maxwell Street fish peddler, Levinsky stood #7 in the rankings of the National Boxing Association.

So great was the interest that it attracted 23,322, breaking the existing record for an indoor sporting event. There was considerable betting interest in the contest, especially in Levinsky's neighborhood. Since no decision could be given, the bookmakers exhumed an old practice that had fallen into disuse. Barring a knockout, the outcome would be decided by a poll of ringside reporters.

Dempsey pressed the action, but his legs were leaden and his punches lacked steam. Levinsky grew bolder as the bout progressed and stood toe-to-toe with Dempsey in the final frame. Eighteen of 24 ringside reporters scored the fight for Levinsky, two favored Dempsey, and four had it a draw. Dempsey fulfilled the remaining exhibitions on his docket, but wisely abandoned his comeback plans. As for Levinsky, he went on to make a good showing in a 20-round fight with Max Baer in Reno before degenerating into a trial horse. When his best days were behind him, reporters took to calling him "Kingfish" and he took on the coloration of a clod.[6]

The son of an Omaha meat-packer who resettled his family on a ranch near Stockton, California, Max Baer had a Jewish strain on his father's side. But in choosing to banner this component of his lineage, he rubbed Nat Fleischer the wrong way. Fleischer's antipathy toward Baer was intensified by Baer's reputation as a happy-go-lucky ladies' man who spent less time in the gym than in nightclubs. In the May 1934 issue of *The Ring*, Fleischer made a startling accusation: "It is my opinion that Hitler is more of a Jew than Baer."[7] Less damning was the running joke that Max didn't look Jewish in the shower.

Baer was hardly the first marginally Jewish boxer to exploit his Jewish ancestry. The practice became relatively more common as the field of Jewish boxers became fallow. Mike Rossman, the son of Michael DiPiano, adopted his mother's maiden name when he turned professional, wore trunks ornamented with the Star of David, and for good measure adopted the nickname "Kosher Butcher." In 1978, on the undercard of Ali-Spinks II, Rossman defeated Argentina's Victor Galindez to win the WBA version of the lightheavyweight title, becoming the first American-born Jewish boxer to sport a world championship belt since Barney Ross.

## Bummy

On June 1, 1938, an era ended when Henry Armstrong hammered Barney Ross into retirement. Ross would be the last Jewish-American boxer of the 20th century to be denominated an undisputed world champion. Of course, there was no way of knowing this at the time, and Jewish boxing fans were consoled somewhat by the triumph of Maxwell Street welterweight Davey Day in the chief undercard bout. The departure of Ross, however, hardly signified the end of Jewish fighters as big gate attractions. In Brooklyn, a lightweight with an explosive left hook was drawing SRO crowds to neighborhood fight clubs. He fought under the name Al Davis and bore a nickname — not of his own choosing — that would come to be seen as a perfect fit.

Born Abraham Davidoff, Davis was a product of Brownsville, the section of Brooklyn most redolent of the Lower East Side. Brooklyn's main fistic incubator, Brownsville was also the home base of the chillingly ruthless cabal known as Murder Incorporated. Growing up there, Davis had one foot in Brownsville's criminal subculture. His father sold bootleg liquor out of a small candy store; an older brother, nicknamed Little Gangy, would spend most of his adult life in prison. As a boy, Bummy sold vegetables out of a pushcart when he wasn't running with his gang.

The origin of his *nom de guerre* was a corruption of the Yiddish translation of Abraham. To an untrained ear, *Ahvron* filtered through a Yiddish accent sounded like "Boomy." His co-manager Johnny Attell, who ran shows at a Brooklyn nightclub called Ridgewood Grove, took it a step further. When Davis made his pro debut at Ridgewood Grove, he was dismayed to find that his name appeared on the fight poster as Al "Bummy" Davis. At least it was closer to his birth name than Giovanni Pesconi, the handle he had used as an amateur. Too young to fight in AAU tournaments, Davis had pilfered Pesconi's I.D. to circumvent the roadblock.

The Jewish population of boxers was thinning rapidly when Davis launched his pro career on May 22, 1938. Unlike Kid Berg in London or the venerated Benny Leonard across the bridge in Manhattan, Davis was not matched against other Jews right out of the box. But there were other Jews in his weight class on the same career track, and Davis would need to go through them before meeting a ranked opponent. One of those fellows lived right in his neighborhood. Bernie "Schoolboy" Friedkin was not a stereotypical Brownsville boxer. He lived in a single-family home, which branded him as middle class. The well-mannered "school-boy" was a natural for the hard-boiled Davis, who had virtually no schooling at all, and their fight in the summer of 1938, framed as a neighborhood grudge match, was one of the most eagerly anticipated fights in Brooklyn in years. Too big for a venue like Ridgewood Grove, it was placed in a neighborhood park, but wound up at Madison Square Garden when mon-soon-like conditions forced four postponements.

The postponements took much of the air out of the promotion. Barely 6000 witnessed the Battle of Brownsville, but even that turnout was impressive considering that the card did not include a single 10-round fight, a first for a professional boxing show at Madison Square Garden since the passage of the Walker Law in 1920. Friedkin, slightly older and consider-ably more experienced, had lost only one fight in the previous two years and was nubbed a 13/10 favorite. Neither man had an edge through three humdrum rounds, but "Boomy" low-ered the boom in Round 4, ending the contest with a blow that hit poor Friedkin so hard that his head hit the ring post with a sickening thud as he was falling down. The pattern of the bout was consistent with the pattern that Bummy had established in his earlier fights.

Six months later, Davis engaged Mickey Farber of the Lower East Side at St. Nick's Arena in a promotion that *The Ring* called "the most ballyhooed small club fight of the season." Fans of both fighters staged pep rallies in their respective neighborhoods on the eve of the skir-mish. In a corker of a slugfest, Bummy emerged with a majority decision.

The two were immediately inked to a rematch the next month at Madison Square Gar-den in what would be Davis's first 10-round bout. Mike Jacobs predicted a sellout, and might have achieved it if his matchmakers had been more alert and sprinkled the St. Patrick's Day show with a few Irish faces. As it was, Davis-Farber II drew 13,435. In a bout that did not measure up to its prequel, Bummy prevailed by a comfortable margin despite hurting his left hand in the opening stanza while scoring the lone knockdown of the contest.

Bummy was now generally recognized as the toughest Jewish boxer in New York, but he was still a work in progress. In the time-tested manner, his management went out in search of a faded luminary. They didn't need to look far. Tony Canzoneri, a four-time champion in three weight classes, had never been knocked out in a career numbering 174 fights, but was so frayed the New York Boxing Commission was reluctant to let him participate in any more 10-round fights.

Bummy walked right through Canzoneri, knocking him into retirement with a third-round stoppage. He did it in a manner that rubbed many attendees the wrong way. As he battered Canzoneri into a state of helplessness, his moon face was creased with a cockeyed grin.

Canzoneri was the last active fighter who had affixed his name to the roster of champions during the Golden Age of Sports. Although it was disheartening to see him go out this way, it was perversely poetic that a Jew brought down the final curtain. In his Madison Square Garden debut, Canzoneri had stamped himself an up-and-comer with a victory over undefeated Danny Terris. In title fights, he had defeated Benny "The Little Fish" Bass, Al Singer, Jackie Berg, and Al Roth.

Davis's next opponent, Tippy Larkin, was a solid professional who boasted a 66–5 record and had never been stopped. Larkin baffled Davis through four rounds, but Bummy found his opening in Round 5 and terminated the bout with a paralyzing left hook to the body. With this victory, Davis advanced his record to 37–0–2 and earned a non-title match with lightweight champion Lou Ambers. The match acquired a brighter hue when Davis was arrested for the felonious assault of one Harold Mersky, who wound up in the hospital after their fracas in a Brooklyn candy store. This incident cemented Davis's reputation as a bully and prompted reporters to append a euphonic tailpiece to his name: "Bummy Davis, the Brownsville Bum...." From this point on, whenever Davis walked through the floodlights into the ring, the boos drowned out the cheers.

Dubbed the Herkimer Hurricane, Ambers (90–6–7) had recently ended the 46-fight winning streak of Henry Armstrong. He had competed extensively in Brooklyn, where he had killed a man in the ring. Their bout on February 23, 1940, drew a sellout crowd of 20,586, the largest gathering at Madison Square Garden in several years.

An 11/5 favorite, Ambers outclassed Davis, winning the decision by a comfortable margin. Despite the one-sidedness, the bout was crowd-pleasing. Those that bet Ambers never felt safe, cognizant that Bummy's left hook could reverse the tide in a flash. Bleeding from his nose and mouth, Davis was in tears when he left the ring. Nat Fleischer assuaged his hurt with a favorable review of his performance. "If [Davis] ... trains faithfully, gives up bad company and uses socks only in the ring," wrote Fleischer, "he may yet become a world champion."[8]

Back to the drawing board, Bummy scored three wins to earn another date in a featured bout at Madison Square Garden. He was matched against Tony Marteliano, a good technician who had suffered only two losses in 50 fights. Davis pulled the fight out of the fire by decking Marteliano seconds before the final buzzer. The victory — a split decision — put him in line for what would be his career-defining fight, a non-title match with welterweight champ Fritzie Zivic.

One of five fighting brothers from Pittsburgh, Zivic had sheared the welterweight crown from Henry Armstrong. A veteran of 130 fights although yet only 27 years of age, Zivic was recognized as one of the dirtiest fighters in the game. He was adept at using his thumbs to impair the vision of an opponent, knew how to un-stanch a cut by using the laces of his glove as an anti-coagulant, and was actually admired for this aptitude. Fritzie was the boxing version of a baseball pitcher who earns kudos for his guile in doctoring the ball. Pundits tagged the upcoming battle "Bummy versus Thumby," a prescription for trouble.

Davis approached the fight as if he had already been victimized by Zivic's transgressions.

It would be written that Zivic reddened Bummy's eyes with some sleight-of-hand during an opening round clinch, although newspaper accounts of the fight make no mention of it. Regardless, Zivic did something to get Bummy's goat and Bummy went berserk. In Round 2, he launched a salvo of punches aimed squarely at Zivic's groin. At least ten landed before the referee was able to stop the bombardment. Bummy erupted again when it dawned on him that he had been disqualified and kicked the referee as he charged across the ring at his stricken foe. As the police were restoring order, the ring was pelted with all manner of debris. *New York Times* scribe James P. Dawson called it one of the most disgraceful exhibitions in the history of boxing. At the next meeting of the Athletic Commission, Bummy was suspended for life.

Bummy was not about to accept his disfellowship without a fight, but was persuaded to join the Army and let others fight the battle. The commissioners were in an awkward position because they had undermined their authority by looking the other way when Bummy added two years to his age to meet the minimum age requirement for 10-round bouts. His case was not atypical. Perhaps in fear of yet more discomfiting revelations, the regulators struck a deal. They would approve a Zivic-Davis rematch, but only as a benefit for the Army Emergency Relief Fund.

The military was more than happy to grant Bummy a furlough for a charity bout. Anticipating a large crowd, the promoters potted the rematch in the cavernous Polo Grounds, choosing the date of July 1, 1941. Bad weather hurt attendance — the bout was pushed back a

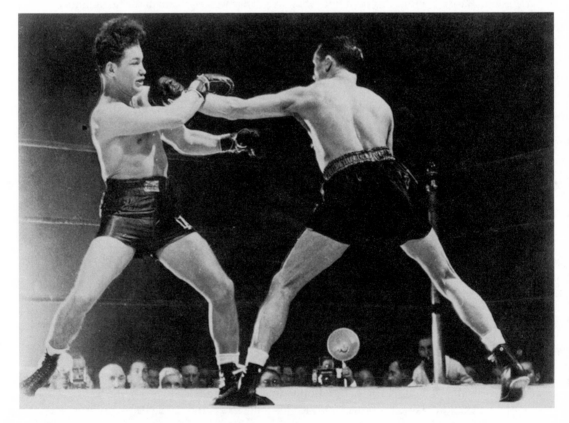

The volatile, ill-fated Bummy Davis (left) fared poorly against Fritzie Zivic in their second meeting. *Antiquities of the Prize Ring.*

day by rain — as did the late starting time. The first preliminary did not go until 9:30, a concession to military enlistment centers, which remained open until 9 P.M. Barely nine thousand paid to see Zivic thrash the bad boy from Brooklyn, who was identified by the ring announcer as hailing from Camp Hulen, Texas. The foul-free and monotonously one-sided contest was stopped in the tenth round. As a precaution — and perhaps also to extend his furlough — Bummy spent several days after the fight in a hospital.

The Army let Bummy go before his hitch was up. No reason was given for the early discharge, but the skinny was that his insolent demeanor had become a red flag for Jew-baiters and that his expulsion was deemed necessary for company morale. Flabby and overweight, he resumed his boxing career, building himself back into condition with a series of bouts at small clubs outside New York. On February 18, 1944, he returned to Madison Square Garden, where he was matched against Bob Montgomery. A talented lightweight, Montgomery had TKOed formidable Ike Williams in his most recent bout.

Although Bummy was bigger and theoretically stronger, it looked like an easy workout for the more skillful Montgomery, who attracted heavy play and went to post a 9/2 favorite. However, while Bummy was on the decline — and never an exceptional fighter in the first place — his left hook was as potent as ever. Bummy landed several in the opening minute of the contest, the last of which unbuckled Montgomery's knees, knocking him erect, out on his feet. For a pregnant moment Montgomery looked like a statue, and then pitched face-first into the canvas — sweet redemption for Davis, whose last outing at this venue had brought on a "lifetime" suspension.

The shocking 63-second blowout was a springboard to Bummy's most lucrative fight and two other nice paydays, but he would never defeat another name fighter. His bout with popular Beau Jack broke the existing Madison Square Garden record for gate receipts for a show with a non-heavyweight main event. Large throngs saw Davis get knocked unconscious by Henry Armstrong and then lose a Pier 6 brawl with Rocky Graziano. He quit boxing after being held to a draw by a fighter with a losing record and purchased a saloon. His manager had negotiated a fight for him at Madison Square Garden with Morris Reif, a fellow Brooklynite whose career was on the up-tick, but Bummy had been down that hard road before and was travel-weary. Who was Morris Reif anyway, but the incarnation of Schoolboy Friedkin in the guise of a different name? Been there; done that.

As a teenager, Bummy was a Pied Piper for neighborhood boys who turned out in droves to watch him train at Beecher's, a small gym attached to a pool hall that sat across from an elevated subway station. Now a washed-up fighter in his mid-twenties, he had lost his magnetic pull. Business never took off at his tavern and he quickly dumped it, using the proceeds to buy an interest in three racehorses.

There were a few loose ends that needed to be tied up before the buyer had clear title to the establishment. That is how Bummy came to be there at 2:45 A.M. on the morning of November 21, 1945. There were four other people in the bar — the new owner, Arthur Polansky, an off-duty policeman, Edward Fritz, the bartender, George Miller, and a fellow passed out in a stupor at a corner table. Then four young men on a stick-up spree burst in with guns drawn.

Davis reportedly tried to reason with the intruders: "Why don't you guys give us a break? This fellow here just bought the joint and he's having a rough go of it." The leader of the gang responded with a profanity that discomposed Bummy like a thumb in the eye, throwing him into a blind rage.

The *New York Times* was not in the habit of sensationalizing crime news. Thus, the paper's account of what transpired next was probably a fairly accurate blow-by-blow description of Bummy's final altercation.

> The impulsive Davis ... came out of his chair. His famous left hook smacked against the hold-up man's face and the man reeled. The door guard and the two other hold-up men seemed to get panicky at this startling interruption. They fired, but the shots went wild.
>
> Davis shoved the table away, kicked the chair aside, and blindly rushed the four armed men, swinging and crying out oaths in his rage. They backed away from him hastily, through the door, but he still charged.
>
> The guns blazed again. Three bullets hit the fighter. One went through his neck and cracked his spine, one went through his back into his left lung, and a third lodged in his right arm. He kept swinging with his left.
>
> The hold-up men jumped into their car after a spurt across the gravel. The motor roared and they were gone. The policeman got into his car and chased them, but they were quickly out of sight.
>
> Davis, dazed and blinded, stumbled toward his own car, apparently intending to join the chase. A few steps from the barroom threshold he staggered and fell flat on his face in the sand. He was dead before an ambulance came.[9]

Officer Fritz fired several shots at the getaway car as he was giving chase. One of the bullets struck one of the desperadoes, leading to the apprehension of all four culprits. They were members of a gang of Irish and Italian toughs who called themselves the Flatbush Cowboys.

Bummy Davis left behind a wife and two-year-old son. His funeral attracted a crowd that spilled out onto the sidewalk. Newsreel photographers took pictures at the gravesite where Abraham Davidoff was laid to rest. His name faded quickly and the circumstances of his murder got muddled with the passage of time. Those that vaguely remembered hearing about the holdup had difficulty recalling whether the boxer was one of the good guys or one of the bad guys. The confusion was understandable. A Brownsville Bum doesn't figure to die a hero.

The mourners at Bummy's funeral must have been vaguely aware that he was a symbol of the old Brownsville, a world that was disappearing before their eyes. In the immediate post-war Brownsville, young Jewish boys were less coarsened by melting-pot friction and poverty. Similar developments elsewhere meant that Jewish boxers were fast becoming an endangered species. Jews would never disappear completely from boxing, but their numbers would dwindle to next-to-nothing. By 1990, Jewish boxing trainers had also vanished, a foreseeable development since trainers, with few exceptions, were ex-boxers.

There is a poignant moment in John Harding's biography of Jack Berg when the author and his subject are motoring to a boxing show in a London suburb. Harding remarks that one of the fighters on the card happens to be Jewish and adds that he is the only homegrown Jewish boxer competing at the professional level in all of Great Britain. The old Whitechapel Whirlwind, now a 79-year-old part-time cab driver, is flabbergasted. After expressing his surprise, he lapses into silence with a lump in his throat.

When "Kid" Berg was a young man, boxing was part of the Jewish cultural mosaic of London. The golden era of the Jewish boxer was here and gone in a heartbeat in cosmological time, but it was seismic while it lasted.

# CHAPTER 10

---

# Hard Times and Hoaxes

Three hundred policemen were on duty outside Madison Square Garden on the frigid Thursday morning of January 10, 1929. The occasion was the funeral of Tex Rickard. In an ecumenical service conducted by two Protestant clergymen, a Catholic lawyer, and a Jewish appellate court judge, Rickard was eulogized before an estimated ten thousand mourners.

Those in the multitude who had profited from Rickard's promotions—bucket carriers, stagehands, concessionaires, ring officials, sportswriters, etc.—were both doleful and apprehensive. Rickard was the man most responsible for elevating boxing into the realm of high finance. Without him there was bound to be a rollback. These qualms would prove to be well founded, but the severity of the slide would be even greater than feared.

During the Depression years (1930–35), seven heavyweight championship fights were contested on American soil. The aggregated box-office receipts amounted to less than the 1927 Tunney-Dempsey rematch alone. At Madison Square Garden, a sharp reduction in ticket prices failed to stem declining attendance. There were thirteen fewer shows in 1933, the height of the Depression, than in 1928, Rickard's last full year.

MADISON SQUARE GARDEN BOXING STATISTICS

|      | Shows | Avg. Attendance | Avg. Gate |
|------|-------|-----------------|-----------|
| 1928 | 32    | 13,224          | $51,807   |
| 1933 | 19    | 9,687           | $16,095   |

While revenues declined substantially, there was no concurrent drop in activity. Name fighters fought more frequently to compensate for reduced purses and amateur fight clubs became more abundant. Most were amateur in name only. It was an open secret that the prizes, typically cheap gold watches, could be redeemed for cash at the conclusion of the show. Bouts were short, typically three rounds, and many amateurs boxed several times a week, sufficient to earn maybe forty dollars, a good weekly wage at a time when many Americans were reduced to living on welfare. Many pro fighters supplemented their earnings by fighting as amateurs under assumed names. Adding to the glut was the expansion of intercollegiate boxing. The first national tournament was held at Penn State University in 1932.[1]

Reduced revenues meant fewer perks for sportswriters. When former Yale football star Colonel John Reed Kilpatrick was named president of the Madison Square Garden Corporation in 1930, he eliminated the slush fund for sportswriters and cut back sharply on complimentary tickets. But for many sportswriters, this was the least of their worries. The economic downturn led many newspapers to freeze or reduce salaries and slash staff. There was a hyphenation of newspaper names as morning and afternoon dailies were blended into one edition. The pool of American fighters increased during the Great Depression, but downsizings and mergers diminished the pool of sportswriters.

The trend set in motion by the Walker Law — heightened regulation of boxing — was another hurtful development for sports scribes as it translated into fewer moonlighting opportunities. The sportswriter-cum-referee faded into antiquity, displaced by the "professional" referee, a man certified by the boxing commission. Established organizations like the Amateur Athletic Union fought successfully to remain autonomous, creating a loophole for shoestring promoters who redefined their product as amateur to skirt oppressive regulatory fees. Amateur clubs could name their own officials and set their own pay scales. Examining the newspapers of this era, one is struck by the amount of space devoted to quasi-amateur shows. Undoubtedly sportswriters were reciprocating favors extended by maverick promoters who did business the old-fashioned way.

The heavyweight championship changed hands five times in the years 1930–35. The title-holders that came through the revolving door would come to be lumped as "caretaker champions" — usurpers keeping the throne warm until the arrival of Joe Louis. The third of the five caretakers, Primo Carnera, won and lost the heavyweight title in a span of fifty weeks, but occupied the throne the longest as measured by the number of successful title defenses (two). Carnera came to be seen as the face of an era rancid with human degradation.

Born in 1906 in the village of Sequals, Italy, Carnera was a physical anomaly, a raw-boned, lantern-jawed, ham-fisted giant of a man with a remarkably well-proportioned physique. He was barely seventeen years of age when he left his village to work as a strongman for a small French traveling circus where he was discovered by Leon See, an Oxford-educated hustler with ties to the leading promoters in Europe. Abetted by a slick publicity campaign that exaggerated his enormousness, Carnera attracted a large crowd of curiosity-seekers for his boxing debut in Paris and was a headline attraction while still a raw novice.

In his eighth fight, Carnera was matched against a fighter of little merit named Moise Bouquillon. Carnera copped the decision after ten monotonous rounds, but never hurt Bouquillon despite an 80-pound weight advantage. In the audience was vacationing Paul Gallico, who attended the fight as a diversion. Gallico would be the first American sportswriter to declare that the over-hyped Italian was a fraud.

Carnera's first name opponent was W.L. "Young" Stribling. They met in London on November 18, 1929, and again three weeks later in Paris. Jefferson Dickson, the leading promoter in France, made both matches. An ex-G.I. from Natchez, Mississippi, Dickson had stayed on in Paris after the war.

The pride of Macon, Georgia, Stribling was only two years older than Carnera, but vastly more experienced. The son of carnival entertainers, he had been boxing almost literally from the day he learned to walk. As a toddler, slapstick fights with his older brother were incorporated into his parents' variety act. In time, he became one of the best-known fighters of his day, earning acclaim as the all-time knockout king, a distinction he acquired before he had reached his twenty-fifth birthday. Dickson billed him as the American lightheavyweight champion, a claim that had some validity as he had won three non-title bouts against reigning lightheavyweight champions.

The first fight between Carnera and Stribling filled Royal Albert Hall to capacity. The

For publicity purposes, Primo Carnera was photographed with short people. This photograph, taken at an unidentified ballpark circa 1930, was likely doctored. *Reproduced from the original held by the Department of Special Collections of the University Libraries of Notre Dame.*

Prince of Wales, later King Edward VIII, was among those in attendance. The fight was a spirited affair — both fighters were on the canvas in the third stanza — but ended on a sour note when Stribling was disqualified for a low blow in the fourth round. The rematch in Paris lasted into the seventh round before Carnera was disqualified for hitting after the bell. Stribling was ahead on points but was clearly tiring.

Neither fight raised much of a stink. European referees were stricter than their American counterparts. But both bouts were almost certainly rigged. An injury to either fighter in London would have ruined the Paris promotion, which was locked in as part of a two-fight deal. The outcomes were beneficial to both parties. Stribling embossed his reputation with a "W" against a colossus, but did so without despoiling Carnera's marketability.

Young Stribling was undeniably talented, but his entire career was largely a hoax. The all-time knockout king scored many of his knockouts against carnival roustabouts. In most of his important fights, he was hampered by ineffectual power punches. Stribling was essentially a booth fighter who built his reputation in the boondocks. Atypical of the breed, however, he was sufficiently clever to defeat most of his name opponents, albeit usually by slim margins in dull fights.[2]

Fixed or not, the Carnera-Stribling fights of 1929 set the tone for Depression-era boxing, an era characterized by an epidemic of fouls and an unusually high number of suspicious fights at the upper level of competition. It was hardly coincidental that boxing in this period became more closely hitched to the world of the carnival midway, a world of deception and fabrication. Primo Carnera and Young Stribling were products of this world.

The month following his second fight with Stribling, Carnera launched a tour of the United States. It began at Madison Square Garden, where 17,896 turned out for his match with Clayton "Big Boy" Peterson. The contest was a travesty. Victorious in only three of his previous 16 fights, Peterson hit the deck four times in the opening round, but each knockdown was the result of a shove. On his last trip to the mat, Peterson appeared to hit himself on the jaw as he was toppling backwards. "He had too much integrity to take a dive without being hit," wisecracked Paul Gallico.

Carnera's tour lasted 37 weeks, during which he had 24 fights. Only five went beyond the third round. How many of these fights were bogus will never be known, but Carnera's sworn testimony would be worthless. "The poor floundering giant was duped along with the spectators," wrote Gallico. "He was permitted, in fact encouraged, to believe that his silly pawings and pushings, when they connected, sent men staggering into unconsciousness and defeat. It was not until late in his career ... that he ever knocked anyone out on the level."[3]

Wherever Carnera appeared, a packed house was the rule. The *New York Times* reported that he earned $103,391 for his first ten American fights, an incredible sum considering the economic climate and the poor caliber of some of his opponents.

Carnera's appeal owed partly to the fact that he was a monstrosity. He was not six-foot-ten, as reported by the *London Times*, nor was he six-foot-eight-and-a half, as reported in the first articles about him in New York papers. But while his true height was closer to six-foot-six, this was an extraordinary height circa 1930 for a man with such a powerful physique.

His appeal was also enhanced by his ethnicity. Immigration to America from overseas declined after World War I, but the decline was less pronounced for Italy, which became the chief producer of immigrants from Europe. Italian-American fighters of earlier vintage tended to adopt Irish ring names. This practice largely stopped after Carnera arrived on the scene.[4]

Carnera's tour ended in Boston, where he was saddled with his first true defeat, losing a decision to local product Jim Maloney (his previous losses were on disqualifications). Before beginning another U.S. tour in 1932, he suffered two more defeats, these coming at the hands of top-tier opponents Jack Sharkey and Larry Gains. The fight with Gains, an African-Canadian fighter based in England, drew a record crowd of 70,000 to London's White City Stadium.

Carnera began his second U.S. tour by avenging his loss to Maloney, but early into it he

W.L. "Young" Stribling gives his son an airplane spin in this undated photograph. Note the roller coaster in the background. The all-time knockout king, Stribling had many of his fights at country fairs and amusement parks. *Antiquities of the Prize Ring.*

was defeated again, losing a bout in Newark against Stanley Poreda, a fighter trained by Joe Jeanette. When Carnera signed to fight Ernie Schaaf at Madison Square Garden on February 10, 1933, his reputation had become so tattered that Schaaf was installed a 2/1 favorite.

A 24-year-old fighter from Boston, Schaaf was coming off a victory over Poreda, but he had suffered 12 losses during a career numbering 67 bouts. The previous summer, he had fought a vicious fight with Max Baer. After fighting Baer on even terms through nine stanzas, Schaaf was battered from pillar to post in the final round and then knocked out cold by a punch that landed two seconds before the final gong.

In common with all of Carnera's fights, there was talk that the outcome against Schaaf was prearranged. Those suspicions were heightened when a late surge of money on Carnera resulted in a switch of favorites.

It seemed as if the scuttlebutt was true when Schaaf slumped to the canvas in Round 13 after an exchange of seemingly light punches. Up to that point, the bout had been relatively tame. There were catcalls as Schaaf was carted out of the ring by his cornermen. But this was no fake — Schaaf was unconscious and something was terribly wrong. In a coma for several days, he died after a three-hour operation to remove a blood clot from his brain.

Carnera's detractors had difficulty believing that he was capable of killing a man with his fists. They suspected that Schaaf's death was related to his beating at the hands of Baer. An inquiry revealed that Schaaf had recently been hospitalized with a severe case of influenza. Blind to this fact, the New York boxing commission deemed him suitable for a 15-round bout with an opponent who outweighed him by 60 pounds.

The deplorable ring fatality was a career-booster for Carnera, pushing him into a title bout with former opponent Jack Sharkey, who had wrested the title from the shoulders of Max Schmeling.

Primo knocked out Sharkey in the sixth round and went on to successfully defend his diadem in route-going bouts with Paulino Uzcudun in Rome and Tommy Loughran in Miami before losing his title to Max Baer in a grotesquely one-sided affair. Fighting on a twisted ankle that became badly swollen, Carnera was on the deck eleven times before the referee halted the slaughter in Round 11. Adding to his misery — he sobbed uncontrollably after repairing to his dressing room — some reporters altered his nickname from the Ambling Alp to the Leaning Tower of Gorgonzola.

The Baer-Carnera fight was profitable, but Carnera's previous fight against Laughlin set two inglorious records. Carnera's 86-pound advantage was the largest differential in a championship fight to that point in time. The gate receipts totaled $39,361.60, easily the lowest figure for any heavyweight title bout contested with gloves. Carnera reportedly received $15,000, but how much of it he got to keep is anyone's guess.

Leon See was forced to take on partners when he brought his freak fighter to America. Speakeasy owner Big Bill Duffy, an ex-felon, was Carnera's official co-manager for his big New York fights, but more than a dozen people purportedly had pieces of him, most notably Owney Madden. The nephew of an Irish booth fighter, Madden was the principal owner of Harlem's famous Cotton Club.

See was eventually elbowed out by Carnera's American backers, but enough fingers remained in the pie so that it was inevitable that Carnera would be shortchanged. His purses for all of his fights through his match with Ernie Schaaf — a total of 80 — amounted to nearly a million dollars, but he was constantly short of funds and hounded by bill collectors. Primo's creditors bayed loudest as he was preparing for the second fight with Jack Sharkey. To keep them at arm's length, he filed for bankruptcy, listing assets of $1,182 and liabilities of $59,829. The numbers were incomprehensible since he was not a big spender. His career in America ended in 1936 when he suffered back-to-back knockouts at the hands of Leroy Haynes, a Philadelphia-based campaigner with a spotty record. He recuperated from his second bout with Haynes in a New York hospital where he was admitted with temporary paralysis in his left leg.

Carnera was the model for Toro Molina, the Argentine protagonist of Budd Schulberg's *The Harder They Fall*, and Mountain Rivera, the Anthony Quinn character in the movie adaptation of Rod Serling's *Requiem for a Heavyweight*. Both works were influenced by Paul Gallico's 1938 book of reminiscence, *Farewell to Sport*, which for many years was a standard text in college journalism classes. In the book, Gallico portrays Carnera as a simple-minded oaf who was carrion for callous, mob-connected vultures who tossed him aside like garbage when he had outlived his usefulness.

Gallico chose to believe that Carnera captured Sharkey's title in a fixed fight, but few of his colleagues shared this opinion. Almost everyone who followed Carnera's career agreed that he improved as he gained more experience. The punch with which he ended Sharkey's brief title reign was a vicious uppercut in the eyes of many ringsiders. Moreover, there was nothing about the betting that hinted at skullduggery. According to the *New York Times*, the late money was actually skewed toward Sharkey. The *Times* reported that Carnera was a 6/5 favorite when Broadway bookies closed shop at 6 P.M. An hour later, bookies working the crowd were quoting Sharkey the favorite at odds of 7/5.

Perhaps no fighter was ever surrounded by as many shady people, but the view from here is that Gallico's widely read portrait of him was overly harsh. As champions go, Carnera was distinctly substandard, but he was hardly a tomato can. He was a courageous fighter, surprisingly nimble for a man his size (although prone to lapses of clumsiness), and his stamina was remarkable. Nor did his saga end with him living out his days in abject poverty in the village of his birth, the scenario that Gallico envisioned. He returned to the United States after World War II to launch a new career as a grunt-and-groan wrestler. Boxing purists considered this undignified, but Carnera was paid well for his exertions and, by all accounts, his disposition was cheerful.

All five "caretaker champions" would become fodder for Joe Louis. The so-called Brown Bomber would be credited with restoring the integrity of boxing. No one who had lived through the era of Jack Johnson could have foreseen this development.

# CHAPTER 11

# Boxing and Blacks

Joe Louis rocketed into celebrityhood. Within a year of his pro debut he vanquished Primo Carnera, the most recognizable name in his sport. He had been fighting professionally for less than fifteen months when he engaged in a bout that generated a gate of nearly a million dollars, a welcome blast of fresh air.

Louis had one spill during his dash to the title, but he quickly regained his momentum. Two months after his setback to Max Schmeling, he was back in the ring at Yankee Stadium, where he TKOed Jack Sharkey in the third round.

The Louis-Sharkey fight was staged two days after the closing day of the 1936 Berlin Olympics. At those games, 10 African American track athletes combined for 16 medals (seven gold), a cornucopia that became an ongoing story. The vexing question was whether this was an aberrational phenomenon, a bumper crop, or whether it was something more.

Heightened curiosity about black athletes in general, coupled with the growing fame of Joe Louis, prompted Nat Fleischer to create a series of books for his magazine's mail-order bookshop. The first installment of the five-part *Black Dynamite* series was released in 1938.

In setting down the history of blacks in pugilism, Fleischer wrote that he was amazed at how many fables had been incorporated into facts. But he cited no concrete examples and made no effort to separate the wheat from the chaff—the truth from the folklore. Moreover, his credentials were such that years would elapse before scholars questioned the accuracy of what appeared under his byline. The owner of a massive collection of boxing memorabilia that included shoeboxes of old newspaper clippings, and the publisher of the world's most influential boxing monthly, Fleischer was recognized as the foremost authority on matters pugilistic. In his publication, his editors frequently referred to him as the *official* historian of the ring.

Volume 1, which covered the bare-knuckle era, was rich in information about Tom Molineaux. An American slave by birth, Molineaux turned up in England about 1810 and quickly became one of the most talked-about ring personalities. His two fights with champion Tom Cribb were two of the most celebrated fights of the Regency era. Cribb's triumph in their second encounter in 1811 inspired a glut of poetic tributes.

Fleischer informs us that the ship that took Molineaux to England docked in Liverpool and that Molineaux walked from there to London. At John Jackson's gym, he caught the eye of Bill Richmond. An important trainer, Richmond took Molineaux under his wing and arranged a match with a man named Burrows, a prizefighter from Bristol. Molineaux passed this test easily and then, four weeks later, passed a more difficult test, vanquishing Tom Blake, a fighter known as Tom Tough. Somehow that was sufficient to propel him into a match with Cribb.

Molineaux was thought to be too raw. The most popular wager was on whether he would still be standing after 15 minutes. But the interracial angle alone made the bout intriguing, and the intrigue was heightened by Molineaux's nativity. The strained relations between England and her former colony were especially taut and would shortly erupt in the War of 1812. In the British mindset, the boxing champion of England was the champion of mankind and it was unthinkable that a foreigner would appropriate that distinction, particularly on British soil.

An estimated five thousand turned up to watch the fight, braving a torrential December rain. Molineaux gained the upper hand near the 30-minute mark. A few falls later, Cribb was too incapacitated to come to scratch but his seconds, chief among them John Gully, used various subterfuges to prolong the rest period and bullied the referee into letting the contest continue. Cribb got his second wind and turned the tide. Struck by innumerable low blows, Molineaux was all in after 55 minutes.

Molineaux demanded a rematch. When negotiations bogged down, he took a fight with a newcomer named Heskin Rimmer. Fighting before a large gathering at Moulsey Hurst, Molineaux had an easy go. Rimmer collapsed after taking a punch to the stomach.

The second meeting between Molineaux and Cribb was staged on September 28, 1811, in a field near the midland village of Grantham, close to where three counties abutted. It would be written that on the eve of the fight there wasn't a bed to be found within twenty miles of the battleground. Cribb was bet up from a 3/2 to a 3/1 favorite amidst reports that Molineaux—who had broken from his trainer—had been lax in his preparation. There were no such worries about Cribb, who trained in the highlands of Scotland under the stern watch of England's foremost long-distance runner Robert Allardyce, a man known to the Fancy as Captain Barclay.

Molineaux started fast, drawing first blood and raising a lump above Cribb's eye that required lancing, but the pace was too fast for him. Cribb brought the fight to a halt in the twentieth minute with a wicked shot that broke Molineaux's jaw in two places and then showboated by performing a Scottish jig.

Molineaux faded fast outside the ring too, descending into alcoholism and a life of petty crime. He died in Ireland in 1818, a victim of tuberculosis at age thirty-four.

As the first man of his race to fight for the title, Molineaux occupies a special niche. One thirsts to learn more about his background.

*Black Dynamite* regurgitates the info that Molineaux was the son of America's first storied prizefighter. Tom's father Zachary Molineaux and Zachary's four fighting brothers were prominent pugilists during the days when plantation owners were wagering enormous sums on their best fighting slaves, pitting them against slaves from rival plantations. Tom wins his freedom from bondage in one of these inter-plantation slave fights. Manumission is his prize for winning his master a fortune. Before shipping off to England, Tom has a series of fights with sailors that lead him to be hailed as the champion of the docks.

The problem with this far-fetched portrait is that it is totally lacking in documentation. Betting on horses was a popular pastime among plantation owners, especially in Virginia. During the eighteenth century, there were numerous match races that attracted huge wagers, events documented in newspapers, almanacs, diaries, and court reports. But nowhere in these strongholds of slavery does one find evidence of inter-plantation slave fights.

Molineaux carried about 200 pounds on a five-foot-nine frame. Dark-skinned, his facial features were fairly concordant with insulting caricatures of African natives. This undoubtedly was an asset to him in securing bookings, as the Brits then had a morbid fascination with "jungle people." In England, Molineaux traveled extensively on the fair circuit, where he was part of a community of human anomalies — snake charmers, bearded ladies, etc. All led amazingly adventurous lives, at least according to the cheap pamphlets that fair-goers were encouraged to buy to learn more about them. The core "facts" of Molineaux's early days in America — indeed, the entire body of American slave fight folklore — probably originated in these fabricated biographies. (Molineaux's tale most closely parallels the tales of damsels rescued from the harems of Turkish sultans. The biographies of these so-called "Circassians" were chock full of harrowing adventures.)[1]

Writers might not have found his story as compelling if it did not resonate with readers at both poles of the racial divide. He was plainly cheated out of the title in his first match with Cribb. This treachery, heaped onto other corrosive indignities, was psychologically devastating, pitching him into a tangle of pathology. His story also plays into the stereotype of the intemperate Negro who is unequipped to handle fame and fortune.

If not for these parabolic threads, perhaps more would have been written about his black benefactor, a far more interesting man.

As was true of Molineaux and bare-knuckle blacks in general, conflicting accounts would be written about Bill Richmond's boyhood in America. According to one account, he hailed from Richmond, Virginia, the derivation of his last name. A more popular version states that he was born in the New York county of Richmond, consisting of Staten Island, where he was raised in a parsonage where his mother worked as a live-in housekeeper. In both versions, Richmond is a lad of about thirteen when he first demonstrates his fighting prowess, repelling a gang of British soldiers who attack him without provocation. Supposedly news of the incident is relayed to General Earl Percy, commander of the British occupational forces, who insists on meeting the precocious fisticuffer and then informally adopts him. Initially Percy's valet, Richmond is subsequently apprenticed to a cabinetmaker, a middle-class occupation.

The tale doesn't jibe with what we know of Richmond's early years in England. If he was that good with his fists, it figured that Percy, a prizefight patron, would have apprenticed him to a boxing professor. Richmond became great pals with Lord Camelford, a lout who was associated in the public mind with his dog Trusty, England's foremost fighting bulldog. He undoubtedly had several "turn-ups" while serving as Lord Camelford's bodyguard and likely a few more while defending his honor in the face of racial slurs, but he did not have his first recorded prizefight until he was in his late thirties.

Throughout most of the bare-knuckle era, there were no preliminary fights. There were, however, frequent "post-liminaries," called bi-battles. After the main go, other pugilists might have a go of it. They would pass the hat for a purse and stood to make more money from a second pass of the hat if their match was crowd-pleasing. Bi-battles were most likely to occur if a prizefight ended quickly.

Richmond made his debut in one of these secondary bouts. He came up short, but made a good showing and was soon competing against top-raters. Pierce Egan would write that Richmond was unsurpassed at "milling on the retreat." The impression is that Richmond was a counterpuncher who let his opponent do the leading, but he was actually more of a bumblebee. When an opening appeared, he would spring forward and unleash a flurry of punches, then dart out of harm's way. At five-foot-eight, 165–170 pounds, Richmond was usually matched against bigger men and would have been overpowered if he had milled toe-to-toe in the conventional manner.

Richmond was a notch below championship caliber, but became one of the most important men in the pugilistic subculture. He leased rooms at the Fives Court, a sparring hall that was something of a co-op for boxing instructors. One of his pupils, William Fuller, opened boxing gyms in the United States and was an important intercontinental link. Richmond was also the landlord of a popular drinking establishment, was in constant demand as a second, and had a flourishing sideline as a booking agent. A man of color added spice to a fairgrounds boxing tent; fight caravans usually included one black face. If a promoter wanted a black fighter, he was the man to see. One of his most in-demand fighters was Sambo Sutton, a versatile entertainer who danced, sang, and performed acrobatic stunts.

Reading about Richmond, one is struck by the ease with which he circulated in a predominantly Caucasian environment. The proprietor of a boxing-themed pub was expected to do more than serve drinks and make small talk. He was expected to be something of a cheerleader, leading the chants that venerated ring titans. Egan relished his companionship, noting that Richmond was good-natured, witty, and conversant on almost any subject. While it would be ignorant to think that Richmond was undamaged by racism, whatever wounds were inflicted on his psyche left no outward marks, at least none visible to a man with blue eyes. It's reasonable to think that his name would have been more enduring if he had got caught up in some scandal.

There was a constant stream of black fighters in England during the 19th century. Few had the opportunity to fight for a large purse, but several distinguished themselves as trainers. James Wharton, reportedly from Morocco, sometimes used the handle Young Molineaux. As a trainer, he worked with such notables as Bendigo and Big Ben Caunt. Despite an ugly history of racial discrimination, boxing has been largely free of the drivel that blacks lacked the skills to become effective teachers and motivators.

Of all the black heavyweights that came to the fore before 1900, none came to be praised as lavishly as Peter Jackson. Born on the island of St. Croix in 1861, Jackson arrived in Australia about 1875. When his parents returned to St. Croix, disillusioned at failing to cash in on the gold rush, Jackson stayed behind. In the most fanciful account of his early years in Australia, his flair for aquatic sports was so great that he earned a handsome living from the stipends of his backers. Said to be a tremendous rower and diver, Jackson purportedly set distance records for underwater swimming. It would even be claimed that he invented the Australian crawl stroke. In a more moderate sketch, he worked as a seaman before finding his way to Larry Foley's boxing academy. Located in a back room of the White Horse Inn on the Sydney waterfront, Foley's gym was then the richest spawning ground of pugilistic talent in the world.

Jackson was knocked out by Melbourne foundry worker Bill Farnan in his first stab at the Australian heavyweight title in 1885 — a bout omitted from his ledger by his American biographers — but captured the title the next year, defeating Farnan's conqueror Tom Lees in Sydney. Although the bout lasted nearly two hours, Lees was so completely outclassed that Jackson had difficulty finding new opponents. In 1888, he sailed off to America. His reputation preceded him, but his profile became larger when W.W. "Big Bill" Naughton hired on as his tub-thumper. Born in New Zealand, Naughton hooked on with the *San Francisco Examiner* in his adopted country, rising to the post of sports editor, and was instrumental in boosting the careers of other boxers in the Australian wave.

Jackson came in search of a fight with John L. Sullivan, but the powers that be insisted that he first test his mettle against a man of his own race. On August 24, 1888, he defeated *Police Gazette* "Colored Heavyweight Champion" George Godfrey in a bout sponsored by San Francisco's California Athletic Club. A small heavyweight of indeterminate age who had come to acquire the cognomen Old Chocolate, Godfrey quit after nineteen rounds.

Jackson easily defeated two other name opponents — Joe McAuliffe and Patsy Cardiff — at San Francisco venues before accepting an offer from the Pelican Club to fight Jem Smith, the same Jem Smith who had fought a 106-round draw with Jake Kilrain. After a series of exhibitions around England to build up interest in the match, Jackson had an easy go with Smith, who fouled out in the second round. Before returning to the United States, he had more fights in the British Isles. In two of the more notable, he knocked out British Navy champion Sailor White in the third round at Portsmouth and scored a second-round stoppage of Peter Maher at Dublin, an outcome that would be seared with irony when Maher got to fight Bob Fitzsimmons in a bout billed for the heavyweight title.

In 1890, after a stay in Australia, Jackson returned to San Francisco to resume his campaign for a bout with Sullivan. But Sullivan turned a deaf ear to his *defi*, compelling him to take a match with the city's rising fistic star, Jim Corbett.

Several weeks before the match, Jackson injured his leg when a carriage in which he was riding overturned, but he went ahead with the fight anyway, confident that he could beat the smaller and less experienced Corbett with one good leg. However, the injury, which Jackson made no attempt to conceal, was so severe that the odds favoring him tumbled from 5/1 to 10/7.

A hybrid fight — a fight to the finish under Queensberry rules — the contest lasted 61 rounds, acquiring the trappings of an epic, although in truth it was largely a big bore. Jackson entered the ring with his bad leg swaddled in bandages, an incentive for Corbett to turn the match into a track meet. He did that, more or less, allowing Jackson to dictate the pace, and vigorous exchanges became briefer and less frequent as the bout degenerated into a test of endurance. Eventually both men were reduced to posturing, too arm-weary to launch an assault. By then, some of the spectators had gone home and others were asleep in the bleachers. Deciding that it was pointless to continue, the referee asked the officers of the club for permission to declare the match a draw. Against the protestations of Corbett, who was less droopy, the request was granted.

The purse was ten thousand dollars, $8500 to the winner. When the match ended inconclusively, the purse was slashed in half and divvied up equally. The chiseling was particularly hurtful to Jackson, as he had a lower income ceiling without John L. Sullivan in his future. Fortunately, he had a legitimate claim to the title of British Empire champion, and interest was building overseas for a match between him and Frank Slavin, a former sparring partner known as the Sydney Cornstalk. Slavin had been on a roll since taking up residence in London, recording a string of quick knockouts, and was considered superior to Jackson in some respects, an opinion that rested partly on the supposition that Jackson could never be his old self after his marathon fight with Corbett.

The Jackson-Slavin match had been kicking around for five years. They were originally scheduled to meet in 1887 in Sydney, but the bout fell out. Stoked by reports that they had come to blows over the affections of a woman, the contest at the National Sporting Club gripped the sporting crowd of England. "The speculative fever of the Capital spread through the country, and the voice of the Layer was heard in the land," reminisced NSC co-founder A.F. Bettinson.

After three even rounds, the fight turned viciously one-sided. Jackson gave Slavin a terrible beating before putting him down for the count in the tenth frame.

Jackson was no stranger to strong drink or loose women, but like Jim Corbett was packaged as a man of refinement. Some writers hailed him as the whitest black man who ever lived, a characterization intended as a supreme compliment. A.C. Hales, an Australian writer of novels for young readers, used Jackson as the model for "Young Prince Peter," one of the first adventure stories in which the protagonist is black. But the bouquets would be of no solace when Sullivan bypassed him and risked his title against Corbett, who had "earned" the opportunity by holding his own with a man in no condition to show his true ability. And when Corbett became the title-holder, he drew the color line as effectively as had Sullivan.

Jackson's victory over Slavin was his last significant ring triumph. Over the next six years, he appeared frequently on the stage as the title character in the play *Uncle Tom's Cabin*, earning rave or hostile reviews, depending on one's source. In 1898, he returned to San Francisco to meet a powerful up-and-comer named James J. Jeffries. Rusty, poorly conditioned, and beginning to exhibit signs of ring damage, Jackson, now 37 years old, was belted out in the third round. He then returned to Australia, where he took to drinking heavily and began to exhibit signs of schizophrenia. The decline in his health was undoubtedly hastened by the toxicity of racism. He had played the game by the white man's rules, aspiring to reach the mountaintop, but had succeeded only in climbing high enough to read the sign on the summit: "Whites Only." Jackson died of tuberculosis at the age of forty.[2]

Blacks competing in lighter weight classes had opportunities that were denied Jackson. Smaller men were less threatening to the white establishment and the belts for which they competed had less symbolic importance.

In Jackson's day, few fighters had a larger profile than George "Little Chocolate" Dixon, who won the world bantamweight title in 1890 and the featherweight title the following year. Dixon was such a stylish boxer that he fairly invented the category of best pound-for-pound. In 1902, Joe Gans and Barbados Joe Walcott ruled the lightweight and welterweight divisions simultaneously. Walcott, barely five-foot-two, failed in three chances to win a world title before finally succeeding, but on the way up he knocked out Joe Choynski and defeated the estimable George Gardner, who would go on to knock out future heavyweight champion Marvin Hart. Barbados Joe would be credited with coining the saying "The bigger they are, the harder they fall."

The opportunities afforded smaller fighters, however, were certainly less than that afforded their white counterparts. To secure matches, blacks were often compelled to compete at less than their optimal weight. More commonly, they were thrust into matches against bigger men at catch-weights. Against this backdrop, skullduggery was rampant. All prominent turn-of-the-century black fighters in America, save perhaps Jack Johnson, lost one or more interracial bouts that were fixed, at least in the court of public opinion. For a black fighter, circa 1900, putting food on the table often meant "doing business," a Catch-22 if he wasn't a good actor, as a fighter with a tainted reputation was flawed merchandise and less able to command top dollar for his services down the road.

Both Gans and Walcott fought Sam Langford, the Boston Tar Baby, a cult fighter with a gnome-like appearance. As would be true of the colorful FDR-era baseball pitcher Satchell Paige, Langford stood as a metaphor for an entire community of segregated athletes. A middleweight who fought "squirts" like Gans and Walcott but was more often pitted against larger men, Langford was the man most closely identified with boxing's "Chitlin' Circuit."

In common with George Godfrey and George Dixon, Langford was born in Nova

Scotia and had most of his early fights in Boston, benefiting from that city's relatively benign policy toward blacks, a residuum of the days when Massachusetts was the axis of the abolitionist movement. He competed from 1902 to 1926, reputedly having more than 400 fights, of which 314 have been verified. Near the end of his career, when he campaigned extensively in Mexico, Langford was almost totally blind.

While a few Caucasian fighters of his era were comparably active, none answered the bell for as many rounds. A more striking feature of Langford's career is that he kept fighting the same men over and over.

Langford purportedly had more than thirty fights with Harry Wills. Researchers have located seventeen, while also documenting fifteen bouts with Sam McVea and fourteen with Joe Jeanette. However, in some of these fights, the opponent was likely an imposter. Several fighters of his day adopted the handle Young Peter Jackson. There were presumably at least two Battling Jim Johnsons. In newspaper accounts of his fights in Boise, Battling Jim is described as a fighter standing five-foot-eleven with conspicuously short arms, but he has been referenced as the most massive fighter on the Chitlin' Circuit.

Black fighters were often made to pull their punches when meeting a white opponent, but this practice of holding something back, called "fighting under wraps," was hardly limited to their interracial matches. Almost all of Langford's bouts with Wills, McVea, and Jeanette went the full distance, averaging 13.5 rounds. A contributing factor was that black fighters were less likely to be paid in full if they made short work of an opponent and the crowd felt cheated.

While Langford almost certainly fought under wraps in bouts with some of his Caucasian opponents, most notably Stanley Ketchel, he tended to be at his most formidable in interracial matches. In 1909, he scored a clean knockout of fan favorite Iron Hague at London's National Sporting Club, and he was one of only three men to stop Philadelphia Jack O'Brien, a man who had more than 200 bouts. But big paydays were rare. In a 1944 interview, Langford, then living in squalor in a Harlem boardinghouse, estimated that his purses averaged three hundred dollars.

Early in his career, Langford was out-pointed by Jack Johnson in a 15-round bout at Chelsea, Massachusetts. Johnson went on to become the most renowned — and most reviled — fighter of his generation.

Born in Raleigh, North Carolina, in 1878, Jack Johnson was raised in Galveston, Texas, where his father found work as a school janitor. Early into his career, he developed rivalries with John "Klondike" Haines, Hank Griffin, and Sam McVea. The latter extended him the distance in three 20-round fights billed for the Negro Heavyweight Title. Johnson was accorded the winner in each meeting, solidifying his reputation as the top fighter in his colony.

Johnson routinely taunted opponents before knocking them groggy, behavior that incited a torrent of invective if the opponent happened to be white. Outside the ring, he fancied gaudy jewelry and expensive cars. The sportsman he most admired was stunt driver Barney Oldfield, the first man to travel a mile in under a minute. Johnson imagined himself to be Oldfield when he went for a spin and his name would come to be identified with reckless driving. Public indignation was intensified by his habit of motoring in an open-air car with an attractive blonde snuggled at his side.

A shrewd self-promoter, Johnson campaigned hard for a match with Jim Jeffries and chummed the water more vigorously after Jeffries retired and the title passed into the hands of Tommy Burns. His campaign took him to Australia, where Burns was held in higher repute than in the United States. In 1907, Johnson knocked out two of Australia's top fighters, Peter

Felix and Bill Lang, in bouts at Sydney and Melbourne. Felix fell in the opening round of a match billed for the World Colored Heavyweight Title.

There was little chance that Burns would risk his title against Johnson in America. The match was certain to generate a big gate, but opposition to interracial fights, and to Jack Johnson in particular, was so strong that no promoter would touch it. But Johnson was a more sympathetic figure in Australia, where there was a residue of anger over the unfair treatment accorded adopted son Peter Jackson. An energetic young promoter named Hugh McIntosh was keen on making the match. A former racing cyclist and amateur boxer, McIntosh would go on to become a theatrical impresario on a par with James Brady. He was the driving force behind Sydney's new sports stadium. The arena fronted Rushcutter's Bay.

McIntosh made the fight for December 26, 1908. This was Boxing Day in the British Commonwealth, a national holiday, but in this particular year it was also a day in which it was known that the city of Sydney would be teeming with American sailors on shore leave.

A Canadian from the province of Ontario whose given name was Noah Brusso, Burns stood five-foot-seven. Initially regarded as a mediocrity, he forced a reconsideration of that appraisal with eleven successful title defenses. Theoretically at his peak at age 27, Burns had 34 knockouts to his credit in 52 bouts, an exceedingly high ratio, and was accorded the better chance of bringing the bout to a conclusion with a single punch. One could build a case for him without filtering one's impressions through fashionable stereotypes, and the case became stronger when it became known that his good friend McIntosh would referee the contest. It was plain that Johnson was more physically gifted, but the odds favoring Burns (7/4 the consensus) were ridiculous only in hindsight.

Having McIntosh serve as the referee was actually Johnson's idea. He reasoned that the promoter would be scrutinized so closely that he would not dare allow Burns any liberties. But this precaution was unnecessary. Johnson knocked Burns to the canvas in the second frame and then methodically beat him to a pulp, all the while taunting him to make a better showing. Near the end of Round 14, a police captain seated at ringside decided he had seen enough and signaled that the fight was over.

The next morning, white America awoke to learn that a man derided as a "flash nigger" sat on the throne reserved for the most important deity in the pantheon of sports. Among the most incensed was Jack London, who covered the fight as a ringside correspondent for the *New York Herald.* He concluded his dispatch by imploring Jim Jeffries to come out of retirement and wipe the smile from the face of the new champion. With this exhortation, London opened the floodgates of the White Hope era. Jeffries was eventually swept into the current.[3]

Born on a farm in Ohio, James Jackson Jeffries was the first heavyweight champion whose parents were born in the United States. He first attracted attention while working as a sparring partner for Jim Corbett. A big target, seemingly impervious to punishment, he was ideally suited to this role. The word most often used to describe him was ungainly. However, he became more fluid and his defense improved tremendously when he learned to box from a crouch with his forearms guarding his face in somewhat of a peek-a-boo style.

In his thirteenth professional fight, Jeffries claimed the heavyweight title with a mild upset of Bob Fitzsimmons. He had a rough go with Tom Sharkey in his first title defense, prevailing after 25 brutal rounds, but encountered progressively less trouble in his subsequent bouts and was seemingly at the top of his game when he retired at the age of 30, leaving the scene with a record of 18–0–2. By then he had acquired an aura of indestructibility fostered by hackneyed stories that played up his athleticism. It was written that he once ran the 100-

yard dash barefoot in under 11 seconds and that he could jump as high as his shoulders from a standing start.

Jeffries had no desire to heed London's plea. He had let his weight balloon to 285 pounds. But he succumbed to the proverbial offer that he couldn't refuse. It came from Tex Rickard, whose outfit outbid three rival consortiums with a $101,000 guarantee, 60 percent to the winner, plus a percentage of the movie rights. The deal was sealed when Rickard agreed to pay off a $12,000 marker that Jeffries owed to a Reno casino.

The chasm between the races in America appeared to have widened since Jack Johnson had been made to travel all the way to Australia to get a crack at the heavyweight title, but opposition to the Johnson-Jeffries match was mitigated by the cheerful expectation that the black man would get his comeuppance. Johnson had been less than impressive in a match with Philadelphia Jack O'Brien, a man he outweighed by 44 pounds, and had been decked by Stanley Ketchel in a match where he had a 30-pound advantage. Now the roles would be reversed and he would be the smaller man. But Johnson had no doubt that he could defeat Jeffries. At his training camp in Reno, he violated one of the oldest strictures of his profession by entertaining female visitors, two of whom — Belle Schreiber, a Chicago prostitute, and Etta Duryea, a divorced Long Island socialite — came to figure prominently in his life.

Jeffries had the weight of an army on his shoulders. The editor of a London fight journal captured the prevailing mood in the white community: "[A win by Johnson] has become a contingency almost too awful to contemplate. Should Johnson win, not only he, but all of the colored inhabitants of the United States would commence strutting at once. And this would be a serious state of affairs."[4]

The worst-case scenario was that Johnson would toy with the ex-champion, flogging him at his leisure with a smirk on his face and this, as it turned out, was exactly what came to pass. It was obvious from the onset that Big Jeff was nowhere near the fighter he had been prior to his 70-month layoff. At the 2:20 mark of the fifteenth round, his corner tossed in the towel. Six months after the fight, Johnson married Etta Duryea. She was the first of his three white wives.

Too controversial for American promoters, Johnson spent most of 1911 in England, where he polished a vaudeville act that consisted of telling a few jokes in an anecdotal vein, playing a few tunes on a bass violin, and sparring a few rounds with a member of his ensemble. A match was arranged with Billy Wells, a young British fighter who went on to become enormously popular, but the Home Office disallowed it. The reason given was fear of uprisings by blacks in colonial territories, but Johnson hurt his cause with a series of incidents. During his stay in London, he was issued a summons for using excessive profanity in public, was a frequent no-show at music halls where he was scheduled to perform, and had a well-publicized spat with his landlady, who had him evicted for nonpayment of rent and obtained a judgment against him for the destruction of home furnishings. The broken crockery in his vacated flat was construed as evidence of marital discord.

Johnson returned to the U.S. in 1912 to look after his business interests. It was an eventful year. In September, Etta Duryea Johnson committed suicide, shooting herself in the head with a revolver. Shortly thereafter, it came to light that Johnson was romantically involved with his 19-year-old white secretary, Lucille Cameron, whose mother accused Johnson, now 34, of having hypnotic powers over her daughter. Federal agents investigated her claim as a possible violation of the White Slave Traffic Act of 1910, better known as the Mann Act, but dropped the matter when Johnson married her. They then turned their attention to Johnson's on-again, off-again paramour Belle Schreiber, who acknowledged taking money from

Johnson during periods when she wasn't employed in a house of prostitution. Arrested at his Chicago cabaret, the Café de Champion, Johnson spent four days in jail before his attorneys finagled his release. Antagonism toward him was now at such a high pitch that he literally put his life in danger each time he ventured out in public.

On June 4, 1913, Johnson was found guilty of violating the Mann Act. Facing a year in prison, he fled the country. During his years in exile, he moved freely about Europe and South America, staying solvent with music hall engagements and phony fights with circus wrestlers. In Paris, where African American musicians were better appreciated than in their native country and black prizefighters had a somewhat similar cachet, Johnson risked his title twice, boxing a 10-round draw with Battling Jim Johnson (no relation) and earning a 20-round decision over Frank Moran, an ex-sailor from Pittsburgh.

A hastily arranged affair, roundly ignored by the American press, the Johnson-Johnson bout was yet noteworthy in that it was the first heavyweight title match in which both contestants were black. Battling Jim wasn't in the same class as Langford, Jeanette, or McVea, but he had no difficulty staying the course against the fugitive champion, who was poorly conditioned and emerged from the dissatisfactory bout with a broken arm.

Johnson's last meaningful fight in exile was ultimately the last meaningful fight of his career. On April 5, 1915, the day after Easter Sunday, he opposed Jess Willard at Havana's Vedado Racetrack. A six-foot-six former cowpuncher with a 23–5–1 record, supposedly 27 years of age (he was actually seven years older), Willard had been lured into boxing in 1911 when the search for a White Hope was at its zenith. Shrewdly managed by Tom Jones, a former barber, Willard hailed from Pottawatomie County, Kansas, and was nicknamed the Pottawatomie Giant.

Scheduled for 45 rounds, the bout ended in Round 26 when Willard put Johnson down for the count. As the referee tolled off the final seconds, a photographer caught the moment. Lying on his back with his knees raised, Johnson appeared to be shielding his eyes from the sun. This would be presented as evidence that the fight was fixed, but a more popular opinion was that Johnson had simply quit. Blowups of the photo came to ornament the walls of many saloons. It conveyed the message that blacks weren't welcome.

On July 20, 1920, Johnson returned to the United States to face the music. Although the Mann Act was aimed at brothel-keepers and organizers of prostitution rings, Johnson was sentenced to a year and a day in the federal prison at Joliet. Then, for one of the few times in his life, he got lucky. The Illinois facility was full (owing partly to zealous enforcement of the Mann Act) and he was reassigned to Leavenworth, where former Nevada governor Denver Dickerson wielded clout with the administration. According to Johnson, Dickerson had won a large bet on him and showed his gratitude by allowing him to dine apart from other inmates, eating food prepared by a personal chef.

Johnson served two-thirds of his sentence and was released on good behavior. Resuming his career, he fought sporadically into the decade of the 1930s, ending up as a trial horse on the tank town circuit. For every fight that he had in his professional dotage, at least that many were canceled, some at the behest of politicians yielding to pressure from the Ku Klux Klan. In his twilight years, Johnson worked intermittently as a human curiosity at a flea circus in Times Square.

Jess Willard was the first of eight Caucasians to rule the heavyweight roost during the 22-year interregnum between Jack Johnson and Joe Louis. There were many good black heavyweights during this period, but they were shut out of title fights. The discrimination was rationalized as Jack Johnson's fault; he had left such a terrible stench that others, through no fault

At the age of 56, Jack Johnson still cut a dashing figure. This photograph was taken in 1934 at Madison Square Garden. Johnson never boxed at Madison Square Garden, where he was informally blackballed. *New York World Telegram and Sun/Library of Congress/History Image.*

of their own, were forced to bear the consequences. The man that came closest to cracking this barrier was Harry Wills.

A native of New Orleans who acquired the nickname Brown Panther, Wills was the youngest of the great Chitlin' Circuit heavyweights treadmilled by a virus of racism made more virulent by anti–Johnson hysteria. In 1919, he settled in Harlem, where he quickly became a socially prominent member of a growing and vibrant black community. A third-round knockout of Fred Fulton at Newark in 1920 — Wills' first encounter with an important Caucasian fighter — spawned a grass-roots movement for a match between him and Jack Dempsey that evolved into a *cause celebre* in 1924 when *The Ring* named Wills the top heavy-weight contender in its first published set of rankings.

The tired argument that a black heavyweight champion would dishonor his sport and attenuate racial friction did not wash in the case of Wills. A health faddist faithfully married to a smart businesswoman, he was completely free of scandal. He had an honorable manager in Harry Mullen, but his loyalty to Mullen may have hurt him in the long run as Tex Rickard was never able to lock him into a multi-fight contract. The reality was that he was already on the downgrade when Dempsey was pressured to fight him, his knockout power depleted by brittle hands. His top placement in the ratings was more a lifetime achievement award than an assessment of current form.

Rickard succeeded in matching Wills with Luis Angel Firpo. Staged at Boyle's Thirty Acres, the fight drew a reported 80,000. It was roundly understood that Firpo would be accorded a rematch with Dempsey if he survived this test, but Wills, a slight underdog, won the decision by a comfortable margin in a dull fight. New York Athletic Commission chairman James A. Farley then issued an edict that made Wills the mandatory opponent for Dempsey's next title defense.

A political gadfly who would become chairman of the National Democratic Committee and postmaster general under Franklin D. Roosevelt, Farley had an ulterior motive. Blacks were becoming a significant voting bloc. Their allegiance was skewed heavily toward the Republican Party, the party of Abraham Lincoln. Support for the Brown Panther was calculated to siphon votes away from Republican candidates in the next round of elections.

Wills and Dempsey actually came to an agreement to fight in Benton Harbor, Michigan, but Doc Kearns knew that the match could not be made without involving Rickard, so the news conference announcing the fight was likely nothing more than a ploy by Kearns to stifle talk that he was losing his grip on his meal ticket. Rickard was then working to eliminate the potholes in the road to a match between Dempsey and Gene Tunney. With Rickard's tacit encouragement, Tunney cut a deal with Timothy J. Mara, promising Mara a piece of the action if he could eliminate the obstacles to a bout with Dempsey in New York, one of the few states to permit both 15-round fights and official decisions. Most states allowed only 10-round fights; the longer distance favored Tunney, a slow starter.

Behind the scenes, the Wills-Tunney tug-of-war was a battle between Irish-American power brokers. The son of a small-town saloonkeeper, James A. Farley would go on to be recognized as the most influential coalition builder in the Democratic Party since Andrew Jackson. But he met his match in Tim Mara, a bookmaker from a humble background who would be best remembered as one of the founding fathers of the National Football League.[5]

When the smoke cleared, Dempsey was allowed to bypass the Brown Panther without being stripped of his title. Farley saved face by keeping the match out of New York, a Pyrrhic victory as the bout drew a gate of $1,895,733 in Philadelphia, denying the Empire State an enormous tax windfall. As for Wills, he took to the ring three months after the Dempsey-

Tunney fight and suffered a tremendous loss of prestige. At Ebbets Field, he was roundly out-pointed by Jack Sharkey.

For blacks in pro boxing, the Golden Era was a misnomer — nay, a hoax. In the period between the ratification of the Treaty of Versailles and the stock market crash of 1929 — convenient Golden Era bookends — there were 121 fights across the eight standard weight divisions that would be certified by *The Ring Record Book* as legitimate title fights. In only three of these bouts was the challenger a man of color. Lightheavyweight Battling Siki, middleweight Theodore "Tiger" Flowers, and bantamweight Alphonso "Panama Al" Brown were victorious in their first title fights. Of the three, only Flowers, who fought out of Atlanta, was born and raised in the United States.

Flowers's early record is murky, but he acquired the profile of a windmill fighter with a china chin. In his most curious defeat, he suffered a fifth-round knockout at the hands of 43-year-old Fireman Jim Flynn in Mexico City. He then reeled off a 21-fight winning streak before losing a newspaper decision to middleweight champion Harry Greb in a non-title fight. But in a mild upset, he avenged this defeat when he fought Greb for the title in February of 1926. A rematch produced the same result. The nod went to Flowers after fifteen lusty rounds.

Because most of his early fights were in Southern rings, it was widely assumed that Flowers had a battle royal background. Boxing promoters operating below the Mason-Dixon line were far more likely to spice their shows with battle royals. The participants — almost always black and typically teenagers — engaged in a free-for-all until only one was left standing. Sometimes they were blindfolded. This was called a battle-blind.

Rooted in the ancient sport of cockfighting, battle royals have been depicted as frightfully savage. This is more folklore than fact. Battle royals with seasoned campaigners were expositions of "hippodroming." The term, which has fallen into disuse, denotes a slapstick charade. Hippodroming was manifest in the choreographed comedy of barnstorming teams like the Harlem Globetrotters and Indianapolis Clowns.

At grunt-and-groan wrestling shows, battle royals were often curtain-closers, but in boxing the battle royal was more likely to be the lid-lifter. The idea was to get the crowd in a jolly mood and perhaps soften the disappointment that might follow if the conventional bouts were humdrum. The time allotted to the segment was elastic; the plug would be pulled if the crowd started to lose interest.

An occasional injury was inevitable. It's easy to lose one's composure in a make-believe fight. Off the vaudeville circuit, battle royals were often slapped together with volunteers, producing a predictably clumsy exhibition. First-time participants were particularly accident-prone as they had little practice in pulling their punches and were less versed in gentlemen's agreements. However, there is no record of a fighter ever being seriously injured in a battle royal.

Battle royals were outlawed in New York in 1911, and in many other jurisdictions thereafter. Their doom was hastened when Ralph Ellison's *The Invisible Man* became a best seller. In this powerful 1952 novel, a battle royal is unmasked as a defilement of dignity that illustrates the moral depravity of the white establishment. But battle royals would not disappear completely until they lost their pull as a gimmick for reversing sagging attendance at fight clubs outside major cities.

It's uncertain whether Tiger Flowers ever participated in a battle royal, but he had a penchant for clowning, suggesting that he was schooled in the hippodrome tradition. This penchant may have cost him his title when he risked it against Mickey Walker at the Chicago Coliseum in December of 1926. After 10 bloody rounds, referee Benny Yanger, an ex-fighter from the old school, awarded the decision to Walker.

The verdict was well received by the predominantly white audience, but roundly denounced by the ringside press. Westbrook Pegler called it the worst decision of all time. The brouhaha prompted the Illinois Boxing Commission into following the examples of New York and Pennsylvania by adopting the use of three scorekeepers.

Flowers had an ironclad contract for a rematch, but Walker's manager Doc Kearns disregarded the compact. Four days after a bout in New York with journeyman Leo Gates, Flowers died during a routine eye operation. His memorial service in Atlanta reportedly drew the largest crowd ever in that city for a man of color, a turnout unsurpassed until the funeral of Dr. Martin Luther King, Jr. A deeply religious man, Flowers left a large estate.

Despite the brambles, the number of African American boxers increased dramatically during the Great Depression. A major push factor was the growth of amateur boxing in the form of newspaper-sponsored tournaments. A tournament sponsored by the *Chicago Tribune* in 1926 was the blueprint for the Golden Gloves tourney sponsored by the *New York Daily News* the following year. Other papers in other regions of the country jumped on the bandwagon. These tournaments were uniquely open-door. The most decorated of the black amateurs were welcomed into the stables of well-connected managers.

For a black fighter in a lighter weight class, the most open state was California. Those unable to get matches with talented Anglo cohorts might yet build a following at the expense of Mexicans and Filipinos, whose ranks were thick. No one capitalized more than Henry Armstrong, who snared the featherweight, welterweight, and lightweight titles in that sequence in New York rings after a six-year apprenticeship on the West Coast circuit.

Armstrong won his titles within a 10-month span and briefly held all three belts simultaneously. He accomplished this remarkable "hat trick" during a 46-fight winning streak that circumscribed a skein of 27 knockouts. Coming up the ladder, however, he was less than a world-beater. Prior to launching the streak, his ledger was 58–11–7, an excellent record but hardly the template of a man who would come to be rated among the very top pound-for-pound fighters of all time.

Armstrong's high-octane attack made him a welcome addition to any fight card. As was true of Primo Carnera, an awkward comparison, the on-the-job repetitions sharpened his skills more effectively than tutorials in the gym. He struggled early in his career with gritty Perfecto Lopez, but gradually got the upper hand, winning inside the distance in their seventh meeting. A higher-stakes five-fight rivalry with "Baby" Arizmendi followed a similar drift. But while Armstrong evolved into a sparkling gem of a fighter, it's unlikely that he would have crossed the threshold into national stardom without influential backers. His big break came when the famous entertainer Al Jolson purchased his contract and hooked him up with Eddie Mead.

A colorful character who knew all the right people in New York, Mead fit right in with the new wave of fight managers nudging aside the old guard, a shift advantageous to a few favored black boxers who were carefully matched to pad their record, a luxury denied blacks of previous generations who were invariably matched tough from the very onset of their careers. In October of 1939, Armstrong defended his welterweight diadem four times in a span of only 18 days, but these were title fights in name only as his opponents were hardly in his league. The men calling the shots for Joe Louis adopted the same tack in 1941, launching Louis on a fight-of-the-month tour while all the talk was about his imminent showdown with Billy Conn.

Born on May 13, 1914, in a sharecropper's shack in Alabama, Joe Louis (Joseph Louis Barrow) learned to box at the Brewster Recreational Center in Detroit. Blessed with a

Eddie Mead stands between Al Jolson and Henry Armstrong in this photograph circa 1938. *Antiquities of the Prize Ring.*

paralyzing punch, he won 41 of his 54 amateur fights inside the distance. When he turned pro, he was accorded advantages unprecedented for a novice of African ancestry. His backers gave him a monthly stipend, set him up in a nicely appointed Chicago apartment, and remanded him to the trainer that had guided lightweight Sammy Mandell and bantamweight Bud Taylor to world titles, Jack Blackburn. What made this even more unusual was that the men behind Joe Louis—John Roxborough and Julian Black—shared his color.

Roxborough was the policy king of Paradise Valley, the largest area of black settlement in Depression-era Detroit. Julian Black, less involved in Louis's day-to-day affairs, controlled a policy wheel in Chicago. As was true of all numbers barons, they had diffuse business interests. Roxborough had a thriving bail bond agency and published guidebooks to finding winning lottery numbers based on the interpretation of dreams. Black was involved with funeral homes and had run speakeasies. (Another numbers banker, dairy owner Marshall Miles of Buffalo, supplanted Roxborough in 1941 when the Detroiter was snared in a sting of municipal corruption, but Roxborough would return to the fold with no diminution in status after serving a 30-month prison term.)

Louis launched his pro career in 1934 on the Fourth of July—a splendidly appropriate day in light of future developments—dispatching a sacrificial lamb from Bremerton, Washington, inside two minutes. Fighting on average every two weeks, Louis owned a 16–0 record when Mike Jacobs entered the picture, binding Team Louis to an exclusive promotional contract.

Before casting their lot with Jacobs, Roxborough and Black laid down the law. They would brook none of the dishonesty that had hamstrung black fighters for decades. There would be no fighting under wraps and no fixed fights to build up the gate for a rematch. Operating on the premise that the heavyweight sultanship was restricted to men palatable to white America and fearing that any indiscretion would be blown out of proportion, they also set down rules for Louis. They forbade bad-mouthing an upcoming opponent or gloating over a fallen opponent and they insisted that he never be photographed alone with a white woman. A top-tier Chitlin' Circuit fighter in his younger days, Blackburn projected the wrong image, but his teaching skills trumped other considerations. A closet alcoholic whose face was disfigured by a mean razor scar, Blackburn had served time for manslaughter.

Mike Jacobs was versed in all the established gyps. He had taught Rickard how to stretch an arena by the expedient of adding rows lettered AA, BB, etc., thereby doubling the number of seats in the priciest sections. But Jacobs had some unorthodox ideas. By his reckoning, a champion with staying power, black or white, was a far more valuable commodity than a charismatic white champion susceptible to flaming out quickly.

Jacobs was like Rickard in one important aspect. He believed in coddling the press. For Louis's first fight under his promotional banner, Jacobs took a contingent of sportswriters to Detroit, where Louis had his coming-out party against Natie Brown, a rugged but marginally skilled Jewish fighter. Louis had an off night and was extended the distance in a dull fight, but the writers on the rail junket had a splendid time and reciprocated by oiling the wheels for a more ambitious promotion: Joe Louis vs. Primo Carnera.

On the comeback trail after his dreadful showing against Max Baer, Carnera was coming off a 9th-round stoppage of six-foot-eight Ray Impelletiere. A sure-fire box office hit, the Louis-Carnera confrontation was transformed by events overseas into a morality play for black America. Italy's fascist dictator Benito Mussolini was mobilizing troops for an invasion of Ethiopia, a huge news story in black-owned newspapers where Ethiopian emperor Haile Selassie—the Nelson Mandela of his day—was portrayed in terms befitting a man inspired by Providence.

The bout at Yankee Stadium on June 25, 1935, attracted a crowd of 62,000, which was nearly double the attendance for the Baer-Braddock heavyweight championship fight two weeks earlier. An estimated 10,000 blacks were in attendance, an unofficial U.S. record for a boxing event with a biracial crowd. An 8/5 favorite, Louis hammered "Mussolini's man" to the canvas three times in the sixth frame, impelling the referee to stop the match and triggering a tumultuous celebration in black ghettoes across America. Precocious Joe Louis, a professional boxer for less than one full year, was only a contender, not yet a champion, but he was suddenly The Man.

Two months after routing Carnera, an estimated 95,000 (84,831 paid) turned out at Yankee Stadium to see Louis fight Max Baer in a non-title fight. Baer's popularity had soared following a surprisingly apt performance as the leading man opposite Myrna Loy in the 1933 hit movie *The Prizefighter and the Lady*, and he was still rated top-notch despite his shocking loss to Jimmy Braddock.

This was the largest crowd to ever witness a sporting event in New York. Broadway betting commissioner Jack Doyle pegged the wagering handle in New York City alone at more than $5 million, the highest in his memory for a fight that did not involve Jack Dempsey. The big plungers were squarely behind Louis, as were members of the Fourth Estate, but reportedly nine of every 10 bets were written on Baer. A 2/1 favorite, Louis dominated from the opening bell. The dispassionate Baer went down for the count in the fourth round.

This was an eventful day in the life of Joe Louis. On the afternoon of the fight, he wed 19-year-old Marva Trotter in a ceremony performed by her brother, an ordained minister. A secretary employed by the *Chicago Defender* newspaper, Marva appeared to be a nice catch. The presumption was that she would motivate Joe to keep his nose to the grindstone. In deference to her, it was decided to slow the pace. Louis fought only twice in the next eight months, making quick work of overmatched opponents. Then he was thrust against a beetle-browed German, Max Schmeling.

Held at Yankee Stadium on June 19, 1936, Louis vs. Schmeling attracted barely half as many people as had witnessed the Louis-Baer fight. Inclement weather was a contributing factor, but one could have predicted a low turnout by examining the odds. Louis was an 8/1 favorite to win by any scenario and a 4/1 favorite to win by knockout inside five rounds. Schmeling was no slouch — he would have been a formidable heavyweight in any generation — but he had won the title on a disputed foul, relinquished it in his first defense, and had lost three of his last four fights in American rings. The odds also hinted at Louis's emerging status as a hero to black *and white* America.

There was one knowledgeable fellow who rated Schmeling a very live underdog. Jack Johnson, still very much a public figure, volunteered that Louis was too flat-footed and leaned forward to an excessive degree when he probed with his jab, making him vulnerable to a right-handed sharpshooter, a description that fit Schmeling to a tee. Few people paid Johnson any heed, attributing his observations to jealousy. It was known that he had been turned away at functions where Louis was the guest of honor and he was proud of his distinction as the only black face in the montage of heavyweight champions. But Johnson was a very astute handicapper.

In the second round, Louis dropped his left as he prepared to launch a right hook, but Schmeling beat him to the punch with a stiff right lead. In Round 4 it happened again and this time Louis landed on the canvas, suffering the first knockdown of his career. Fighting with great composure with his mouth bleeding and one eye swollen nearly shut, Schmeling repeatedly wobbled Louis in the ensuing rounds and ended the bout in Round 12 with a volley of punches that put the Brown Bomber down for the count.

This photograph of Max Baer was likely taken in 1933 at an MGM studio lot. Fodder for Joe Louis, Baer was noted for his womanizing and renowned for his lethal punches. *Reproduced from the original held by the Department of Special Collections of the University Libraries of Notre Dame.*

Louis had little time to brood over his humbling defeat. He was back at Yankee Stadium two months later, matched against Jack Sharkey. Some questioned whether it was wise to send him out against a name fighter so soon, but his advisors had little fear of Sharkey, a clever boxer who had scored only 15 knockouts in a 54-bout career and was on the downside at age thirty-four. A 4/1 favorite, the Brown Bomber rebounded in a big way, sending Sharkey into permanent retirement with a third-round stoppage. Louis won six more bouts over the next six months as Jacobs finalized arrangements for a match with title-holder Jimmy Braddock.

A product of Joe Jeanette's gym in Jersey City, Braddock was the most implausible of heavyweight champions. He had shown great promise early in his career, but had hit the skids, beginning with a loss to lightheavyweight champion Tommy Loughran in 1929. He won only 11 of his next 33 fights and hit rock bottom in 1933 when he severely injured his right hand in a bout with journeyman Abe Feldman. The injury was a double whammy as his day job unloading cargo from ships required two good hands, and Braddock, a family man with three young children, was compelled to swallow his pride and apply for public relief. The injury proved to be a blessing in disguise, however, as Braddock was reinvigorated by his furlough. Returning to the ring after a 9-month layoff, he scored three minor upsets and then capped his fairy-tale comeback with a shocking upset of Max Baer, winning a 15-round decision.

Braddock let two years go by without defending his title. A contributing factor was that his manager, Joe Gould, knew that he was nothing special and that his next big payday would probably be his last. Gould wasn't about to sell the belt for less than what he considered fair market value and kept stalling until someone was willing to meet his inflated price. Braddock was content to wait it out because he had money rolling in from personal appearances. The public identified with his pluck and thought more highly of the "Cinderella Man" when it came out that he had repaid the state of New Jersey the money he had received while on the dole.[6]

The Louis-Braddock fight was placed in Chicago, where Louis had scored his biggest amateur wins and launched his pro career. Louis was a mere 2/1 favorite, a price compatible with the understanding that the deck was invariably stacked against men of color in world title fights. Braddock, a veteran of 74 fights, had never lost inside the distance except once on cuts, and it was roundly conjectured that he would filch the decision if he lasted the distance, not merely because of his race but because judges in title fights were predisposed toward the incumbent.

Braddock came out winging, thrilling the Comiskey Park throng with a flash knockdown in the opening stanza, but Louis quickly gained the advantage and methodically cut Braddock to ribbons before finishing him off with a vicious right to the jaw at the one-minute mark of the eighth round. The lion-hearted but badly outclassed Braddock would fight only once more before calling it quits.

The biggest fight out there for the new champion was a rematch with Max Schmeling, but Louis's management chose the path of least resistance, opting for quantity over quality on the logic that a series of little fights would produce as much revenue as one blockbuster, and with less jeopardy. Louis's first title defense would be against Tommy Farr, a reddish-haired bruiser from a coal-mining village in Wales. Described by one reporter as having a face like a blasted cliff, Farr was only 23 years of age but claimed to have fought 253 fights, the majority in carnival booths.

Farr was far tougher than expected, extending Louis the distance in a reasonably close fight. Less rugged were Nathan Mann and Harry Thomas, both belted out early in low-budget title fights at indoor venues. Thomas, from Eagle Bend, Minnesota, was so lightly regarded that ringside seats in Chicago Stadium were priced at only $10, the cheapest price ever for a heavyweight title fight in a public building. The discount was consistent with Thomas's frank acknowledgement that his chances boiled down to landing a lucky punch.

Louis might have continued along this well-manicured path a tad longer, but the Schmeling rematch became a matter of great urgency as the rumblings of war became louder and louder. In the spring of 1938, it became obvious that if the match were not made quickly, it would likely never happen. Jacobs was in an awkward position as he was Jewish and his coreligionists favored a boycott of German imports, including prizefighters. Aggravating matters, Schmeling had been photographed shaking hands with Hitler and had tremendous value to his country as a propaganda tool. Working tirelessly behind the scenes, Jacobs lobbied anti–Nazi groups to let his promotion proceed without interference, all the while racing the clock as relations between the U.S. and Germany became more strained with each passing day.

Although Schmeling had mastered Louis in 1936, the would-be avenger was a 12/5 favorite in the rematch. This owed partly to the fact that Schmeling, eight years older than Louis at age 32, wasn't getting any younger and Louis was judged to be at his peak. It was reliably reported that Louis was training hard and would be totally focused, a departure from the first meeting when he was distracted by a newfound passion for golf.

Held at Yankee Stadium on June 22, 1938, the bout was barely a minute old when Louis

Max Schmeling and Joe Louis at the weigh-in for their 1936 bout. Standing to the right of Schmeling smoking a cigar is his colorful Jewish-American manager Joe Jacobs. *New York World Telegram and Sun/Library of Congress/History Image.*

trapped Schmeling on the ropes and threw a right to the body that connected as Schmeling was swiveling his torso. The punch fractured two vertebrae in Schmeling's lower back. Fighting in a fit of concentrated fury, Louis pressed the attack and Schmeling had no antidote. He was prostrate and twitching convulsively when the referee interrupted his count and declared Louis the winner.

In the first fight, Schmeling had received the warmer reception in the pre-fight introductions. He received a cooler reception in the rematch because many had come to view him as the symbol of an evil dictatorship. The fight was broadcast on the radio in four languages: English, German, Spanish, and Portuguese. In the United States, the ratings went through the roof, rivaling the top-rated broadcasts of all time, the FDR fireside chats. When the broadcast was finished, there were spontaneous street celebrations in black communities, none more exuberant than in Detroit, where revelers rejoiced under a banner that read "JOE LOUIS KNOCKED OUT HITLER." The 124-second blowout would come to be recognized as the most internationally important fight ever and would be allegorized in America as a victory for humanitarian principles.

At this juncture, Louis had been a professional boxer for barely five years. His championship reign would last another decade, encompassing 21 more wins in title fights, but his blowout of Schmeling would forever overshadow his other conquests. With the skies now cleared of the Schmeling cloud, Louis's advisors concentrated on opponents that fit the Harry Thomas mold. Beginning in December of 1940, Louis had a title fight in each of seven consecutive months, all but two outside New York. His adversaries came to be lumped into the "Bum of the Month Club."

The characterization was cruel, tainting some industrious men who were actually quite good. Bob Pastor (Robert Pasternak) was an excellent boxer, although too small for a powerful foe like Louis. Johnny Paycheck (John Pacek) was legitimate, but his name invited derision and reporters made fun of him. However, some of the "bums" accorded title shots were ridiculously overmatched. A 35-year-old electrician at Warner Brothers Studio who appeared as an extra in dozens of movies, Jack Roper had won barely half of his 99 fights. Tony Musto, a bartender by trade, carried 200 pounds on a five-foot-eight frame, but was a powder puncher with only six knockouts to his credit in 36 fights. Beefed-up middleweight Al McCoy (Florien LaBresseur) had lost seven of his last 11 starts and was 39–17–6 in bouts outside his native Maine.

Billy Conn was a beefed-up middleweight too, but he was no bum. The last man to challenge Louis in the septet of monthly fights, the 23-year-old Conn was a nimble fighter with an excellent jab who had built himself into a lightheavyweight champion after losing six of his first 14 fights. He seemingly had the style to frustrate Louis, who had eaten a lot of leather in a bout with ponderous Abe Simon, a former ice truck driver who looked like Boris Karloff. There was considerable buzz when Louis was matched against the so-called Pittsburgh Kid at the Polo Grounds on June 18, 1941.

In a memorable performance that vaulted him into the Boxing Hall of Fame, the 174-pound Conn put on a boxing clinic for 12 rounds. He was actually winning on two of the scorecards — and winning comfortably in the minds of most eyewitnesses — until he got reckless in Round 13 and Louis lowered the boom. Smirched but still champion, Louis had three more fights before Uncle Sam took charge of his daily regimen and reconstituted him into a poster boy for the war effort.

Four years, two months, and twenty-three days elapsed before Louis returned to the ring. The war effectively closed one chapter of his career and the end of his hitch begat another.

The first chapter would be the most copious, crammed with all of Louis's most exhilarating triumphs and a slew of wins in soft title defenses against opponents who would become mere footnotes in the abridged versions of the Joe Louis story. One of those soft defenses, however, was sociologically important. The 1939 match between Louis and reigning lightheavyweight champion John Henry Lewis was a graphic illustration of the importance of gambler-businessmen in the sporting life of black America.

At the age of 16, in just his third professional fight, Lewis killed a man in the ring. He became less of a banger after this tragedy, eroding his gate appeal. His career followed the same tack as Henry Armstrong. A native of Prescott, Arizona, he fought exclusively in western rings coming up the ladder, and his migration east dovetailed with a change of management.

In 1935, Lewis came under the wing of Gus Greenlee, a Pittsburgh numbers banker who had branched into boxing full-bore, building a gym on the grounds of his spacious home with dormitories for fighters and trainers, the first step in his master plan to manufacture a champion in each weight class. His ambition far exceeded his reach, but Greenlee navigated Lewis into match with lightheavyweight titlist Bob Olin and Lewis rose to the occasion, winning the bout on points. The most notable of his five successful title defenses was a match in Madison Square Garden with Jock McAvoy. With McAvoy hailing from the land of Tom Cribb, much was made of the fact that Lewis was the great-great-grand-nephew of Tom Molineaux. The dubious ancestral link was likely the brainchild of Nat Fleischer.

Louis and Lewis knew each other socially. Greenlee occasionally borrowed Jack Blackburn to help Lewis prepare for an important test and he was well acquainted with his counterparts, Roxborough and Black. Each had a good-sized piece of the national numbers action and it's likely they had occasional business dealings of a lay-off nature, trading bets to round their books.

In January of 1939, Joe Louis was seven months removed from his annihilation of Schmeling and perhaps at the absolute peak of his physical prowess. There was little doubt that he would destroy Lewis, who wasn't fast on his feet. The odds were even-money that the Brown Bomber would win inside four rounds despite the fact that John Henry had never been knocked out in 104 fights.

Those that faulted Greenlee for sending his fighter into the lion's den didn't know the full story. Lewis's eyesight was rapidly deteriorating. The match was basically a charity fight, with Lewis the beneficiary. What was amazing about John Henry's career was that he had 51 non-title fights during his 39-month title reign, the most of any champion who came along after the no-decision era. His purses from these fights didn't amount to a hill of beans. The best payday of his career evaporated when Domenick "Two Ton Tony" Galento contracted pneumonia, forcing the cancellation of their fight in Philadelphia with more than $100,000 already in the till. Lewis couldn't wait around for Galento to get healthy because time was of the essence. The only way to recoup the lost income was to fight Joe Louis.

Lewis's crucifixion wasn't painless, but at least it was quick. Louis clubbed him to the canvas three times before the referee stopped the fight barely two and a half minutes into the opening round. Lewis never fought again, although he attempted to duck in one more payday. His match in London with Len Harvey fell out when he failed his eye exam. Pushed into retirement at the age of 25 with a record of 103–8–6, Lewis would be roundly disesteemed by many of the same historians charmed by Billy Conn. His African American manager would fall through a bigger crack into greater obscurity, a terrible oversight, as the trailblazing William Augustus "Gus" Greenlee was a remarkable promoter.

Joe Louis and John Henry Lewis at their contract signing. Standing left to right: Julian Black, John Roxborough, Mike Jacobs, Gus Greenlee, unidentified. The man seated in the middle is New York State Boxing Commissioner John J. Phelan. *fighttoys.com.*

A large, lumpy man with a tint of red in his hair, reportedly born to one of the wealthiest building contractors in North Carolina, Greenlee pyramided his earnings from the numbers business into extensive real estate holdings in Pittsburgh's black belt. He owned the Crawford Grille, one of America's classiest integrated supper clubs, and an intimate red brick stadium that he built from scratch in 1932. By some accounts the first sports park in America with permanent artificial lighting, Greenlee Field had a ready-made tenant in Greenlee's Pittsburgh Crawfords, a team whose roster for a brief period numbered five eventual Hall of Famers, most notably Satchell Paige and Josh Gibson, the most venerated black players of the Jim Crow era.

Greenlee's grandest promotion was the East-West Negro League All Star Game. An important event on the black social calendar, the event was staged at Chicago's Comiskey Park. The 1943 game drew a fashionably dressed, well-mannered crowd of 51,000 that included a large sprinkling of whites. The lords of baseball could not help but take notice.

According to Wendell Smith, a renowned sportswriter in the world of African American journalists, Greenlee badgered his friend Branch Rickey, owner of the Brooklyn Dodgers, to take the initiative in breaking the color line. Rickey bought into the idea, making Greenlee his Negro League scout, but swearing him to secrecy. Integrating baseball would be controversial enough without exposing the involvement of a man who bore the stamp of a racketeer. Working behind the scenes, Greenlee set the wheels in motion, a selfless gesture, as he had the most to lose if the "Grand Experiment" succeeded.[7]

According to Smith, Negro League team owners, predominantly black numbers barons, let out a collective curse on hearing the news that Jackie Robinson had signed with the Dodgers. They knew that this spelled the death knell for Negro League baseball. While good for the soul of America, integration had bad economic repercussions — at least in the short term — for black communities in cities with Negro League teams.

Greenlee died in 1952 at age 55, taking to his grave the satisfaction of knowing that he was the first black man to manage an internationally recognized boxing champion and was instrumental in making the first black-on-black world heavyweight title fight held in the United States; more than that, the first championship bout in which all of the purse money, including managers' percentages, stayed within the black community. Of far greater significance, he was arguably the man most instrumental in hastening the integration of major league baseball.

Joe Louis's next interracial fight didn't come off until after the war, when he was matched against Jersey Joe Walcott. Before meeting Walcott, Louis had a stroll in the park against Billy Conn in their overhyped rematch and scored a first-round knockout of Bronx bartender Tami Mauriello, fights that suggested he was undiminished by his wartime sabbatical.

To the contrary, Louis was starting to fade, with developments outside the ring a contributing factor. Jack Blackburn had died while Louis was at boot camp. Louis didn't have the same rapport with his replacement, Manny Seamon. His marriage had ruptured beyond repair, notwithstanding the birth of daughter Jacqueline, named in honor of Blackburn. Louis had been careful to philander discreetly, but hadn't been able to hide all of his many affairs, and his marriage had been rocky from the start. Complicating matters, the government was hounding him for back taxes and cracks were developing in Mike Jacobs' empire, with Jacobs less able to keep the buccaneers at bay as his health deteriorated.

The public had been slow to notice that Louis had been carefully steered away from good fighters of his own color, but this was now becoming a source of embarrassment. To keep this from becoming a bigger topic of discussion, Jacobs matched him with Walcott, bypassing other worthy black fighters considered more treacherous.

Ultimately the last top-tier fighter to adopt the name of a legendary black pugilist, Walcott seemed like a safe choice. He wasn't a hard puncher, was a bit on the small side, had the appearance of being significantly older than his years, and had a style that did not curry favor with judges. But Jacobs hedged his bets and audaciously framed the match as a 10-round exhibition. Public disapprobation was swift and the press raised hob, forcing the promoter to recast the mill as a title fight. The bookmakers, however, considered it little more than an exhibition. Louis was established a 10/1 favorite and the over/under set at four rounds.

It has been theorized that Jersey Joe abandoned his birth name — Arnold Raymond Cream — because it encouraged his detractors to call him a cream puff. Whatever the motivation, he was anything but a cream puff when he locked horns with Louis on December 5, 1947. He decked the Brown Bomber in the opening round, decked him again in Round 4, and appeared to have an insurmountable lead when he switched gears late in the fight and backpedaled his way to the finish line. A chorus of boos greeted the announcement that Louis had retained his title on a split decision, but this was a moot point for many of the bookies as the action was lopsided on the "over." The sharp bettors knew that Walcott had been a part-time fighter throughout most of his career, working day jobs to support his growing family, and that his three losses inside the distance were in fights in which he had merely run out of gas.

Mike Jacobs privately doubted that a bout between two blacks was economically viable in a ballpark. He revised this opinion when the Louis-Walcott fight drew 18,194 to Madison Square Garden on a chilly evening despite poor advance sales. The fight was televised, magnifying the indignation and the clamor for a rematch. Presto, a big ballpark show fell right into Jacobs' lap, a show that became more compelling when Louis announced it would be his last fight.

The rematch was dreadfully dull. Walcott was ahead on two of the scorecards after ten uneventful rounds when he obeyed the referee's command to pick up the pace and walked into a pulverizing punch. The turnout of 42,667 at Yankee Stadium was below expectations, but impressive considering that the fight was on home TV and had to be pushed back two days because of rain.

The skeptics predicted that Louis's retirement would be brief. It appeared that they might be wrong when he signed on as an advisor to the new International Boxing Club, a salaried position that promised generous bonuses. But his earnings were hardly sufficient to reverse a negative cash flow related to ill-advised business ventures and worsened by an ever-mounting tax debt.

Inactive for 27 months, Louis returned to the ring on September 27, 1950, at Yankee Stadium. Without the benefit of a tune-up fight, he was thrust against the man that now wore his crown, Ezzard Charles. Known as the Cincinnati Cobra, Charles had 39 knockouts to his credit in 74 bouts and had killed a man with his fists, but he was a tactical fighter whose style invited comparisons with Gene Tunney, poisoning his box office appeal.

An 8/5 favorite, Louis was soundly defeated. In grave danger of being knocked out in the 14th stanza, he stayed the course but lost a lopsided decision. The stadium was two-thirds empty and the crowd was subdued.

Still in need of fresh funds, Louis soldiered on, winning eight fights in the next eleven months, most notably a sixth-round knockout of Lee Savold, a 35-year-old journeyman from Minnesota who was recognized as the heavyweight champion by the British Boxing Board of Control. Held at Madison Square Garden on June 15, 1951, the Louis-Savold fight was beamed into theaters in six cities (Albany, Baltimore, Pittsburgh, Chicago, Cleveland, and Washington), where it played to capacity crowds, marking the first time that a bout attracted more paying customers off-site than on-site. Regular movie prices prevailed, except at the segregated Lincoln Theatre in Washington, where blacks were charged a steeper admission fee than whites viewing the same telecast at a theater a few blocks away. Ticket prices ranged from 64 cents to $1.30.

Louis showed flashes of his former brilliance in that fight and was established a 7/5 favorite over his next opponent, Rocky Marciano. Marciano wrote the epitaph to Louis's career with a brutal eighth-round knockout.

It had been an amazing career, extending from the depths of the Great Depression through the most horrible of wars and stretching into the decade of the 1950s, when American life was revolutionized by the miracle of television, and it ended for Joe Louis on a most inglorious thud. Marciano's final punch knocked him through the ropes and onto the ring apron, so thoroughly unhinging his senses that the referee waived the fight off without the formality of starting a count.

In Harlem, where the Brown Bomber had inspired so much revelry, the streets were eerily quiet. It was as if a wraith had appeared with news of a death in the family.

# CHAPTER 12

# Marcianomics

Rocky Marciano came to prominence at a time when boxing was at one of its lowest ebbs. On the night he hammered Joe Louis into retirement, the reigning heavyweight champion was Jersey Joe Walcott, a retread who had won the title in his fifth attempt and was contractually bound to a rematch with uninteresting Ezzard Charles. But the woes that plagued the fight game ran deeper than a defective mainspring. The sport was under siege from reformers amidst damaging revelations of racketeering, and small fight clubs were shutting down at an alarming rate.

During World War II, there were no grand promotions but yet the sport was vibrant. Dozens of fight clubs around the country staged weekly or bimonthly shows. By one count, there were 74 fight clubs in New York and New Jersey in 1944, twelve located within a 25-mile radius of Times Square. Eight years later, New Jersey was virtually bereft of boxing clubs and the number in New York City had dwindled to five. Concurrently, the pool of licensed boxers declined sharply.

Although not recognized at the time, the popularity of boxing during the war years was a product of external forces. Many consumer goods were in short supply, leaving more money to spend on entertainment. Wartime restrictions on rubber and petroleum curtailed the popular pastime of pleasure driving. The fuel shortage became so severe that many annual sporting events were discontinued.

Boxing was uniquely positioned to pick up the slack. Most fight clubs were easily accessible by public transportation. The local neighborhood often supplied the fighters, at least for the undercard bouts, making it easier to comply with federal travel restrictions. As had happened in 1918, boxing benefited publicity-wise from a less cluttered sports landscape, albeit this was mitigated somewhat by reduced sports coverage in newspapers during the later war years, the by-product of a paper shortage.

Guided by the example of the post–World War I boom, promoters presumed that the sport would skyrocket in popularity when the soldiers returned home and prominent fighters filtered back into action. Among those whose titles were frozen during the war years were Joe Louis, Gus Lesnevich, and Tony Zale, the champions in the three highest weight classes. When boxing fell on hard times after the war — the exact opposite of what was anticipated — the blame was placed squarely on television. In 1953, *New York Daily Mirror* boxing writer Dan Parker went so far as to call for a one-year moratorium on televised fights "to nourish withering roots."

It was obvious even before the war that boxing was going to be modified by live broad-casting. In 1939, NBC and CBS conducted experiments with mock fights. That same year, the British lightweight title bout between Arthur Danahar and Eric Boon was beamed into two cinemas in London, marking the advent of simulcasting. Further progress was stalled by the war, but the die had been cast. By 1952, all four major American networks (NBC, CBS, ABC and Dumont) were airing weekly boxing programs. It wasn't as if boxing was all the rage, but the sport was neatly suited to the infant, money-strapped medium because the drama was confined to a small area that required little furbishing other than brighter illumination, keeping production costs low.

With boxing beamed into living rooms and neighborhood taverns on an almost nightly basis, diehard fans were less inclined to attend the fights. Casual fans developed new loyal-ties to their favorite TV programs. Small clubs were hit the hardest, but important venues also suffered. At Madison Sqaure Garden, average attendance for the Friday night boxing show declined from 12,324 in 1946 to 6,869 in 1952 despite a one-third reduction in the num-ber of dates. But the shibboleth that television ruined boxing by giving the product away for free was too simplistic. A host of other factors were at play.

As television was coming into vogue, Americans were increasingly moving to the sub-urbs, a trend abetted by low-interest mortgages for ex-servicemen under the G.I. Bill. Fight fans caught up in the drift were no longer in proximity to established boxing venues and their leisure time, in most cases, was constricted by a longer commute to the workplace and new responsibilities foreign to renters, such as landscape maintenance. Labor-saving household appliances, scarce during the war, were in ready supply; keeping up with the Joneses siphoned money from entertainment budgets. Jews unmoved by the pull of suburbia were less loyal to neighborhood fight clubs because of a severe drop in the number of Jewish boxers.

During World War I, military tournaments spawned a new generation of boxers and cre-ated new fans among soldiers. During World War II, the concerns of the brass were more nar-rowly focused on destroying the enemy and far fewer tournaments were staged. It didn't help matters when the most eagerly anticipated postwar fights turned out to be duds. The Louis-Conn rematch was a tepid affair until the Brown Bomber found his range. The early rounds were likened to a mortician's wake. This was the first fight where a ringside seat cost $100 (a fourfold increase over the first meeting), begetting howls of price gouging.

In May of 1950, a U.S. Senate committee chaired by Estes Kefauver (D-Tenn.) launched a sweeping 15-month investigation of organized crime that threaded into fresh campaigns to clean up boxing. During the course of the hearings, the New York boxing statute that barred licensees from associating with convicted felons was broadened to prohibit them from con-sorting with gamblers "or persons of similar pursuits."

In September of 1951, as the Department of Justice was processing an indictment of the International Boxing Club for violation of the Sherman Anti-Trust Act, New York Governor Thomas E. Dewey axed boxing commission head Edward P.F. "Eddie" Eagan and replaced him with Robert K. Christenberry. A Yale and Oxford educated scholar who won Olympic gold medals in boxing (1920) and bobsledding (1932), Eagan was held up as a great role model, but Dewey — a failed presidential candidate who had made his reputation as a racket-busting district attorney — felt he was too lax in rooting out unsavory characters.

A Presbyterian Sunday School teacher who had lost the stem of his right arm in a World War I grenade explosion, Christenberry plunged into his new post with the zeal of FBI paragon Elliot Ness. To rally public support for his mission, he authored a scathing expose of boxing that was published in the May 26, 1952, issue of *Life,* America's top-selling weekly magazine.

The piece was accompanied by mug shots of alleged underworld boxing czar Frankie Carbo and five associates — Frank "Blinky" Palermo, Felix Boccicchio, Eddie Coco, Champ Segal, and James Plumeri. According to Christenberry, these were the top extortionists in an organization he dubbed "The Combination."

Carbo had served time for manslaughter for a 1924 shooting in a Bronx pool hall and had been indicted but never convicted of a 1939 Los Angeles contract killing. His chief lieutenant Palermo was a Philadelphia numbers baron with a long rap sheet of gambling-related arrests. Through kickbacks, Carbo and his cronies in the Combination acquired a hidden interest in dozens of fighters.

Chistenberry's article downplayed the influence of James Dougan "Jim" Norris Jr., the true big cheese in the fight game. The son of a revered Canadian sportsman, Norris and family business partner Arthur Wirtz owned the Detroit Red Wings hockey team and controlled through outright ownership or lease six sports arenas, including Chicago Stadium and the Detroit Olympia. Norris was also the largest single shareholder in the Madison Square Garden Corporation, having upped his investment when he formed the International Boxing Club in 1947 while seizing the remains of Mike Jacobs' empire.

Then in his mid-forties, Norris was an unreformed rapscallion drawn to the same sorts of people that fascinated Damon Runyon. Like Runyon, he was a betting man who openly hobnobbed with bookies. This was not very smart considering the temper of the times. A spate of point-shaving scandals in college basketball cast bookies and bettors in a very harsh light. Inevitably, cleanup campaigns curved into the corridors of boxing.

When Averell Harriman was elected governor of New York in 1954, he borrowed a leaf from his predecessor Dewey and shook up the boxing commission. Harriman deposed Christenberry in favor of Brooklyn District Attorney Julius Helfand. As a parting shot to Christenberry, Helfand dressed him down publicly for being overpermissive in dealings with racketeers. The allegation shadowed Christenberry during his unsuccessful run for mayor of New York.

Bookmakers at boxing matches became more furtive and then faded from the scene, but there were other factors at play besides tighter constraints. Many bookies were first-generation Americans with a special aptitude for figures. Their sons were drawn to more respectable avenues of risk-taking. However, the thread between boxing and betting remained strong, as evidenced by the Rocky Marciano story. The Rock was a financial angel to more than a few folks in his decaying hometown, a queer development as he was an extremely tight-fisted fellow.

Born Rocco Francis Marchegiano in Brockton, Massachusetts, Marciano's first love was baseball. A stalwart semi-pro catcher, his dream of playing professionally was dashed when he was cut from a rookie league affiliate of the Chicago Cubs after a three-week tryout in 1947. Prior to the tryout, he had competed in a few amateur boxing tournaments, compiling an 8–4 record, and had one bout that came to be catalogued as his first professional fight. Using the alias Rocky Mack, he scored a third-round knockout of one Lee Epperson on a card in Holyoke, Massachusetts.

In his most maladroit showing at the amateur level, Rocky was roundly outclassed by an African American boxer named Henry Lester. A three-time regional Golden Gloves champion who never turned pro, Lester won inside the distance when Rocky, near the point of exhaustion, kneed him in the groin and got disqualified. That taught Marciano the importance of conditioning. Late in his career, even his detractors acknowledged that no fighter was ever more faithful to his training regimen. Marciano actually seemed to welcome the hardships imposed on him when he was cloistered away from family and friends.

In 1948, Marciano, then nearly 25 years old, wangled an audition with veteran corner-man Charlie Goldman. The wizened, Warsaw-born Goldman, who stood barely five feet tall, trained fighters controlled by Madison Square Garden matchmaker Al Weill. A great fight character, he had a favorite expression: "A hard punch is a shortcut to the money."

Thick-legged with short, stumpy arms, Marciano had two left feet. But his punches were hurtful. Sparring partners were uncommonly sore after a session with him, a mystery considering that they absorbed few punches. Sufficiently intrigued, Goldman advised Weill to add Marciano to their stable.

Weill hedged his bet by subcontracting Rocky to a promoter in Providence, a city within an hour's drive of Brockton. This meant that Rocky could live at home and Weill could save on expenses. With Weill calling the shots, Marciano had 21 fights, all but two in New England, before he was deemed ready for New York. In his Big Apple debut at Madison Square Garden on December 2, 1949, he was put into an 8-round fight with Pat Richards, a fighter from Ohio with a 22–6–5 record. Marciano flattened Richards in the second round and was brought back four weeks later to meet Carmine Vingo, a six-foot-four brawler from the Bronx with a 16–1 record.

Knocked down in the first and second rounds, Vingo slugged his way back into contention, but in the sixth frame Marciano knocked him comatose with a short left hook. A priest administered the last rites before Vingo was removed from the ring on a stretcher. On the critical list for six days, he recovered and became a security guard.

This was Marciano's first fight with a published betting line. The oddsmakers had rated the match a near toss-up, installing Rocky a 7/5 favorite.

Twelve weeks later, Marciano was back in action at Madison Square Garden against Roland LaStarza. A 22-year-old college student, LaStarza lacked a big punch but was unbeaten in 37 pro fights. Framed as a crossroads fight between undefeated heavyweights, this was an attractive pairing, but a match that was psychologically all wrong for Marciano. He had been badly shaken by the Vingo incident. In La Starza, he was meeting another Bronx Italian.

Cognizant that fighters often fought without passion in the aftermath of a ring tragedy, the pricemakers installed LaStarza a slight favorite. The rationale was sound, but Marciano — who uncharacteristically shifted into a defensive mode and lost the middle rounds after scoring the bout's lone knockdown — came on in the homestretch to win a hair-thin decision.

The close shave prompted Weill to send Rocky back to the New England circuit for a refresher course. He was gone almost sixteen months before Weill brought him back to New York to fight Rex Layne.

Hailing from Lewiston, Utah, Layne (34–1–2) had become a fan favorite in New York, where he had won over his detractors with wins over Jersey Joe Walcott, Cesar Brion, and Bob Satterfield, the latter a China-chinned lightheavyweight from Chicago feared as a one-punch knockout artist. Once again Marciano found himself cast as the underdog. The odds favoring Layne peaked at 2/1 on the day of the fight. And once again, Rocky upset the form sheet. He put Layne down for keeps in the sixth round with an explosive right hand.

After defeating Layne, Marciano fulfilled a commitment in Boston and then began training for his match with Joe Louis. His smashing knockout of the Brown Bomber triggered a tumultuous celebration in downtown Brockton that contrasted sharply with the somber scene in Harlem. A few days later, Rocky was feted with a parade.

The reaction was overcharged considering that Louis was an old warrior, ripe for the taking, and Rocky had done nothing more than bump himself up another notch in the ratings. But to his townsfolk, the man that sportswriters were now calling the Brockton

Blockbuster was more than a native son; he was the personification of Brockton itself—a rugged, hard-working, meat-and-potatoes kind of guy who rubbed elbows with glamorous people but was umbilicized by choice to the community that hewed him.

The Brockton of Marciano's day was a rusting, blue-collar city of approximately 65,000. The leading industry was shoe manufacturing. The city was also a major producer of carpet tacks, storage batteries, and burial vaults. Brocktonites of Rocky's generation were mostly the children of European immigrants. Italians were the largest ethnic group, but the melting pot was seasoned with Lithuanians, Poles, Irish, Swedes, and French Canadians. The locals, by and large, were avid supporters of high school and sandlot teams. Sports were the great leveler, promoting an esprit de corps that crossed ethnic boundaries.

Rocky's parents Pierino and Pasqualena Marchegiano were born in Sicily and educated in Brockton's public elementary schools. Pasqualena, a homemaker, sprinkled her conversations with Italian words and phrases. Pierino, called Pete by his co-workers at the shoe factory, had a wider circle of friends and was more fully Americanized. Rocky, the oldest of five children, less insulated within the Italian community than his parents, married a girl of Irish stock, the daughter of a Brockton policeman.

The Italians in Brockton tended to be the most passionate about boxing. One of Rocky's most vivid memories was of a bonfire lit by neighbors to celebrate Primo Carnera's victory over Jack Sharkey. In defeating Louis, Rocky restored the luster of Italian-American boxers. The stylish featherweight Willie Pep (Gugliemo Papaleo) was then under suspension in New York after quitting on his stool in an unruly bout with his great rival Sandy Saddler. Joe Louis had turned a slew of Italian fighters into putty. The list of his knockout victims included Al Ettore, Nathan Mann (Manchetti), Tony Galento, Gus Dorazio, Tony Musto, and Tami Mauriello.

In defeating Louis, Marciano earned a crack at the winner of the forthcoming heavyweight title fight between Ezzard Charles and Jersey Joe Walcott. An unforeseen development dictated an intervening bout.

Jack Hurley, a Seattle-based promoter, was pushing to get a big-money fight for his latest protégé, Harry "Kid" Matthews. With the IBC under scrutiny for monopolistic practices, Hurley took to bellyaching that his fighter was the victim of an illegal lockout. It was a fusty complaint, but ripe for the times, and Hurley found political allies in Harry Cain (R–Washington) and Herman Welker (R–Idaho), who aired his grievance on the floor of the United States Senate. As an appeasement, the IBC proposed matching Mathews with lightheavyweight champion Joey Maxim, but Hurley held out for a match with Marciano that would be framed as a title eliminator.

A native of Ola, Idaho, Matthews had looked good out-pointing rising contender Bob Murphy in his lone previous appearance in a New York ring, but his magnificent record — 96 wins, 3 losses, and 6 draws, according to news stories — was largely a sham as he had been fed a steady diet of boondock fodder. He hadn't tasted defeat since returning from the Army in 1946, but that said less about him than about Hurley, a wildcat promoter since 1918 who was something of a poor man's Doc Kearns, constantly searching for the next Dempsey while building the best of his finds into gate attractions through astute matchmaking and a steady stream of ballyhoo. (Hurley was the model for Doc Carroll in W.C. Heinz's *The Professional*, rated by some critics as America's best boxing-themed novel.)

Most of the wiseguys thought Marciano would overpower Matthews, but enough punters were smitten with Jack Hurley's mystery fighter so that the odds favoring Rocky held steady at 2/1 until the weigh-in, when there was a light surge of Marciano money following the revelation that Matthews weighed only 179 pounds. The fight at Yankee Stadium on July 28, 1952, attracted 31,189, less than half capacity, but a good turnout for a non-title fight on a blisteringly hot and muggy night in a year when the shows at Madison Square Garden routinely drew crowds under 5000.

Matthews outboxed Marciano in the opening round, jabbing effectively while easily parrying Rocky's lunges, but Marciano connected with a straight right hand under Matthews' heart as the bell sounded, a nondescript punch from a distance that stunned the Idahoan, who lost track of his whereabouts and started toward the wrong corner. Early in the next round, Marciano connected with a sweeping left hook that floored Matthews for the full count.

Seven weeks later, Marciano met Walcott at Philadelphia's Municipal Stadium. Weill preferred a different locale — Walcott resided across the river in Camden, New Jersey, and had enjoyed great success in Philadelphia rings — but Jersey Joe's manager Felix Boccicchio was blackballed in New York for his reputed mob ties.

Walcott was at least 38 years old. His record was smirched with 16 losses. Considering these facts, it was a bit strange that Rocky was only a 3/2 favorite. However, many sharp bettors favored Walcott, a late bloomer with a 7-inch reach advantage who was appearing in his sixth title fight. Marciano's pro record was unblemished, but rare was the fight in which there were not moments when he looked like a rank amateur, a disposition likely to manifest itself for a long stretch against a cagey fighter like Walcott. Moreover, although Rocky was building a fanatical following, many people had a warm spot in their hearts for Jersey Joe, a genuinely nice guy with six children who had overcome lean times, staying the course in the storybook fashion of New Jersey's original Cinderella Man, Jimmy Braddock. It was widely assumed that the judges would give the old-timer the benefit of the doubt if the fight went to the scorecards.

For the first twelve rounds, the fight followed the script envisioned by the pro–Walcott prognosticators. Rocky was knocked down in the first round, his mouth was bloodied, and he returned to his corner with a swollen left eye. But he continued to press the action, winning several rounds by sheer aggression. Heading into Round 13, Marciano trailed on all three cards. Walcott, pacing himself smartly, needed only to stay out of harm's way to retain his title. But Marciano would not be denied. When he finally lowered the boom, it was with a short right hand that was caught by the camera at the point of impact, a frightfully explosive punch that contorted Walcott's face into a grotesque mask, pitching him back against the ropes and then forward where he landed unconscious with his face buried in the canvas.

Rocky Marciano, the Brockton Blockbuster, ca. 1953. *Antiquities of the Prize Ring.*

Well-wishers rushed forward from every corner of the ballpark, overwhelming the security detail. In Brockton, there was bedlam too. The match was blacked out of radio and television coverage, so thousands of locals had gathered outside the *Enterprise-Times* building on Main Street, where round-by-round summaries were relayed to the crowd from the news ticker via loudspeakers. The delirium there did not subside until after midnight. The parade for Rocky a week later attracted such a large turnout that police from neighboring communities and state troopers were conscripted to help keep things orderly.

Marciano Mania lured writers to the soot-stained city that Rocky called home. W.C. Heinz, preparing a story for *Cosmopolitan*, discovered that Rocky's popularity owed to more than vicarious ego-identification, which Rocky cultivated by wearing the Brockton High School colors on his boxing robe. Affection for him was also rooted in material benefits. Folks outside Brockton were eager for inside dope on Rocky, a boon to the city's traveling salesmen, who had an easier go landing new accounts. More than that, Heinz discovered that Rocky was a cash cow to many Brocktonites, some of who morphed into big plungers whenever he was in action.

The first person to make Heinz aware of this phenomenon was the taxi driver that drove him to his hotel. The cabbie told Heinz about an elderly Italian couple that put up their house as collateral to borrow money to bet on Rocky. Another person told Heinz about an elderly Italian woman who had stashed away $500 in a coffee tin. She bet it all on Rocky against Rex Layne, increasing her assets more than twofold.

"A lot of people in this town are a lot better off because of Marciano," said another person that Heinz interviewed. "There are families that have suddenly moved into brand new homes. They say 'Where does he get the money to buy a house like that?' It's obvious. They've been betting on Rocky. And these guys who have pyramided their cars. They started out with old rattletraps when Rocky started fighting in Providence in 1948. They borrowed what they could on their cars, they won, and bought better cars and borrowed again. Today they're driving high-priced automobiles that are paid for."[1]

More evidence of Marcianomics came from Rocky's mother: "I walk on the street and a woman come up to me. She say 'God bless you, Mrs. Marchegiano. My son and my son-in-law, they make a fortune on your boy.' Who is this woman? I go in a store. In the store the man say, 'If you need credit, Mrs. Marchegiano, you get credit. Your son make a lot of money for us.'"[2]

Heinz wasn't the only reporter to unearth evidence of aggressive wagering. According to Marciano biographer Everett Skeehan, Rocky's maternal uncle, Pete Piccento, a factory worker, had $40,000 on his person when he arrived in Philadelphia for the Walcott fight, a fair amount of it collected in odd lots from friends and co-workers who wanted a piece of the action. He was able to get down the entire amount at Lew Tendler's restaurant. Piccento reportedly reinvested all of his winnings at every opportunity, pyramiding his original $500 bankroll more than twentyfold even before his nephew's first title defense. Anecdotal accounts of betting are invariably skewed toward the high side, but this anecdote is plausible because Rocky was not rated very high by betting men outside New England until relatively late in his career.

There weren't any more "steals" after Marciano's coronation. His first defense was a rematch with Walcott at Chicago Stadium. Although Jersey Joe had won most of the rounds in the first meeting, Marciano was a solid 5/1 favorite. The theory that Walcott had been psychologically ruined by the paralyzing punch that terminated the first fray was born out when Jersey Joe was belted out in the opening frame, succumbing to a short right uppercut that was only visible from one side of the ring. Walcott looked tense as he awaited the opening bell, leading some to posit that he simply quit out of fear of another concussion. In the fashion of Joe Louis, he would never fight again, earning Marciano the distinction of knocking two heavyweight champions into retirement.

Rocky next fought Roland LaStarza, who had fought him to a virtual standstill in their previous meeting. A 5/1 favorite, Rocky carried the fight to La Starza, inflicting considerable damage until the bout was stopped in the thirteenth round. A crowd of 44,452 turned up at the Polo Grounds, ending a run of six straight heavyweight title bouts outside New York, the longest skein since the implementation of the Walker Law.

Next up for Marciano was former champ Ezzard Charles. Now 32 years old, Charles could boast that he had scored nine wins in bouts labeled heavyweight title fights, but most of those fights were box-office duds, making him the most prominent symbol of the postwar decay.

Marciano was the antidote to Charles's unpopularity. An intriguing contest of contrasting styles, their match drew 47,585 to Yankee Stadium. Those in attendance were treated to a rousing good skirmish climaxed by a marvelously entertaining final round. Rocky retained his title by unanimous decision, but Charles, fighting with unanticipated verve, earned the respect of the crowd and was accorded a quick rematch.

A middleweight when he entered the professional ranks in 1940, Charles beefed up seven pounds for the sequel. The extra weight was meant to make him stronger, but was interpreted in some quarters as a sign of sloth. A 7/2 favorite in the first meeting, Rocky was 11/2 for the rematch.

Charles was sluggish. Rocky bulled him about the ring as he pleased. But the affray turned suspenseful in Round 6 when Rocky's nose was badly gashed during an exchange at close range, most likely from a wayward elbow (slow-motion replay had not yet been invented). Propelled by a sense of urgency, Rocky stormed after Charles and broke through his defense, ending matters with an eighth-round flurry. Charles disintegrated quickly after this match. He lost 13 of his last 23 bouts.

A deep incision, the cut to Rocky's nose was slow to heal. Eight months elapsed before Marciano had another fight. With the heavyweight division lacking men that excited the public, Rocky was afforded the luxury of a potboiler. The main selling point for his match with British Empire Heavyweight Champion Don Cockell (61–11–1; six losses inside the distance) was that he had never fought a foreigner. The bout drew poorly on a chilly May Monday at San Francisco's Kezar Stadium, but was a useful exercise from Marciano's standpoint. He showed well in a crowd-pleasing rumble, beating the flabby Englishman to a pulp after a slow start en route to a Round 9 stoppage. More importantly, he emerged unscathed.

Marciano vs. Cockell was profitable only because of revenue from theater television, but Marciano's next fight versus reigning lightheavyweight champion Archie Moore was an on-site bonanza, drawing 61,574 to Yankee Stadium despite a 26-hour postponement occasioned by the threat of a hurricane. Among Moore's many distinctions, he had the longest tenure of any man in *The Ring* rankings, having first crashed the ratings as a middleweight in 1940, but the promotion would not have been as successful if Moore hadn't learned the importance of good press relations during his years of struggle.

The United Press correspondent who covered Moore's first world title fight in 1952 wrote that Moore was born in Toledo, Ontario (presumably he meant Toledo, Ohio), was 36 years of age, and had a professional record of 103–5. All of these facts were wrong, but that was par for the course. Most articles about Moore were peppered with falsehoods. Born Archibald Lee Wright in Benoit, Mississippi, likely in 1913, Moore had at least 160 fights under his belt when he finally got to fight for a world title. A more accurate record for him was 132–19–9.

Before Doc Kearns entered his life, Moore's career harked to Sam Langford. Fighting good black boxers over and over again, he had fierce rivalries with six-time opponent Jack Chase (aka Young Joe Louis) and five-time opponent Jimmy Bivins. The only multiple opponent whose nut he never cracked was Ezzard Charles, against whom he was 0–3.

A peripatetic boxer whose wanderlust led him to Australia, Panama, Argentina, and Uruguay, Moore was still fighting for moving-around money when lesser fighters were earning big purses. Fighting only twice in New York rings in his first fourteen years as a professional, he was the last of the top-notchers active in the Truman administration to fight in a nationally televised bout. But when he finally commanded the attention of important East Coast sportswriters, he had a storehouse of anecdotes to share with them that translated into copious ink. By then, the fighter nicknamed "Mongoose" by San Diego sportswriter Jack Murphy sported a goatee and wore a beret, a combination that gave him the appearance of a beatnik poet. Jimmy Cannon likened him to the old ragtime pianists who were slow to gain recognition for their artistry.

Moore was also good copy because he was a man of contradictions with a mysterious background and embodied the virtue of stick-to-itiveness. A man with a mellow disposition, he had virtually no formal schooling, but was an erudite person with an expansive vocabulary and a vivid imagination heightened by his association with Doc Kearns. Reporters were curious how he was able to bounce back and forth from the heavyweight to the lightheavyweight division, gaining or losing a significant amount of weight depending on the circumstance. Moore claimed to have been taught secrets of weight control by Aborigines he befriended in the Australian outback. But while he was spinning tall tales, the fighter now known as the Old Mongoose was aging like fine wine. Archie rode a 21-fight winning streak into his confrontation with Marciano on September 21, 1955.

Bettors paid little heed to Moore's momentum. The late money was skewed toward Marciano, who closed a 4/1 favorite. Rocky rewarded his backers, but there were moments when it seemed as if their bets were lost.

In the second stanza, Moore knocked Marciano to the canvas with a short right hand that many reporters called a sneak punch, an allusion to the stealth of a mongoose. Rocky bounced right up but his eyes were glazed as he waited out the standing 8-count. In Round 6, Marciano decked Moore twice, but it was Archie getting the best of the milling as they exchanged haymakers near the end of the round. Both were rubber-legged as they returned to their corners. Round 8 ended with Moore on his haunches, posed to rise from yet another knockdown, but looking completely worn out. Rocky was a wretched sight, bleeding from his nose and from cuts above both eyes, but he had cornered his prey. In Round 9, he sank Moore for keeps with a salvo of punches.

Moore blamed his misfortune on referee Harry Kessler, who had erred by giving Rocky a standing 8-count, a rule customarily waived in title fights. A multimillionaire metallurgist whose primary home was in St. Louis, Kesssler was an odd choice to referee the bout, as he had never worked on a stage this large. To his dying day, Moore would be furious at Kessler for robbing him of the prize that he most coveted, but most folks thought Marciano won squarely and dismissed Archie's complaint as sour grapes.

In defeating Moore, Marciano pushed his record to 49–0. Now 32 years old, he was theoretically past his prime, but not in the eyes of his trainer Charlie Goldman, who still considered him a work in progress. But Marciano decided that it was time to hang up his gloves.

He announced his retirement on April 27, 1956, telling reporters that his decision was prompted by a desire to spend more time with his family.

Other factors were likely more salient. Marciano had come to detest Al Weill, a mendacious man who worked both sides of the fence. Privately Marciano had accused Weill of cheating him out of perks like press-row tickets, a commodity that could be sold on the black market or bartered for other kinds of perks. Those closest to him were aware that he always got the willies when he saw a punch-drunk fighter and speculated that his decision was influenced by fears that he might wind up in the same condition. Whatever the actual motives, the cynics were confident that he would eventually return to the ring. They always come back, don't they?

Marciano in retirement was a strange duck. Abandoning his Spartan regimen for extra helpings of pasta, he developed a big potbelly. Incorrigibly restless, he was constantly on the go. He acquired a new set of friends, mostly Italian businessmen who brokered deals in cash, the sorts of men who had lines of credit in Las Vegas and Havana casinos and always knew where to find the best "broads." His parsimony began to take on the dimensions of a compulsive disorder. (The piece of wire he carried in a shirt pocket was a tool that allowed him to hot-wire a pay phone and skirt the 10-cent charge for a local call.) But with each passing day, as it became more apparent that his retirement was permanent, his legend grew larger.

Thirteen years after announcing his retirement, Marciano was lured back to the ring for a mock "Battle of the Century" with 27-year-old outcast Muhammad Ali. Impelled by pride and vanity, Marciano shed 50 pounds for the betiding.

This would actually be Marciano's fifth in a series of fantasy fights. In 1967, clever Miami promoter Murray Woroner concocted a tournament to determine the all-time greatest heavyweight. A panel of experts rated 16 fighters on 129 variables. The data were fed into a computer and then sculpted into 15 docudramas that aired on hundreds of radio stations. In the grand finale, Marciano knocked out Jack Dempsey in the thirteenth round.[3]

Woroner's tournament generated a lot of buzz, prompting him to adapt the concept to the big screen. In the summer of 1969, he leased Chris Dundee's Miami gym, converted it into a movie set, and filmed Marciano and Ali in a simulated battle, in all 75 one-minute sessions, some spliced with fake knockdowns and fake blood. The final cuts were cobbled with fabricated and archival material into a film that would be shown in more than 1500 theaters. A number of different endings were filmed. Neither man was apprised of the outcome that would ultimately make the final cut.

The footage was eventually doctored to produce two separate endings. In the version that aired in Great Britain, Ali emerged victorious when the bout was stopped on cuts. The version shown in the United States was a close facsimile of Marciano's first fight with Jersey Joe Walcott. His face smeared with blood, Marciano rallied from the brink of defeat to stop Ali in the thirteenth round.

Ali, then undefeated in 29 pro fights, purportedly developed a high opinion of Marciano's skills during the taping, but when the movie came out his pride was wounded. He characterized Woroner's state-of-the-art computer as a Mississippi redneck. Many knowledgeable boxing fans shared his indignation.

Marciano never fought a good black heavyweight who was in the prime of his career, the best yardstick for measuring a fighter's merit. Moreover, Rocky never tested his mettle against a big, raw-boned heavyweight of any hue, albeit fighters of this description were then in short supply. Considering these facts, one could reasonably infer that he arrived on the scene with exquisite timing and would have quickly fallen into the rubble in a different era.

The case against Marciano is compelling, but one fact stands out among all others: *He never lost!* Not even the immortal racehorse Man O' War (20 wins in 21 tries) was as trustworthy. And those that faithfully bet on Marciano were undefeated too.

Marciano's favored mode of travel was a small airplane. He was a fearless flyer, unfazed by turbulent weather.

On the evening of July 31, 1969, Marciano boarded a 4-seat Cessna at Chicago's Midway Airport. His destination was Des Moines, where he was booked to make a public appearance arranged by his friend Louis Fratto, a Des Moines beer distributor who had been grilled by the Kefauver Commission regarding his ties to the Chicago mob. Fratto's 22-year-old son accompanied him. At the controls was an inexperienced pilot.

A budding storm became full-blown as the plane was in flight. The wreckage was discovered in an Iowa cornfield. There were no survivors. Marciano died before learning the outcome of his mock fight with Ali and legend has it that his heirs never learned the whereabouts of most of the money that he had squirreled away for his twilight years.

# CHAPTER 13

# Floyd and Sonny

When it became plain that Rocky Marciano was unlikely to return any time soon, Jim Norris met with his advisors to map out a plan for determining a new champion. The situation dictated some sort of tournament and it was agreed that the field must include Archie Moore. The Old Mongoose was popular with sportswriters, had enhanced his stock with his spunky performance against Marciano, and had stayed busy in the aftermath, winning a string of non-title bouts in western rings while retaining his laurel as the world's lightheavyweight champion. Marciano had ruined most of his opponents, but not ancient Archie, a medical marvel.

The "tournament" came to consist of three entrants — Moore, Tommy "Hurricane" Jackson, and Floyd Patterson. Moore got the bye.

The inclusion of Patterson was somewhat unexpected because his manager Constantine "Cus" D'Amato was a sworn enemy of Norris and his International Boxing Club. But Norris could scarcely afford to exclude him as he was under pressure from federal prosecutors to disband the good-ol'-boy network, and young Floyd, a gold medal winner at the Helsinki Olympics, had the media on his side. D'Amato let it be known that he would have no further business dealings with the IBC once Patterson became champion, but this was putting the cart before the horse and Norris was confident that he could persuade D'Amato to change his tune.

Hurricane Jackson, a formless fighter who threw punches from all angles when he wasn't preening for the crowd, had attracted a nice following while building a 27–4–1 record. Patterson found him a difficult nut to crack, but copped the verdict on a split decision.

The Patterson-Moore fight was stalled when Doc Kearns took Archie to Toronto to fight Canadian hopeful James J. Parker, a fighter controlled by Jack Solomons, the kingpin of boxing promoters in Great Britain. Although outweighed by 25 pounds, Moore had no trouble with Parker, scoring a 9th-round stoppage in a bout packaged as a world heavyweight title fight.

Patterson-Moore was finally made for November 30, 1956, at Chicago Stadium. Although neither man was viewed as a full-fledged heavyweight, it was yet an intriguing pairing between a grizzled veteran and a baby-faced upstart barely half his age. The only smirch on Patterson's record was a disputed 8-round loss to iron-chinned veteran Joey Maxim, a man that Moore had defeated three times. The "Maxim variable" loomed large in shaping the odds. At post time, the Old Mongoose was a 9/5 favorite.

Patterson upset the odds with a dominating performance, becoming the youngest man to win the heavyweight title. The fight was stopped in the fifth round.

Patterson's first title defense against Hurricane Jackson failed to generate much of a buzz. Acquaintances as schoolboys, both now resided in the borough of Queens. There was a parochial flavor to the promotion that diminished its stature as a world title fight. Patterson had added more muscle since the first meeting, whereas Jackson had eroded his gate appeal with uninspired efforts in two interim bouts. Fighting before a sparse crowd at the Polo Grounds, Patterson, a 5/1 favorite, won every round before halting Jackson in the tenth frame.

The promotion was noteworthy in that it was the first true heavyweight championship fight in many years in which neither Mike Jacobs, now deceased, nor Jim Norris had a piece of the pie. D'Amato and his silent partners had effectively disenfranchised the Combination, albeit the feds had already sucked much of the air out of the tire. But the iconoclastic D'Amato was hardly a blast of fresh air. In short order, he would be scorned for feeding Patterson a succession of chumps and behind the scenes it was business as usual.

A mere 24 days after his rematch with Jackson, Patterson was back in action, defending his crown in Seattle against Pete Rademacher, a fighter *making his professional debut!* The balding 28-year-old Rademacher, a former Washington State University football player, had achieved a measure of fame the previous year by winning the gold medal in the heavyweight class at the Melbourne Olympics.

The promoter of record for this oddment was Jack Hurley, but the driving force was Rademacher, who raised Patterson's $250,000 purse by selling shares in his future ring earnings. The investors threw their money into a sinkhole. Rademacher caught Patterson off-balance and knocked him down in the second stanza, but the Apple State novice was in over his head. Patterson put him down for keeps with a body punch in the sixth round.

Patterson-Rademacher was roundly denounced as an insult to fans of the Manly Art, but D'Amato was merely doing what fight managers do — getting the most money for the least risk — and he had a handy excuse: his options were limited because Patterson's most worthy opponents were IBC pawns. With his manager refusing to play ball with the old guard, Patterson was on the shelf 20 months before his next fight, during which time there was considerable jockeying for his services by would-be promoters with insufficient financing to make any headway. Then Bill Rosensohn entered the picture. Schooled in the closed-circuit production side of the boxing business, Rosensohn sold D'Amato on the idea of staging a fight in Los Angeles between Patterson and Roy Harris. The match would be a tough sell, necessitating a slick advertising campaign.

Harris was undefeated in 24 fights but he had never appeared on national television or fought outside his native Texas. His ledger showed only nine stoppages, consistent with the inside dope that he didn't pack a hard punch, but he did have one thing going for him: he was born and raised in Cut and Shoot, an unincorporated hamlet on the fringe of the Big Thicket, approximately 40 miles north of Houston. A good publicist could concoct a heady brew with that place name alone. A college graduate who would go on to become an elementary school teacher and then a lawyer, Harris was fermented into a backwoods hillbilly in the mold of the comic strip character Li'l Abner.

*Sports Illustrated* featured a barefoot Roy Harris on its August 18, 1958, cover. The accompanying puff piece by Joe David Brown said that Harris was from "a fine old family of knife, knee, and knuckle fighters." Harris's father, according to Brown, had once ax-handled 16 people to the hospital during a disagreement at a local dance hall. Harris practiced his craft in his yard in a homemade ring with barbed wire on one side (this much was true), but it took a leap of faith to swallow the claim that his kinfolk shanghaied his sparring partners from honky-tonks.[1]

The L.A. sportswriters played along with the charade. (The *Los Angeles Times* wasn't yet affiliated with the *Washington Post* and had somewhat of a tabloid sensibility.) Ned Cronin wrote that Rosensohn was bombarded with calls from wealthy Texans requesting him to broker their bets and that the odds favoring Patterson had been trimmed to 7/2.[2] Planting a rumor that big plungers were lurking in the weeds with satchels of money to bet on a mystery fighter was an old connivery. In reality, the odds were closer to 7/1 with few takers on either side.

Contested before an announced crowd of 22,000 at Wrigley Field, the Patterson-Harris fight would be described as a hog butchering, a reference to the wild hogs that roamed Harris's front yard. The hog was Harris. He had a brief moment of glory when Patterson was on the wrong end of a flash knockdown in the second round, but Patterson deposited him on the deck four times before his corner tossed in the towel in the twelfth round.

Reporters covering the fight wrote favorably of Patterson, but admonished him to step up his caliber of opposition, an entreaty blithely ignored. For his next opponents, D'Amato looked to the arid soil of Europe, procuring Brian London and Ingemar Johansson. Represented by the same London booking agent, D'Amato acquired them in a package deal. Johansson was the more credible, dictating that London go first.

The son of a former British Empire heavyweight champion, London was such a crude brawler that the British Boxing Board of Control refused to recognize the match as a title fight and actually took steps to scuttle it, suspending London for insubordination in a lame attempt to save British boxing from further humiliation. Held at the Indianapolis Fairgrounds as an adjunct to the big auto race, Patterson vs. London ran true to form. Floyd was far in front when London was rescued from further punishment in the eleventh round. Although always in command, Patterson was far from sharp. With Johansson sitting ringside, there was speculation that Floyd had purposely held something back.

Patterson and Johansson were first introduced in Helsinki at the 1952 Olympics. Bidding to become the first Swede to win a gold medal in boxing, Johansson reached the finals in the heavyweight competition, where he was disqualified for fighting too meekly. Turning professional, he won the European title in his fifteenth pro bout and successfully defended it twice against British invaders on Swedish soil. These wins carried no currency outside Europe, but Johansson's countrymen were sufficiently enthralled to turn out 55,000 strong in Gothenburg for his match with undefeated (24–0, 18 KOs) Eddie Machen, the top heavyweight contender in *The Ring* ratings.

A 25-year-old ex-convict from Redding, California, Machen had virtually no chance of copping the decision if the bout went to the scorecards, but it was commonly assumed that he would blow right through Johansson. He had fought much stiffer competition. The list of his knockout victims included Nino Valdez, a fighter noted for having a cast-iron jaw. But in a shocker, Machen was easy prey for the Swede. Johansson belted him out in the opening round.

Johansson finished up his training for Patterson at Grossinger's, the Borscht Belt resort in the Catskill Mountains that had been Rocky Marciano's favorite place to train for a big fight. With him were his parents, his two brothers, and three buxom young ladies. The Swedish pastries, as some drooling reporters called them, were his 16-year-old sister, a brother's girlfriend, and his stunningly attractive fiancée, Birget Lundgren. During his last days at Grossinger's, Ingemar eschewed sparring in favor of dancing with his bride-to-be. This strengthened the case for Patterson, lengthening the odds in his favor to 5/1.

Staged on June 26, 1959, at Yankee Stadium, the summertime fight would be the first installment of a brutal trilogy with no intervening bouts for either man. The first meeting would inspire the most rehashes because the outcome was the most shocking. In the third round, the Swede knocked Patterson to the deck seven times. Patterson was on the mat a combined 42 seconds before referee Ruby Goldstein stopped the slaughter.

To build up interest in the fight, Johansson was fitted with a "Toonderbolt," the name given his supposedly lethal punch. To the surprise of the tub-thumpers, the hyperbolization was prophetic. Johansson first uncorked his looping right hand near the end of the first round, but the punch landed too high to do any damage. The next sighting of it was in Round 3 and Patterson, knocked flat on his back, was a cooked goose.

The rematch simmered for almost a year, stalled by an investigation into D'Amato's ties to underworld characters. When the match finally came to fruition, Johansson was an 8/5 favorite, an absolute steal in the estimation of savvy *New York Daily News* scribe Dick Young. To avenge a narrow defeat was one thing, but to avenge a terrible beating was quite another, and Young anticipated that Patterson would melt as soon as he entered the ring, his discomposition the product of flashbacks. However, contrarians found an ample number of reasons to rate Floyd a very live underdog. His work ethic was superior, he had fewer outside distractions (Johansson owned a construction company and a commercial fishing boat), and he was still judged to have faster reflexes. For all purposes, he had been knocked down only once in the first meeting. The other knockdowns were extensions of the first. Patterson could theoretically avoid a repetition by turning the bout into a chess match, or by smothering Johansson with a blizzard of punches so that the Swede couldn't get proper leverage behind his vaunted punch, which had acquired a second nickname, the Hammer of Thor.

His face never furrowed with signs of worry, Patterson pressed the action from the opening bell. He was rattled in the second round, but stayed upright and recovered quickly. He won the third and fourth stanzas decisively and in Round 5 he put Johansson on the mat twice with picture-perfect left hooks, the second of which knocked Ingemar cold. As he lay on the canvas, his left leg twitched convulsively. Distracted by the celebration in Patterson's corner, most in attendance were blind to his distress.

Johansson made a full recovery, but was so thoroughly demythologized that Patterson would be installed a 7/2 favorite in the rubber match at Miami Beach, odds that shot higher when the Norseman came in ten pounds above his best fighting weight. The third meeting produced more fireworks. Both fighters were on the canvas in the opening round. But Johansson quickly ran out of gas and did not get up after being felled in Round 6 by a rabbit punch.

As the trilogy was unfolding, Sonny Liston was moving up the charts. A Liston-Patterson fight figured to generate a hefty gate, but D'Amato wasn't about to thrust Floyd into a difficult fight on the heels of his three encounters with the treacherous Swede. Searching for a softie, D'Amato found the perfect die in Tom McNeeley, a Bostonian whose 24–0 record was fashioned against motley opposition. Unable to get licensed in New York, D'Amato attempted to stage the match in Boston but was rebuffed when he insisted on naming the referee. The fight went to Toronto. For closed-circuit viewing, another mismatch was bundled with it. The co-feature, staged in Philadelphia, was Sonny Liston vs. Albert Westphal.

The innovative double-header was intriguing only because Liston and Patterson were on a collision course and this was likely the final opportunity to assess their respective forms. Liston was awesome, whacking out his overmatched German opponent with the first serious punch he threw. Patterson's fight was a complete farce. McNeeley was up and down like a yo-yo before referee Jersey Joe Walcott waived the fight off in the fourth round.

Born in the impoverished Delta region of Arkansas, Charles "Sonny" Liston was reportedly the son of a man who fathered 25 children. Sonny was part of the second batch, born to his father's second wife, a woman who would leave the homestead during World War II for work in a St. Louis war plant. Sonny, the second youngest of her eight children, was a strapping 13-year-old man-child when he caught up with her there in 1945. Akin to Archie Moore, born in the same general area, Liston had no birth certificate and was presumed to be older than his professed age.

Unable to read but strong enough to do a man's work, Liston was soon earning his keep as a construction worker. When work was slow, he resorted to robberies. Three months shy of his 18th birthday, he was sentenced to five years in the Missouri State Penitentiary, where he took up boxing at the behest of the prison's Catholic chaplain.

Liston showed such great promise that word of his prowess leaked outside prison walls. Paroled after 29 months, he was sent to an amateur boxing club in St. Louis where he quickly became the cock of the walk. A brooding hulk of a man with a sullen disposition, Liston had a crisp left jab, a powerful left hook, and a malevolent stare that could spook an opponent ashen before any punches were thrown.

Liston had three early fights in Detroit, where he was matched against tough local fighters who were further along in their careers. He won two narrow decisions over Johnny Summerlin, but was less fortunate against Marty Marshall, the so-called Michigan Bomber. Liston had Marshall on the run as the final seconds ticked out, but his jaw had been broken earlier in the fight and he lost an 8-round decision. He went on to win his next 25 fights, 21 by knockout. In the process, he twice avenged his loss to Marshall and had a noteworthy fight with Roy "Cut 'N' Shoot" Harris. The first heavily hyped interracial fight in Texas since the lifting of a ban on mixed matches, the Liston-Harris bout drew an SRO crowd to Houston's Sam Houston Coliseum. The intrepid Harris was gunned down in the opening round.

Climbing the ladder, Liston was periodically sidelined by legal problems. His 15th and 16th pro fights were spaced almost two years apart. The interruption stemmed from a shouting match between a white St. Louis policeman and a black taxi driver. A bystander, Liston butted into the spat, a scuffle ensued, and the policeman suffered a broken leg. Sonny was arrested and sentenced to nine months in the city workhouse.

Liston was a marked man after this incident. He left St. Louis for Philadelphia and then resided briefly in Denver, but couldn't escape police harassment. Motoring about in his flashy Cadillac, he was invariably pulled over on some pretext. To most of white America, however, the cops were merely being proactive. Often seen in the company of unsavory characters, Liston was perceived to be an incorrigible troublemaker.

Patterson had been in trouble too. Born in a log cabin in the Blue Ridge Mountains of North Carolina, Patterson had been remanded at the age of 10 to a reform school in upstate New York for chronic truancy. When he was returned to his family in Brooklyn, he was enrolled in a school for students with behavioral problems. At age 14, he began to accompany his older brothers to D'Amato's Gramercy Street Gym in lower Manhattan. A skinny welterweight when he first laced on the gloves, Floyd was compelled to spar with bigger and older boys. These sessions were confidence-boosters. Painfully shy, he began to emerge from his shell. Concurrently, his schoolwork improved, as did his "citizenship."

Seemingly hoed for the fast lane, Patterson was just the opposite. Abstemious in his habits, he came across as a fellow who would just as soon stay home at night and curl up with a good book. Unobtrusive in dress and demeanor, soft-spoken and well spoken, the boyishly

**Floyd Patterson and Cus D'Amato (photograph undated).** *Antiquities of the Prize Ring.*

handsome boxer was most of all introspective. Reporters twice his age were drawn to him because he was the altar boy in a room full of dead-end kids.[3]

Patterson's relationship with D'Amato began to sour after the first Johannson fight when D'Amato was stripped of his New York boxing license for associating with racketeers. Some young reporters, notably Howard Cosell, continued to paint D'Amato as a white knight, but even before his suspension he had fallen from grace with a thud in the court of public opinion. "His phony pretenses of doing good for boxing is so much bunk," wrote Al Goodrich. "Cus is a power-mad little piker, with an overly loud mouth. He's as phony as a four-dollar bill."

The suspension forced D'Amato to reconfigure his formal relationship with Patterson to that of a business advisor, a semantic ploy that had self-fulfilling ramifications when others began to exert greater sway in plotting the path of Patterson's career. When Patterson signed to fight Sonny Liston, there was a presumption that he pushed for the match that D'Amato would have stalled indefinitely.

Akin to Jack Dempsey's fights with Gene Tunney and Rocky Marciano's fights with Jersey Joe Walcott, the Patterson-Liston fight could not be staged in New York because some of those with a stake in the promotion were on the outs with the commission. The preferred alternative was Philadelphia, but Liston had run afoul of the law there, drawing citations for impersonating a police officer, disorderly conduct, and resisting arrest. None of the charges would stick, but putting the fight in Philadelphia would open doors that had best remained shut. The fight landed in Chicago at Comiskey Park.

Civil rights leader Ralph Bunche, the head of the Urban League, expressed his dismay at the specter of a Sonny Liston sitting on the heavyweight throne. With the fight framed as a morality play, there was pressure on Patterson to play his part more vigorously by enumerating Sonny's moral shortcomings, but Floyd would not be a party to it. "I made mistakes too," he told reporters. "I hope you fellows will give Sonny a chance. There's good in all men, and I think if you look closely, you will find there's lots of good in Sonny Liston." But Patterson's diplomacy merely accentuated the perceived differences between them.

The case for Liston was elementary: He was a brute who would use his ham-hock 14-inch fists to pummel Patterson into quick submission. The case for Patterson rested on a multiplicity of factors. He had faster reflexes, was judged to be more resourceful, was more accustomed to dealing with the pressure of a big fight, was the younger man by at least three years, and had dispelled concerns about his punching power in his second bout with Ingemar Johansson. There was also a school of thought that Patterson's frame — at five-foot-eleven and 190 pounds, he was two inches shorter and 25 pounds lighter than Liston — was closer to optimal for a man in his weight class. His tale of the tape invited comparisons with Corbett and Dempsey and especially Ezzard Charles, who had overcome an even bigger weight disparity on the night he out-slicked Joe Louis.

In analyzing the bout, sportswriters accorded more space to the man with the most theoretical edges, painting themselves into a corner where Patterson became the concordant pick. In an Associated Press poll, 64 of 102 reporters picked Floyd. The odds favoring Liston dropped to 7/5. In England, where off-course bookmaking had recently been legalized, Liston was a larger favorite.

All the edges in the world were useless to Patterson. When he entered the ring, he looked frightened. In a fight reminiscent of Marciano-Walcott II, another Windy City dud, the contest was over before many of the latecomers had found their seats. Patterson was shorn of his title in 126 seconds without landing a significant punch. The fight played out before fewer than 19,000 paying customers in a stadium that accommodated nearly three times that number.

The courts had recently overturned legislation that prohibited rematch clauses, so Liston was legally bound to fight Patterson again. The rematch went to a small city on the Mojave Desert where no heavyweight title fight had ever been staged before.

We will go there too, hunkering down for a long spell. We're off to Las Vegas.

# CHAPTER 14

# Tank Town Boxing in Las Vegas

The Ballpark Era of heavyweight championship boxing began with the Dempsey-Firpo fight. Over the next forty years, every genuine heavyweight title fight was staged in a major city. The skein was broken when the Liston-Patterson rematch went to Las Vegas, a community that for most of the 20th century was merely another tank town.*

The first documented boxing match in Las Vegas was held on July 4, 1919. Staged in a ring erected on a baseball diamond built by railroad workers, the contest was part of a holiday sports festival. The leather-pushers, identified only by their last names — Silk and Hernandez — fought three lively rounds. The master of ceremonies pronounced it a draw.

In 1910, the first year that Las Vegas was canvassed by census takers, the population was 3,321. By 1919, there were about 5000 residents. On September 13 of that year, a meeting at a Methodist church gave birth to a branch of the American Legion. In a development mirrored in many other communities, the organization acquired a de facto monopoly on the right to promote boxing matches. The Legion held tight to this "entitlement" for the better part of the next four decades.

In 1926, the Legionnaires slapped up some bleachers behind their meeting hall. Two days following the first Dempsey-Tunney extravaganza, the runty arena — Legion Stadium — was christened with a boxing show. The bouts were lively, prompting a writer for the *Las Vegas Age* to crow that "125,000 people sitting in the rain (in Philadelphia) had less of a thrill and the enjoyment of the boxing game than the Las Vegas people enjoyed last night."[1]

Boxing in Las Vegas during the decade of the 1920s was not as vibrant as in many similar-sized communities. Activity slowed to a crawl or ceased entirely during the summer when the oppressive heat discouraged outdoor activities. More often than not, turnouts were disappointing. A contributing factor was that the local crop of fighters included no men with a reasonable expectation of making waves in bigger ponds. The busiest main-event fighter, Mickey Wallace, was good enough to get a match with middleweight champion Mickey Walker, but not good enough to show well in such distinguished company. In their non-title fight in Fresno, Wallace was knocked out in the third round.

On January 10, 1929, the *Age* blazoned the news of a forthcoming megafight. The highly

---

*"Tank town" was vaudeville slang for a town where the tallest building was the municipal water tank. In the lexicon of prizefight organizers, the term, which connoted a village of rubes, took on an even more cynical connotation.

anticipated rematch between Mickey Walker and Ace Hudkins was projected to pump $50 million into the Las Vegas economy. Walker had turned back Hudkins the previous year at Chicago's Comiskey Park, retaining his middleweight title in a spirited rumble. Walker-Hudkins II, pegged for the Fourth of July, would command the building of a 50,000-seat arena. The deal was seemingly sealed when Hudkins and his manager Tom Kennedy came to Las Vegas and affixed their names to the Articles of Agreement in a formal ceremony at the mayor's office.

To the cynics, it appeared that Walker's manager, Doc Kearns, had discovered another Shelby, a place where the townsfolk had visions of grandeur and were ripe for the fleecing. However, there were reasons to think that little Las Vegas might actually pull off the fight and reap benefits from it. Construction would soon begin on Boulder Dam, the most ambitious engineering project since the Panama Canal. The great man-made wonder, already drawing curiosity-seekers, was expected to transform Las Vegas into another Niagara Falls. The local backers drew up a plan whereby a ticket to the fight entitled the bearer to a free excursion to the dam site.

In what would become a recurrent theme in Las Vegas boxing, the promotion died on the vine. (Perhaps that wasn't such a bad thing. The temperature in Las Vegas on July 4, 1929, was 112 degrees.)

Dam construction began in 1931. Virtually overnight, a bustling community emerged around the site, a community almost as populous as Las Vegas itself. During the early days of dam construction, fights were staged at the workers' enormous mess hall. The first card, held on January 14, 1932, under the auspices of the American Legion, was a mixed bag of boxing and wrestling matches. Many subsequent cards were similarly structured. The commingling was a reflection of the times. Wrestling nationally was enjoying one of its periodic booms.

The Boulder Dam project expanded the customer base for boxing and augmented the local pugilistic fraternity with a badly needed infusion of new blood. Ted "Stecher" Jensen, a U.S. marshal, developed a following as a wrestler, dabbled in matchmaking, and helped organize the drive to build Boulder City's first privately owned athletic arena. Eddie O'Brien, a dam construction worker, developed a keen rivalry with the top homegrown fighter, Indian Johnny Smith, and had the distinction of winning Las Vegas's first 15-round fight. Staged at Legion Stadium on November 10, 1932, the match between O'Brien and unknown Curley Mines was billed for the Nevada welterweight title.

Dam construction had barely started when Nevada legalized gambling, approving the measure on March 11, 1931. Sponsored by a legislator in Winnemucca, a cow town near the Oregon border, the bill received only lukewarm support in Las Vegas. Opponents did not view gambling as a big stimulus to tourism, reasoning that the Dam would draw visitors with or without it and that the beautiful scenery would then draw them back. There was also the concern that Monte Carlo-style gambling would destroy the cowboy town synergy, a fear that would be borne out, although the Depression and World War II slowed this development. Without gambling, Vegas would not have become the fight capital of the world, but the immediate impact was negligible.

Johnny Sikes, a fighter from Bismarck, North Dakota, supplanted O'Brien as the foremost fighter among the dam workers and became an important cog in the local boxing apparatus. A rough-hewn fighter who would be classified today as a super-middleweight, Sikes was the most peripatetic of the fighters domiciled on the Boulder City federal reservation, traveling as far as Seattle for ring engagements. Between fights, he stayed busy as a referee and matchmaker. Two noteworthy facts about Sikes are that he participated in the first fight in Las Vegas where one of the principals was actually famous, and he refereed the fight that resulted in southern Nevada's first ring fatality.

Sikes fought "Slapsie Maxie" Rosenbloom at Legion Stadium on February 12, 1936. Then living in Hollywood where he was cultivating a career in show business, the former lightheavyweight champion had reached the stage of his career where he was coasting on his reputation, but was he yet too resourceful for Sikes and was accorded the decision after 10 uneventful rounds. Sikes fared much better when he was matched against Rosenbloom two weeks later in Tonopah, but was robbed of the decision by the referee. The arbiter was a member of Rosenbloom's traveling party.

The fatal fight, pitting California welterweights Domingo Lopez and Ernie Duarte, was the main event of a June 18, 1936, show at Legion Stadium. Lopez fell into a coma after being nailed with a short right cross in the second round. Carted off to Los Angeles in a passenger train, Lopez died 17 days later at an L.A. hospital without regaining consciousness.

The Legion opened a new arena in 1939. A 1200-seat facility situated behind a tavern near the railroad depot, the venue attracted only two SRO crowds before falling into disuse. The allurement of the first sellout was guest referee Jack Dempsey. The second sellout, on September 6, 1942, was accorded much more than the usual amount of hype in the daily paper and had the advantage of being positioned on Labor Day, a favorable day for sports promotions of all kinds.

There were actually two boxing shows in Las Vegas on that particular day. The local paper snubbed the later-starting show, notwithstanding the fact that the headliner was the renowned Henry Armstrong. While Armstrong was matched against a stooge, the cold shoulder bore witness to the fact that his appearance was arranged without obeisance to the good-ol'-boy network. Inside that network, no one was more powerful than Al Cahlan. The Nevada State Commander of the American Legion, Cahlan was the founding owner of the *Review-Journal*. (The *Las Vegas Age* had gone belly-up.)

Al Cahlan's younger brother John F. Cahlan covered the sports beat. He was forever gushing that Las Vegas had landed a fight that would have created a big buzz in larger precincts, but his only references to Armstrong's impending visit were words of disparagement. Cahlan told his readers that Hammerin' Hank was half-blind and had "bees in his noggin." He also had some choice words for former bantamweight champion Joe Lynch, Armstrong's new manager: "Mr. Lynch is desirous of expanding his territory to the 'tank' towns and has eyes on numerous spots in the desert. We would advise him that frontier communities are not as gullible as they appear to be, and six shooters still are unholstered on occasions. They may fire blanks, but the effect is the same."[2]

It was true that Armstrong was past his prime. He had been badly mauled by Fritzie Zivic in a title fight at Madison Square Garden, and was on the comeback trail after a 16-month layoff. However, at age 29 he was still a formidable fighter, as he would demonstrate seven weeks after his stopover in Las Vegas, winning his third encounter with Zivic at San Francisco before the largest Bay Area boxing crowd in fourteen years. Armstrong was pilloried only because he was the pawn in a territorial dispute.

During the war years, the number of boxing shows in Las Vegas fell off dramatically, but there was yet an upgrade in the caliber of fighters that appeared in Las Vegas rings. Gains in air transportation were a contributing factor, as was the arrival of casino developers with deeper pockets.

In 1942, the Last Frontier Hotel opened on a largely naked stretch of road that the locals called the Old Los Angeles Highway. On the expansive grounds, the owners built a replica of a western mining village with a functional rodeo corral. On April 23, 1943, the corral became the site of the first boxing show staged on property abutting the thoroughfare that would become famed as the Strip. Shows were held there intermittently over the next fourteen years, first at the corral and then at the so-called Sportsdrome that displaced it, an oval advertised as the world's fastest jalopy track. Prominent heavyweight Jimmy Bivins fought at the Last Frontier, as did Art Aragon, a teenage whirlwind from New Mexico who went on to become a box office sensation in California.

Attempts to run regular shows at the Last Frontier were aborted by poor attendance, but spot promotions featuring top contenders attracted good gates. The venue, however, was too small for a fight of major import. In 1947, a ballpark named Cashman Field was built to house the city's first minor league baseball team. It would be the site of the first Las Vegas boxing event to receive international press coverage. The principals were Archie Moore and Geraldo "Nino" Valdes. The promoter was none other than Doc Kearns.

## Catching Up with Doc Kearns

Although his name would be forever linked with his golden goose Jack Dempsey, Kearns managed scores of other fighters. Dempsey was still active when Doc latched hold of Mickey Walker. The so-called Toy Bulldog seemingly had his best days behind him, but under Doc's management he recaptured the middleweight title, defeated several top-shelf heavyweights, and became a far larger gate attraction. Doc also had a hand in plotting the comeback of Benny Leonard. During this final phase of his career, the former lightweight champion engaged in a series of sham fights.

Kearns was a fixer-upper who had little use for neophytes, although he was quick to make an exception for a promising white heavyweight or a fellow with a colorful life story. One could have foreseen that Doc would grab a piece of Enzo Fiermonte, a lady-killer married to *Titanic* survivor Madelaine Talmadge Force, the widow of John Jacob Astor IV. A top-of-the-line middleweight in Europe, Fiermonte was out of his element fighting bigger men in the U.S. His career ended on an inglorious note when trial horse Les Kennedy knocked him out with a punch described in news reports as accidental. Fiermonte had a longer and more profitable career as a screen actor in his native Italy.

Doc went through a rough patch during the Joe Louis era. During the early years of Louis's title reign, he co-promoted several poorly attended shows that were stupidly packaged as White Hope tournaments. Jimmy Adamick, his most heavily hyped heavyweight, was forced to quit boxing in 1938 after suffering a near-fatal head injury in a bout with Roscoe Toles, a fighter from the same Detroit neighborhood as Joe Louis.

Doc got back on track when he acquired Joey Maxim. A powderpuff puncher with a wealth of stamina and a granite jaw, Maxim couldn't draw flies without an interesting opponent, but Doc guided him into big-money fights with Freddie Mills and Sugar Ray Robinson. Maxim turned into a tiger when he fought Mills in London, knocking the defending lightheavyweight champion into retirement with a 10th-round stoppage. Maxim vs. Robinson drew 47,983 to Yankee Stadium on June 20, 1952.

In boxing lore, many fights were contested in sweltering heat that came to be more sweltering with each retelling. Jack Johnson's April fight in Havana with Jess Willard came to be described as bathed in a sauna. But the heat and humidity were truly oppressive on this particular night in the Bronx. Out on his feet after ten frames, referee Ruby Goldstein yielded his post to "bullpen reliever" Ray Miller. The 32-year-old Robinson, bidding to become the third fighter in history to win world titles in three weight classes, held a commanding lead on the scorecards when he too went limp. Badly dehydrated, he quit on his stool after the 13th round and had to be assisted from the ring. The result would go into the books as Robinson's only defeat inside the distance in a career that eventually numbered 200 fights.

When Maxim retained his belt by virtue of being the last man standing, Kearns caught a big break. He owned a fighter whose wheels were about to fall off (Maxim won only four of his next 11 fights), but that fighter was now more marketable than ever. Doc reportedly finagled $100,000 for a bout for Maxim in St. Louis with Archie Moore.

Moore's cut was reportedly $800, but the bout would be the turning point of his long career. After 15 uneventful rounds, he had Maxim's belt and a new manager to boot. Officially it was Charlie Johnston, an old-timer who had fronted fighters for his Boy Bandit brother and then managed wrestling troupes, but one didn't need special glasses to see that it was actually Kearns. With Moore and Maxim under his thumb, Doc did the logical thing and ordered a rematch and then another rematch after that. Both bouts were dull and neither was deemed very newsworthy, but Doc was the laying the foundation for a match between Moore and Rocky Marciano.

# CHAPTER 15

# The Doctor Makes
# a House Call

On May 16, 1955, Rocky Marciano retained his heavyweight title at the expense of Don Cockell. When the bout was signed, the top-ranked contender in both *The Ring* and National Boxing Association ratings was Nino Valdes, a fighter from Cuba managed by New York gym operator Bobby Gleason. Archie Moore's quickest route to Marciano was through Valdes. Kearns made the match before locking in a venue.

Doc had already booked a fight for Joey Maxim in San Francisco. The Marciano-Cockell fight would be staged in the same city not quite five weeks later. It made sense for Doc to put the Moore-Valdes fight inside this 33-day window and as near San Francisco as possible. Las Vegas was on his short list of possible staging grounds, as were several cities in California, but then Moore was diagnosed with a possible heart ailment, impelling the California commission to suspend his license.

Despite its relatively small population, Las Vegas had several pluses. The fight game there had slowed to a crawl. Anxious to jump-start a revival, the commissioners could be bullied into making concessions. Cashman Field had become a white elephant. The landlord was willing to rent it cheap. New hotels were sprouting on the Strip. The owners could be counted on to purchase large blocks of tickets. And it mattered greatly that Las Vegas was becoming more easily accessible by air.

Doc had promoted a fight for Mickey Walker in Louisville on the eve of the 1930 Kentucky Derby. Hitching a boxing show to an unrelated sports event was an ancient practice. Las Vegas offered the same opportunity. The Desert Inn Golf Tournament of Champions, benefiting the Damon Runyon Cancer Research Fund — the first recurrent athletic event in Las Vegas with national interest — was set to conclude May 1. Prominent newspapermen like Walter Winchell would be in town and Doc was assured of good press coverage. Important British boxing writers would already be in San Francisco covering Cockell's pre-fight workouts and Doc knew them well enough to know that they would welcome a side trip to Las Vegas.

The *Review-Journal* paid scant attention to the fight until both fighters arrived in town. This was understandable considering that Las Vegas had been repeatedly teased with false promises of a big fight, but Doc, with the encouragement of Hank Greenspun, invited the cold shoulder by snubbing the American Legion crowd. A former arms dealer and hotel publicist from Brooklyn, Greenspun had founded a rival daily in 1950, the *Las Vegas Sun*. This begat one of the nastiest newspaper feuds in American journalism.

Greenspun's paper devoted copious ink to Doc's promotion. The ink flowed more copiously following a damning disquisition by John F. Cahlan that ran in the *Review-Journal* on Sunday, April 10. Cahlan implored the boxing commission to send Kearns packing, postulating that Archie Moore might suffer a fatal stroke in the heat of battle with bad repercussions for tourism.

"[The fight] is probably the greatest event for the town since the government started using the area for atom bomb tests," fulminated Greenspun in rebuttal. "If Mr. Cahlan's head was half as sound as Moore's heart, he wouldn't be filling his lying newspaper with that sort of drivel.... It is possible that 'Doc' wouldn't fall for some shakedown which the *Review-Journal* usually maneuvers with anyone who tries to do something in Las Vegas."[1]

After anointing the match the Fight of the Century in a *Sun* editorial, Greenspun contrived a sappy contest to promote the fight. The contest took the form of a short essay. The winner pushed the right button by writing that the fight "should be a stirring contest with either man likely to win."

In point of fact, Moore and Valdes had met once before. Moore got the nod in a snoozer. Valdes had rebounded with wins over four ranked contenders, but his record in U.S. rings (12–5–1) was unspectacular and it was unlikely that he would fight with fury against a cagey fighter like Moore, especially as he had never gone fifteen rounds and a fast pace might be withering. The big Cuban was stereotyped as lazy. It was written that his preferred method of training was rumba dancing.

Valdes was younger and taller than Moore — he normally tipped the scales at about 215 pounds — but Kearns always tilted the playing field in favor of his guy. In 1946, Joey Maxim won an unpopular decision over Jersey Joe Walcott in Camden, New Jersey. The lone scorekeeper, referee Paul Cavalier, was an old friend of Kearns who had served as a sparring partner for Jack Dempsey and Mickey Walker. That kind of arrangement was always best for the Doctor — a referee with whom he was socially acquainted and no judges, as they couldn't be trusted to render the right decision and normally expected to be paid.

When the Nevada Boxing Commission was formed, the state adopted the rule of three scorekeepers, the referee and two judges. But Kearns never felt obligated to follow dictates not of his own devising. He refused to countenance judges and announced that he was bringing in Jimmy Braddock from New Jersey to referee the contest. He even went out and found his own ring announcer, a second-rate lounge comic who volunteered his services for free. To save face, the commissioners extracted a promise from Kearns that Braddock would score the bout on the 10-point must system, which the commission had recently adopted.

Advertised in promotional materials as a world heavyweight title fight, the Moore-Valdes tiff began shortly after 6 P.M. A 12/5 favorite, Moore won the early rounds by pinning Valdes against the ropes so that he was squinting directly into the sun. The Cuban came on strong in the middle rounds while Archie was methodically working on the lump that had formed above Valdes's left eye. The eye shut completely in Round 13, whereupon Moore shifted into a higher gear, scoring with effective combinations.

Paying no heed to the dictate of a 10-point must system — perhaps because he found the math too cumbersome — Braddock awarded the fight to Moore by a score of 8–5–2. While most ringsiders concurred with the verdict, the folks in the bleachers — too far from the action to appreciate Moore's clever inside work — let loose a torrent of boos. Valdes burst out crying and his manager screamed that they had been double-crossed.

Attendance was announced at 10,800, but the turnout was conspicuously smaller. The gate receipts were announced at $102,608, another figure that appeared to have been pulled out of thin air. Moore and Valdes were each guaranteed $50,000. While Doc's guarantees were elastic, he could not possibly have covered his nut considering his obligations to the undercard fighters and other expenses. The fight was aesthetically disappointing, and on the surface it appeared that Kearns in his dotage had lost his Midas touch.

In actuality, it was a slick piece of work. Although the turnout was disappointing, it more than doubled the previous high for a boxing show in Las Vegas despite steep ticket prices, unseasonably chilly weather, and negative to lukewarm previews in the established newspaper. Moore's performance was unexceptional, but the Old Mongoose was lauded for fighting a very intelligent fight, imparting a bull-and-matador sheen to his proposed match with Rocky Marciano. As noted, Marciano vs. Moore was a blockbuster, earning both men the largest paydays of their careers.

Greenspun predicted that Las Vegas would become a big fight town. His crystal ball was crystal-clear, but the Moore-Valdes fight wasn't an important catalyst. One could sense that Las Vegas was fast ripening into a port for major sporting events, but Kearns's unbridled shenanigans bore witness that Las Vegas circa 1955 was still very much a tank town.

## Postscript

Doc Kearns returned to Las Vegas in 1963 and took up residence at the Hacienda Hotel. An octogenarian now and a teetotaler, he scarcely resembled the rambunctious fellow whose name repeatedly surfaced in memoirs of the speakeasy era. However, he was no less obsessed with finding the next Dempsey, which led him to acquire the contract of Jefferson Davis, a fighter developing a strong local following. A lanky cruiserweight from Mobile, Alabama, Davis was a solid prospect. He had advanced to the 1960 Olympic trials, only to be defeated by Cassius Clay. Chumming the water for a rematch with Clay, who was soon to adopt the name Muhammad Ali, Doc told reporters that his latest find was a direct lineal descendent of the president of the Old Confederacy. It would not have mattered if Doc had known that the famous Civil War leader had no male heirs.

Davis sported a 17–2 record when Kearns repaired to the home of his son, a Miami fireman, to recuperate from a bout of pneumonia. He died there on July 7, 1963. Without Doc, Davis devolved into a building block for European fighters the likes of Henry Cooper and Karl Mildenberger. Doc's last Great White Hope retired with a 28–13–1 record after suffering a fifth-round knockout at the hands of up-and-comer Joe Frazier.

# CHAPTER 16

# Las Vegas: The Transition Years

Five years elapsed between the Moore-Valdes match and the first genuine world title fight in Las Vegas. The major development during this period was the opening of the Las Vegas Convention Center in 1959. Within walking distance of the hotels on the most densely developed portion of the Strip, it had a 9000-seat rotunda and smaller halls suitable for club fights. A parallel development was the formation of the Silver State Sports Club.

The founders of this new promotional entity were craps dealer Mel "Red" Greb and Jack Doyle, an engineer by trade who owned a popular tavern on the outskirts of town. Greb, a relative newcomer to Las Vegas, had spent virtually his entire life in boxing, working his way up from an errand boy to a matchmaker for influential Newark-based promoter Willie Gilzenburg. He had strong contacts and was familiar with all the little details involved in staging a boxing show. Doyle, a longtime resident who had served on the state boxing board, was a great facilitator. He had the juice to cut through red tape.

The second SSSC promotion, on January 11, 1960, featured heavyweights Charlie Powell and Lamar Clark in separate bouts. A schoolboy track and baseball star, Powell had played in the National Football League directly out of high school and was fairly touted as the best all-around athlete in the history of boxing. Clark, a farm boy from Cedar City, Utah, had attracted national attention while ringing up a string of 42 knockouts, one short of the record set in 1947 by Blackjack Billy Fox.

Powell managed only a draw against Reno journeyman Howard King, but their action-packed fight fumigated the building after Clark's 59-second knockout over a mystery opponent who was a very poor actor. The event attracted a paid crowd of 3,346, a new Las Vegas high for an indoor boxing show, emboldening Greb and Doyle to pursue bigger game.

The timing was right. In response to various pressures, the Madison Square Garden Corporation was farming out fights to organizers around the country, co-promoting these events to keep the lion's share of the TV money. SSSC, in tandem with Madison Square Garden, arranged a welterweight title defense for Don Jordan. The match between him and Bernardo "Kid" Paret came to fruition at the Convention Center on May 27, 1960.

An ill-humored man of uncertain lineage, Jordan competed as Geronimo Kid during his early days on the southern California circuit, a name attached to him because of his Native American features. Reportedly from a family of 19 children, Jordan acquired a taste for boxing on the streets of East Los Angeles and in reform schools. In his 59th pro fight, he upset title-holder Virgil Akins at the Olympic Auditorium. The L.A. papers enhanced his profile by proclaiming him the first Los Angeles-born fighter to win a world title. (In later years, Jordan avouched that he was born in the Dominican Republic, but reporters never knew if he was telling the truth.)

Tangled in a web of distractions, the promotion was touch-and-go right up to the opening bell. Marching to the beat of his own drummer, Jordan lost a tune-up fight in Baltimore that he arranged without consulting his managers. Happy to be rid of him, they reached an agreement to sell his contract to a young entrepreneur named Kirk Kerkorian. The transaction, ultimately consummated, was put in limbo when Jordan's ex-wife attempted to garnish his purse for delinquent alimony and child support. Nevada boxing regulators saw to it that her petition was filed in a wastebasket, but there was talk that Jordan would pull out to spite her.

The odds favoring Paret rose from 7/5 to 3/1. Paret justified the shift, winning Jordan's title via a unanimous decision in a lackluster bout. (Although seemingly far from finished, Jordan lost 11 of his next 13 fights before retiring into obscurity. Paret, born into poverty on a sugar plantation in Cuba, suffered fatal injuries in a match with Emile Griffith at Madison Square Garden on March 24, 1962, making him the first man to die a violent death during a live national TV broadcast, a distinction that would have otherwise gone to Lee Harvey Oswald.)

A messy promotion and a flop at the gate, Jordan vs. Paret was yet a breakthrough. Aside from being the first championship fight in Las Vegas, it was also the first fight from Las Vegas to be nationally televised. The production was glitch-free, paving the way for more fights of national significance. Of course, it mattered greatly that Las Vegas was an island in the desert. Nationally televised fights were customarily blacked out for a radius of 50–250 miles to protect the live gate, an arrangement that negatively affected the sale of TV ads. In Las Vegas, the impact of a blackout was negligible.

Having passed the initiation, so to speak, Greb and Doyle were rewarded with Robinson-Fullmer IV, a surefire moneymaker.

After his debilitating fight with Joey Maxim, Robinson retired with a record of 131–3–2. He was out of boxing for two and a half years, during which time he formed a variety act. His rope-skipping routines were mesmerizing, but the Sugar Man was nothing special as a singer, drummer, or tap dancer, and his agent had difficulty securing repeat bookings at the better nightclubs. In common with his friend Joe Louis, his unretirement was hastened by IRS trouble.

Robinson went on to recapture the middleweight title with a quick stoppage of Bobo Olson, a man he had defeated twice previously. His first bout with Gene Fullmer was his first bout at Madison Square Garden in almost a decade. Much was made of the fact that Robinson was returning to the venue where he had dazzled the sportswriters as a rising contender and where he had won his first championship belt. The match packed the fabled Eighth Avenue sock palace to capacity. An estimated five thousand were turned away at the gate. But Fullmer, the younger man by 11 years, spoiled Sugar Ray's homecoming, winning the gory fight by a decisive margin. Robinson won the rematch with a spectacular one-punch knockout and the rubber match was ruled a draw.

Named Gene (not Eugene) in honor of Gene Tunney, Fullmer hailed from West Jordan, Utah, home to Marv Jensen, a mink rancher who operated one of the busiest gyms in the country and promoted dozens of low-budget shows in nearby towns. Jensen's stable was full of ham-'n'-eggers, but Fullmer, a gritty and guileful fighter with great stamina, was legitimate. A relatively short and short-armed middle-weight, he was something of a miniature Marciano. He ate a lot of leather, but was stubbornly aggressive and won many of his fights on sheer tenacity.

Most observers thought that Robinson was robbed in his third meeting with Fullmer. In an informal poll of ringside reporters, the tally was 14–6–3 for Sugar Ray. The fourth installment of their rivalry, staged at the Las Vegas Convention Center on March 4, 1961, was free of controversy. Saved by the bell in round three, Robinson, now 40 years old, fought back valiantly in a rough and bloody fight, but Fullmer, a 2/1 favorite, was a clear-cut winner.

With hundreds of Utahans in attendance, Fullmer had a "home field advantage," but Robinson had built a good local following during his stay at the Dunes Hotel, where his afternoon workouts attracted overflow crowds. His encampment there was noteworthy in itself. Until March of 1960, when local NAACP officials and Strip hotel owners hammered out an anti-segregation decree, blacks

Don Jordan circa 1959. Jordan lost his welterweight title in the first world championship fight staged in Las Vegas. *Cyber Boxing Zone.*

were denied accommodations in the better Strip hotels. African American boxers, even the illustrious Archie Moore, were set up in rooming houses in the black section of town. Famous for traveling with a large retinue, Robinson arrived at the Dunes with his mother, manager, trainer, assistant trainer, bodyguard, chauffeur, valet, traveling secretary, personal barber, and two sparring partners, all of whom were black. More than likely, this was the largest African American group domiciled at a major Strip resort to this point in time.

It was during Robinson's stay at the Dunes that the name Irving "Ash" Resnick first appeared in blurbs about boxing in the local press. A Dunes casino executive with a hidden interest in the Silver State Sports Club, Resnick became an important figure on the Las Vegas boxing scene, notwithstanding a shadowy background. A renowned athlete in his native Brooklyn who rose to the rank of captain while serving in the Army, Resnick had been barred from racetracks in Florida and his name had been linked to college basketball point-shaving scandals. Howard Cosell pronounced him "one of the original hardboiled guys of the world."[1]

To the sporting crowd, Resnick was the concierge with the "power of the pen," meaning a fellow authorized to give away freebies (rooms, restaurant meals, stage shows, etc.) at his whim. In most cities, the cost of hotel rooms was rising faster than inflation, making it prohibitively expensive to lodge out-of-town fighters and their entourages. In Las Vegas, where Ash Resnick established the ground rules, these costs were defrayed with the understanding that the fighters were obligated to socialize with big gamblers.

During Resnick's heyday as a sachem on the Las Vegas boxing scene, it was normative for the principals in a big fight to show up three weeks before the event. Their afternoon workouts in hotel ballrooms — open to the public either free or for a nominal fee — were listed under lounge shows. A residual benefit was strong newspaper coverage as the fighters were available on a daily basis for bull sessions with reporters. SSSC promotions received extensive and generally fawning coverage in both Las Vegas dailies.

(The *Review-Journal* had passed into the hands of a media conglomerate headquartered in Arkansas. The sale of the paper to an out-of-town company severely undermined the influence of the American Legion in Las Vegas.)

Bouncing from the Dunes to the Thunderbird, Resnick turned his new workplace into a haven for the fight fraternity. During his stay there, SSSC promoted eight championship fights at the Convention Center, the last of which fell out a mere three days before the appointed date when the closed-circuit exhibitor failed to post the required bond. In each instance, one of the principals — champion or challenger — held open training sessions at the Thunderbird.

The aborted fight, scheduled for October 23, 1964, warrants a mention because it begs a "what if?" The match pitted Joey Giardello in a middleweight title defense against Rubin "Hurricane" Carter. In his workouts at the El Cortez, Carter looked sensational. A 7/5 favorite to dethrone Giardello, Carter was repositioned the underdog when the match — delayed seven weeks — was transplanted to Philadelphia, Giardello's hometown. Inspired by a partisan crowd, Giardello outworked Carter in the late rounds to retain his belt. Carter's subsequent incarceration on two questionable counts of murder brought him more notoriety than anything he accomplished in the ring, spawning several books, a Bob Dylan song, and a Norman Jewison movie that earned an Oscar nomination for Denzel Washington. Had the bout been held in Las Vegas as scheduled, perhaps Carter's life would have taken a different turn.

Resnick was great pals with Joe Louis. He put the Brown Bomber on the Thunderbird payroll as a greeter and kept him on in that capacity at his next places of employment, the Aladdin and Caesars Palace.[2] Resnick's paternal relationship with Louis cast him in a positive light, but his subsequent busom-buddy association with Sonny Liston redounded to his discredit. Liston's mysterious death in late December of 1970 — officially a heroin overdose — smacked of foul play since Sonny was known to be deathly afraid of needles. In the eyes of conspiracy theorists, Resnick emerged as a prime suspect. He had no perceptible motive, but a man of his reputation didn't need one.

Liston had the distinction of appearing in the first heavyweight championship fight in Las Vegas when he risked his title in a rematch with Floyd Patterson on July 22, 1963. The fight drew only 6,689 paid, somewhat surprising as Patterson (at the Dunes) and Liston (at the Thunderbird) drew large turnouts for their pre-fight "lounge shows." The first meeting had lasted 126 seconds. The mirror-image rematch went four seconds longer.

Championship boxing in Las Vegas slumped following this stinker. Only six world title fights were staged during the years 1964–1974. A contributing factor was that it became harder to secure good dates at the Convention Center, which came to be used more and more for its intended purpose — conventions and trade shows. Also, beginning in the mid–1960s, more foreign fighters achieved top-contender status, pushing more title fights overseas. Carlos Monzon, a brilliant fighter from Argentina, participated in 15 middleweight title fights between 1970 and 1977. Monzon fought only once on American soil, defeating Tony Licata at Madison Square Garden in 1975.

As big fights were becoming more sporadic, the local club scene exploded. Las Vegas became the top fight town in America as measured by the sheer quantity of shows. The spearhead of this development was Bill Miller. A native of Elmira, New York, Miller ran the Thoroughbred Lounge, a mid–Strip tavern situated next to a bookie parlor. Befitting its name and location, the Thoroughbred Lounge had a horseracing motif, but the overriding synergy was boxing, particularly after Miller put boxing equipment in the basement for fighters appearing on his cards. When the equipment was put to use, the sounds vibrated into the bar.

A licensed pilot, Miller was known to go get the fighters he needed to flesh out a card, sometimes returning in his aircraft with both battlers in a particular match. An indefatigable promoter who was as resilient as the sport to which he was addicted, Miller would eventually be able to boast that he was the only person in America still staging a weekly show, a feat more noteworthy as he operated in an open city where other promoters were constantly challenging his hegemony.

On October 4, 1960, Miller initiated a weekly series of fights at the La Vista Supper Club, a 24-hour drinking and dining establishment with an outdoor swimming pool by the rear entrance. (In the wee hours, one might encounter a cocktail waitress in her underwear taking a dip in the pool before calling it a night.) Miller erected the boxing ring on wooden slats laid over the pool, inviting hackneyed jokes about fighters taking a dive.

The La Vista shows led to Miller's "Strip Fight of the Week." After stopovers at three rival properties, the show had a long run at the Silver Slipper, a two-story gambling saloon and burlesque house that was originally an annex of the Last Frontier. The fights were held in an upstairs auditorium that had fallen into disuse as a western dance hall.

Silver Slipper food and beverage manager Art Lurie, an intermittent member of the athletic commission, encouraged and facilitated the transfer of Miller's weekly show to its new location. Lurie would recollect that his bosses were worried that boxing would attract the wrong element, but that their misgivings were vaporized by a stranger who turned up at the inaugural show (July 18, 1966) and blew seven thousand dollars shooting craps. This was a rare windfall for the Silver Slipper, a grind joint whose clientele consisted mostly of slots and keno players. Management quickly extended Miller's contract, shifting his shows to Wednesdays, the slowest night of the week.

The ambience at the Silver Slipper harked back to an earlier era. Spectators showered the ring with "nobbins" in the form of gambling tokens whenever a bout was especially entertaining. Hard-core ringside gamblers bet man-to-man. A regular patron straight out of Damon Runyon circulated through the crowd between bouts, shouting out "seven to five but I get to pick first, who wants a piece of it?"

Bill Miller, more than anyone, was responsible for making Las Vegas a leading hub of boxing. During the dam-building years and again during World War II, the local pool of fighters consisted of men drawn to Las Vegas by employment unrelated to boxing. They were semiprofessional fighters. But during Miller's heyday, the town became a magnet for individuals that derived most or all of their income from boxing. Undercard fighters and trainers could not support themselves on purses alone, but there were supplemental income streams. Managers of important fighters increasingly looked to Las Vegas for sparring partners. Promoters elsewhere were constantly in need of manpower on short notice; enterprising cornermen earned commissions as freelance booking agents. The activity nourished a small but vibrant pugilistic subculture.

Miller's most utilitarian "house fighter" was Irish Denny Moyer, a stocky, baby-faced fighter from Portland, Oregon. A comet coming out of the amateur ranks, Moyer defeated five former world champions in nationally televised fights before his twenty-second birthday. In 1962, he laid claim to the vacant light middleweight (154-pound) title by virtue of outpointing Joey Giambra in a 15-round contest refereed by reigning heavyweight champion Sonny Liston.

**Sugar Ray Robinson has his blood pressure checked by Dr. Alexander Schiff as Denny Moyer looks on. Moyer split two fights with Robinson prior to becoming the busiest main event fighter on the Las Vegas Strip. Photograph taken in 1961 or 1962.** *Cyber Boxing Zone.*

Moyer's best years were behind him when he hunkered down in Las Vegas in 1965, but he was a name-brand commodity who invariably drew good crowds. While always identified as a Portland fighter, the stylish but feather-fisted Moyer participated in more fights in Las Vegas than in his native Oregon. His record in Nevada rings was 26–3–1.

Moyer attracted other good fighters in his weight class to Las Vegas. The most notable of those that set down roots were Ferdinand "Ferd" Hernandez, who hailed from Sydney, Nebraska, and Freddie Little, a native of Picayune, Mississippi.

Hernandez lost two hairline decisions to Moyer in the summer of 1965, but rebounded under Miller's smart matchmaking to become a top contender. Miller both promoted and managed Hernandez, employing him as a bartender to keep him in steady coin and helping him acquire a referee's license. Hernandez officiated many fights while still active, the last Las Vegas-based fighter to hold this distinction.

Boxing was a profitable sideline for Freddie Little, a schoolteacher with a degree from Dillard University. In his first Las Vegas fight, he knocked out Moyer, a stepping-stone to title fights in Korea and Italy and to eventual recognition as the junior middleweight champion. Little remained active for a while after taking a high government post in Carson City. He finished his career with a record of 51–6.

A drumbeater for the infant World Boxing Council and one of the founding fathers of the North American Boxing Federation, Miller accomplished a number of firsts that in hindsight were important transitional developments in the history of boxing in Las Vegas. He was the first local promoter to secure a multi-fight television contract. The fights were beamed into southern California. He was the promoter of record for the first Las Vegas fight aired on *ABC's Wide World of Sports*. Staged at the International Hotel (the original name of the Las Vegas Hilton) on December 6, 1969, it pitted Sonny Liston against Leotis Martin in a bout billed for the vacant NABF heavyweight title.[3] Miller was also the point man for Bob Arum and Don King in their earliest Nevada promotions. He greased the skids with the regulators and arranged the undercard bouts.

A hot-tempered workaholic, Miller died in 1976 at age 49 during open-heart surgery. In other places, the loss of a go-getter like Miller would invariably bring a downturn, but the Las Vegas club scene was percolating. Shows at the Silver Slipper continued but became less frequent as boxing was implanted at new venues, notably the Showboat. In the grand scheme of things, however, this was of little importance. A new era was dawning, an era resplendent with megafights.

# CHAPTER 17

# The Rise and Fall of Ali

Bob Arum and Don King had widely different backgrounds. The son of a Brooklyn accountant, Arum graduated with honors from Harvard Law School. The son of a steelworker who died in a smelter explosion, Don King graduated from the Marion (Ohio) Correctional Institution, where he served four years for the fatal Cleveland sidewalk stomping of a numbers runner with whom he had a business dispute. King had previously shot a man to death, but the victim was attested to be a would-be robber and the shooting was ruled a justifiable homicide.

Arum was first involved in a boxing promotion in 1966, six years before King, but their rivalry would be so long-lasting that it was as if they bubbled forth simultaneously. In a sense they had, as both were drawn to the fight game by the realization that Muhammad Ali was a font of untapped wealth. There would be interludes of outward harmony when neither could manufacture a big fight without involving the other, but these periods of reconciliation invariably opened new sores. By and large, King's accomplishments were greater because he had his hooks into more fighters, promoted across a wider swath of the globe, and exerted far more sway over the heavyweight division.

Arum forayed into Nevada in advance of his Brillo-haired rival. Arum's company, Top Rank, handled the closed-circuit telecasts for Ali's fights with Jerry Quarry and Bob Foster and then promoted Ali's February 14, 1973, fight with Joe Bugner at the Las Vegas Convention Center. Ali vs. Bugner was the first boxing event sponsored by Caesars Palace and the first Las Vegas show to attract a large block of tourists from overseas. An estimated 1500 Brits crossed the pond to cheer on Bugner, a British citizen born in Hungary, and his stablemates John Conteh and John Stracey, future titlists who were victorious in supporting bouts.

King's first Nevada promotion was Ali's title defense against Ron Lyle on May 16, 1975. King also promoted the January 24, 1976, non-title bout between Lyle and George Foreman, a fight of larger historic significance. Housed in the newly constructed Caesars Palace Sports Pavilion, an armory-styled building located behind the tennis courts, Foreman vs. Lyle was the first boxing card staged on the actual grounds of Caesars Palace. A wildly successful promotion as measured by the action in the casino pit, this wildly entertaining slugfest came to be seen as the fight that birthed the Casino Era of boxing.

Coming off a 15-month layoff, Foreman was making his first start since his "Rumble in the Jungle" in Kinshasa, Zaire. He stopped Lyle in the fourth round, and then defeated three lesser opponents en route to a fight with Jimmy Young in San Juan. A "cutie" from Philadelphia with a 20–5–2 record, Young's main claim to fame was that he had gone 15 rounds with Muhammad Ali, losing a razor-thin decision in what was expected to be an Ali cakewalk.

Inexplicably lethargic, Foreman was out-pointed by Young. In his dressing room after the fight, he experienced an epiphany. Akin to the bare-knuckle bruiser Bendigo, he renounced the world of the prize ring and set out, Bible in hand, to spread the gospel of the New Testament.

The Foreman-Young fight was framed as an eliminator. The prize for the victor was a rematch with Muhammad Ali. But Don King reneged on the deal and thrust Young into a second eliminator against Ken Norton. On November 5, 1977, Norton defeated Young by split decision at Caesars Palace. World Boxing Council president Jose Sulaiman promptly decreed that Ali must fight Norton within six months or his title would be stripped.

Ali was in attendance, openly cheering for Young. While he had no inclination to fight Young again, Ali was more chagrined at the prospect of fighting Norton, who had extended him the full distance in all three of their previous engagements, breaking his jaw in the first encounter. Ali knew that he would still be recognized as the people's champion if he countermanded Sulaiman's edict, which held no sway with the World Boxing Association, the older of the two organizations.[1]

Ali's disinclination to renew hostilities with Norton played into the hands of Bob Arum, who offered Ali an alternative in Leon Spinks. A gold medalist at 178 pounds in the Montreal Olympiad, Spinks was one of several fighters from the 1976 U.S. team to launch his pro career under Arum's Top Rank banner. His first pro fight, staged in Las Vegas at the Aladdin Theatre for the Performing Arts, was nationally televised with Olympic teammate Sugar Ray Leonard providing the color commentary.

Leon Spinks had only six pro fights under his belt when the match was proposed and was coming off a draw with journeyman Scott LeDoux. The WBA could not certify Ali-Spinks as a title fight unless Spinks achieved a Top 10 ranking, which dictated that he defeat a ranked opponent. Arum chose Alfio Righetti to play the role of the stepping-stone. A traffic policeman in Rimini, Italy, Righetti was not quite in Leon's league despite his 27–0 pro record. On November 18, 1977, in a relatively close fight, Spinks won a 10-round decision from Righetti in the first boxing event in the new sports pavilion at the Las Vegas Hilton.

Arum had carved out a multi-fight deal with the Hilton that spelled competition for Caesars Palace and was indicative of the fact that boxing in the city had taken a new turn. The early Convention Center fights were promoted as communal events. Casino operators were encouraged to support them as a token of civic-mindedness. In the souvenir programs, there were advertisements for taverns, bookie joints, jewelry shops, and other locally owned businesses. Now major casinos were corralling fights for their own narrow benefit.

Twenty-five days before the Ali-Spinks dust-up, Caesars Palace hosted a fight between Roberto Duran and Esteban De Jesus. It was the fourth meeting between the dynamic lightweights. The suspenseful fight was stopped in the twelfth stanza moments after Duran unhinged his Puerto Rican adversary with a picture-perfect right hand. The event—the first universally recognized world championship fight on the grounds of a Las Vegas gambling resort—attracted a lusty, flag-waving crowd fairly evenly divided in its allegiance. The atmosphere inside the arena was supercharged and the noise was deafening.

This contrasted starkly with the last big ballpark fight, the Ali-Norton rubber match at Yankee Stadium on September 29, 1976. The event was shrouded by a labor dispute between the city and the police union. Outside the stadium, there were squabbles between picketing off-duty cops and colleagues working the event. In this chaotic environment, there were numerous purse snatchings — acts described by a police spokesman as the work of feral children. Out-of-towners sheltered from the lawlessness were still exposed to the eyesore of the Bronx as they were motored to the fight. The area around the stadium had become badly decayed. The bout was a nail-biter — dead even on two scorecards after 14 rounds — but yet rather tame, and the enthusiasm of the crowd was blunted by a chilly breeze. Since the days of Tex Rickard, New York was considered the optimal location for a major fight, in part because the city had the best attractions for the female companions of sporting men, notably great places to shop. But as New York City lost its luster, Las Vegas became a relatively more attractive destination. The shopping was inferior by a New York yardstick, a situation that would change dramatically, but the entertainment was top-shelf and Las Vegas had the added amenity of sunbathing nearly year-round. Both "push" and "pull" factors were changing the ecological dynamic.

Ali vs. Spinks was roundly lampooned. The certification of the contest as a championship match stoked the disapprobation. Now 36 years of age, Ali was ripe for the taking, but presumably not by a fighter as unschooled as Spinks. Moreover, there was scant reason to think that Leon would have an edge if the bout turned into a test of stamina. A notorious night owl, he was known to order a beer with his breakfast. In the handicapping of the match, the shadow of Pete Rademacher loomed large, but a more popular school of thought was that Ali would toy with Spinks until, through his own carelessness, his pride was wounded, whereupon he would get serious and terminate matters in a hurry, akin to Jack Johnson's fight with Stanley Ketchel.

As a sop to his critics, Arum braced the match with an ambitious undercard. The list of preliminary fighters included such notables as British middleweight champion Alan Minter, featherweight titlist Danny "Little Red" Lopez, top-rated lightheavyweight contender Eddie "The Flame" Gregory, Michael Spinks, and Gerry Cooney, a hot heavyweight prospect who was developing a cult following. All were victorious, as was Leon Spinks, who sprung the biggest upset in a heavyweight title fight since Braddock defeated Baer, upending Ali by a split decision. The verdict was controversial only because almost everyone thought it should have been unanimous.

Spinks came from a terrible place, the squalid Pruitt-Igoe housing project in St. Louis. An ex–Marine with three young children, he was a classic rags-to-riches story, but reporters did not write favorably of him. A poor vocabulary, a bad appearance — he was missing his upper front teeth — a happy-go-lucky disposition, a lackadaisical approach to paying bills, and a propensity for missing appointments branded him a knucklehead. There was no sympathy for Leon when half of his crown was stripped from his head, ending his reign as the *undisputed* champion after only six weeks.

Jose Sulaiman, who hadn't yet come to be seen as a puppet of Don King, had backed down on his threat to strip Ali of his title, but with the proviso that Ali fight Norton next. The shocking upset compounded the anarchy. Arum immediately set about making a rematch. Judging the WBC blessing superfluous, he left Sulaiman out of the loop. Sulaiman countered by retroactively anointing the Norton-Young fight a title match, thereby making Norton the heavyweight champion by fiat. In his first defense of the WBC title, Norton was made to fight Larry Holmes, a King-controlled fighter from Easton, Pennsylvania.

Norton had heightened his high profile with a smashing knockout of Duane Bobick in a bout at Madison Square Garden. An Olympic boxer from a small town in Minnesota, Bobick had forged a 61-fight winning streak during his amateur days and was 38–0 as a professional.

Fighting under the management of Joe Frazier's syndicate, he was much more than a generic White Hope, or so everyone thought until Norton blew him away in 58 seconds.

Coming up the ladder, Larry Holmes was lightly regarded. His brief amateur career was marred by a loss to Bobick and he was routinely identified as a former Ali sparring partner, a designation that carried the implication that he was run-of-the-mill. But in his 27th pro fight, he turned heads with a virtuoso performance against Earnie Shavers, a knockout artist who had starched 20 opponents in the opening stanza. Summing the scorecards, Holmes won 35 of the 36 rounds.

Staged on June 9, 1978, Norton vs. Holmes was such a hot ticket that a Caesars Palace ballroom was converted into an annex for closed-circuit viewing. By all accounts, this was the first instance of a closed-circuit theater bobbing up under the same roof where the telecast originated.

The general public favored Norton, a 13/10 favorite, but most of the smart money was on the 28-year-old challenger. Holmes's showing against Shavers was full of positive omens. He had exhibited great stamina, an iron chin, and most conspicuously a caustic jab, his signature punch, the effectiveness of which was enhanced by his 81-inch reach. There was also the general feeling that Holmes would be the hungrier fighter. He was only a few years removed from driving a delivery truck, a job he began full-time when others his age were high school underclassmen. Norton had an acting career to fall back on.

Norton vs. Holmes was a humdinger. Through 14 rounds, the bout was even on all three scorecards. Both fighters appeared to sense that winning the last round was imperative and cranked up the intensity. Holmes got the best of it, although one of the judges saw it differently. No fighter ever began a long and illustrious title reign with such a hard fight.

Holmes made seven successful defenses in the next 25 months, all but two at Caesars Palace. Those wins, however, did little to enhance his stature with casual fans. His opponents were unexceptional and Muhammad Ali, who had avenged his loss to Leon Spinks, was still rated the top dog, notwithstanding his insistence that he had hung up his gloves for good.

Unfortunately, Ali would fall prey to the siren song that lures so many great fighters back to the squared circle after their well has run dry. Muhammad Ali vs. Larry Holmes would be a grand spectacle without precedent in Las Vegas boxing. Portended by events of increasing magnitude — tremors on the local boxing seismographic — this was the big bang.

It was all of this only because Ali was one of the principals. To better appreciate his magnetism, let's briefly chronicle his tumultuous career using his Las Vegas fights as avenues of ingress.

**Larry Holmes circa 1992. A great champion, Holmes was underappreciated.**

## Duke Sabedong (June 26, 1961)

Cassius Marcellus Clay had six pro fights under his belt when he headlined a card at the Las Vegas Convention Center. In the opposite corner was Kolo "Duke" Sabedong, a six-foot-six Hawaiian garbed with a 15–8 record after four of his losses were erased from the press release. Clay tattooed him with an assortment of punches, but Sabedong stayed upright the whole while. An estimated three thousand were in attendance.

At the 1960 Olympics in Rome, Clay had charmed reporters with his wide-eyed wonderment and effervescent personality. He was the unofficial mayor of Olympic Village. In Las Vegas, his comportment was no less beguiling.

This was his first scheduled 10-rounder. Of greater import, he was inspired during his visit to adopt a more flamboyant persona. The impetus was a wrestling card that he attended as a favor for promoters Mel Greb and Jack Doyle. The marquee match paired Gorgeous George against Fred Blassie. Reporters had already begun calling him the "Louisville Lip," but the loquacious teenager kicked his act up a notch after watching the audience go bonkers over the histrionics of Gorgeous George.

## Floyd Patterson (November 22, 1965)

When he next appeared in a Las Vegas ring, Ali was far more famous and far more controversial. In notable events during the interim, he stopped venerable Archie Moore in four rounds, predicting the exact round of Moore's demise in a slab of his poetry, sold out Madison Square Garden during a newspaper strike for a bout with lusterless Doug Jones, made new fans and enemies in London where he cut Henry Cooper to ribbons, and twice defeated Sonny Liston, winning and retaining the world heavyweight title. The first Ali-Liston fight was held at the Miami Beach Convention Center and the second in the rink of a recreation center run by Dominican priests in Lewiston, Maine.[2]

Ali's bout with Jones marked his first appearance in a New York ring. Despite advantages in height, weight, and reach, he made a poor showing, winning by a 1-point margin on two of the scorecards. Based on this effort, Nat Fleischer judged that he was at least two years away from making a credible showing against Liston. "He could no more stop Liston than the old red barn could impede a tornado," opined *The Ring* oracle in advance of their first meeting.[3] Most of the boxing writers shared this assessment. Forty-three of 46 picked Liston in the UPI survey, an unprecedented degree of deviation.

As he was preparing for this fight, there were rumbles that he had joined the Nation of Islam, an Islamic sect founded by Elijah Muhammad, a sect viewed by much of white America as a Ku Klux Klan in blackface. Ali officially confirmed the rumor at the post-fight press conference, a bombshell that fractured his fan base. In conformance with Elijah Muhammad's dictate, he reluctantly abandoned his birth name, calling it a slave name. Long after he legally adopted the name Muhammad Ali, reporters continued to call him Cassius Clay. (The original Cassius Marcellus Clay was an anti-slavery activist who served as Abraham Lincoln's ambassador to Russia.)

On his first visit to Las Vegas, Ali had been as convivial as a politician on the stump. This time he was all business, keeping strangers at a distance behind a posse of unsmiling bodyguards. His afternoon workouts at the Stardust Hotel were open to the public for a $1 donation, but he was quick to leave the premises at the end of these sessions. Ali and his entourage stayed in a block of adjoining rooms at a small non-gaming hotel called the El Morocco, a place that afforded greater privacy.

Patterson had scored five wins since his encounters with Sonny Liston. Although his reputation had been scarred beyond repair, he remained one of America's best-liked athletes. He referred to Ali as Cassius Clay, but in a manner that suggested an oversight rather than a slur. Ali, a 7/2 favorite, vowed to punish him for this discourtesy and was a man of his word.

There were times when Patterson was almost out, but Ali prolonged his torment. The referee finally halted the match in the 12th round. The mood inside the arena was made more uncheerful by tight security. An estimated 100 members of the Nation of Islam stood watch, providing ballast, as it were, for a large detail of hired security guards who were viewed by the Muslims with suspicion. As a sidebar, a rainstorm forced an early closure of the airport, stranding many invited guests in Los Angeles. Elizabeth Taylor and her husband Richard Burton were among the celebrity no-shows.

## Jerry Quarry (June 27, 1972)

The Muhammad Ali saga took many twists and turns in the six-and-a-half year chasm that separated his second and third Las Vegas fights. After thrashing Patterson, Ali had had four consecutive bouts outside the United States, defending his title in Toronto, London twice, and Frankfurt. He had two fights at the Houston Astrodome, each witnessed by more than 35,000, establishing and breaking the attendance record for a boxing event at an indoor venue. On April 22, 1967, he knocked out Zora Folley at Madison Square Garden. Six days later, within hours after Ali disobeyed an order to step forward for classification at an Army induction center in Houston, the New York Boxing Commission suspended his license, igniting a spasm of suspensions in other jurisdictions. Ten days after this commotion, Ali was indicted for draft evasion by a federal grand jury. He remained free while the case was on appeal, but was prohibited from traveling outside the country.

In his exile, at least the early portion of it, Ali was the most reviled athlete — perhaps the most reviled man — in America. In the eyes of the many, he was both a segregationist and a traitor. His famous pronouncement "I ain't got no quarrel with them Viet Cong" was made more unpalatable by the trappings of his wealth: stretch limousines, airplane flights in private planes, lodging in penthouse suites.

During his banishment, Ali appeared frequently on TV and radio talk shows, lectured at dozens of colleges and universities, briefly starred in an off-Broadway play, and filmed his simulated fight with Rocky Marciano. Tempering his militancy with humor, Ali was a smash on the college lecture circuit, particularly at elite schools where he was embraced as an anti-establishment hero. Students with no interest in boxing became keenly interested in Ali, indirectly oxygenating boxing in general, at least in the United States, where the sport's adherents were becoming increasingly older than the national average.

Ali eventually won his appeal for conscientious objector status. In a separate action, he triumphed over the New York Boxing Commission, which was reprimanded for acting capriciously and contrary to law in rescinding his license. His 43-month furlough from boxing ended on October 26, 1970, when he met Jerry Quarry in Atlanta. That bout and his next match with Argentina's Oscar Bonavena were tune-ups for the big showdown with the man who had "stolen" his crown during his expatriation, Joe Frazier. Billed as the first bout in history between undefeated heavyweight champions, Ali vs. Frazier was a classic bull-and-

The repartee between Howard Cosell and Muhammad Ali was great theater. This 1965 photograph was taken at the WABC radio studio. *New York World Telegram and Sun/Library of Congress/History Image.*

matador confrontation cunningly steeped in metaphor. Staged at Madison Square Garden on March 8, 1971, the bout was witnessed by millions at closed-circuit venues where advance sellouts were the norm.

Contested at a furious pace, the match was hugely crowd-pleasing, although there was little uncertainty about the verdict after Frazier knocked Ali down with a frightful left hook in the 15th round, a punch that almost instantaneously afflicted Ali with what appeared to be a severe case of the mumps. The great fight was an even greater spectacle. The SRO crowd was studded with celebrities and "peacocks" whose outrageous sense of fashion added glitter to the fanfaronade. Writing in the next day's *New York Times*, longtime columnist Arthur Daley wrote that the epic "was worth every glorious, heartbreaking penny." Pete Hamill, who covered the bout for *Harper's Bazaar*, called it the most spectacular event in sports history.

Ali's advisers were in no hurry to line up a rematch. The fight was the sort that shortens a man's career and a string of easy wins would soothe his hurt while ratcheting up his popularity. The road to a rematch wended through Houston, Zurich, Tokyo, Vancouver, and then Las Vegas, where the opponent was old foe Jerry Quarry.

In his amateur days, Quarry was special. In 1965, he set a National Golden Gloves Tournament record by winning all five of his fights by knockout. But Quarry had the misfortune to arrive on the scene during the Golden Era of heavyweights. He had a treacherous left hook and boundless courage, but wasn't as big or as quick as the top heavyweights of his generation. He had been badly cut in his first skirmish with Ali, forcing the fight to be stopped after only three rounds, but Ali, with his superior reflexes, had landed many more punches. Aware that Quarry's pigmentation and strong regional following were insufficient to generate a strong gate, Bob Arum noosed the rematch with a somewhat more intriguing contest between lightheavyweight champion Bob Foster and undefeated Mike Quarry (36–0), Jerry's younger brother. Foster was being positioned as a future opponent of Ali.

To the delight of autograph hounds, Ali's comportment in Las Vegas was in marked contrast to his behavior preceding the Patterson fight. He conducted his public workouts at Caesars Palace but made several trips to the Tropicana to good-naturedly heckle the Quarry brothers at their afternoon sparring sessions. His Nation of Islam phalanx was smaller and stayed in the background. As expected, Ali, a 5/1 favorite, had no trouble with Quarry, stopping him in the seventh round. Mike Quarry, the youngest man to fight for the lightheavyweight title, was likewise overmatched. Foster knocked him unconscious in the fourth stanza.

## Joe Bugner (February 14, 1973)

Eight months after the Quarry fight, Ali — with three more wins now affixed to his ledger — returned to Las Vegas to fight European heavyweight champion Joe Bugner. At six-foot-three and 220 pounds, the 22-year-old Bugner (43–4–1) was considerably bigger than Jerry Quarry, but reputedly slower, suggesting that he was an English-Hungarian incarnation of Duke Sabedong. Ali was installed a 7/1 favorite. The odds were 4/1 against the fight going the full 12 rounds.

Ali won a clear-cut decision, but Bugner was never hurt and his stock rose considerably. After the fight, Ali said that he planned to fight Joe Frazier again, and would then retire. He predicted that once he took his leave, Bugner would rise to the top.

## Ron Lyle (May 16, 1975)

Barely six weeks after defeating Bugner, Ali was out-pointed by Ken Norton in Norton's adopted hometown of San Diego. Reporters interpreted this as a sign that Ali was near the end of the trail, but that appraisal was premature. Ali turned the tables in a rematch with Norton and achieved mythical status the following year with victories over Frazier and George Foreman.

The second Ali-Frazier fight at Madison Sqaure Garden drew a crowd of 20,758 and a gate of $1,053,688, breaking the arena records for a non-title fight. As in the first encounter, the crowd was overwhelmingly pro–Ali. The fight was not imbued with the same aura as the first meeting, but was every bit as robust, albeit three rounds shorter. A 7/5 favorite, Ali won a unanimous decision.

Ali's stock gimmick was the Ali Shuffle, which he unveiled in a 1966 bout at the Astrodome against Cleveland Williams. Robert Lipsyte described the affectation as a Mexican hat dance on a waterwheel. In his bout with Foreman, he unveiled his next great artifice, the Rope-a-Dope. Using his arms as a shield, Ali lay on the ropes and — against the protestations of his horrified cornermen — invited Foreman to flail away, occasionally answering

Foreman's punches with a volley of swift jabs, but basically biding his time until Foreman had punched himself out. Near the end of the eighth round, Ali seized the initiative, knocking Foreman off his pins with a swift combination. Foreman, a 7/2 favorite, rose on unsteady legs but was unable to beat the count.

Roundly out-pointed in an earlier fight with Jerry Quarry, Ron Lyle wasn't considered in Ali's league, but his history of violence outside the ring imbued the match with a thin layer of intrigue. One of 19 children born to deeply religious parents, Lyle had suffered a near-fatal stabbing while serving a 7½-year hitch in the Colorado State Penitentiary for murder. He was facing domestic battery charges (subsequently dropped) that augured another long prison stretch. The angle for the publicists was that Lyle had nothing to lose by throwing caution to the wind.

This was not one of Ali's stronger efforts. Fighting without passion, he was trailing on the scorecards when he hit Lyle with a big right hand in the 11th frame. Ali quickly went for the kill, pummeling Lyle until referee Ferd Hernandez threw himself between the fighters to stop the mill.

## Leon Spinks (February 15, 1978)

A mere six weeks after defeating Ron Lyle, Ali was back in action against Joe Bugner in Kuala Lampur, Malaysia. The sturdy Bugner was more passive than in the first meeting, seemingly content to last the distance. Because the fight was so tame, there was speculation that the next fight on Ali's docket, a rubber match with Joe Frazier, would likewise be a disappointment. To the contrary, the "Thrilla in Manila" was a hypnotically savage bout. Ali absorbed terrific punishment but was ahead on the scorecards when Frazier's corner threw in the towel following the 14th round.

In common with most great champions, Ali was constantly avouching that his next fight would be his last. Many of his admirers now clamored for him to make good on his promise and let the "Thrilla" be the capstone of his legacy. Ali ignored the admonition and had six more fights before his encounter with Spinks. The most ballyhooed was his Yankee Stadium rubber match with Ken Norton. As in their second meeting, Ali skirted defeat by winning the final round, but the decision was controversial.

Hard-core boxing fans cared less about the Ali-Spinks fight than about the forthcoming fight between Norton and Larry Holmes, but Ali had become such an icon of pop culture that his fight with Spinks attracted more advance ink. The significance of Ali-Spinks for Las Vegas was that it was the first boxing event to attract a horde of writers from large-circulation magazines that did not regularly cover sports. The most obtrusive person on press row was gonzo journalist Hunter Thompson, the eccentric wordsmith for *Rolling Stone*.

## Larry Holmes (October 2, 1980)

Ali was more insistent than ever that he would walk away from boxing following a rematch with Spinks. Nearly 70,000 turned out for his "final recital" at the Louisiana Superdome and an estimated 75 million tuned in on ABC. What they got was a mediocre fight that was yet great drama. Fighting methodically against an uninspired opponent, Ali scored a unanimous decision, becoming the first three-time heavyweight champion. Although Ali went to post a

2/1 favorite, he was symbolically the underdog because he was fighting a much younger man and fighting the ghosts of legendary champions who had failed in similar situations. Moreover, surveys of knowledgeable boxing insiders had shown a pronounced preference for Spinks.

Ali retired with a 56–3 record that included a 5–0 mark in rematches against the only three men to defeat him, but he did not retire as champion in that corner of the universe inhabited by Don King and the World Boxing Council. In that corner, the champion was Larry Holmes. Pressure began to build on Ali to come back and humble his former sparring partner.

Ali had other options if he chose to fight again. Arum pestered him to fight WBA title-holder John Tate, and then pushed for a fight with Mike Weaver after Tate lost to Weaver in his first title defense. However, the inarticulate Tate had no drawing power and Weaver, a late-blooming Adonis with a soft beard, was not a compelling opponent because of his 22–9 record. Ali had no interest in any match that was not a surefire blockbuster, and that eliminated everyone but Holmes. Caesars Palace wanted the fight, but there was one major stumbling block. Although the live gate would be dwarfed by closed-circuit revenue, the fight was yet too big for the Sports Pavilion. Indeed, Ali vs. Holmes had the earmarks of such a huge attraction that there were talks about holding it at Maracana Stadium in Rio de Janeiro, a facility built to accommodate a crowd of 180,000.

To get the fight, Caesars Palace built a temporary 25,000-seat stadium in its parking lot. The arena would be almost completely sold out before the carpenters nailed the last board in place.

Although he was the challenger, Ali reportedly received an $8.5 million guarantee versus $3.5 million for Holmes. The $8.5 million was spent on damaged goods.

Ali had only 59 professional fights, but had answered the bell for 515 full or partial rounds. Of those rounds, 347 had come after his exile when his reflexes were slower, at first only a millisecond slower, but the start of an inexorable decline. He had also fought hundreds of rounds in the gym. In an interview that ran in the November 1975 *Playboy*, Ali said: "I let my sparring partners beat on me about eighty percent of the time. I go on the defense and take a couple of hits to the head and body, which is good: You gotta condition your body and brain to take those shots." That interview was conducted while he was preparing for his third bout with Frazier, a battle in which he absorbed 440 punches, many of them vicious left hooks. Eight more fights would precede his showdown with Larry Holmes; six of them went 15 rounds.

Behaving as if his brain were a muscle rather than an intricate circuit board encased in a thin shell, Ali was clearly a prime candidate for pugilistic dementia. Worse, there were clear signs that the mutation had already begun.

Buffalo sportswriter Steve Weller sounded an early alarm. Observing that the steam had evaporated from Ali's bluster, Weller wrote: "His pronunciamentos are delivered in the slow, slightly slurred monotone of a man worn out by his profession." At this point, Ali vs. Holmes was still in the rumor stage. Nearly 14 months would pass before the fight became a reality.

In the summer of 1980, after the contracts were signed, Dr. Ferdie Pacheco, formerly Ali's personal physician, went public with his information. "Slurred speech, blood in the urine, slowness in reacting to questions, mumbling, all are already appearing," Pacheco told reporters, adding that the damage was irreversible and accelerating with age.[4]

Although Ali's workouts were lackluster, lending credence to the notion that his reflexes were shot, there were times when he was as loquacious and playful as ever, and he was always cocksure that he would win the fight. His positive attitude was contagious. Those in his entourage knew that was taking a prescribed drug to burn off the suet that flabbed his torso, and some of them chose to believe that it was the medication that was making him occasionally dopey and that he would recapture his vigor as soon as he stopped taking it.

At the El Cortez, venerated Brownsville-born oddsmaker Bob Martin opened Holmes a 5/2 favorite. A publicist there drew up a press release inviting Ali to come down and bet on himself, to put up or shut up. The release said that Ali was welcome to bet a million dollars provided that he made the wager in person.

Pacheco avouched that Ali had only two chances: "if Holmes drops from a sudden diabetic coma or if the fight is fixed." Prominent sports gambler Lem Banker, then writing a weekly column for the *Review-Journal,* declared that a bet on Holmes was one of the top investments of the decade. Nonetheless, the betting would be tilted against the undefeated (35–0) Holmes, a fighter in the prime of his career. By one estimate, the sports books in Las Vegas wrote 30 tickets on Ali for every one ticket on Holmes. The larger bets were on Holmes, but the weight of all the small bets depressed the odds from 5/2 to 7/5.

The lemming-like stampede bore witness that Ali in his pugilistic dotage had taken on the nimbus of a comic book superhero. This was true in the literal sense. In 1978, Ali defeated Superman in the pages of a tabloid-sized, special edition D.C. comic. (After their match, Ali and Superman joined forces to vanquish alien invaders, saving the planet from destruction.) It would be supercilious to think that anyone betting serious money was influenced by the comic book or the humbug of Ali's trainer, Angelo Dundee — "my guy will win because he's not an ordinary earthling" — but the overall effect was to reinforce an opinion expressed by UPI sportswriter Milton Richman: "If there's a way to win, he'll find it. He's the most adroit, most resourceful, and most inventive individual at devising ways and means to come out on top that I have ever run into in the entire realm of sports."

A development that definitely impacted the betting line was rampant speculation of skullduggery. While murmurs of a fix almost always accompany a heavyweight megafight, the murmurs were particularly loud in this instance. British scribe Hugh McIlvanney recalled the mood in the preface to his 1982 anthology: "The bars of Las Vegas were brimming with characters who knew that arrangements had been made for Muhammad Ali to defeat Larry Holmes, and those of us who argued that Ali had no chance were regarded as bumpkins who should be humoured."

A final dose of hokum was injected into the promotion with the news that Ali planned to undergo hypnosis before entering the ring. The hypnotherapy — which supposedly would improve Ali's concentration and suppress fatigue (mind over matter) — was to be administered by Jimmy Grippo, the unofficial court jester at Caesars Palace. A renowned magician, Grippo was a long-time pal of Ali, a relationship rooted in Ali's fascination with sleight-of-hand tricks. No stranger to boxing, the 86-year-old Grippo had once owned a stable of fighters, the ranks of which included Melio Bettina, briefly a lightheavyweight champion. Known to a tight circle of friends as an astute fight prognosticator, Grippo's involvement actually discomfited some of the sharp bettors who were poised to bet big on Holmes when the odds stabilized.

After the bout, Grippo's friends would tease him that he had forgotten the buzzword for deactivating the trance, levity that did little to erase the bad memory of Ali's pathetic effort. Early in the fight, Ali did his Shuffle and his Rope-a-Dope and the crowd responded with laughter and applause, confident that his posturing was contrived as the prelude to a Garrison finish, but the cheers turned to jeers when it became plain that Ali was too parched to switch gears into an offensive mode. He retired on his stool to a chorus of boos after ten dreary frames without winning a round or landing a meaningful punch. Reminiscent of the backlash to Jim Jeffries' inept showing against Jack Johnson, the press turned on Ali viciously. It was as if he had purposely set out to defraud the public.

The fight was a charade, but not by design. Ali was fighting something more insidious than Father Time. More than a solid investment, a bet on Holmes was a lead-pipe cinch. Incredibly, Ali fought yet one more time, losing a 10-round decision to Trevor Berbick in Nassau, the Bahamas.[5]

Although Holmes vs. Ali was a sad and sordid affair, the promotion was a smash from the beancounters' perspective. Staged on a Thursday, the event artificially induced a four-day holiday weekend that energized the entire city. On the day of the fight, every hotel on the Strip was reportedly sold out. Up and down the boulevard, hotels sought to rope in fight-goers with boxing-themed allurements. The free midafternoon "lounge show" at the Frontier was a documentary movie about the life of Rocky Marciano. The gaiety had a fairgrounds flavor and everyone seemingly had a good time until the timekeeper hit the gong to signal the start of the fight and ruined everything.

The extravaganza begat a series of big outdoor fights in Las Vegas, elevating the erstwhile tank town into the fight capital of the world. Overshadowed in the tumult was the advent of a new game at the host property that accelerated a boom of a different sort. On the day before the big fight, Caesars Palace got the green light from the Nevada Gaming Commission to accept wagers on sporting events and began taking bets at a hastily erected kiosk in a pedestrian corridor. The bare-bones setup was the forerunner of the plush Olympiad Race and Sports Book. In short order, the old freestanding bookie joints fell by the wayside. While there were larger contributing factors, the big fights hastened the growth and glamorization of sports betting in Las Vegas.

# CHAPTER 18

# Parking Lot Extravaganzas

As Muhammad Ali entered the twilight of his career, reporters were in general accord that the sport would wither without him. But when Ali finally let the final curtain fall, it was clear that his sport would survive quite nicely, at least in the short run. The heavyweight division was bereft of charismatic personalities, but a stylish welterweight named Sugar Ray Leonard had developed a rabid following and boxing was enjoying a renaissance on television.

Once scorned as the scourge of boxing, television had come to be seen as the savior — inflating purses, enhancing the fame and magnetism of the top competitors, and nurturing the soil as every TV card was underpinned with off–TV preliminaries, ensuring a steady stream of fresh faces. Moreover, television was evolving into a multi-tiered medium. A new subscription channel, the Entertainment Sports Programming Network (ESPN), was sponsoring a series of tournaments for up-and-comers, top-shelf fighters were accorded major network exposure, and bouts of major importance were aired on closed-circuit. The stratification harked back to the days when fighters started out at neighborhood clubs, the most talented advancing to Madison Square Garden and from there to a big fight in a ballpark.

Ray Charles "Sugar Ray" Leonard was a wonderful fighter, but his rapid ascent to big-money bouts was a product of fortuitous timing. He came to the fore at the 1976 Montreal Olympics, where he won the gold medal in the 140-pound class. Because Montreal was in the Eastern Time Zone, ABC was able to televise more events as they were happening at hours when large numbers of television sets were in use. When he entered the pro ranks, the division in which he competed was bubbling with talented performers, several of whom were on the same career plane.

Five U.S. boxers won gold medals at the 1976 Olympiad. The Most Outstanding Boxer award went to Long Island lightweight Howard Davis, Jr., but Leonard acquired a larger following. Boyishly handsome, he was more photogenic. He competed with a picture of his girlfriend taped to one of his boxing shoes, a gesture that endeared him to women of all ages. Well spoken, personable, and intuitively media-savvy, he also made for good interviews. He seemed sincere when he maintained that he would quit boxing as soon as he had enough money to buy his parents a better home and pay for his college education. He did not have what some sports fans may have considered the preferred pigmentation, but otherwise Sugar Ray was a publicist's dream — a baby-faced assassin with old-fashioned virtues to boot.

In his first pro fight, Leonard scored a 6-round decision over Luis Vega at the Baltimore Civic Center. The fight was nationally televised. Leonard's $40,000 purse was the highest ever for a fighter making his pro debut.

With Angelo Dundee on board as a matchmaker and apple-polisher (a trainer who turns up in the final days before the fight), Leonard progressed swiftly. After only thirteen pro fights, he was pitted against a ranked opponent, Floyd Mayweather. He passed this test with flying colors, scoring a ninth-round TKO. In his next bout, he easily out-pointed Randy Shields, the last man to defeat him as an amateur. In the summer of 1979, he headlined three cards at Caesars Palace, demonstrating increased power with quick stoppages of worthy opponents. That bumped him into a match with welterweight titlist Wilfred Benitez. Staged at the Caesars Palace Sports Pavilion on November 30, 1979, the fight — conjoined with a middleweight title bout between Marvin Hagler and Vito Antuofermo — was an immediate sellout.

**Sugar Ray Leonard (1989).** *Top Rank file photograph.*

A Bronx-born Puerto Rican, Benitez won his first title at age 17, wresting a junior welterweight belt from 86-fight veteran Antonio Cervantes. He was still eight months shy of his 21st birthday when he added a welterweight diadem to his dossier, out-pointing Carlos Palomino. A successful defense against Harold Weston, who had held him to a draw in an earlier encounter, prefaced his Las Vegas showdown with Sugar Ray.

Benitez (38–0–1) had never tasted defeat, but his reputation as a party animal seemed to portend a short career. Leonard, the challenger, older but less experienced, was a solid 7/2 favorite. Too slick for Benitez, Sugar Ray was leading by a comfortable margin when the referee curiously stopped the 15-round contest with only six seconds remaining. Leonard advanced his record to 26–0.

The pelt of the *wunderkind* Benitez — the youngest man ever to win a world title — was a plum acquisition, but a more prestigious belt was shimmering in the background. Roberto Duran had relinquished his lightweight title after twelve successful title defenses to campaign as a welterweight. Nicknamed "Manos de Piedras" (Hands of Stone), Duran boasted a 71–1 record and had twice avenged his only defeat. Not yet 30 years old, he was already hailed in some quarters as the best lightweight since Benny Leonard and in other quarters as the best lightweight ever, bar none.

Leonard vs. Duran was compelling because of their contrasting styles, but more so because of their contrasting personalities. Sugar Ray was perceived to be a reluctant warrior, fighting only as a means to an end and only because he had been gifted with a special talent that a man his size could not profitably channel into other athletic endeavors. Duran, raised by a single mother in the worst slum in Panama City, was a street fighter by nature, a man of seemingly boundless pugnacity. Unschooled and vulgar, Duran needed no prodding to participate in the obligatory exchange of insults that were prologues to all of his big fights. When a reporter asked Leonard a question about his wife, the girlfriend of his amateur days, Duran threw in his two cents, calling her a *puta* (prostitute).

Bob Arum planted the Leonard-Duran fight at Montreal's Olympic Stadium, the venue associated with the greatest day in the history of U.S. amateur boxing. The event drew 46,317, an all-time high for a boxing show in Canada.

A 3/2 favorite, Leonard went quickly on the attack. Duran was able to sidestep his rushes and smother him against the ropes. In the very first round, Duran hurt him with a left hook to the liver. An overhand right dazed Leonard in Round 2, and from there Sugar Ray had an uphill struggle. He was the busier man in the late rounds, but Duran garnered the decision, winning unanimously by an aggregate four points. (One of the judges, an Italian, scored ten rounds even.) Duran returned to Panama a national hero. Schools, banks, and government offices were ordered shut on the day of his homecoming parade.

Leonard was faulted for fighting a stupid fight, sacrificing lateral movement to get more leverage behind his punches, but in defeat he dispelled any questions about his fighting heart. Neither man had an intervening fight before renewing hostilities at the Louisiana Superdome on November 25, 1980.

In the rematch, Leonard held a 1-point lead on all three cards through seven rounds. In Round 8, Duran inexplicably stopped fighting, uttering the words, *"No mas"* as he turned back to his corner, waving his right glove in a gesture of disgust. Whether afflicted by cramps or simply flustered by Sugar Ray's windmill combinations and uncharacteristic showboating, Duran had done the unthinkable, branding himself a quitter.

In his next fight, Leonard defended his title with a 10th-round stoppage of Larry Bonds at the Syracuse Carrier Dome. Then it was on to the Houston Astrodome, where he assumed the role of the challenger in a match with 154-pound titlist Ayub Kalule, an undefeated Ugandan based in Copenhagen. Leonard stopped Kalule in the ninth frame. Although this was a title fight, it was also a tune-up for the showdown brewing with a fighter showcased on the undercard. A Detroiter born in Memphis, his name was Thomas Hearns.

Detroit had a lattice of neighborhood recreation centers named for the councilmen in whose districts the centers were built. In an earlier era, most of the good black fighters in the city bubbled out of Brewster, the rec center that spawned Joe Louis and Hall of Fame trainer Eddie Futch. Hearns lived closer to the after-school activities center named after councilman John Kronk. It was there at the age of 14 that he was introduced to boxing by Emanuel Steward, an electrician by trade and former National Golden Gloves champion who moonlighted as a $35 per week boxing instructor.

With long skinny arms and pipe-stem legs, the six-foot-one Hearns had the appearance of a praying mantis. But his beanstalk physique was deceptive, as he was a terrific hitter, boasting one-punch knockout power. He brought a 28–0 record into his first important contest against Isidro "Pipino" Cuevas, a veteran of eleven title bouts. Cuevas never got inside Hearns' rapier jab and was pole-axed into dreamland with a straight right hand in the waning seconds of the second round.

Staged in the outdoor stadium at Caesars Palace on Wednesday, September 16, 1981, Leonard vs. Hearns had all the grandeur of the Ali-Holmes spectacle and was a significantly larger event as measured by the betting handle. Although most sportswriters favored Sugar Ray (34 of 48 in the UPI survey), big gamblers were bunched in almost equal measure on both sides of the fence. Hearns went to post a slight favorite, but most wagers were sealed at even money.

Leonard (30–1, 21 KOs) had more plusses on the handicapping checklist. He had fought stiffer competition, was judged to be more resourceful, and was accustomed to the circus atmosphere of a big fight. Having Angelo Dundee in his corner was considered a major plus. Steward had made Kronk the most respected name in amateur boxing, but Hearns was the first of his pupils to turn pro. In contrast to Dundee, Steward was a tinhorn.

The case for Hearns (32–0, 30 KOs) was simply that he had better physical equipment. When the fighters were posed for the pre-fight face-off, old-timers were reminded of Sandy Saddler and Willie Pep. Saddler, a beanpole featherweight, was a sharpshooter with explosive power in his long, sinewy arms. Pep had taken him to school in their second meeting — "the greatest boxing exhibition I ever saw" rhapsodized the great journalist W.C. Heinz — but Saddler had won their other three meetings inside the distance, suggesting that the value lay with the so-called Motor City Hit Man.

Unlike the Ali-Holmes debacle, Leonard vs. Hearns would be a fight for the ages. His vision blurred by a puffed right eye, Leonard turned the tide with a big thirteenth round. Hearns was slumped on the ropes, his eyes glazed, when the referee rescued him at the 1:45 mark of Round 14. The discordant note was the scoring of the three Las Vegas judges. Their cards favored Hearns by margins of 2 to 4 points through the completed rounds, whereas ringside reporters were almost unanimous in their opinion that Leonard had the advantage. But this was a moot point. Sugar Ray's whirlwind finish arrested the budding brouhaha.

*Sports Illustrated* named Leonard the Sportsman of the Year, an honor previously given to only two other boxers, Ingemar Johansson (1959) and Muhammad Ali (1974). In his cover story, Frank Deford noted that Sugar Ray had deposed four title-holders in a span of only 22 months, and that these title-holders — Benitez, Duran, Kalule, and Hearns — were a combined 177–1–1 going in.

Had there been an annual award for the best sporting venue, a parking lot would have been a worthy candidate. In his three fights immediately prior to his match with Hearns, Leonard had fought in three of the four largest indoor arenas in the United States. How bizarre that these facilities were merely way stations for a more momentous event on a patch of asphalt in the Mojave Desert!

Gerry Cooney's frightful 54-second knockout of Ken Norton in a nationally televised Monday night fight was the flash that set the pins in place for the next Las Vegas megafight. To house Cooney's match with Larry Holmes, Caesars Palace commissioned a 32,000-seat stadium. .

The son of a Long Island ironworker, Cooney carried 160 pounds on a six-foot-four frame when he won his first amateur title in the sub-novice competition of the New York Golden Gloves. Prior to his demolition of Norton, his most notable wins had come at the expense of faded veterans Jimmy Young (KO 4), and Ron Lyle (KO 1). Heading into his match with Holmes, he had answered the bell for only 86 rounds in a pro career that numbered only 25 fights. However, there was something beyond his explosive left hook that seized the imagination of the public. A lantern-jawed man who now stood six-foot-six, he had a Paul Bunyan quality about him. His managers — Long Island real estate speculators Mike Jones and Dennis Rappaport — leveraged his popularity to obtain a $10 million purse — the same amount accorded Holmes, who was making his twelfth title defense.

Holmes was understandably nettled. When Cooney began reaping a rich harvest in endorsements, he was unable to hold his tongue. "I crawled before I walked," he told reporters, "Gerry Cooney jumped ahead because he's white."

Holmes' resentfulness underscored the racial subplot, which representatives of both camps took pains to downplay. But it was inevitable that the racial factor would come into play. Twenty-one years had elapsed since a white man (Ingemar Johansson) wore the heavyweight crown, and he was a flash in the pan.

The fight had to be pushed back twelve weeks when Cooney tore a muscle in his left shoulder. Qualms about the injury factored into the odds, as did Holmes' greater experience and superior athleticism, and the credentials of his handlers. Gone was long-time trainer Richie Giachetti, a Don King crony from Cleveland. In his stead, Holmes had the double-barreled counsel of 67-year-old Eddie Futch and 82-year-old Ray Arcel, grand masters who had schooled twenty-five champions between them. Cooney's chief handler Victor Valle had been mentoring boxers since 1938, but mostly on a part-time basis. Valle's only previous fighter of note was Alfredo Escalera, briefly a lightweight titlist.

Despite the longer list of theoretical edges for Holmes, bettors were overwhelmingly pro–Cooney. Reportedly, eight of every ten bets in Las Vegas were written on Cooney. The pattern was a silhouette of Holmes vs. Ali, but the betting was not as heavy and the odds did not plummet as drastically. Holmes closed a 7/5 favorite.

Holmes vs. Cooney was the first heavyweight championship match pitting undefeated fighters since Frazier-Foreman in 1973, and the first fight of this description on American soil since the first Ali-Frazier fight. The match was also a good test of a vexing question that had provoked an acrid debate many years ago: How would Jim Jeffries have fared against Jack Johnson if Big Jeff had been in his prime?

Cooney had his moments, although he was stiff in his movements and never uncorked his vaunted left hook. Mystifyingly, he directed most of his punches at Holmes' midsection. Enough landed south of the border to cause the referee to deduct three points for low blows. Game to the end, Cooney lasted until the thirteenth round, when Holmes knocked him woozy with ten unanswered punches. As Cooney was lurching into the ropes, his left glove brushed the canvas, dictating a standing 8-count. The referee had barely started the count when Valle bounded into the ring. That disqualified Cooney, but Holmes would be credited with a TKO.

Holmes was ahead on all three cards heading into Round 13, but two of the judges had him up by only two points. Contrastingly, in a UPI survey of 20 experienced newspapermen, only six awarded Cooney more than two rounds. *New York Times* columnist Dave Anderson wrote that what the judges saw was a "*pigment* of their imagination," an opinion echoed by Howard Cosell and many others.

When the fight was replayed on *ABC's Wide World of Sports*, Cooney came off better than in the newspaper summaries. The controversy quickly died, but not before the abstract Las Vegas boxing judge had become fodder for TV and nightclub comics. Peculiar scoring would continue to be an intermittent thorn in the side of Las Vegas boxing, with bad decisions by out-of-town officials tainting the local pool of judges as the casual fan often failed to make the distinction.

The official attendance was 29,214, but thousands more were present, including an international press contingent that numbered almost eight hundred. It was the largest gathering at a boxing match in the history of Nevada, and has retained that distinction. (At the Meadowlands Racetrack in New Jersey, 52,974 turned out for the closed-circuit telecast.) On the afternoon of the big battle, the walkways into Caesars Palace were a gridlock of humanity. Inside the noisy casino, where the minimum wager was $100 at the least restrictive dice and blackjack tables in the main pit, it was New Year's Eve in Times Square.

Cooney was inactive for more than two years after this setback and had only five more fights his entire career. His last bouts were in Atlantic City, where Michael Spinks and George

Foreman knocked him out in fights spaced almost three years apart. Because his managers fast-forwarded his learning curve, Cooney left the sport without knowing how good he might have been. Decades from now, historians may lump him with the cheesy white hopes of Jack Johnson's era. It will seem odd that he was the lightning rod for the most heavily attended sporting event on the Las Vegas Strip.

Expansion projects at Caesars Palace swallowed up the land needed to stage more fights in an arena as large, but the management remained strongly committed to the sport and built a permanent multi-purpose outdoor arena to house future shows. The debut show in the new arena was a lightweight title match between Ray "Boom Boom" Mancini and Duk Koo Kim.

A perpetual motion machine from Youngstown, Ohio, Mancini was a great human-interest story. His father Lenny Mancini, a barrel-chested welterweight of the World War II era, was headed toward a title match when he was drafted into the Army and sent overseas, returning with a Silver Star. The younger Mancini completed his father's journey, winning a share of the lightweight title in his twenty-fifth pro fight. The unknown Kim had never fought outside the Orient, but "Boom Boom" had such magnetism that the bout was aired live on ABC.

On the eve of the Mancini-Kim fight, Aaron Pryor successfully defended his welterweight title in a showdown with Alexis Arguello at Miami's Orange Bowl. A great ebb-and-flow fight, this tiff ended in the fourteenth stanza with Arguello so badly hurt that he lay motionless on the canvas for seven minutes. Eerily, Mancini vs. Kim was nearly a carbon. The no-name Korean was anything but a pushover, exhibiting tremendous spunk and courage until he was battered to the canvas in Round 14. But unlike Arguello, Kim never regained consciousness.

At the next meeting of the Nevada Boxing Commission, a measure was passed that elongated the break between rounds from 60 to 90 seconds. The proposal could not be implemented without the approval of the state legislature and never took flight. However, the tragedy had big repercussions. At its next annual convention, the World Boxing Council eliminated 15-round fights. The WBA and IBF followed suit in 1987. Cynics believed that these measures were TV-related. A 12-round fight could be formatted to an hour-long broadcast. However, the death of Duk Koo Kim would come to be seen as the catalyst. (Maverick organizations continued to sanction 15-round fights. In the last fight of this description on American soil, Jose Alfredo Flores out-pointed Eric Holland at a convention hall in Ruidoso, New Mexico. The date was June 7, 1997.)

At Caesars Palace, a six-month moratorium on boxing was put on hold to avoid a legal hassle with Don King, who had locked in a show featuring Mike Weaver and Michael Dokes. At stake would be Weaver's WBA heavyweight title.

Weaver vs. Dokes lasted all of 63 seconds. Habitually a slow starter, Weaver was in no imminent danger when referee Joey Curtis halted the contest, provoking angry shouts of "Fix! Fix!" that continued for a full 20 minutes after the ring had been cleared. Curtis conceded that he was spooked by the visualization of another ring fatality, but suspicions that he had an ulterior motive were attenuated six weeks later when Weaver and Dokes fought 15 rounds to a deadlock — the first draw in a heavyweight title fight in 69 years. A Las Vegas building contractor, Curtis was never permitted to work another fight.

Dokes-Weaver II, coupled with a second title fight between Larry Holmes and Tim Witherspoon, was staged in a 20,000-seat outdoor stadium at the Dunes, marking the first big outdoor show at a Las Vegas Strip property other than Caesars Palace. Within a matter of months, however, the Roman-themed gambling emporium that adopted the motto "Home of Champions" reclaimed its status as the city's preeminent boxing venue.[1] Figuring prominently was "Marvelous" Marvin Hagler, a headliner in four outdoor shows at Caesars Palace between 1983 and 1987.

The product of a broken home, Hagler spent his early years in the slums of Newark. The race riot of 1967 prompted his mother to seek out a better environment in which to raise Marvin and his six siblings. She chose Brockton, Massachusetts, where the streets were less menacing. At age sixteen, Hagler wandered into the Petronelli Brothers gym. Under the tutelage of Guerino "Goody" Petronelli, he went on to win an AAU title before turning pro under the management of Pat Petronelli on a card held in the Brockton High School gym.

Hagler brought a 46–2–1 record into his first title fight. His toughest fights had come in Philadelphia, a hornets' nest of tough middleweights hardened by that city's famously fierce gym wars. Hagler defeated hometown favorites Bennie Briscoe and "Cyclone" Hart in Philadelphia rings, but lost a dubious decision to Bobby Watts in the first of their three meetings and was fairly out-pointed by Willie Monroe. In one of his most impressive showings, he knocked out Sugar Ray Seales in the opening round. The only U.S. gold medal winner at the 1972 Olympics, Seales had previously boxed Hagler to a draw. This bout was contested in Seattle, an advantage to Seales, who hailed from the Puget Sound area.

Hagler's bout with rugged Vito Antuofermo, the defending middleweight champion, was ruled a draw. The decision was so unpopular that reporters took to calling Hagler the people's champion, a label no longer necessary when Hagler stopped Antuofermo's conqueror Alan Minter in the third round at London's Wembley Stadium. Hagler needed a police escort to get back to his dressing room and numbered himself fortunate that he wasn't hit squarely by any of the projectiles that showered him.

Over the next three years, Hagler made seven successful title defenses. Viable opponents were in short supply, but in hindsight Hagler was biding his time until the top welterweights moved up into his line of fire. The first to test his mettle was Roberto Duran.

Written off as finished after losing a decision to unheralded Kirkland Laing, Duran bounced back with stoppages of Pipino Cuevas and 154-pound titlist Davey Moore. The bout with Moore (no relation to the former featherweight champion of the same name) was his finest hour since his conquest of Sugar Ray Leonard in Montreal. A 5/2 underdog, Duran methodically destroyed Moore, taking control in the first round with a tactical thumb to the eye that reduced his adversary to a fumbling Cyclops. More shocking was the attendance. The first sellout at Madison Square Garden in nine years, the gate receipts were the third highest in the history of the arena, topped only by the two Ali-Frazier affairs. The presumption that "*No mas*" had permanently eroded Duran's marketability was shown to be a fallacy, and his ruthless decomposition of his previously undefeated opponent was fence mending of the most reconciliatory kind.

Hagler vs. Duran was a dull fight that, if anything, redounded more to the credit of Duran. The former lightweight king took Hagler to the brink, if only in the eyes of the two foreign judges that had the fight even entering the fifteenth round. In his next outings, Hagler atoned for his flat performance with stoppages of respected campaigners Juan Roldan and Mustafa Hamsho, setting the stage for an eagerly anticipated match with Thomas Hearns. The Detroiter had won eight straight since his setback to Sugar Ray. His most notable victory during this run was a second round blastout of Duran. The "Hit Man" knocked the Panamanian unconscious with a devastating right hand.

The Hagler-Hearns fight, staged at Caesars Palace on April 15, 1985, was the first fight in Las Vegas in which the *least expensive* seat was priced at $100, double the established rate for a big outdoor fight. This was the more noteworthy in that the date coincided with the final day for filing income taxes, traditionally one of the deadest days of the year for casino operators. The late money was tilted slightly toward Hagler, a 13/10 favorite.

Hagler and Hearns were contractually bound to hold public workouts in the Caesars Palace Sports Pavilion. Hagler copped out, fleeing to a small storefront gym run by a crusty, old-time fight character named Johnny Tocco. Located in a seedy commercial district in a flood zone near a railroad trestle, the gym was a dank and smelly place without air conditioning.

This was in character with Hagler's no-frills persona. In 64 fights spaced across a dozen years, his fighting weight had never deviated more than three pounds from the middleweight limit, a testament to his unwavering dedication. Hagler was also admired because he kept his entourage to a minimum and stayed loyal to the Petronelli brothers. Don King offered him a big bonus conditional on his breaking the triangle, but Hagler declined it.

Although barely eight minutes long, Hagler vs. Hearns was a rock 'em-sock 'em classic that drew comparisons to the Dempsey-Firpo ripsnorter of 1923. Hagler, badly cut above his left eye, had Hearns out on his feet when the referee stopped the contest.

A scrap this exhilarating begged for a fast rematch, but Hagler had bypassed top contender John Mugabi to fight Hearns and could not do so again without the hassle of having his title stripped. A Tampa-based Ugandan controlled by London fight manager Mickey Duff, Mugabi, nicknamed "The Beast," was 26–0 with 26 knockouts, but yet relatively obscure.

Pat Petronelli and Goody Petronelli are all smiles as Richard Steele raises Marvin Hagler's hand in triumph following his sensational bout with Thomas Hearns. Hagler stayed loyal to the Petronellis, but the brothers later had a falling out. *Antiquities of the Prize Ring.*

The promotion needed window-dressing and acquired that trapping when Hearns was added to the card and matched against unbeaten James Shuler. Originally set for November 14, 1985, the show was pushed back almost four months when Hagler suffered a broken nose in training.

Hagler was slow out of the gate, but finally disposed of Mugabi in the eleventh round. Hearns dismissed Shuler with a scorching one-two combination in the opening stanza. The stage was now set for Hagler-Hearns II, but Sugar Ray Leonard had ideas of his own.

No prominent athlete rattled out of retirement as often as Sugar Ray Leonard. The start of his pro career was even prefaced by a retirement. He retired again in November of 1982, six months after surgery for a detached retina, and again seventeen months later after a comeback fight with Kevin Howard, a bout in which he scored a ninth-round TKO but looked very ordinary, suffering the first knockdown of his career.

Few people had any inkling that Leonard was planning another comeback, but he had become obsessed with the idea of fighting Marvelous Marvin and started training for the match even before his representatives sent out feelers to the Hagler camp. When the fight was formally announced, it created a sensation. The April 6, 1987, Caesars Palace promotion was sold out four months in advance.

On paper, Sugar Ray had bit off more than he could chew. His performance against Kevin Howard was consistent with the precept "rest makes rust." He had never locked horns with a full-fledged middleweight, nor entered the ring carrying more than 153 pounds, and — because laser surgery was relatively new — the suspicion persisted that his eyesight was impaired. He was younger than Hagler by two years, but Hagler, by all indications, was still at the top of his game after twelve successful title defenses. There was also the general opinion that Hagler would be more motivated. Coming up the ladder, he was overshadowed by Leonard, who commanded hefty purses while he was still fighting for small purses. (Their careers had first intersected on June 10, 1977, in Hartford. Leonard, in his third professional bout, was paid $50,000 for fighting one Vinnie DeBarros. Hagler, then a veteran of 36 fights, appeared on the undercard and fought for a purse of $1500.) Weighing these factors, the pricemakers installed Hagler a 4/1 favorite.

The fight would go the full twelve rounds without producing an indelible moment, but the tension in the air was thick and grew thicker as Sugar Ray held tight to his game plan. Fighting with cool precision, he built an early lead and then seemed content to simply frustrate the constantly stalking Hagler with his will-o'-the-wisp defense, playing to the judges by fighting with more bravado in the waning seconds of rounds when the bell would save him from any bad consequences. These gusts were met with great applause. The final round ended with Hagler chasing Leonard about the ring without landing a hurtful punch.

The bout was difficult to score. The least controversial verdict would have been a draw, but two of the judges favored Leonard. (Astoundingly, the foreign judge, Mexico's Jo Jo Guerra, gave Hagler only two rounds.) A majority of ringside reporters had Leonard ahead, but there was wide disagreement. The Associated Press scorecard favored Hagler 117–112. The verdict would be debated for years.

Eleven days after the fight, a sportscaster at WNEV-TV in Boston told his viewers that a big gambler with $300,000 riding on Leonard had bribed one of the judges. The alleged fixer was quickly identified as Billy Baxter. Best known as a high-stakes poker player, Baxter owned a small stable of fighters, the most successful of whom was Roger Mayweather.

Nevada's Attorney General investigated the allegations. Baxter and the judge with whom he was allegedly in cahoots were cleared of any wrongdoing.[2]

It was speculated that the source of the malicious gossip was Bob Arum, and that he had planted the story in collusion with prominent Boston barrister Morris Goldings, Hagler's attorney. But if Arum was hoping to kindle a rematch, his machinations backfired. Leonard was initially cool to the idea of fighting Hagler again, and his opposition stiffened when aspersions were cast on the integrity of his triumph. Always his own man, Sugar Ray was not about to be pressured into a fight that was not of his own choosing. On May 26, 1987, three days before the results of the investigation were made public, Leonard announced yet another retirement, telling the press that he had sated the burning desire that drew him back to the ring.

Hagler had no incentive to fight anyone but Sugar Ray and retired without fanfare, moving to Italy, where he began a second career as a movie actor. In common with Brockton's other great champion, Rocky Marciano, he defied the cynics and never returned to boxing. If there had been a second fight, Hagler would have been a solid favorite again. Lethal in rematches, Hagler left the sport with a record of 62–3–2. Both draws and two of the losses were controversial and his ledger could have easily been 66–1. Of course, all this is idle speculation. Who's to say that Leonard would not have befuddled Hagler again?

Nineteen months later, the mercurial Leonard was back in the squared circle at Caesars Palace. In the opposite corner was Donny LaLonde, a fighter from Winnipeg whose long, bleached-blond hair gave him the appearance of a California surfer. Smartly managed by David Wolf, a former editor at *Life* magazine, LaLonde held the WBC lightheavyweight title, a nice bauble for Leonard's trophy case but not a practical acquisition as Sugar Ray was too much of a minnow to swim with lightheavyweights. But LaLonde was willing to drop down to 168 pounds and the WBC 168-pound title was conveniently vacant.

The promoter of record was Mike Trainer, Leonard's attorney and financial advisor, but one could fairly say that Leonard promoted the contest himself and sanctioned it at his whim. Fortified with an intriguing match between Roger Mayweather and Vinny Pazienza, the promotion went head-to-head with *Monday Night Football* but drew an announced crowd of 13,241 at ticket prices that ranged from $200 to $1000. LaLonde, whose ambidexterity was reduced by a pin in his left shoulder, the result of a boyhood hockey injury, bloodied Leonard's nose and knocked him down in the fourth round, but Sugar Ray gradually found his groove and stopped him with a vicious assault in Round 9.

Rumors flew before this fight that Leonard was dickering for a rematch with Thomas Hearns. The rumor had substance. Leonard-Hearns II was staged at Caesars Palace on June 12, 1989.

Leonard-Hearns I was a classic, but the rematch lost luster while simmering eight years on the backburner. Leonard and Hearns now had greater name recognition, but both were judged to be on the downgrade, especially Hearns. The Hit Man had been playing the same game as Leonard, gilding his resumé with synthetic belts that allowed him to pose as a champion or former champion of multiple weight classes, but his reputation had been badly tarnished by his performance in his most recent fights. A knockout loss to Iran Barkley could be dismissed as a fluke — Hearns was winning by a mile when he was clocked by a wild right hand — but there were no excuses for his poor showing against James Kinchen. Hearns prevailed by split decision, but the verdict was lustily booed. Twenty-eight of 31 sportswriters surveyed by the *Review-Journal* favored Leonard, a 7/2 favorite. Of the three dissenters, two wrote for Detroit papers.

Hearns scored knockdowns in the third and eleventh sessions, but Leonard came on strong in the final stanza to salvage a draw. At the final gong, the Hit Man was holding on for dear life. The bout was not nearly as memorable as the first meeting because there were fewer toe-to-toe exchanges.

Sugar Ray had one more fight on the table that was too lucrative to pass up. Although he had avenged his loss to Roberto Duran, the circumstances were such that he hadn't removed all doubt that he was the better man.

At age 38, Duran scarcely resembled the fierce warrior that had stormed like a cyclone through the colony of lightweights. He had lost his last four fights in Nevada rings, most recently a 10-round decision to Robbie Sims, Marvin Hagler's moderately skilled half-brother. Yet Duran could still make the turnstiles hum. He was the first Hispanic fighter to command a following across five time zones. His appeal to Mexicans had zoomed following the revelation that he was Mexican on his father's side. His biological father, a former merchant seaman, was discovered working as a short-order cook in Flagstaff, Arizona.

Duran was also a cat with nine lives, periodically turning back the clock with flashes of brilliance that were mindful of his heyday. Five years and eight months after resurrecting his career at the expense of Davey Moore, he turned the trick again with a bravura performance against middleweight titlist Iran "The Blade" Barkley. Duran defeated the 28-year-old Barkley in stirring fashion, rallying from a big deficit to cop the decision in a robust fight before a wildly enthusiastic crowd at the Atlantic City Convention Center.

Staged on December 27, 1989, the Leonard-Duran rubber match was the climax of grand opening festivities at Steve Wynn's Mirage. Credited with reinventing gambling casinos by melding the sensibilities of Bugsy Siegel and Walt Disney, Wynn packaged the event along the lines of a Hollywood premier, parading celebrities into his 16,305-seat outdoor stadium on a red-carpeted runway. After the last of the preliminary bouts, the arena went dark for an extravagant fireworks show.

The big shebang attracted so many rubberneckers that Wynn was impelled to cull the herd. Late on the afternoon of the fight, only hotel guests, fight-goers, and members of the media were allowed access to the property, a lockout believed to be without precedent in the history of legal gambling in Nevada. At the conclusion of the fight, ten Mirage baccarat crews were pressed into service, a record number for a single shift.

Considering the hubbub, perhaps it was inevitable that the fight would be a dud. Duran had looked sensational against the free-swinging Barkley, but wasn't able to vex Leonard, who was content to stay out of harm's way and pile up points with light jabs and counterpunches. Leonard-Duran III was dreary and one-sided. Chilly weather worsened the tedium.

This was the last important bout of the 1980s. Named the Fighter of the Decade by the Associated Press, Leonard achieved the honor without ever fighting in Madison Square Garden. More so than anyone, his name signified the transformation of American boxing into a casino sport.

# CHAPTER 19

# The Iron Mike Express

A few days after his eighteenth birthday, Michael Gerard Tyson made his first visit to Las Vegas. The occasion was the Olympic Box-Off at Caesars Palace, the final hurdle to the 1984 summer games in Los Angeles. Competing at 201 pounds, Tyson lost a mildly unpopular decision to a 24-year-old ex-convict from Los Angeles named Henry Tillman. Repairing to his dressing room, Tyson broke down in tears and bolted outside to the famous parking lot to regain his composure. Barely three years later, he was the undisputed heavyweight champion of the world.

In mapping out his future, Tyson's managers were guided by the example of Joe Louis. The Brown Bomber had 27 pro fights before his first encounter with the vastly more experienced Max Schmeling. Those fights were compressed into only 18 months. Tyson had precisely the same number of fights inside the same window of time before taking on battle-tested Trevor Berbick.

JOE LOUIS — MIKE TYSON
THE FAST TRACK COMPARISON

|  | FIRST PRO FIGHT | 27TH PRO FIGHT | WINS | KNOCKOUTS |
|---|---|---|---|---|
| Joe Louis | 07/04/34 | 01/17/36 | 27 | 23 |
| Mike Tyson | 03/06/85 | 09/08/86 | 27 | 25 |

Joe Louis was matched against more name opponents and had two big paydays in ballpark fights during the first 18 months of his career, but otherwise their paths dovetailed almost perfectly, begetting equivalent hymns of praise. Among twentieth-century heavyweights, only Louis and Tyson were judged to be unbeatable while their careers were still in the warmup phase.

Tyson was only fifteen fights into his pro career when he made the cover of *Sports Illustrated*. The front-page caption said "Kid Dynamite — The Next Great Heavyweight." With a strikingly thick neck hinging his head to a thick, muscular torso, Tyson certainly looked the part. Better even than the photo was the truth-is-stranger-than-fiction story about him, an old-fashioned yarn about a dead-end kid sidestepping the pitfalls of instant fame and fortune through the sway of elders that had his best interests at heart. In the process of molding a champion, Tyson's mentors were also molding a rudderless child into a solid citizen, or so it seemed.[1]

Tyson's first mentor was Cus D'Amato, who assumed the role of a surrogate father. Best remembered for piloting the careers of Floyd Patterson and lightheavyweight champion Jose Torres, D'Amato had been off the radar screen for so long that most casual fans would have guessed he was dead. But he had merely left the big stage, retreating to bucolic Catskill, New York, where he occupied his time running a gym above a police station that produced a few fighters for amateur smokers.

In 1980, a counselor at a reformatory in upstate New York touted D'Amato on a pugnacious 13-year-old inmate who was incredibly strong for his age. D'Amato followed up on the lead and was so thunderstruck by the boy's potential that he inquired about becoming his legal guardian. On his 14th birthday, Tyson was paroled into the care of the 72-year-old confirmed bachelor, taking up residence in the large Victorian home that Cus shared with long-time companion Camille Ewald, the sister of a sister-in-law. It was a radical departure for the man-child from Brownsville, who had never known his father and had spent all of his nights in slum tenements or detention facilities.

In his younger days, D'Amato would have retained sole proprietorship, but he was cash poor and no longer had the stomach for waging another lonely war against the boxing establishment. When Tyson was ready to turn pro, D'Amato called on trusted friends Jim Jacobs and Bill Cayton, the original managers of Wilfred Benitez, whose business partnership was an extension of their shared hobby of collecting rare fight films. The day following Tyson's twelfth pro fight, D'Amato died of pneumonia.

Jacobs, a walking encyclopedia of boxing, believed that most of the storied pre–World War I fighters were unexceptional, but it was a point that he no longer cared to debate. In an article in *The Ring,* Jacobs wrote: "[The] fans of old time fighters are the most amazingly uninformed individuals in any area of sport. But the problem is that debating anything with an old time boxing fan is tantamount to arguing with an earthquake."[2]

In obeisance to old-time boxing fans, Tyson was fashioned into the idealization of an antiquarian pugilist, a no-frills fighting man who was all business when the bell sounded. There would be no silk boxing robe, not even socks. Tyson's ring attire would consist of only the bare essentials — trunks and boots, both solid black, and a plain white towel draped on his shoulders. Jacobs and Cayton also encouraged his interest in pigeons, a hobby that was good bait for sportswriters. Budd Schulberg's famous fictional boxer Terry Malloy — played by Marlon Brando in *On The Waterfront* — manifested his underlying decency in the tender way that he cared for his pigeons.

An incorrigible truant as a schoolboy, Tyson surprised Jacobs and Cayton with his intellectual curiosity. He roamed the stacks of Jacobs' vast boxing library, so to speak, acquiring knowledge of ring titans who competed long before he was born. Armed with this knowledge, he charmed veteran sportswriters who had become increasingly annoyed with hotshot athletes who knew almost nothing about the trailblazers that smoothed their paths. In unstructured bull sessions with writers, he was exceedingly cordial.

During his days with Patterson, D'Amato had a stormy relationship with the press. Some reporters were beguiled by his philosophical musings, but others dismissed them as the vapors of a gasbag. In general, older reporters were most antagonistic. Few were still around when D'Amato re-emerged with Tyson in tow. By then, Patterson and Torres had vindicated him by their seamless transition to life after boxing. Considered something of a renaissance man, Torres had earned critical acclaim for a 1971 biography of Muhammad Ali and was the chairman of the New York State Boxing Commission. Patterson, something of a suburban squire, would eventually be appointed to the same post. As Patterson had also spent time in a reform school, it was easy to visualize Tyson someday working for the betterment of boxing in some administrative capacity.

While Joe Louis provided the blueprint for Tyson's timetable, his ring aura harked back more to Jack Dempsey. Akin to the young Dempsey, Tyson was likened to a jungle cat for the way he pounced on his prey at the opening gong, often leaving his sufferer sprawled in a heap before the audience had time to exhale. Tyson even bobbed his head like Dempsey, slipping punches as he pressed forward. Coming up the ladder, Tyson would be extended ten rounds by trial horse James Tillis and by Harlem street tough Mitch "Blood" Green, but the image from television that resonated was his 30-second wipeout of 16–1 Marvis Frazier, a man from whom big things were expected if only because he was Joe Frazier's son.[3]

With Tyson drawing attention away from his lackluster stable of heavyweights, Don King thought it prudent to manufacture a tournament to unify the title. Tyson was initially excluded, but pressure from others with a financial stake in the tourney forced King to bring Tyson into the fold. Tyson's first fight in which King had his hands in the pot was a tune-up with Alfonso Ratliff. Pinned to an IBF title fight between Michael Spinks and Steffan Tangstad, it was staged in the convention hall of the Las Vegas Hilton on September 6, 1986.

Ratliff stood six-foot-five, had an 85-inch reach, and was sufficiently talented to have won a piece of the cruiserweight title, but he was a better orator than a boxer. Likening Tyson to a government mule in a pre-fight sermon full of bravado, Ratliff turned milquetoast at the sound of the opening bell. Retreating all the while, he survived the first round but not the second. Spinks, also matched soft but against a far less docile opponent, retained his belt in the co-feature, stopping his Norwegian adversary in Round 4.

Spinks withdrew from the tournament for a rich payday with Gerry Cooney, producing a flood of lawsuits, but this was of no immediate consequence for Tyson, who drew WBC title-holder Trevor Berbick as his next opponent. The last man to defeat Muhammad Ali and the second man to go fifteen rounds with Larry Holmes, the emotionally erratic 33-year-old Berbick had acquired the reputation of a spoiler. He had knocked Greg Page from the ranks of the unbeaten when Page was considered the best of the new crop of heavyweights, and he was coming off an upset of previously undefeated Pinklon Thomas. Nonetheless, the 20-year-old Tyson, who had answered the bell for only 74 rounds at the pro level, went to post a 9/2 favorite, a degree of favoritism unprecedented for a challenger in a heavyweight title bout.

Tyson rocked Berbick with combinations in the first round and finished the job in the next stanza, creating another indelible image when his punches sent Berbick lurching about the ring like a drunken sailor. With the victory, Tyson was hailed as the youngest heavyweight champion in history, but to validate that claim he would need to acquire all three belts.

WBA title-holder James Smith was up next. A pleasant, soft-spoken ex-serviceman with a college degree, raised on a North Carolina tobacco farm, Smith bore a striking resemblance to Jersey Joe Walcott. A TKO victim in his pro debut, Smith had gone through a rough stretch of four losses in five fights, but King maneuvered him into a title bout with Tim Witherspoon and Smith knocked him out in the opening round. The more mundane the name, the more essential a catchy nickname, and Smith had a good one — Bonecrusher — acidly reformulated to "Boneclutcher" after a hollow performance in which he tagged Tyson with only two punches of consequence, both in the waning seconds of the final round when the motivation was simply to save face.

Tyson needed one more belt to unify the title, but there was a snag. The IBF had defrocked Michael Spinks when he pulled out of the tournament. The organization wanted to fill the vacancy before letting Tyson have a go at it, thereby pocketing one more sanctioning fee. Eventually it was decided that Tyson would risk his belts against Pinklon Thomas on a card where Tony Tucker and James "Buster" Douglas would battle for the IBF diadem.

Tucker (34–0) kept his unbeaten record intact, but Douglas made things dicey before running out of wind, leaving him vulnerable to the chopping right hand that put him down for the count in the 10th round. Tyson stayed on course. Game but outgunned, Thomas was finally a goner in Round 6.

Tyson vs. Tucker was seemingly a natural blockbuster. Two undefeated fighters were competing for the right to be called the *undisputed* heavyweight champion of the world. However, there wasn't a fighter on the planet then considered in Tyson's league, save perhaps Michael Spinks. Earlier in his career, Tucker had struggled to repel Eddie "The Animal" Lopez. A crude fighter with a Tyson-like physique, Lopez was able to get inside Tucker's jab and rough him up before the contest was stopped on cuts. Never before in heavyweight title history had the less experienced man been chalked the favorite in a match of unbeatens, but Iron Mike (the Kid Dynamite tag never stuck) went off a 6/1 favorite.

Staged at the Las Vegas Hilton on August 1, 1987, the fight started out as if it would be a pip. Tucker tagged Tyson with a wicked uppercut midway through the opening round, effectively traded punches in Round 2, and parried Tyson's lunges smartly in the next frame while landing enough punches to win the round. But then Tucker went into a survivor's mode, where he stayed until the final stanza when he borrowed a leaf from the notebook of James Smith, stunning Tyson with a combination just before the final bell. The overall effect was disappointing and many spectators left the arena without bothering to wait for the announcer to read the scores.

While the fight was in progress, workers — some dressed in Elizabethan frippery and others in beefeater costumes — were preparing a Hilton ballroom for a grand post-fight party themed as a coronation ball. While Tyson was pained that Cus D'Amato had not lived to share the moment, he had a special someone to make the occasion more special. Seventeen months older than Mike, the stunningly attractive Robin Givens had attended *haut monde* Sarah Lawrence College and was a celebrity in her own right as one of the stars of a popular TV sitcom.

After two title defenses — knockouts of Tyrell Biggs and Larry Holmes in bouts in Atlantic City — Mike married Givens in a quiet ceremony in Chicago, inheriting a 42-year-old mother-in-law, Ruth Roper, who became sauce for the tabloids when she charged baseball star David Winfield

Mike Tyson circa 1991.

with infecting her with a sexually transmitted disease and sued for damages. In short order, Givens came to be seen as the *femme fatale* that is a staple of every boxing B-movie.

Tyson's first bout as a married man was against Tony Tubbs on March 21, 1988, in Tokyo. The icebreaker event at a domed stadium dubbed the Big Egg, the bout started at 12:20 A.M., a concession to American television, yet drew an announced crowd of 51,000. The bout was halted near the end of the second stanza with Tubbs semiconscious, blood streaming from a nasty cut above his right eye.

Jim Jacobs was unable to accompany Tyson to Tokyo. Three days after the event he died of leukemia at age fifty-five. While Tyson had never warmed to Bill Cayton, something of a cold fish, he had a close relationship with Jacobs. A legend in the sport of handball, Jacobs's athletic background was useful in bridging the generation gap.

Jacobs had already signed off on a match for Tyson with Michael Spinks. Before he pulled out of the unification series, Spinks had come to be recognized as the linear heavyweight champion. Jacobs felt that reattaching the umbilicus was important to Tyson's place in history.

The experts had accorded Spinks little chance when it was announced that he would fight Larry Holmes. It was elementary. A good little man didn't beat a good big man, and it figured that Spinks would be outweighed by about 40 pounds. Approaching his 36th birthday, Holmes was getting long in the tooth, but at 48–0 he was only one win removed from tying Rocky Marciano's record and not likely to have picked a treacherous opponent for such an historic fight. But Spinks spoiled the soup, winning a hair-thin unanimous decision in an arena constructed in the parking lot of the Riviera Hotel — literally a stone's throw from the Hilton Center, where older bother Leon had wrested the heavyweight title from Muhammad Ali. Spinks repeated the feat seven months later, upending Holmes on a split decision in a competition that closely mirrored the first meeting.

Akin to his older brother, Spinks was an unorthodox fighter — a darter who was somewhat herky-jerky and threw punches from funny angles — but their differences were more pronounced than their similarities. Leon was loud, foolish with his money, and notoriously nocturnal. Michael was unobtrusive, a squirrel with his money, and by all accounts, early to bed and early to rise.

During Spinks' 62-month reign as a lightheavyweight titlist, the sport became balkanized like never before, a condition that worsened in 1984 when Larry Holmes cut off all ties except to the upstart IBF. The shifting coterie of heavyweight title-holders in this pot of alphabet soup had a propensity for acquiring "love handles." Budd Schulberg acidly observed that a new classification had been born: the overweights. Investigative reporter Jack Newfield faulted King for this development, postulating that the fighters contractually bound to him had become so demoralized by his double-dealing that they lost all incentive to stay in shape. Newfield was sympathetic to Tim Witherspoon, who coined a neat phrase when he described himself and his cohorts under King's thumb as the "lost generation" of heavyweights.

Michael Spinks put the "overweights" to shame. More than distinctly disciplined, he was the product of a revolutionary training regimen. In the summer of 1982, his manager Butch Lewis brought him to the Sports Performance Clinic at St. Jude's Medical Center in New Orleans, where Mackie Shilstone customized a fitness and nutritional program for him.

From the days of Tom Cribb, long-distance running was a staple of a fighter's routine. A self-styled sports performance enhancer who would go on the work with dozens of prominent athletes, Shilstone believed that this was pointless unless one needed to burn calories to lose weight. Noting that boxing was a series of cycles — three minutes of intense activity followed by a short interval of rest — Shilstone mapped out a program heavy on wind sprints and explosive calisthenics. His program also included weight training. Shilstone believed that working with weights added to a fighter's flexibility if done with a full range of motion, a credo that was sacrilege to old-time trainers who believed that lifting barbells produced the opposite result.[4]

The addition of a fitness guru to Team Spinks allowed trainer Eddie Futch to concentrate on what he did best; plot strategy to exploit an opponent's weaknesses. Futch, born in 1909, was initially wary of Shilstone, but he tipped his hat in wonderment when Spinks grew into a full-fledged heavyweight while simultaneously reducing his body fat. Jaws dropped when Michael stood on the scale at the weigh-in for his first meeting with Holmes. While his physique was not outwardly much larger, he had put on 25 pounds, stifling comparisons to Billy Conn.

From a stylistic standpoint, Tyson vs. Spinks had a Sullivan-Corbett contour. There was a sentiment that Tyson would blast Spinks out of the water in sudden fashion, but the number of people inclined toward this viewpoint shrank with each new tidbit about Tyson's personal life. It had become generally known that his marriage was stormy and that King was steering him away from Bill Cayton, an act of piracy abetted by Tyson's wife and meddlesome mother-in-law, now more luridly painted as gold diggers. He was described in the press as confused and rudderless, logically a plus for his undefeated, even-keeled adversary, who had never been knocked down in his 31 pro fights. In Las Vegas, where Tyson had opened a 9/2 favorite, the early money was all Spinks.

The fight was staged in the Atlantic City Convention Center, a timeworn property now connected by an overhead walkway to the Trump Plaza. Well into the next century, Tyson vs. Spinks would stand as the greatest boxing spectacle in the history of the seaside resort city, but those that witnessed it didn't get much bang for their buck. Spinks, who entered the ring wearing a look of foreboding, was knocked out clean in 91 seconds. He would never fight again.

After an eight-month layoff, Tyson returned to Las Vegas to meet Frank Bruno, an Englishman of Jamaican lineage who had briefly owned the WBA belt. This would be Tyson's first fight without Kevin Rooney. A Cus D'Amato protégé who was still an active fighter when he assumed the role of Tyson's chief trainer, Rooney, a gruff taskmaster, had been replaced by low-key Aaron Snowell, a man considered little more than a nine-to-five drone at King's training center on the grounds of his Orwell, Ohio, estate. Although their divorce wasn't yet official, Robin Givens was also gone. This was viewed in a positive light.[5]

Despite the intrigue occasioned by the departure of Rooney, Tyson went to post a 14/1 favorite. His performance would be inartistic — his punches were often wild — but he knocked Bruno out in the fifth round. In his next outing, Tyson blasted out Carl Williams in 93 seconds.

The next big fight brewing for Tyson was against Evander Holyfield. King sealed the deal before taking Tyson off to Tokyo for a tune-up with Buster Douglas. By this time, the Las Vegas sports books had taken Tyson's fights "off the board," reluctant even to post an "over/under." There would be no betting line on Tyson vs. Douglas save at the Mirage, where mischievous bet-taker Jimmy Vaccaro established Tyson a 27/1 favorite. At its highest point, those inclined to bet Tyson were required to lay 42/1.

Buster Douglas was not without virtues. He was big and athletic and came from fighting stock. His father Billy "Dynamite" Douglas, a fringe middleweight contender, was known for taking hard fights on short notice. However, Buster had problems managing his weight, and his ledger (29–4–1) was marred by slipshod performances against modestly skilled opponents. An 8-round draw with Steffan Tangstad, a much smaller man, was an especially unsightly wart. He rarely fought with passion, although there were a few exceptions. Against Tex Cobb — best known for going 15 rounds with Larry Holmes without winning a single frame — Buster skirted defeat with a big rally in the final round. Most of his recent fights were on the undercards of Don King promotions, creating the false impression that his manager was Carl King, Don's stepson and front man.

Douglas had weighed a puffy 242½ in his last assignment, a drab but victorious effort against then unknown Oliver McCall. He came in 11 pounds lighter for Tyson and tunnel-visioned to the task at hand. The images that stand out are Douglas taking charge early by being the far busier man, then Tyson, his left eye swollen nearly shut, seemingly pulling the fight out of the fire with a wicked uppercut that knocked Douglas off his feet near the end of Round 8, and then Douglas regaining command, landing the harder shots in a spirited ninth frame and putting Tyson away for good with a textbook three-punch combination in the next stanza.

The famous fight would come to be numbered with the great upsets of all time, not just in boxing but across the entire spectrum of sports. The betting line became a major thread in post-fight stories. By quantifying the magnitude of the upset, Mirage pricemaker Vaccaro enjoyed a brief moment in the spotlight. He told *Review-Journal* sportswriter Stephen Nover that three big plungers went down the tubes with Iron Mike. Their ill-advised wagers were in the amounts of $56,000 at 28/1, $64,000 at 32/1, and $143,000 at 39/1. The largest wager on Douglas was a $1500 bet that yielded a profit of $52,500.[6]

The shocker threw the heavyweight division into an immediate state of chaos. Inside the Big Egg, the shameless King was wheeling-and-dealing as the reporters were filing their copy. As for Tyson, he was reeling toward big trouble, but would go on to have four more fights before his career screeched to a lockout.

Tyson's setback scuttled his impending encounter with Holyfield. For his first comeback fight, King selected amateur nemesis Henry Tillman. The fight was a natural for the parking lot at Caesars Palace, where a tearful Tyson took refuge following his loss to Tillman in the Olympic Box-Off, but ticket sales were bound to be sluggish without a strong undercard, as Tillman's credibility had depreciated. His 24–4 record was marred by a stoppage at the hands of journeyman Dwain Bonds.

The embellishment would be George Foreman, who was paired with Adilson Rodriguez, a marginally skilled Brazilian. A big bear of a man, Foreman had returned to boxing after a decade-long hibernation and had thrust himself back into contention with a quick knockout of Gerry Cooney.

The bouts went as expected. Tyson dispatched the petrified Tillman in 167 seconds. Foreman, carrying 263 pounds — *43 pounds* more than he had weighed for Muhammad Ali — stopped Rodriguez in Round 2.

Tyson's next opponent, Alex Stewart, was another "deer in the headlights." Tyson dismissed him in 147 seconds, but yet his performance drew bad reviews. He telegraphed his punches and all but a few were wide of the mark. For his next bout with Donovan "Razor" Ruddock at the Mirage, Tyson was "only" an 11/2 favorite. Richie Giachetti, a gruff and slovenly man who had had a nice run with Larry Holmes, had become Tyson's chief trainer following the disaster in Tokyo. He closed Tyson's training sessions to the press, more fodder for the notion that Tyson had lost something.

A Canadian born in Jamaica, Ruddock had been stopped early in his career by third-rater David Jaco, but had won 16 straight and was coming off a brutal fourth-round KO of fearsome Michael Dokes. He took Tyson into the seventh round before referee Richard Steele decided that he had seen enough. The stoppage was highly controversial — Ruddock was upright and did not appear to be in immediate danger — and provoked a nasty free-for-all inside the ropes that was hugely embarrassing to the boxing commission, which had stubbornly refused to replace Steele when the Ruddock camp protested his appointment. A lay preacher, Steele was a man of unimpeachable integrity, but he worked as a pit boss at Steve Wynn's Golden Nugget, raising questions about his neutrality.

Tyson and Ruddock had another go at the Mirage three months later. This time the stakes were higher. The winner would get the next crack at the new heavyweight champion, Evander Holyfield.

Tyson-Ruddock II was free of extracurricular scuffles, but the fight was almost as inelegant as the scrum that followed the first meeting. Both had points deducted for hitting after the bell and Tyson was penalized twice for low blows. Although Tyson won convincingly on the scorecards, he never bobbed his head while pressing forward and was unable to put Ruddock away despite breaking his jaw. The saving grace of the show was an entertaining match between talented featherweight titlists Jeff Fenech and Azumah Nelson, but that encounter produced catcalls when the decision was awarded to Nelson.

At the pre-fight press conference, Tyson guttersniped that he would make Ruddock his girlfriend. Early into his career, Tyson had appeared in commercials for Diet Pepsi and Kodak and had even done a recruiting advertisement for the New York Police Department. But he had fallen out of favor as a corporate pitchman and his "girlfriend" slur — a jailhouse *defi* so beyond the pale that it didn't even lend itself to a mirthfully sarcastic retort — foreclosed any possibility that he might reopen those doors.

Despite his growing reputation as a two-bit punk, Tyson was still the biggest draw in boxing and his forthcoming fight with Holyfield would easily surpass his bout with Spinks as the richest in history. Then a complication developed. Authorities in Indianapolis issued an arrest warrant for him for the alleged rape of 18-year-old Desiree Washington. She represented Rhode Island in the Miss Black America pageant, the event that drew Tyson to that city.

The promoters blithely barreled ahead, staging a gala news conference at the Waldorf-Astoria to announce that the Tyson-Holyfield fight would be held on November 8, 1991, at Caesars Palace. An advertising campaign was launched, posters and programs were produced, and a betting line was established (Tyson 5/1).

To the great dismay of those with a stake in the promotion, the complication was hardly a hiccup. Tyson and Holyfield would eventually get it on (oh boy, would they ever), but it wouldn't happen in 1991. Prosecutors in Indiana made certain of that.

# CHAPTER 20

# Buster Craps Out

When Mike Tyson fought Buster Douglas, Don King had options on both fighters. Regardless of the outcome, he would still be the lord of the heavyweight manor. But it wasn't as if King was without a rooting interest.

In the chess game of boxing, promoters are always thinking a few moves ahead. Buster was frocked as Tyson's stumbling block to a megafight with Evander Holyfield, but King never considered the possibility that Tyson might actually lose and he had no contingency plan. A Tyson-Douglas rematch would be huge. As a sales hook, the storyline of redemption is most powerful when a deposed champion is seeking to wipe away his only blemish. However, a victory by Douglas would give his manager John Johnson an enormous wedge in the negotiations and King didn't need the hassle.

During the contest, King was observed rooting openly for Tyson. When Tyson scored his knockdown, it appeared to King that the referee accorded Douglas the luxury of a slow count, an impression that did not register with unbiased observers. After the bout, King browbeat WBC president Jose Sulaiman and his WBA counterpart Gilberto Mendoza into reversing the outcome. King's rationale was that the first knockout invalidated the second knockout. Reporters raised such a snit that King and his lackeys were forced to back off and allow the original verdict to stand.

Steve Wynn followed these developments with a keen interest. His first venture into boxing was bittersweet. Leonard-Duran III had succeeded handsomely as a spectacle, but the fight was a dud and it struck him that he had overpaid the promoter (Bob Arum) for the right to host the event. Promoting a big fight is a complicated undertaking, but Wynn reasoned that his in-house personnel were up to the challenge. Dealing directly with fight managers that were not legally beholden to a promoter, Wynn could cut out the middleman, a major cost savings.

With Wynn's backing, Douglas sued to have his contract with King invalidated. The gist of the suit was that King had breached a fiduciary responsibility with his post-fight antics in Tokyo. King protested that he was merely stirring the pot for a rematch, but the excuse was lame. An out-of-court settlement gave King promotional rights to a Tyson-Douglas rematch, but first Douglas would defend his title against Evander Holyfield at the Mirage, a promotion in which King would have no direct pecuniary interest.

While Wynn envisioned a windfall in casino winnings, he had other motivations for horning in. He was feuding with Donald Trump, who had spirited away several of his top casino executives. Trump was becoming a force in the sport through his cozy relationship with King, and Wynn relished the opportunity to diminish his influence. Douglas had value that went beyond his usefulness as "whale bait." He was the Joe Blow that knocked out Superman and won the big jackpot, making him the perfect poster boy for a gambling establishment.

Raised in Atlanta, Evander Holyfield first attracted notice as a member of the 1984 U.S. Olympic team. Competing in the 178-pound class, he advanced to the semifinals where he was disqualified for hitting his outclassed opponent — New Zealand's Kevin Barry — after he was commanded to break. It was a borderline call that redounded into a larger controversy when a countryman of the Yugoslavian referee won the gold medal. A deeply religious man, Holyfield accepted it as God's will.

Holyfield made his pro debut on a card at Madison Square Garden that included five of his Olympic teammates. Twenty months later, with only 11 pro fights under his belt, he captured his first title, dethroning 190-pound titlist Dwight Braxton by split decision in a 15-round contest in Atlanta that ranked among the best fights of the year. He went on to unify the cruiserweight title before stepping up in weight. Fighting as a heavyweight, he stopped six foes, extending his record to 24–0. The most difficult of those bouts was against Michael Dokes. Holyfield had several anxious moments before taking Dokes out in the 10th round.

To an even greater extent than Michael Spinks, Holyfield embraced revolutionary notions about sports conditioning. Old-school trainers Lou Duva and George Benton were second fiddles to his Houston-based fitness guru Tim Hallmark. If Holyfield had been a basketball player, he would have been the kid that cadges a key to the gym so that he can practice in solitude while his teammates are sleeping. To prepare for Buster Douglas, he expanded his network of advisers with the addition of a ballet instructor. By contrast, Douglas had only one trainer, his uncle J.D. McCauley. During his days as a professional fighter, McCauley won only four of his 22 fights. All but three of his defeats were of the knockout variety.

Douglas had gone through some tough times in the weeks preceding his encounter with Tyson. Twenty-three days before the match, his mother had suffered a fatal stroke. His wife had left him and a former girlfriend with whom he had a child was terminally ill. It figured that these tribulations would translate into a poor showing, but somehow they had the opposite effect, strengthening his resolve.

There were different kinds of stresses after he won the title. He was not a good public speaker and was something of an introvert, but yet he was constantly pushed into situations where protocol dictated a short speech and schmoozing with strangers. Don King publicly called him an ingrate, an opinion that strained some of his personal relationships. The crown on his head was an imaginary cornice, but it was as real as a tight-fitting truss. And whenever the pressure was acute, Buster found comfort in food.

There was considerable speculation about Buster's weight as his date with Holyfield drew near. He conducted all of his on-site workouts wearing a thick sweatshirt, a tip-off that he was making little headway in his battle of the bulge. There was also talk that he was less than diligent in doing his roadwork, abbreviating his runs after oversleeping. Johnson deflected questions about his fighter with elocutions of Buster's brilliance. Briefly an assistant football coach at Ohio State University, Johnson had worked the back roads of boxing before striking gold with a fighter from his own backyard, but he was up to the challenge. The purse he cadged from Steve Wynn was reportedly $24 million.

At the Mirage, Holyfield opened a 9/5 favorite. The early money was on Douglas, but the flow reversed in the last few days of betting and the trickle turned into a tidal wave when

Douglas came in at a blubbery 246½ pounds versus a lighter-than-expected 208 pounds for Holyfield. Jimmy Vaccaro reported taking a $500,000 bet on Holyfield within moments after Douglas stepped on the scale, the largest wager of his bookmaking career.

The fight started slowly. From the very onset, it appeared that Douglas was going through the motions. In the third round, he missed with a looping right hand and Holyfield countered with a right hook that landed flush but didn't appear to be especially powerful. Douglas went down and lay on his back, his eyes wide open. As the referee completed his count, Buster moved his right hand in front of his face as if shielding his eyes from the sun. In this repose, he bore an uncanny resemblance to Jack Johnson taking the count in Havana in 1915.

The tale of Buster's dishevelment acquired a seriocomic postscript. The scuttlebutt in Las Vegas fight circles was that Douglas and those in his crew were evicted from their plush suites at the Mirage even before the arena was locked down. The house magicians, Siegfried and Roy, made jungle beasts disappear on command, but no one was able to prune a smidgeon of suet from the man identified in the public mind as Steve Wynn's pet bruiser. To a perfectionist like Wynn, this must have been infuriating. If he did not command his bouncers to give Buster the heave-ho, the thought must have certainly crossed his mind. What is a fact is that Wynn would never again lavish such a huge sum on a boxing promotion.

On February 10, 1992, Mike Tyson was found guilty of committing an act of rape in his room at the Canterbury Hotel in Indianapolis in the pre-dawn hours of July 19, 1991. Sixteen days after the verdict was rendered, Judge Patricia Gifford sentenced him to six years in prison.

When a boxer of great renown takes his leave, the sport customarily suffers a decline, a finding that is something of a tautology. But while no one could generate revenue like Iron Mike, the heavyweights making waves as he went to trial were a more interesting lot than the ephemera that claimed pieces of the title as he was coming to prominence. Holyfield had a name that stood out in a phone book, a physique the envy of a Chippendales dancer, and it was plain that he was highly skilled. If Evander was merely an interloper, there were others that looked as if they might be the real deal, notably Riddick Bowe, Lennox Lewis, Michael Moorer, and Ray Mercer, all of whom were still amateurs when Tyson unified the title. The highly marketable Tommy Morrison was also in the picture despite a bad loss to Mercer the previous year, and then there was George Foreman, the amazing Rip Van Winkle of boxing, who had won legions of new fans with a buoyant performance that dumbfounded the experts.

The person most directly affected by Tyson's departure was Don King. Without his top attraction, King was forced to do some scrambling. Julio Cesar Chavez was bumped up the totem pole.

# CHAPTER 21

# Mariachi Salsa

A featherweight when he first burst on the scene, Julio Cesar Chavez had two strikes against him: casual fans were indifferent to boxers his size and he never achieved sufficient command of the English language to bolster his appeal via appearances on English-language TV and radio shows. But Chavez had attributes that sent his stock soaring and made him an icon in his native country. In common with most great Mexican fighters, he was a terrific body puncher with great stamina and an iron chin, but what set him apart was a relentless will to win that translated into an attention-grabbing winning streak. That Chavez became the top dog in Don King's kennel was partly an accident of good timing, but it was also a triumph of substance over style. One might also say that it was a half-century in the making. Mexican fighters had a long row to hoe before a member of their brigade reached that pinnacle.

In 1984, Bonanza Books released Bert Randolph Sugar's *The 100 Greatest Boxers of All Time,* a richly illustrated book that became a popular reference source. Sugar's Top 100 included only two fighters born in Mexico, Carlos Zarate (68) and Salvador Sanchez (86).

Among those left out, few had stronger credentials than Alberto "Baby" Arizmendi. Born in Torreon (some accounts say Tampico), Arizmendi won the California and New York versions of the featherweight title and scored two wins over five-time rival Henry Armstrong. Among other distinctions, Arizmendi was the first fighter born in Mexico to achieve a #1 ranking in *The Ring* ratings and the first native Mexican to see his name atop the marquee at Madison Square Garden.

Arizmendi competed from 1927 to 1942. He came to the fore at the Olympic Auditorium, where he headlined 33 shows. He had 90 documented bouts on American soil, but only six at venues east of Galveston. In his day, the glass ceiling for Mexican fighters was nearly impenetrable. When Arizmendi quit boxing at the age of 38, he enlisted in the U.S. Navy.

Built specifically for boxing events, the Olympic Auditorium opened in August of 1925. Over time, the 10,096-seat arena on South Grand Avenue in central Los Angeles became a shrine to fighters of Mexican descent. Arizmendi was the first fighter from Mexico to achieve a loyal following there. He blazed the trail for others, the best of whom were able to climb the ladder more swiftly.

Ten months after Arizmendi's farewell fight, Enrique Bolaños made his pro debut. Bolaños surpassed Arizmendi in popularity, drawing SRO crowds to the Olympic even after repeated

*Left to right:* Rodolfo "Baby" Casanova, Kid Azteca, Alberto "Baby" Arizmendi, unidentified, in 1933 or 1934. Fighters from Mexico energized the California boxing scene during the Depression. Azteca, born Luis Villanueva Paramo, had 200 documented fights in a career that spanned 30 years. *Reproduced from the original held by the Department of Special Collections of the University Libraries of Notre Dame.*

failures in his most important fights. A man easy to caricature because of his prominently long nose, Bolaños had a style that invited comparisons with Willie Pep.

In his 24th pro fight, Bolaños was matched against former featherweight titlist Albert "Chalky" Wright. A seasoned veteran whose career took an upward turn when actress Mae West took an interest in him, Wright was likely born in Durango, Colorado, but he was referenced as a native of Durango, Mexico. Bolaños also hailed from the Mexican city of Durango, or at least his family had roots there. The "Battle of Durango" was a hot ticket. Bolaños's final sparring sessions at the Main Street Gym reportedly drew more rubberneckers than had come to see Joe Louis prepare for his title bout with Jack Roper.

Bolaños came up short, losing a 10-round decision, but avenged the defeat in two subsequent meetings. He went on to have three fights with lightweight titlist Ike Williams. Bolaños showed well in defeat in the middle match, which drew a crowd in excess of 25,000 to L.A.'s Wrigley Field, but Williams beat him to a pulp in their first and third encounters.

Four months after his third fight with Williams, Bolaños was out-pointed by undefeated New Orleans cutie-pie Maxie Docusen in a bout billed for the California lightweight title. They were rematched for February 14, 1950, at the Olympic Auditorium, but Docusen was a late scratch and the promoters substituted Art Aragon. A swaggering Don Juan often seen

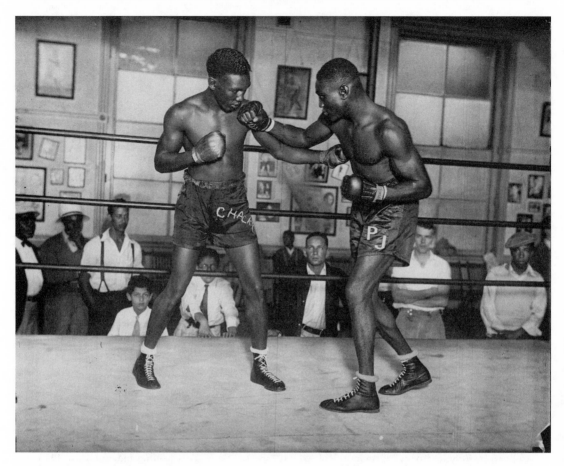

Albert "Chalky" Wright sparring with lightweight contender Young Peter Jackson circa 1938. Fluent in Spanish, Wright had 200 documented fights and motored about Hollywood with Mae West, and yet his background is shrouded in mystery. *Reproduced from the original held by the Department of Special Collections of the University Libraries of Notre Dame.*

in the company of Hollywood starlets, Aragon had an unexceptional 38–9–3 record, but he was a good action fighter who had a star quality about him, befitting his cognomen Golden Boy.[1]

Assumed to be of Mexican extraction, Aragon wanted it known that his ancestors came from Spain, insinuating that Mexicans were beneath him. This fueled more interest in a bout that would have drawn well without this prod. When Bolaños made his entrance, he was greeted with thunderous applause; Aragon drew mostly catcalls. However, at the conclusion of the rousing slugfest, stopped in the twelfth round, the victorious Aragon received a tremendous ovation. It was wisecracked that he entered the ring a Spaniard and emerged a Mexican, which was quite true, as Mexican fight fans came to embrace him as one of their own.

Aragon and Bolaños were matched again five months later. Although Bolaños was showing the effects of too many hard fights, the match at the Olympic Auditorium was California's biggest boxing event of the year. "You can't get a ticket for love or money unless you know somebody who knows somebody who knows somebody," wrote *L.A. Times* columnist Al Wolf.

Aragon knocked out Bolaños in the fourth round and went on to become an even bigger ticket-seller than the man he conquered. His November 14, 1951, bout with lightweight titlist Jimmy Carter entered the trivia books as the first nationally televised fight from California. His 1958 bout with Carmen Basilio at Wrigley Field broke the existing California record for gate receipts. The Golden Boy lost both fights. He extended Carter the 15-round distance, but Basilio chewed him to ribbons en route to an eighth-round stoppage.

Baby Arizmendi and Enrique Bolaños had their first documented fights in U.S. rings. Both were conversant in English, which widened their appeal. Raul "El Raton" Macias, a fighter from Mexico City who was Cuban on his father's side, brought a new dimension to the L.A. boxing scene. One of the first Mexican boxers to be accorded wide TV exposure in his native country, Macias was the first fighter to bring significant dollars into Los Angeles from south of the border. His bout with bantamweight champion Alphonse Halimi on Wednesday, November 6, 1957, drew 20,060 to Wrigley Field despite chilly weather and the threat of rain. Promoter Cal Eaton puffed that fight fans in Mexico City flooded the American Embassy for 8000 visas, a dubious assertion, although the crowd was thick with Mexican tourists. The new demographic was attributed to wider penetration of Mexico by international airlines and improved economic conditions on both sides of the border.

The California boxing industry south of San Francisco had become increasingly salsa-flavored, but Macias vs. Halimi was a more peppery salsa. Many of Macias's rooters brought musical instruments and many wore sombreros that concealed liquid spirits. *L.A. Times* correspondent John De La Vega noted that one of the scribes in the Mexican press contingent had taken the precaution of wearing a helmet.

The Paris-based Halimi, an Algerian Jew from the slums of Constantine, came on with a rush to cop a split decision. The mood of Macias's supporters was made more somber when

A great ladies' man and a hell-for-leather fighter, Art Aragon earned his nickname "Golden Boy." *Cyber Boxing Zone.*

Jose Becerra suffered a shocking knockout at the hands of L.A. schoolboy Dwight Hawkins in the walkout bout. Becerra, from Guadalajara, was being prepped for a match with Halimi in the event that Halimi retained his title.

Becerra rebounded with a 15-fight winning streak that elevated his ledger to 66–4–2. In the process, he avenged his loss to Hawkins. On July 8, 1959, he was pitted against Halimi in the icebreaker event at the new L.A. Sports Arena. A 9/5 underdog, Becerra fought Halimi on even terms through seven action-packed rounds and then knocked him cold as the crowd went delirious.

The Becerra-Halimi rematch was planted in the L.A. Coliseum, where it drew 31,830. An estimated 15,000 were Mexican tourists, but there was a large sprinkling of Hollywood celebrities. Reporters called it the most star-studded crowd in California ring annals. Becerra, a 2/1 favorite, was trailing on all three scorecards when he brought the bout to a sudden conclusion with a lightning-bolt left hook in Round 9, thrilling his partisans.

Becerra appeared destined to meet South American bantamweight champion Eder Jofre, a fast-rising Brazilian who would come to be ranked among the greatest fighters of all time. However, seven months after his second encounter with Halimi, Becerra walked away from boxing. His retirement at age 24 followed a TKO loss in a Juarez bullring to journeyman Eloy Sanchez, but a larger contributing factor was a tragic tune-up fight in Guadalajara between his two bouts with Halimi, a fatal encounter for his opponent, a young West Virginian, Walter Ingram. National pride prodded Becerra to go ahead with the rematch, but his heart was no longer in the game. A bout with Jofre would have provided the true measure of his greatness.

During Jofre's 55-month title reign, there were two big outdoor shows in Los Angeles featuring fighters from Mexico City. Ultiminio "Sugar" Ramos, a Cuban who resettled in Mexico midway through his career, wrested the featherweight title from Davey Moore on a card that drew 26,450 to Dodger Stadium, a turnout thinned by a five-day postponement wrought by incessant rain. The bout was fatal for Moore, whose brain stem was whiplashed against the bottom strand of rope when he was knocked down in the 10th frame. Barrel-chested Vicente Saldivar, who deposed Ramos by TKO in Mexico City, made his first defense against L.A.-born dockworker Raul Rojas at the L.A. Coliseum. Salvidar dominated the fight en route to a Round 15 stoppage.

The opening of the L.A. Forum in 1968 coincided with a resurgence of interest in Mexican bantamweights. Jesus "Chucho" Castillo (31–7) and Jesus "Little Poison" Pimentel (61–3) christened the new venue on June 14. The turnout, 15,380, was a California indoor record. Castillo won the 12-round non-title fight with surprising ease, out-pointing his countryman by a wide margin to earn a crack at the bantamweight title held by lanky Lionel Rose, a 20-year-old Australian aborigine. This bout, a "pick-'em" fight projected by local reporters to be a ring classic, was held at the Forum on December 6, 1968.

Castillo drew huge crowds to his Sunday afternoon public workouts in a ballroom of the Alexandria Hotel. In the fight, he pressed the action, but the Melbourne-based Rose retained his title on a split decision. The verdict ignited the greatest riot in Los Angeles boxing history. The referee, who voted for Castillo, was badly gashed by a flying bottle. Up in the nosebleed sections, partisans of Castillo started 11 fires. The next bout on the card, one of two scheduled 10-round "post-liminaries," was aborted at the start of the fourth round when emergency workers arrived and ordered an evacuation. The firemen saved the building, but it was speculated that things would never be the same. Influential boxing official Jim Deskin, the former chairman of the Nevada Commission, stated, "I think that the time has come to bar Mexican national fighters from the rings of California and Nevada."[2]

Cooler heads prevailed. Twenty-two months later, the indoor record was shattered again when an overflow crowd of 18,712 turned up at the Forum for an all-bantamweight card powered by a showdown between Castillo and the new bantamweight champion, Ruben Olivares, who had sheared the title from Rose with a fifth-round knockout.

Castillo and Olivares traveled in the same circles in Mexico City. What set them apart was their personalities. Castillo was quiet and a man of temperate habits; the outgoing Olivares was an inveterate partygoer. Undefeated in 57 fights and riding a skein of 30 knockouts, Olivares was a cut above, but Castillo had more *sympaticos*.

A 7/2 favorite, Olivares won the decision, but Castillo turned the tables in a rematch, winning on cuts in the 14th stanza. In a rubber match that was less testy than the first two meetings, Olivares won by a comfortable margin.

All three bouts were held at the Forum, giving Los Angeles the distinction of hosting the first great Mexican vs. Mexican trilogy contested on U.S. soil, but there wasn't another place where the series could play out as profitably. Olivares-Castillo I, the biggest of the three battles from a revenue standpoint, was closed-circuited to only seven locales — three in the Los Angeles metroplex, plus San Francisco, Sacramento, San Antonio, and El Paso. Although the bout was televised in Mexico, the lion's share of the revenue derived from box office receipts.

Olivares went on to compete for the featherweight title, losing by TKO 13 to Alexis Arguello, a Nicaraguan making his first appearance in an American ring. On the same L.A. Forum show, Mexico City bantamweight Carlos Zarate made his U.S. debut. In due course, Zarate would come to be recognized as the hardest-punching bantamweight of all time.

Zarate met his Waterloo in hostile San Juan on October 28, 1978, suffering a fifth-round knockout at the hands of local hero Wilfredo Gomez. The next year, Zarate had the distinction of being the first fighter from Mexico accorded top billing on a show at Caesars Palace. His June 3, 1979, contest with ex-stablemate Lupe Pintor produced a weird split decision — the dissenting ballot favored Zarate by 12 points! The unpopular verdict so discomposed Zarate that he quit boxing, remaining inactive for almost seven years. He left the scene with a 56–2 record studded with 55 knockouts.

It would fall to Salvador Sanchez to shift the tide back to Mexico in the battle with Puerto Rico for supremacy in the world of little giants. On August 21, 1981, Sanchez met Wilfredo Gomez at the Caesars Palace Sports Pavilion in a bout that Bert Sugar denominated the greatest inter–Hispanic event in boxing history. The undefeated Gomez, a slight favorite, entered the bout riding a skein of 32 knockouts, but Sanchez, making the sixth defense of his WBC featherweight title, put him away in eight frames.

Raised on a dirt farm in the village of Santiago Tianguistenco, Sanchez was enormously popular in his homeland, his appeal heightened by his humble background and his uncanny facial resemblance to the cartoon character Popeye. Although he didn't speak English, he seemingly had the potential to become a big draw in the United States. He would have almost certainly become the first Mexican to headline a big outdoor show in Las Vegas. However, three weeks after defending his title with a fifteenth-round stoppage of Azumah Nelson at Madison Square Garden, Sanchez perished in a one-car accident near Mexico City. He was only 23 years old. His hometown honors his memory with an annual fiesta.

# CHAPTER 22

# El Gran Campeón de Culiacan

Launching his pro career at the age of 17, Julio Cesar Chavez had 33 fights in Mexico prior to his U.S. debut in a preliminary bout on a card in Sacramento. On September 13, 1984, he acquired his first belt, stopping Mario Martinez in the eighth round at the Olympic Auditorium in a match sanctioned for the vacant WBC 130-pound title. With this victory, Chavez boosted his record to 45–0. (Chavez lost an early bout in his native Culiacan on a disqualification, but his manager got the result overturned.)

In his first nationally televised fight, staged on a Sunday afternoon in the showroom of the Riviera Hotel, Chavez delivered a sensational performance while defending his crown against Roger Mayweather. In the opening round, Chavez absorbed several hard shots to the jaw. In the next stanza, he knocked Mayweather unconscious with a murderous right hook. The punch said less about Chavez than about Mayweather's beard. Chavez wasn't a one-punch knockout artist, but a woodchopper who methodically stalked his opponents while gradually sapping their strength and their will.

After seven more title defenses, Chavez moved up in weight to challenge Edwin Rosario. A New York–based Puerto Rican, Rosario had rebounded from a hotly disputed loss to Hector Camacho with a smashing performance against Livingston Bramble, snatching Bramble's lightweight title with a second-round knockout. Although Chavez went to post an 8/5 favorite, there were a slew of big bets on Rosario, who was judged to be the stronger man.

Staged in an outdoor ring at the Las Vegas Hilton, the bout was a tour de force for the Mexican, who seemingly got stronger with every round. Rosario was bleeding from cuts on his nose, mouth, and right eyebrow, and his left eye was completely shut when his corner tossed in the towel in Round 11. By turning the highly anticipated fight into a rout, Chavez came to be ranked among the top pound-for-pound fighters in the world.

Eleven months later, with four more fights under his belt, Chavez grabbed another piece of the lightweight title at the expense of Culiacan compadre Jose Luis Ramirez. Contested before a near-capacity crowd at the Hilton Center, the fight went into the books as a win for Chavez when the contest was stopped after ten rounds with Ramirez bleeding from a deep cut inflicted by an accidental head butt. Chavez was comfortably ahead on the scorecards when the bout was halted.

Chavez vs. Ramirez was the first pay-per-view (henceforth PPV) fight in which both contestants resided in Mexico. A sidebar to the event was the involvement of Mike Tyson, who was introduced at the pre-fight press conference as the co-promoter. Don King told the press that he was grooming Tyson to be the CEO of his company.

The next bauble that Chavez acquired was the WBC 140-pound diadem, then owned by the resilient Roger Mayweather. Chavez stopped Mayweather in the 10th round at the LA Forum, putting the pins in place for unification match with IBF counterpart Meldrick Taylor. Although steeped in controversy, the Chavez-Taylor fight, contested on March 17, 1990, before a sellout crowd at the Hilton Center, would come to be seen as the career-defining fight of the great warrior from Culiacan.

An Olympic gold medalist at age 17, Taylor was unbeaten in 25 pro fights. The only blemish on his ledger was a draw with Howard Davis, Jr. Taylor had been unwise to take that fight so early into his career, albeit most in attendance felt that he merited the decision.

**Julio Cesar Chavez, around 1990.**

Taylor had quicker hands and was far more elusive than Chavez. He attracted a great deal of so-called smart money, but yet entered the contest an 8/5 underdog. The roles would have likely been reversed if the fight had been potted at an East Coast venue such as Atlantic City. Taylor hailed from Philadelphia.

Heading into the final round, Taylor had a seven-point margin on one of the scorecards and a five-point margin on another. However, judging by their respective appearances, one would have guessed that Chavez was ahead by a mile. He was unmarked except for a nick on the bridge of his nose, whereas Taylor's face was lumpy and his trunks were flecked with blood from a bad cut inside his mouth. Moreover, Taylor was conspicuously more fatigued.

With 24 seconds remaining in the fight, Chavez buckled Taylor's knees with a vicious right to the jaw. With ten seconds remaining, Chavez knocked Taylor off his feet in front of his horrified cornermen. As Taylor rose on unsteady legs, reflexively gripping a strand of rope, referee Richard Steele looked him in the eye and asked him if he was okay. Taylor was unresponsive, prompting Steele to waive off the fight with only two seconds remaining.

Taylor was credited with landing 199 more punches. Although Steele was roundly criticized for taking the fight away from the judges, it was hard to quibble with his argument that one more punch might have been fatal. Badly dehydrated, Taylor was shooed to a hospital where he was diagnosed with a fractured orbital bone. His attending physician estimated that he had swallowed two pints of his own blood.

The next big fight for Chavez would be against Hector Camacho, but an intervening bout with overmatched Lonnie Smith on September 14, 1991, at the Mirage had significant ramifications from a marketing standpoint. This was the first Las Vegas boxing promotion hinged to a Mexican holiday weekend. Although the show wasn't heavily publicized in the local dailies, it drew a big turnout. In subsequent years, many big boxing shows in Las Vegas were timed to coincide with Cinco de Mayo and Mexico's Independence Day.

Hector Camacho was one of the great characters of boxing. A Puerto Rican raised in New York City, he dressed outlandishly, preened like the old wrestler Gorgeous George, trash-talked incessantly, but in a manner that was more playful than mean-spirited, and reveled in his well-earned reputation as a party animal. His euphonic nickname eventually became incongruent with his fighting style, but TV and radio commentators invariably used it when talking about him, striking the impression that his last name was hyphenated: Hector Macho-Camacho. As his career evolved, he became better known for his escapades outside the ring. Pundits had a field day when he was ticketed for speeding in his Ferrari while his girlfriend was astride him.

Camacho devolved into a runner after a bruising tiff with Edwin Rosario. Fourteen of his 16 fights leading up to his bout with Chavez went the full distance. Chavez would be a commanding 11/2 favorite over the mislabeled Macho Man, and yet their 1992 Mexican Independence Day fight sold out the 19,100-seat Thomas and Mack Center. Foreseeably, Camacho lasted the route but Chavez won virtually every round.

The crowd paled in comparison to the crowds at Chavez's next two major fights. His bout with Greg Haugen on February 20, 1993, at Mexico City's Azteca Stadium drew 132,274, breaking the record set by the first Dempsey-Tunney fight, a record that had stood for nearly 67 years.[1] Haugen was no slouch. In appearance and in fighting style, he resembled Gene Fullmer. But Chavez took the starch out of him in a hurry, much to the jubilation of the great multitude. Haugen had goaded them to a fever pitch by declaring that Chavez had padded his record against a bunch of Tijuana taxi drivers.

If the new sports palace in San Antonio had been built to a slightly larger scale, Chavez might have broken the outdoor and indoor attendance records in the same year. Not quite seven months after the Haugen fight, Chavez drew 59,995 to the Alamodome for a bout with Pernell "Sweet Pea" Whitaker, a number surpassed only by Ali-Spinks II at the Louisiana Superdome. Chavez kept his undefeated record intact when the bout was scored a draw. The verdict seemed fair to most of the folks in the arena, but most of those in the U.S. press contingent were of the opinion that Whitaker was robbed.

Only 14,000 witnessed Chavez's next fight in a Juarez bullring, but they braved near-freezing weather to watch their idol pummel a Denver truck driver in a bout best described as an exhibition. Seven weeks later, Chavez drew 45,000 to a Puebla soccer stadium for a match with Andy Holligan, a fighter from Liverpool who was undefeated (21–0) but far out of Chavez's league. The turnout was exceptional considering stronger pulls on discretionary spending with Christmas only seven days away.

In an earlier era, Chavez would have likely stayed in a big-box groove, fighting his most appealing opponents in large open-air enclosures. However, times had changed and the big money was in Las Vegas where it cost less to stage a PPV event and gate receipts were swollen by steep admission prices. Forty-five days after his appearance in Puebla, Chavez headlined the inaugural show at the MGM Grand. The unfoldment of boxing at the MGM Grand Garden — the "municipal auditorium" of the self-styled City of Entertainment — was the most significant boxing-related development in Las Vegas during the period when Mike Tyson was locked away in prison.

The honchos at the MGM Grand wanted to lock in Chavez for Mexican holiday weekends. Don King was agreeable, but only if they purchased an antecedent show. Twenty-nine days after the christening of the Grand Garden with a Barbra Streisand concert, Chavez topped the marquee on a show spiced with big names on the undercard. The roster of participants included Thomas Hearns, Razor Ruddock, Felix Trinidad, and Meldrick Taylor. The card also marked the Las Vegas debut of King's newest find, Christie Martin, a person destined to become the first nationally prominent female boxer.

King matched Chavez with Frankie Randall, a fighter from Morristown, Tennessee. Randall had a strong amateur background and an impressive pro log (48–2–1), but was an enigma. While he had defeated several high-grade opponents, he had suffered a spectacular defeat in a crossroads fight with Primo Ramos—Ramos hit him so hard in Round 2 that Randall was in a fog for nearly 10 minutes. He had won eight straight since serving a brief prison term on a cocaine-trafficking conviction, but his victims, other than shopworn Edwin Rosario, were largely unknown. It was hard to build a case for him, and the case became weaker when two judges with Spanish surnames, a Mexican and a Puerto Rican, were named to work the fight. At the MGM Grand sports book, Chavez was a prohibitive 17/1 favorite.

Early into the fight, it became apparent that Randall had the tools to make things interesting. In Round 11, what had been a nip-and-tuck fight swung sharply in favor of the Tennessean. Chavez was assessed his second point deduction for low blows and suffered the first knockdown of his career when Randall nailed him flush with a straight right hand. While Chavez wasn't badly hurt or deterred from pressing the action, he was now in deep water. But there would be no Meldrick Taylor-like meltdown for Frankie Randall, who finished the fight looking the fresher of the two and copped the split verdict. The dissenting judge gave the nod to his Mexican countryman.

The shocking upset disarranged well-laid plans, but suited the MGM Grand just fine. The most attractive match out there at 140 pounds was suddenly a Chavez-Randall rematch, and the MGM would make it happen on Cinco de Mayo. Randall would again be competing on a field that was not level—a field that would come to be seen as booby-trapped.

In the rematch, Randall cranked it up a notch. Heading into the eighth frame, it appeared that he was beginning to take control. But with only a few seconds remaining in that round, there was a clash of heads as Randall ducked under a looping overhand right. Chavez spun around and walked to his corner, blood streaming from a scythe-shaped gash on his forehead. While it wasn't immediately apparent, the bout was over.

Too many rounds had elapsed to permit a ruling of "no contest." It would go to the judges, with the abbreviated round counting in the tally. Unknown to almost everyone, the WBC had recently modified its rule regarding accidental head butts. The fighter less damaged by the collision was judged to be the guilty party. He was assessed a one-point penalty.

Two judges had Randall leading heading into the fateful round. The dissenting judge was a Mexican. But when the queer new rule was factored into the tally, Chavez emerged the winner by split decision. There was a great deal of confusion while things were being sorted out, and a shower of boos when the result was announced. Even some of Chavez's staunch supporters were embarrassed by the turn of events. Ringside physician Flip Homansky acknowledged that while the cut was bad enough to warrant stopping the bout, he would have allowed the contest to continue if that had been Chavez's preference. There was an element of "No mas" to Chavez's abjuration, diminishing his status as a proud warrior.

The Nevada Athletic Commission took the unusual step of petitioning the WBC for an immediate rematch and by informal decree barred Mexicans from officiating at any of Chavez's future fights in Nevada. Randall's mood was brightened by an assurance that he would be handsomely compensated in the rubber match, but Don King was in no hurry to make it. Until Mike Tyson was free, Chavez was his star attraction. A rematch between Chavez and

Meldrick Taylor was at least as attractive, and far less likely to produce an inexpedient outcome. Thus, Chavez-Randall III was put on the back burner, where it would languish until both men were in their pugilistic dotage and Randall so badly frayed that he had been reduced to fighting for peanuts in jurisdictions where medical screening was lax. (In 2004, Chavez fairly out-pointed Randall in a good action fight in Mexico City that was accorded no mention in most American papers.)

The first Chavez-Taylor bout was a confrontation between enormously talented fighters. The rematch was a contest between lesser men. Akin to the second bout between Sugar Ray Leonard and Thomas Hearns, handicapping the fight boiled down to assessing which man had declined the most in the interim.

Taylor had absorbed such a bad beating in the first encounter with Chavez that it was reckoned that he would never be the same. He won a share of the welterweight title in his second comeback fight, but then things turned sour. In 1992, he suffered harsh knockouts in back-to-back fights with Terry Norris and Crisanto Espana. He then broke ties with his promoter, signing with King, who fed him three soft touches to rebuild his confidence.

Taylor had been campaigning as a welterweight. He dropped back to 140 pounds for the rematch with Chavez. This was deemed to be his natural weight. The odds favoring Chavez dropped from 4/1 to 2/1.

Taylor started fast and won the early rounds, but Chavez gradually found his range and closed the show in Round 8 with a terrific left hook. Three months later, Chavez gave another strong performance. Fighting at a baseball park in Monterrey, Mexico, Chavez scored a 10th round TKO of Tony Lopez, a solid pro from Sacramento.

Next in the line of fire was Giovanni Parisi. An Olympic featherweight champion, Parisi (29–1) figured to give Chavez a good test, but he fought an uninspired fight and was widely out-pointed. Of greater note, Chavez was again reduced to a supporting act. Topping the bill was a WBC heavyweight title fight between Oliver McCall and 45-year-old Larry Holmes. The most heavily hyped of the undercard fights pitted Bruce Seldon against Tony Tucker.

The shift of emphasis was foretokened by the return of Mike Tyson. Fifteen days prior to this show at Caesars Palace, Tyson had walked out of prison straight into King's welcoming arms. Perhaps Iron Mike would never recapture his former glory, but he was more bankable than ever and the crafty promoter had already drawn a hefty advance on his future ring earnings. More so than anyone, Julio Cesar Chavez kept King in clover during the potentially fallow years when Tyson was quarantined behind prison walls, but now the "El Gran Campeón" was merely an afterthought. Chavez had more big-money fights in his future, but King had other priorities and their relationship was about to be ruptured.

# CHAPTER 23

# Iron Mike II:
# Another Vegas Implosion

The trial of Mike Tyson was Page 1 material and the verdict fomented a contentious debate. Was Tyson truly a rapist, or the victim of feminist-driven dogma that blurred the distinction between rape and seduction? To Tyson's loyalists, it mattered greatly that his accuser had voluntarily accompanied him to his room at a late hour where there would be just the two of them — an alluring young woman and a famously concupiscent young man with the animal magnetism of a young Brando. The discussion engaged individuals with no interest in boxing. As a by-product, more people became conversant with Tyson's ring exploits. During the years of his incarceration, his specter devalued the achievements of every important heavyweight fighter.

The renowned Harvard law professor Alan Dershowitz handled Tyson's unsuccessful appeal. Dershowitz hardened the mindset of Tyson's sympathizers in legal briefs, public forums, and in a copyrighted article — "Why Mike Tyson is Innocent" — that ran as the cover story in the October 1992 issue of *Boxing Illustrated*.[1] A taped prison interview of Tyson by *60 Minutes* correspondent Ed Bradley was a ratings bonanza for the popular television program. The interview was the first public display of Tyson's new tattoos. A portrait of Mao Tse Tung adorned one of his biceps and a portrait of Arthur Ashe adorned the other. One didn't quite know how to interpret the message that Tyson was sending.

A number of Don King's rivals made overtures to Tyson while he was in prison, but King was too dogged and too slick for them. During the hiatus, King kept Rory Holloway and John Horne on his payroll. Old pals of Tyson going back to his Catskill days, they were ostensibly his managers. He took the liberty of negotiating a mind-blowing 6-fight deal for Tyson with the MGM Grand. And he praised Tyson at every opportunity, making certain that Tyson was made aware of these encomiums. In a speech to graduate business students at the University of Virginia, King likened Tyson to Thomas Jefferson, the school's founder. The common hallmark, said King, was uncompromising principles.

Tyson left prison with a new Muslim name that he would never use professionally and a new love interest, Monica Turner. (A pediatric intern from a family of high achievers — her brother Michael Steele would be Maryland's first African American attorney general since Reconstruction — Turner cultivated a relationship with Tyson by the quaint method of exchanging correspondence.) Within days, Tyson walked smack into a controversy not of his making when a group of Harlemites held a candlelight vigil to protest a homecoming rally for him at the Apollo Theatre, an event organized by Reverend Al Sharpton. The protestors succeeded in getting the rally called off.

Although there were several outstanding heavyweight fights during Tyson's hiatus and the division was brimming with new talent, the sport had relapsed into a state of disorganization. Twenty men had claimed a piece of the title since Tyson's defrocking by Buster Douglas. Three fighters in particular — Evander Holyfield, Riddick Bowe, and George Foreman — made significant gains in public esteem. Of the three, only Foreman was a titleholder on the day that Tyson left prison. This was incredible.

## Catching Up with George Foreman

George Foreman's 47th and 48th pro fights were spaced ten years apart. During the interim, Foreman evangelized on street corners and then from the pulpit of a small clapboard church in a gritty section of Houston. The second coming of George Foreman began with little fanfare on March 18, 1987, in Sacramento. Steve Zouski fell in the fourth round.

Although Foreman had been out of action for a decade, it seemed much longer. The man with whom he was most closely linked, Muhammad Ali, had slid into decrepitude, dating an entire generation of boxers as relics. In appearance and in fighting style, Foreman scarcely resembled his former self, which had the sensory effect of elongating the gap in his boxing timeline. The new George Foreman shaved his head bald and was more massive. The pounds that he had gained did not bloat his stomach so much as thicken his entire torso. When Big George, as he came to be called, sallied out of his dressing room for his first comeback fight, Graham Houston likened the impression to that of an ancient battleship coming through the mist.

Foreman launched his comeback with former aide-de-camp Archie Moore back at his side. Moore fitted him with a peek-a-boo style calculated to reduce energy consumption. When the national media began to take notice, Foreman brought publicist Bill Caplan back on board. Caplan's job was made easier because Foreman had mellowed. During his first incarnation, George became increasingly prickly toward reporters and increasingly less approachable. He smiled less and less. The reconstituted George Foreman was a good-natured chap, downright cuddly. He developed an amusing schtick that played up a fondness for cheeseburgers and became a popular guest on the talk show circuit, all the while pushing himself the extra mile in his workouts.

Foreman's first bout against a name opponent came at an old stomping ground, the Caesars Palace Sports Pavilion. He scored a seventh-round TKO of Dwight Muhammad Qawi (aka Dwight Braxton), but his performance against the grossly overweight ex-cruiserweight champion was unimpressive. Gauging that he had more rust to shed, Foreman reverted to fighting in towns off the main line, compensating for the poor quality of his opponents by fighting more frequently to keep his name before the public. He had 19 comeback fights under his belt when he was thrust against Gerry Cooney.

Cooney had been inactive for 30 months, making this a crossroads fight for two boxers on the comeback trail. Staged in Atlantic City on January 15, 1990, the match was dismissed in some quarters as a freak fight, but was yet a compelling attraction that generated strong sales. Foreman was chalked the favorite at odds of 3/2, but Cooney was judged to have the better chance of ending the bout with a single punch. Big George had stopped all of his recent opponents with the exception of sturdy Everett Martin, but none of his victims had been knocked out cleanly. Cooney would be the exception. When he hit the canvas for the second time in the second round, he was in such bad shape that a 10-count was superfluous. It was Foreman's most dominating performance since his demolition of Joe Frazier 17 years earlier.

Foreman had been calling out Tyson from the very onset of his return and suddenly the idea wasn't so preposterous. But Tyson had two fights on his docket — Buster Douglas followed by Holyfield — and Foreman would need to wait his turn. Subsequent events scrambled agendas, resulting in a Foreman-Holyfield fight.

While Foreman now boasted a 69–2 record, his age (42) was considered a curse. The scoffers said that the renascence of Big George was a big sham motivated by the specter of bankruptcy and that he wasn't about to spoil his grand payday — reportedly $12.5 million — by taking unnecessary punishment. Looking into the recesses of

George Foreman, the great Rip Van Winkle of boxing, around 1994. *Top Rank file photograph.*

history, the specter of Benny Leonard loomed large. Leonard's similarly plotted comeback ended in a rich payday, but in a fight he had no realistic chance of winning. A scenario that acquired considerable currency postulated that Foreman would come out like a typhoon and fold his tent when he had spent all his bullets, perhaps feigning an injury. The over/under of 4½ rounds was shaped by this supposition.

Foreman vs. Holyfield was a smashing promotion despite all the disparagement, breaking the existing record for PPV buys. And while Foreman came up short, he made a splendid showing. The seventh round was a furious session, and yet somehow Big George still had plenty of steam in his boiler. In the final stanza he actually had Holyfield on the retreat, simply amazing considering that his undefeated adversary, a 9/2 favorite, was 14 years younger and renowned for his vigor. More than a moral victory, the bout elevated Foreman into a national folk hero.

Foreman's next two major fights were staged at the Thomas and Mack Center on the campus of UNLV. He survived a bruising slugfest with Alex Stewart, copping a narrow decision, but was on the wrong end of a narrow decision in his bout with Tommy Morrison, a contest sanctioned for a minor heavyweight belt. A 24-year-old Oklahoman with a fearsome left hook, Morrison dyed his hair a lighter shade of blond to heighten his resemblance to the comic strip boxer Joe Palooka. For good measure, his manager Bill Cayton told reporters that Morrison was related to western movie icon John Wayne.

Although it wasn't obvious at the time, these fights were another turning point on the Las Vegas fight scene, signaling the demise of the big outdoor shows, which had an aura about them that couldn't be recaptured in an indoor arena. One by one, the old battlegrounds had disappeared, the land usurped for new hotel towers, casino expansions, parking garages, and shopping arcades.

Foreman hyped his bout with Morrison as his farewell fight. He had a TV sitcom in production, appropriately titled *George*, the name he shared with his four sons. This would be a major drain on his time, leaving scant room for training. But Foreman wasn't done with boxing yet. The series was canceled after only eight episodes.

On April 22, 1994, Kronk Gym product Michael Moorer kept his undefeated record intact, out-pointing Holyfield at Caesars Palace to become the first southpaw to join the ranks of heavyweight champions. By and large, the sanctioning bodies allowed a freshly minted champion the right to hand-pick his first challenger. As Holyfield had done before him, Moorer tabbed Big George, the consort that figured to generate the most money with the least risk.

Foreman, inactive for 18 months, was now 45 years old. However, beyond the fact that a man of his vintage had no business in the ring, it was hard to get too enthused about the 27-year-old Moorer, a dispassionate workman whose triumph over Holyfield was credited to the in-fight conniptions of his firebrand trainer Teddy Atlas. When Foreman fought Holyfield, virtually all of the big bets that came in late were on Evander. The trend did not manifest itself in the Foreman-Moorer fight, partly because George trimmed down to 250 pounds and partly because Moorer, a tad overweight at 222, gave no indication that keeping his title was a matter of great importance.

The fight was contested at a slow pace. Moorer, a 14/5 favorite, was comfortably ahead on two scorecards through nine frames. Near the two-minute mark of Round 10, Foreman found an opening and broke the tedium, connecting with a stiff right hand that landed flush on the tip of Moorer's nose. It was a classically British punch in execution, delivered straight from the shoulder. Moorer's face went blank and he crumpled to the canvas. As the referee completed his count, Foreman glanced to the heavens and then kneeled in prayer. It was a scene that touched a soft spot in even the most calloused of ringside scribes. Six days after the twentieth anniversary of the Rumble in the Jungle, Foreman had recaptured his crown, or at least a piece of it, capping the most astonishing comeback in the annals of human endurance sports.

To get Foreman in the ring with Tyson, Don King would need to pony up a king's ransom. There were smarter alternatives in King's estimation, and the confrontation that once seemed inevitable would never take flight. Foreman had four more bouts before finally calling it quits, none versus a man of high reputation. He was fortunate to get the nod over Germany's Axel Schulz, and unfortunate in his final ring outing, losing a hair-thin decision to 25-year-old Shannon Briggs at Atlantic City's Trump Taj Mahal. While the verdict was assailed as a heist, sympathy for Foreman was tempered by his tepid performance against a faint-hearted foe. He was now less than two months shy of his 49th birthday and it was plain that he had slowed down to the point where he had run out of miracles.

Although he ended his career on a downbeat note, Foreman left without a whimper of complaint, his coffers bulging with money. His gross income during the decade of the 1990s reportedly exceeded $100 million, the bulk from endorsements, most notably an electric cooking grill that sold so many units that it gave birth to a new paradigm of marketing. The downside to his comeback was that it seduced other mildewed fighters out of retirement with predictable results. A particularly sad manifestation of this backwash occurred in Aurora, Colorado, on October 30, 1992. Jerry Quarry, 15 years removed from his last meaningful fight and showing early symptoms of dementia, lost a 6-round contest to a cruiserweight with a 3–4–1 record. But the second coming of George Foreman was a feel-good story about an amazing athlete.

Three days before Mike Tyson was let out of prison, Peter McNeeley fought Frankie Hines in Fort Smith, Arkansas. McNeeley won in a flash. No one bothered to record the official time, but it was said that "Hurricane Peter" launched his knockout punch six seconds after the opening bell.

Frankie Hines was something less than a trial horse. Indeed, to list his profession as that of a boxer was a bit of a stretch. He was better described as a performance artist, a loose cousin to a slapstick comedian or a mime. When Hines finally hung up his gloves at the age of 44, his ledger was splotched with 77 losses inside the distance. As for McNeeley, he knew in advance that his excursion to Fort Smith — a popular destination for phony fights — was the final prelude to an encounter with Mike Tyson.

McNeeley's trainer-manager Vinnie Vecchione was an old crony of Don King's crusty matchmaker Al Braverman. In designating McNeeley to be Tyson's first post-prison foe, Braverman was returning a favor. *Boston Herald* sportswriter George Kimball unearthed the story.

In January of 1974, Braverman found an opponent for rising lightheavyweight contender Ennio Cometti. When the opponent disappeared at the 11th hour, he conscripted Vecchione to salvage his commission. Vecchione had never had a professional fight, but he dashed off to Milan, Italy, fighting the bout under the guise of Paul Poirier, an up-and-coming middleweight. (Cometti made short work of Vecchione, who went out in the third round.) The episode was vintage Braverman. Sixteen years earlier, he had been barred from promoting fights in Massachusetts for misrepresenting a fighter who was given the name of a fighter in the Army.

McNeeley had no business in the same ring with a man like Tyson, but was otherwise well suited. His pedigree as a third-generation prizefighter suggested that he was a genuine tough guy. His father Tom had appeared on the cover of *Sports Illustrated* (November 13, 1961), a great coup in the annals of fight ballyhoo. In some of the articles written to hype his match with Floyd Patterson, Irish Tom McNeeley was packaged as a former football star at Michigan State University and readers were told that his father — Peter's grandfather — had competed in the 1928 Amsterdam Olympics. Neither assertion was true, whereas Peter McNeeley's 36–1 professional record was merely deceitful, albeit deceitful in the extreme.

McNeeley enlivened the promotion with some good blarney. He vowed to wrap Tyson in a cocoon of horror, but no one familiar with the inner workings of the fight game was fooled. The integrity of what was unfolding was further disambiguated by advances in record keeping.

The demise of Nat Fleischer's record-keeping annual, which lasted from 1942 to 1986, was hastened by the arrival of record books that were far more thorough. The paragon was the *Fight Fax* record book, a derivative of a yearbook launched in 1983 by versatile cut man Ralph Citro. The upgrade encouraged cross-referencing, enabling one to get a good handle on a fighter without seeing him in the flesh. A closer look at Hurricane Peter's log revealed that he had defeated only four men that had a winning record at the time that he fought them. One of these fellows had been inactive for 15 years. But that did not deter the WBA or WBC from shamelessly bumping McNeeley into the Top 10 on the heels of his victory over Frankie Hines.

In a pre-fight media poll, ten of the respondents framed their predictions in *seconds* rather than rounds. Michael Katz of the *New York Daily News* expressed his contempt by guessing that Tyson would win by disqualification in 21 seconds, an estimate that ultimately wasn't far off the mark. The clumsy, free-swinging McNeeley was on the deck before the fight was 10 seconds old. The bout was stopped after 89 seconds when the quick-triggered Vecchione scampered into the ring on a mission of mercy. By then, McNeeley had been on the canvas twice, but he wasn't seriously hurt.

Inevitably, it was rumored that Vecchione had bet that his fighter would not survive the opening round. Four days after the fight, the rumor became louder when the *Boston Herald* revealed that Vecchione had been shot in Brockton in 1985 over an alleged six-figure gambling debt.[2] Testifying before Nevada regulators, who held up his share of McNeeley's $540,000 purse, Vecchione said: "I didn't have any [expletive] money to bet ... our whole team was [expletive] penniless." That satisfied his interrogators, but the postscript merely prolonged the backlash. Typical was the response of Tribune Media columnist Christopher Matthews: "Only a commission shameless enough to countenance such a matchup would have the shame to blame the man who stopped it."[3]

This travesty was a huge moneymaker. The fight was beamed into 1.4 million U.S. homes. In most markets, subscribers paid $49.95. The live gate ($13,965,600) more than doubled the previous Nevada high set by the Holyfield-Douglas fight. Prominent Las Vegas mob attorney Oscar Goodman was escorted out of the arena when it was determined that his ticket was counterfeit. Destined to become the city's colorful mayor, Goodman declined to identify the provider. "I would never give up anybody," he told *Review-Journal* columnist John L. Smith.[4]

The wacky promotion harked back to Primo Carnera's first fight on American soil. Despite forewarnings that the fight was a swindle, Carnera's supporters swelled Madison Square Garden to the brim and few complained when his opponent melted quickly into putty. Similarly, Tyson's rooters packed the Grand Garden to capacity. They were drawn less to a boxing show than to a tribal celebration. The post-fight VIP party at the hotel's short-lived amusement park was the regeneration of the aborted Apollo Theatre gala repositioned in a more glamorous setting. A small group of picketers clotted the sidewalk on the south side of the property, but the women protesting the glorification of Tyson were barely noticeable in the thick pedestrian traffic and their protest failed to capture the attention of the media.

King thought it prudent to manufacture another tune-up for Tyson, but the MGM and his PPV partners opted to sit this one out. Tyson's match with undefeated (20–0) Buster Mathis Jr. was diverted to Philadelphia and aired free on the Fox network. The feather-fisted Mathis fell in the third round, whereupon Tyson returned to the MGM for a match with former opponent Frank Bruno. The perspicacious Bruno had rebounded from some bad losses to win the WBC version of the heavyweight title.

Bruno entered the ring bearing the countenance of a man being herded to the gallows. Tyson was able to shake free of his clutches and blister him with powerful combinations, much to the dismay of the visiting Brits who comprised a large share of the audience and added color to the event with their chants and flag-waving. The referee halted the mismatch in the third round. Many reporters interpreted Tyson's strong performance to mean that he had rediscovered the tools misplaced when his life turned into a soap opera.

Next up for Tyson was WBA titlist Bruce Seldon. An impressively sculpted boxer who had served a four-and-a-half-year hitch for armed robbery, Seldon was seemingly not the sort of fellow that was easily intimidated, but he too turned meek upon entering the ring. Tyson knocked him down twice with punches that didn't appear to be especially hurtful and the bout was stopped after 86 seconds. The lame fight would be remembered primarily as the overture to the assassination of rap star Tupac Shakur. A brief scuffle inside the arena escalated into a fatal drive-by shooting at a nearby intersection.

Tyson now owned two pieces of the heavyweight title. The third share belonged to Michael Moorer, who had recaptured the IBF title vacated by George Foreman. But in the eyes of Don King, a unification fight was less attractive than a match between Tyson and Evander Holyfield. On paper, Holyfield was a far lesser man than when the fight was first signed, but he was still a big draw.

Staged at the MGM Grand Garden on November 9, 1996, Tyson vs. Holyfield was an enormously profitable promotion, a brutally crowd-pleasing spectacle, the prequel to one of the most infamous fights in history, and a bloodbath for Nevada's colony of legal bookmakers.

## Catching Up with Evander Holyfield

The Tyson-Holyfield match was stalled for five years, during which time Evander's stock went up and down. He cemented his status as a future Hall of Famer and then seemingly reached the point of no return.

On the day reserved for his Caesars Palace fight with Tyson, Holyfield opposed Bert Cooper in Atlanta. A late sub built along the lines of Tyson, Cooper had once been a promising cruiserweight, but his career had soured amidst rumors of heavy drug use. He was coming off a good win over rugged Indian Joe Hipp, but he had been stopped four times and had quit on his stool against George Foreman. Yet Cooper was able to hurt Holyfield, staggering him in the third round with two chopping right hands that produced a standing 8-count. Evander went on to stop him in the seventh frame, but was judged lucky to have found an opponent too muttonheaded to press his advantage.

After out-pointing old-timer Larry Holmes, advancing his record to 28–0, Holyfield risked his title against unbeaten (34–0) Riddick Bowe. Held at the Thomas and Mack Center on November 13, 1992, this would be a terrific fight and ultimately the first installment of a memorable trilogy. The 10th stanza was a round for the ages. Holyfield absorbed a terrible beating in the first two minutes, yet somehow mounted such a robust rally that he won the round in the eyes of many observers, including one of the judges. When the smoke cleared, however, Holyfield was clearly beaten, losing the contest by margins of 7, 7, and 3 points.

Holyfield had one intervening fight before his second encounter with Bowe. He decisioned Alex Stewart, a fighter he had previously TKOed. Meanwhile, Bowe rose to a higher pedestal with quick knockouts of Michael Dokes and Jesse Ferguson. A slight underdog in the first meeting,

Evander Holyfield, circa 1995. Holyfield was still active as this book went to press.

Bowe was installed a 5/1 favorite for the rematch. The fight was held at Caesars Palace on November 6, 1993.

Bowe-Holyfield II was another good scrap, although not as violent as the first meeting. Bowe landed more punches and won the final round on all three cards, but Holyfield's punches carried more authority and he recaptured the title, prevailing by a majority decision.

This ranked among the bigger upsets in heavyweight title bouts, but all the post-fight talk was about the interloper who fell out of the sky.

The intruder, James Miller, was first spotted during the preliminaries. He soared above the arena in a lightweight contraption propelled by a fan encased in a wire cage. During the seventh round, he made his landing, arriving in Bowe's corner, where he got tangled in the ropes. The shroud of his parachute braised several ringsiders, Rev. Jesse Jackson among them. Bowe's wife fainted dead away. Miller — instantly immortalized as the Fan Man — was immediately set upon by ringsiders thought to be members of Bowe's private security force. They pummeled him into a state of unconsciousness.

The scene was surreal almost beyond description. It took 21 minutes before the ring was cleared. Bowe had his best moments after the unscheduled intermission, but it would be his opinion that the Fan Man timed his arrival to arrest his momentum, a perfectly sane conclusion considering the weirdness of it all.

Fined $4000 by the Federal Aviation Administration, Miller was sentenced to eight days in jail on a charge of trespassing. He began serving his sentence on April 20, 1994, thereby precluding him from reprising his stunt at the Holyfield-Moorer fight the next night.[5]

Holyfield attended the post-fight press conference following his narrow points loss to Moorer, and then went to a hospital where he was treated for dehydration. Four days later, he had a more thorough checkup in Atlanta, where he was diagnosed with a congenital heart condition, a noncompliant left ventricle that his physician described as a hole in his heart. His career was apparently finished. Seven weeks later, Holyfield attended a rally in Philadelphia led by evangelist Benny Hinn. He left the revival service believing that he had been healed. Cardiologists at the Mayo Clinic subsequently found no evidence of the defect.

After a 13-month period of inactivity, Holyfield resumed his career in Atlantic City, where he won a 10-round decision over Ray Mercer. Then it was on to Caesars Palace for the rubber match with Riddick Bowe. Victorious in four fights since his second meeting with Holyfield, Bowe was coming off a dominating performance against Cuban defector Jose Luis Gonzalez.

Holyfield knocked Bowe to the canvas in the sixth frame, but then mysteriously ran out of gas. In Round 8, Bowe sandbagged him, scoring two knockdowns, the second of which impelled the referee to stop the fight. Evander's fade-out was completely out of character, raising new concerns about his medical condition. His pro log consisted of only 34 fights, but he had answered the bell for 231 rounds while engaging in several wars of attrition with some of the hardest hitters in the game.

Holyfield plowed forward, turning a deaf ear to those that urged him to retire. On May 10, 1996, he returned to the ring to fight Bobby Czyz. Although Evander was judged by some to be almost completely shot, the 34-year-old Czyz wasn't a credible opponent. A popular fighter in his heyday who won titles in two weight classes, Czyz had never competed at the heavyweight level and had been largely inactive since beginning a second career as a TV fight analyst.

Czyz quit on his stool after five lopsided rounds, complaining of a burning sensation in his eyes. The story of the fight, however, was that Holyfield was never able to knock him off his feet.

Tyson -2500

Holyfield +1800

These were the opening prices at the MGM Grand. A one-hundred-dollar wager on Tyson would yield a profit of four measly dollars. A wager of the same amount on Holyfield translated into a potential payout of $1900, of which $1800 would be pure profit.

The folks that ran the MGM sports book knew that the early action would be lopsided in favor of Evander, but this is what they wanted. Money invariably came in against Tyson when he was dressed a double-digit favorite and Iron Mike had never let them down. Some saps had even taken a flyer on hapless Peter McNeeley, a 22/1 underdog when the line settled.

In a big fight, the action intensifies in the last 48 hours of betting. If the action is balanced during this peak period, the bet-taker is virtually assured of overcoming the jeopardy built up during the antecedency of one-sided action. The MGM Grand bet-takers wanted to "need" Holyfield, but more importantly they wanted to be in position to cover the late six-figure bets that would almost surely show on Tyson, bets that could not be turned down for fear of alienating a prized casino customer.

In a development that still defies explanation, the big bets on Tyson never materialized. The line sank to 8/1 at the MGM and as low as 5/1 at other properties. There wasn't a single sports book in all of Nevada that stood to have a winning day if Holyfield somehow emerged victorious.

The oddsmakers blundered badly. However, the blunder would redound to their credit if Tyson won the fight, and there was nothing beyond his confounding disfavor with bettors to suggest that he wouldn't. In the *Review-Journal* media poll, 47 of 48 respondents picked Tyson, all of them forecasting a stoppage in seven rounds or less. The dissident, *Boston Globe* scribe Ron Borges, was one of America's most knowledgeable boxing writers, but what did that matter when all of his Fourth Estate brethren were dead-set against him? The boxing commission had gone to unprecedented lengths to make certain that Holyfield was fit to fight, dictating another round of tests at the Mayo Clinic and dispatching their own doctors to Houston to observe him in training, but wasn't this merely to forestall litigation in the event that he left Las Vegas in a casket?

In the aggregate, Tyson's four bouts following his release from prison lasted less than eight minutes. The three PPV fights were assailed as rip-offs. Fearing a greater outpouring of outrage, some cable companies offered rebates if the fight ended within three rounds. In the same spirit, a cable company in New York priced the telecast at $9.95 per completed round up to a maximum of $49.95.

Early into the bout, one could sense that Tyson was in for a rough go. In the sixth round, Evander put Mike on the deck, turning the bout sharply in his favor. Holyfield had a big 10th round and then finished matters in the next stanza with a volley of 12 unanswered punches. Tyson was upright when the referee intervened, but in no condition to continue.

According to figures released by the Nevada Gaming Control Board, bookmakers statewide lost $4.9 million, a record loss for a single sporting event. Making matters worse for the host property, some of their baccarat players were Holyfield-esque, drubbing the house. Casino winnings for November 1996 dropped 6.3 percent from the same month the previous year, the largest slide in 45 months. In Clark County, home to the Las Vegas Strip, casinos won $33 million less despite a 2.6 percent jump in visitor volume. If there was any silver lining, at least the fight was free of controversy.

A new man was in charge of the MGM sports book when Tyson and Holyfield renewed hostilities on May 28, 1997. Tyson was installed a 3/1 favorite. The line settled at 12/5 after a proactive adjustment for a hot but baseless rumor that Tyson had a shoulder injury.

Tickets for Tyson-Holyfield II were gone in a blink. Those made available to the general public were gobbled up in 24 hours. Requests for media credentials poured in from around the world. On fight night, correspondents for mass-circulation magazines occupied seats normally reserved for mid-rung sportswriters and radio jocks. Even Graham Houston was shunted to the auxiliary press section high up in the arena. The longtime North American correspondent for (British) *Boxing Monthly* and arguably the most respected boxing handicapper in the print media, Houston opted to watch the match on television in the media center, where he would have a better view of the action. Subsequently, he was able to sort out what happened quicker than if he had been seated ringside. The scene in the ring after referee Mills Lane disqualified Tyson in the third round was one of total confusion. It did not immediately register that one of Holyfield's ears was mangled and the other abridged. Tyson had severely bitten both ears.

The media center was a safe haven. Management had sealed the stairways that led outdoors, funneling the egress into the corridor that bottlenecked into the casino. People were wedged together so tight that the procession moved at a snail's pace. A metal walker bobbed above the swell like flotsam, its owner submerged in the congested tide of humanity. Anything that would have triggered a stampede would have produced a calamity of staggering proportions. Fortunately, the logjam loosened before the incidents that sent patrons scurrying for cover.

Over the next few hours, fistfights erupted like brush fires. A champagne bottle exploded in the hotel lobby, producing more bedlam as people fled in panic from what they believed to be a gunfight. According to one report, forty people were treated at area hospitals for minor injuries. Shortly after midnight, two $100-minimum blackjack tables were overturned, resulting in the disappearance of $134,000 in casino chips and prompting a two-hour shutdown of the gaming pit. Many hotel guests aborted their stay. The MGM Grand was reportedly inundated with more than a hundred claims for damages.

Tyson paid dearly for his convulsion. The Nevada Athletic Commission slapped him with a one-year suspension and $3,000,000 fine. When he petitioned to have his license restored, the commission stalled him by mandating a thorough psychiatric evaluation. After the test was performed at Massachusetts General Hospital by a team of psychiatrists, psychologists, and neurologists, the results were made public when it was ruled that the panel's findings fell under the parasol of Nevada's open-meeting law. Predictably, the examiners concluded that Tyson had psychological deficits that may have been present prior to boxing and that his impulsivity was exacerbated by low self-esteem. Their report recommended a regular program of psychotherapy and noted "antidepressant medications can be a useful adjunct." However, the examiners concluded that there was little chance of another flare-up.

Early into his suspension, Tyson dumped Don King, reportedly on his own initiative. This was deemed an encouraging sign by the MGH clinicians, who had noted in their report that a contributing factor in Tyson's malaise was the deep-seated feeling that no one was protecting his interests. Replacing King in the captain's chair was Shelly Finkel, a former rock concert promoter who had played a prominent role in energizing the boxing scene in Atlantic City.

The Las Vegas Hilton informally ordered a moratorium on boxing in the wake of the infamous ear-chomping incident and its ugly aftermath. Under the pretense that promoters Bob Arum and Cedric Kushner had failed to meet their deadline for providing a certificate of insurance, Hilton executives pulled the plug on the forthcoming match between 115-pound titlists Johnny Tapia and Danny Romero. An advance sellout, the fight was diverted to the

Thomas and Mack Center, where Tapia defeated his Albuquerque rival in a good action fight contested without incident before a well-mannered crowd.

The MGM Grand likewise cut ties to boxing promoters until things cooled down. When boxing resumed there after a 566-day quiescence, the headliner was again Mike Tyson, whose period of inactivity ran concurrent. With Tommy Brooks in his corner—his third different trainer in as many bouts—Tyson took on Francois Botha, a fighter from South Africa nicknamed the White Buffalo.

Botha had a fleshy physique and was rough around the edges, but he was yet a sturdy fighter whose style enabled him to fluster more skilled opponents. Against Tyson, he chose to hit and grab, but landed enough hits so that he won the first four rounds. More harrowing for Tyson, he became so frustrated that he was one misstep away from yet another disqualification.

Near the end of the opening round, Tyson clasped Botha's left elbow inside his right arm and pushed Botha back against the ropes with his free hand, seemingly intent on breaking Botha's arm. Seconds after the bell, they were still yoked like cars with locked bumpers and the ring was quickly a jumble of cornermen, boxing inspectors, and security guards. The convulsion had earmarks of Tyson-Holyfield II without the actual earmarks, but order was restored and the bout continued after a two-minute interval.

In Round Two, Tyson twice pulled the same maneuver, but referee Richard Steele was quick to untangle the knots. After the second incident, he penalized Tyson a point for unnecessary roughness. There were no further problems, but Tyson, an 8/1 favorite, looked like a complete amateur until he finally lowered the boom on Botha, knocking him loopy with a thunderous punch to the jaw near the end of the fifth frame. In a bizarre twist to a bizarre fight, Tyson rushed to the aid of the lurching Botha and rescued him from falling out of the ring.

The flare-up at the end of the first stanza had scant chance of boiling over into a bigger conflagration. A larger detail of police was on hand than for any of Tyson's previous fights, 178 uniformed and plainclothes cops in all, plus the in-house security force. Freelance paparazzi and other rubberneckers were swept from the main passageway before the crowd let out. With sales lagging, tickets were offered to MGM employees at steeply discounted prices, swelling the audience with individuals that had a vested interest in a disturbance-free event.

The event had a completely different aura from Tyson's previous post-prison fights at the MGM Grand. At those events, the property was brimming with centerfold-quality strumpets and there was a palpable undercurrent of danger. Grizzled trainer Lou Duva, whose Barney Rubble face was one of the most recognizable in boxing, had his own method for calculating the gravity of a boxing contest. "You can always tell how big the fight is by how many hookers (and pimps) you've got," he told *Toronto Sun* sportswriter Steve Simmons. "At [Tyson-Botha], I got the feeling that I was at a bowling convention."

Tyson's crude performance was attributed to more than ring rust. Weighing heavily on his mind was a court case pending in Maryland that threatened to put him back behind bars. Three weeks after the Botha match, he pleaded no contest to second-degree assault for an act of road rage after a minor traffic accident. Tyson would spend the next three and a half months in a Maryland county jail, backlogging yet another of his fights. His match at the MGM with Orlin Norris was pushed back seven months.

Norris was built along the lines of Tyson but without the muscular definition. Although he was a solid professional, he was yet something of a fringe fighter, overshadowed within his own camp by his harder-punching younger brother Terry Norris, a long-reigning 154-pound champion. Something of a cutie, Norris figured to extend Tyson into the late rounds and was attractive for this reason. Tyson sorely needed a workout that would test his wind under actual fight conditions. Now 33 years of age, he had fought only seven times in eight and a half years, averaging a shade under four rounds per outing.

Tyson vs. Norris drew poorly. Those that paid to see it came to wish that they had saved their money. After a round of mauling, Tyson put Norris on the canvas with a left hook delivered moments after the bell. Norris twisted his knee as he fell and did not come out for the second round. Again there was confusion and catcalls and cries of a rip-off. The commission held up Tyson's purse pending a review of the tape.

Tyson had been assessed a harsh two-point penalty for the late punch, but referee Richard Steele conceded that Tyson might not have heard the bell and the tape did not support the premise that the infraction was intentional. Having already extracted $3 million from Tyson for Nevada's general fund, the commission was reluctant to force another donation, particularly since Iron Mike had mounting debts. No disciplinary action was taken, but Tyson's license was about to expire and the commission made it known that they would not renew it.

Lorenzo Fertitta, the youngest and newest member of the commission, was the most outspoken. Addressing Tyson's attorneys, he said they should "pack Mr. Tyson's bags and take this show on the road." Tyson had recently become a Las Vegas homeowner, purchasing a property that sat adjacent to Shenandoah Ranch, the landmark estate of entertainer Wayne Newton, but professionally he was now a displaced person, about as welcome as toxic waste. As for Fertitta, he went on to become a powerful force in the sport of Ultimate Fighting.

Tyson's multi-fight deal with the MGM Grand had expired during his previous suspension. When that deal was first announced, it appeared that the MGM had been bamboozled. It was subsequently reported that the property lost $15 million on Tyson's five fights, the shortfall between expenses and gate receipts. Besides the red ink, there was the recurrent hassle of damage control. Pundits said that when Tyson was in the building it was advisable to hide the women and children, a quip that cut deep, as the property was then being marketed as a family resort destination. And yet the MGM had welcomed Tyson back with seemingly no hard feelings, cutting a four-fight deal with Shelly Finkel.

The man most qualified to explain this peculiar development was Kirk Kerkorian, but the octogenarian billionaire assiduously avoided the press. The son of an Armenian immigrant fruit peddler, Kerkorian had boxed in the amateurs, reputedly winning 29 of 33 fights. His first incursion into the business side of boxing, way back in 1960, had been an unmitigated disaster. By all accounts, he was suckered into purchasing the contract of Don Jordan, whose upside was tempered by new legislation (subsequently overturned) that prohibited rematch clauses in fight contracts. There is an old saying that a man is drawn to the fight business by visions of wealth and stays in it to get even with those that exploited his naivety. Kerkorian had built three Las Vegas hotels — each recognized at its opening as the largest hotel in the world — but perhaps even he was subject to this aphorism.

While the future of boxing at the MGM Grand was once again clouded, the future of the fight game in Las Vegas was anything but bleak. There was a new player in town, Mandalay Bay. The 43-story, 3300-room establishment was geared partly toward young adults of the stripe that invaded Cancun for spring break, but the operators were yet bullish on the ancient sport of boxing. A fighter of Mexican descent had bubbled into a huge attraction and he figured prominently in their plans.

# CHAPTER 24

# The Golden Boy

Born to working-class immigrants in East Los Angeles, Oscar De La Hoya entered amateur competitions at the earliest possible age and acquired a roomful of trophies, medals, and ribbons. Fighting to please his father, a great admirer of Salvador Sanchez, he had a stronger emotional attachment to his mother, a part-time seamstress. She died of breast cancer when Oscar was seventeen, making his story all the more interesting. Far and away the most ink-drenched member of the 1996 U.S. Olympic boxing delegation, he lived up to his hype in Barcelona, becoming the only member of his squad to win a gold medal. Despite a difficult draw that pitted him against a Cuban in his opening match, he dominated the 132-pound class.

During the latter stages of his amateur career, De La Hoya had a financial angel. Shelly Finkel funneled money to him in return for future considerations. But Finkel was left holding the bag when De La Hoya turned pro. With the inducement of a large signing bonus, Oscar entrusted his future to investment banker Steve Nelson and his partner Robert Mittleman. This arrangement was short-lived. Early into his pro career, Oscar severed the tie. By then, Bob Arum had entered the picture.

Arum then had little interest in Mexican fighters, but De La Hoya was Mexican-American, an important distinction. Keenly attuned to the demographic weathervane, Arum had previously promoted Richie Sandoval and Michael Carbajal. They too were bilingual sons of Mexican immigrants who had represented the United States in international amateur tournaments. Sandoval, whose pro career was aborted by a life-threatening head injury incurred in a bantamweight title fight with Jose "Gaby" Canizales, was a member of the 1980 Olympic team that was demobilized by the U.S. boycott of the Moscow games. Carbajal was a silver medal winner at the Olympic games in Seoul, Korea.

Carbajal had the distinction of appearing in the first flyweight bout accorded top billing on a PPV show. His March 13, 1999, match at the Las Vegas Hilton with Humberto Gonzalez was a savage affair. Carbajal clawed his way out of a deep hole to score a seventh-round knockout. De La Hoya appeared on the undercard, advancing his record to 5–0 with a fourth-round stoppage of 23–2–2 Jeff Mayweather.

Stamped the Golden Boy by boxing publicist John Beyrooty, a former *Los Angeles Herald-Examiner* sportswriter, De La Hoya had a star quality about him that was mindful of Sugar Ray Leonard. Handsome, personable, and clean-cut, he was extremely well-spoken in two languages and blended in easily with people from privileged backgrounds. Inevitably, he came to be seen as the anti–Tyson. An early endorsement deal with the National Milk Council accentuated the polarity.

In his eighth pro bout, De La Hoya needed only one round to eliminate former featherweight titlist Troy Dorsey. While Oscar was expected to win as he pleased, the quick ending was a surprise. Best known for his two sizzling fights on national television with Jorge Paez, Dorsey had gone 12 rounds on five occasions. Pinned to the Foreman-Morrison fight, this match marked De La Hoya's last appearance in a supporting bout.

In his 12th pro fight, Oscar scored a 10th-round TKO over Jimmy Bredahl. A fighter from Denmark, Bredahl held the World Boxing Organization version of the 130-pound title. Arum housed the show at the renovated Olympic Auditorium, which had been boarded up for seven years amidst talk that it would be torn down for a parking garage. The promotion was seen as auguring a rebirth of boxing at that fabled venue. The Golden Boy was the lightning rod.

The WBO bauble carried little cachet and Oscar was fast outgrowing the 130-pound class. Looking down the road, it was easy to envision him winning multiple titles in the fashion of Thomas Hearns. The first legs of that road were pot-holed with others from his pod — the barrio-flavored Los Angeles–area amateur circuit. The situation was reminiscent of the New York boxing scene circa 1930, when crossroads fights often pitted Jew against Jew.

De La Hoya reportedly finished his amateur career with a record of 223–5. Rafael Ruelas, a boy nearly two years older, inflicted two of those defeats. Ruelas went on to win the IBF lightweight title, overcoming early adversity to dethrone Freddie Pendleton in a scorching good fight. Brother Gabriel Ruelas was simultaneously a titleholder, enhancing the profile of Rafael, the younger sibling by nine months. Sportswriters would not have come knocking so often if they weren't getting two interviews for the price of one.

Arum matched De La Hoya and Ruelas at Caesars Palace for May 6, 1995. Although Ruelas (43–1) was a proven commodity, the Golden Boy was yet a 12/5 favorite. The confrontation had echoes of the 1987 match between Mark Breland and Marlon Starling. An Olympic gold medalist with an 18–0 pro log, the highly touted Breland was in too deep against a seasoned campaigner. But Oscar erased the ghost of Breland with surprising alacrity. He dominated Ruelas from the opening gong en route to a second-round stoppage.

In East Los Angeles, America's largest and most heavily populated Hispanic enclave, De La Hoya's most compelling opponent was Genero "Chicanito" Hernandez. An East L.A. product married to a woman from Tijuana, the undefeated (32–0–1) Hernandez was a solid technician who had paid his dues, staying the course after five hand surgeries. While casual Anglo fight fans had difficulty distinguishing one Hernandez from another, Chicanito was extremely popular in his sprawling habitat, where he was respected as a family man who had stayed true to his roots. He and Oscar had attended rival high schools, a fact not lost on Arum, who kicked off the publicity campaign with same-day rallies at both campuses.

Staged at Caesars Palace on September 9, 1995, the fight was a cakewalk for the Golden Boy. After taking the worst of it for six rounds, Chicanito simply quit. It would come out that he had entered the contest with a broken nose suffered in a sparring session with rising contender Shane Mosley. Those privy to the pre–existing condition cashed in big. Oscar was hammered up from a 4/1 to a 17/2 favorite.[1]

Arum was pleased with the returns from the fight, which rubbed against a Mexican Independence Day card at the Mirage the next weekend with Julio Cesar Chavez in the featured bout. The PPV sales were better than anticipated for a promotion belittled as more suitable for the Olympic Auditorium. The returns were a reflection of the fact that Oscar had become a two-sided magnet. He had an ardent following, especially on the distaff side, but there was a growing sentiment among those of his lineage that he had put on airs, an opinion heightened by his new passion for golf. Oscar was increasingly perceived as something of a diva.

This new facet of his persona, which dilated and receded depending on the opponent, meant that a publicist could shade him as a hero or a villain. It fanned the flames for a bout between Oscar and Julio Cesar Chavez. Whatever his character flaws, Chavez could never be described as superficial. He was Mexican to the core, not a cultural hybrid; he was proletarian, Oscar was bourgeois. But that match would have to wait until Arum figured out a loophole for prying Chavez from the clutches of Don King. With Chavez not yet an option, Arum elected to showcase De La Hoya on the East Coast. He pitted him against Jesse James Leija at Madison Square Garden on December 15, 1995.

Oscar De La Hoya, circa 1999. *Top Rank file photograph.*

Hailing from San Antonio, Leija (30–1–2) had defeated the greatly respected Azumah Nelson, but he wasn't a full-fledged lightweight and had scored only three knockouts in his last 18 fights. Oscar blew right through him, stopping him in the second round, but the big story was the turnout. Boxing had been dormant at Madison Square Garden for two and a half years. Ten days before Christmas was hardly an opportune time to launch a revival, and yet Arum's show drew a star-studded crowd of 16,027. The notoriously catty New York writers were favorably disposed to De La Hoya, who said all the right things, avouching that it was an honor to perform in such a hallowed arena. The show was a triumphant homecoming for Arum, whose first big Top Rank promotion (Muhammad Ali vs. Oscar Bonavena) had taken place at the mid–Manhattan landmark 25 years prior — almost to the exact day.

Arum inked De La Hoya and Chavez for June 9, 1996, at Caesars Palace, bucking a Don King lawsuit for tortuous interference that was ultimately decided in Arum's favor. The showdown was prefaced by a whirlwind 23-city, 11-day promotional tour. Arum likened the match to the first meeting between Sugar Ray Leonard and Roberto Duran. The comparison was apt from the standpoint of the financial arrangements. Arum took it off pay TV and made it a closed-circuit commodity, a bold, revisionist maneuver rooted in his irritation with widespread PPV piracy, more specifically his irritation with distributors who were doing little to foil "shoplifters" descrambling transmissions with so-called black boxes.

The pricemakers established De La Hoya an 11/5 favorite. Oscar's pluses were his distinct physical advantages — he was four inches taller and had a six-inch longer reach — and his youth. Perhaps the Golden Boy was still a work in progress, but Chavez, the older man by nearly 11 years, had seemingly crossed the summit to the downhill slope. It was a foregone conclusion that the bet-takers would write many more bets on the Culiacan veteran, a first-time underdog bringing a 97–1–1 record into his milestone 100th fight. It was no less certain that most of the large wagers would be on De La Hoya. The odds were nicked up in the final hours of betting, driven by the revelation that Chavez had suffered a cut in training, leaving him with tender skin on the bridge of his left eyebrow.

The bout was not even two minutes old when De La Hoya sliced open the soft tissue with a caustic jab. The doctor was summoned to examine the wound before the first round had wended its course. Chavez's face was a mask of crimson when the bout was stopped in the fourth round.

The event was unsatisfactory in other aspects. The new multi–story parking garage was behind schedule, forcing many fight-goers to scramble for off-site parking, resulting in a massive traffic jam. The temperature at ringside was 100 degrees at sundown. The sweltering heat exacerbated other irritations.

As it turned out, this would be the last outdoor megafight on the Las Vegas Strip. The Caesars Palace brand would continue to be affixed to some "off campus" fights, but the era that began with the so-called parking lot extravaganzas had come to a close.

De La Hoya went to post five times in 1997, earning a reported $38 million. The biggest of the five fights was a showdown with WBC welterweight champion Pernell Whitaker at the Thomas and Mack Center, a bout hyped for the mythical "best pound-for-pound" title. The 33-year-old Whitaker was coming off an unexpectedly difficult tussle with Cuban expatriate Diosbelys Hurtado, an indication that he was slipping, but both blemishes on his 40–1–1 record were widely considered heists and he could fairly boast that he had never lost a professional bout in the eyes of anyone with 20–20 vision.

Arum hired a mariachi band to welcome Oscar into the ring, an act of favoritism that many reporters considered unprofessional. "Sweetpea" landed the most punches and scored a flash knockdown, but De La Hoya, a 7/2 favorite, was the aggressor throughout and came on strong in the homestretch. An informal poll of the ringside press found a slight majority for Whitaker, but the judges had Oscar a clear winner. De La Hoya's growing legion of female fans greeted the verdict with lusty applause.

Arum selected Hector Camacho to be De La Hoya's next opponent. Camacho had recently decorated his bedpost with two musty but sanctified scalps, winning an unpopular decision over 45-year-old Roberto Duran and TKOing 40-year-old Sugar Ray Leonard, who had been inactive for six years. An 11/1 favorite, De La Hoya chased Camacho around the ring, winning every round on the cards of two of the judges. Camacho saved face by lasting the distance, retaining his distinction of having never been stopped. It was virtually a foregone conclusion that the fight would take this tack, and yet the show was nearly a sellout. The turnout inspired Arum to create another promotion that shaped up as a De La Hoya cakewalk, a rematch with Julio Cesar Chavez.

Chavez had scored four wins since his first meeting with De La Hoya, boosting his record to 101–2–2. Win number 100 had come at the expense of Larry LaCoirsiere in a supporting bout to Tyson-Holyfield II. Few English-language newspapers acknowledged the milestone, understandable as the main go produced an ear-piercing din, and LaCoursiere, the house fighter at a Minnesota tribal casino, was so far out of Chavez's league that the Nevada Commission was reluctant to sanction the match. It reflected badly on Chavez that LaCoursiere was able to last the distance and his subsequent 12-round draw at Mexico City versus countryman Miguel Angel Gonzalez was generally viewed as gift-wrapped.

Eleven years had elapsed since Chavez's brilliant performance against Edwin Rosario and more than eight years had passed since his most memorable scrap with Meldrick Taylor. The fighter that once had the countenance of a choirboy now looked weathered. However, like virtually all fighters of great renown — Sugar Ray Robinson a prime example — Chavez had reached the peak of his earning power after his best days were behind him. Although he had failed to last four rounds in his first meeting with De La Hoya, the unhealed cut on his brow was a handy alibi. His few good moments in that fight had come near the end of the contest. The notion that he was beginning to find his groove was consistent with his history of being a slow starter. Because he attributed his defeat to bad luck, refusing to acknowledge that Oscar was a deserving winner, the sequel could be framed as a grudge match. Arum was so confident that the rematch would be a blockbuster that he explored the possibility of staging the bout at the Rose Bowl football stadium. The ultimate destination was the Thomas and Mack, where the turnout was only 264 short of capacity.

A 9/1 favorite, De La Hoya was dominant from the opening bell. Chavez was bleeding from cuts above both eyes and a severe cut inside his mouth when his corner tossed in the towel after the eighth frame. To Chavez's credit, he threw caution to the wind in what would be the final round, earning a standing ovation as he traded punches with Oscar in the center of the ring. The cheers then turned to boos when Julio failed to come out for Round 9.

The first fighter to defeat Chavez by TKO, Oscar had now turned the trick twice, but reporters were generally unimpressed. When the rematch was announced, Oscar drew criticism for choosing another safe opponent. The same could not be said of the next man on Oscar's docket, undefeated (34–0–1) Ike "Bazooka" Quartey. A citizen of Ghana, the 29-year-old Quartey had been lucky to salvage a draw in his most recent outing, but the presumption was that he just had an off night. He had had three fights fall out in the interim.

De La Hoya-Quartey was pushed back 11 weeks when Oscar suffered a cut above his left eye in training, extending Quartey's period of inactivity to 482 days. The hard-punching African was tentative in the early going, consistent with the expectation of rust, but came on strong after hitting the deck in Round 6, returning the favor more harshly in the very same round. In the final stanza, with the fight up for grabs, De La Hoya floored Quartey with a left hook. He followed up with a furious assault and the bout was in imminent danger of being stopped, but Oscar punched himself out and Quartey stayed the course, landing some damaging punches of his own before the final gong.

The verdict was split, but De La Hoya got the nod. While the suspenseful mill had few toe-to-toe exchanges, it was laced with high drama and reflected well on Oscar, who relied on his heart to overcome a talented and strong-willed opponent. The show was the first boxing card sponsored by Mandalay Bay, a property that hadn't yet opened for business.

Mandalay Bay welcomed its first guests on March 2, 1999. Six weeks later, it unveiled its 12,000-seat performance hall with a concert by Luciano Pavarotti. Dates had been set aside for Oscar De La Hoya before the Italian super–heavyweight had the honor of christening the splendidly appointed facility.

Oscar's conquest of Quartey moved him a step closer to a showdown with Felix Trinidad. However, that match could not be made until Arum and Trinidad's promoter Don King reached an accord, a long-drawn-out wrangle. The first on-site boxing promotion at the new South Strip property would be an appetizer pitting De La Hoya against Kronk Gym alumnus Oba Carr. A veteran of 51 pro fights, the Detroiter made things interesting after a surviving a first round knockdown, but the Golden Boy brought down the curtain in Round 11 with a fierce left hook.

De La Hoya vs. Trinidad, staged at Mandalay Bay on September 18, 1999, was a dream match likened to the fabled showdown between Sugar Ray Leonard and Thomas Hearns. The undefeated Trinidad (35–0, 30 KOs), from Cupey Alto, Puerto Rico, had reigned as the IBF 147-pound champion for more than six years while successfully defending the belt 15 times. De La Hoya, 31–0 (25 KOs), numbered among his victims ten former champions. Born three weeks apart, each was considered at the top of his game and physically they were nearly identical, both standing 5-foot-11.

Trinidad was considered the harder puncher, but Oscar was judged to be quicker and more multidimensional. Under normal circumstances the site would favor De La Hoya, but the major hotels snatched up all of the tickets for their preferred customers, sharply curtailing the number of Mexicans and Mexican-Americans that would have otherwise swelled the arena. Trinidad was no stranger to Las Vegas. He had fought six times there, including a notable fight with Mexico's Luis Ramon "Yory Boy" Campas. Trinidad halted Yory Boy's 56-fight winning streak.

The word "millennium" was in vogue and the promoters seized it, huckstering a generic Fight of the Century into something even more extravagant. Akin to Leonard-Hearns I, the big plungers were almost evenly dispersed on opposite sides of the fence. Some properties opened and closed the fight "11/10 pick," an exceedingly rare occurrence for a heavily bet competition.

The fight did not fulfill its promise. Wary of Trinidad's power, De La Hoya competed as if the bout would be judged on the Olympic scoring system, where punches landed took

**Bob Arum and Don King are all smiles at the pre-fight luncheon for the "Fight of the Millennium"** between Oscar de la Hoya and Felix Trinidad. The man on the far right is Felix Trinidad Sr. The elder Trinidad was a knockout victim of the great Salvador Sanchez. *Photograph courtesy of Larry Grossman.*

precedence over effective aggression. After nine rounds, De La Hoya was so confident that he had built up an insurmountable lead that he went on his bicycle, circling counterclockwise in the fashion of Gene Tunney after the Long Count. It worked for Tunney, but not for Oscar. One of the judges had the fight even through nine frames and another had De La Hoya up by only one point. Trinidad, the stalker, prevailed by a majority decision.

Most ringside reporters scored the bout for Oscar, credited with landing 97 more punches, but his cleverness was best appreciated close up. In the far reaches of the arena, the decision elicited no surprise. Oscar's rooters were less riled by the decision than they were disappointed in his effort. The promotion was a huge success, becoming the first non–heavyweight fight to exceed one million PPV buys. In Las Vegas, the bout was closed-circuited to a record 19 locations. The event fueled a record month for Nevada casinos, which won $819.6 million.

Trindad's victory ignited an all-night fiesta on the streets of San Juan that echoed the scene in Panama City when Roberto Duran conquered Sugar Ray Leonard. In his first public appearance upon returning from Las Vegas, Trinidad declared, "There is no doubt now that the best boxers are in Puerto Rico — pound for pound they have the most heart." De La Hoya vowed to take the fight out of the judges' hands when they met again, but the rematch died on the vine as Arum and King went their separate ways, their mutual loathing more rancorous than ever.

# CHAPTER 25

# Lennox the Lion

Madison Square Garden was the setting for the March 13, 1999, match between Evander Holyfield and Lennox Lewis, a confrontation reasonably touted as the most significant fight of the decade.

Holyfield had fought twice since losing a chunk of his ear, avenging his loss to Michael Moorer with a smashing eighth-round knockout and then winning an easy decision over undistinguished Vaughn Bean. He held the WBA and IBF belts, but Lewis, the WBC belt holder, was the linear heavyweight champion.

Born to Jamaican immigrants in the West Ham district of London, Lewis was uprooted to Canada at the age of twelve and competed under the Canadian flag in the 1984 and 1988 Olympics. In his final amateur fight, he defeated Riddick Bowe. As a professional, he had suffered only one loss in 36 bouts, a shocking knockout at the hands of Oliver McCall that was attributed to carelessness. He had won nine straight since that mishap and was coming off a 95-second blowout of erratic Andrew Golota.

Holyfield vs. Lewis was the first heavyweight title unification match in six years and the first of this description in New York since the storied first battle between Ali and Frazier. Bettors were able to lock in wagers at even money.

The competition was tame, although pleasing to the large British contingent. Lewis landed more punches in every round. But veteran U.K. judge Larry O'Connell scored the bout a draw and his verdict would stand when the other judges were split.

The decision ignited a great brouhaha. Lewis's promoter Frank Maloney called on British Prime Minister Tony Blair to break off diplomatic ties with the United States. U.S. Senator John McCain (R-AZ), the sponsor of a bill calling for a national boxing agency, produced a letter ostensibly written by Muhammad Ali labeling the affair "the biggest fix in fight history."[1] The predominant opinion was that Holyfield's promoter Don King was the invisible hand on the pencil of judge Eugenia Williams, who gave seven rounds to Evander. She represented the IBF, whose executives were under investigation for soliciting bribes to move fighters up in the ratings, a probe that ultimately sent IBF founder Bob Lee to prison for money laundering.

The reaction to a bad decision is proportional to the magnitude of the event. There were a few ringsider reporters, notably Dave Anderson, who actually concurred with the verdict. Folks scoring at home were biased by the round-by-round CompuBox punch stat graphic, which gave the impression that one was watching a horse race wherein the pacesetter steadily lengthens its lead. *New York Daily News* scribe Bob Raissman characterized the media response as "comical, hypocritical, and knee-jerk." If Don King were not involved, noted Raissman, "the level of outrage from all the headline-grabbing politicians and media-pontificators would be far less vociferous."[2]

It would come out that Williams, a Newark municipal clerk, had recently filed for bankruptcy, listing $33,000 in credit card debt. The *Sunday Mirror* of London added fuel to the fire with allegations that she made deposits to two hidden bank accounts shortly before and after the fight for amounts in excess of her fee for judging the bout. (The imputations provoked Williams to file a slander suit against the paper that was resolved in her favor.)

The firestorm was another black eye for the New York Boxing Commission. The previous year, it was revealed that commission head Floyd Patterson had significant memory loss. Cross-examined by attorneys seeking to lift New York's ban on Ultimate Fighting, Patterson was unable to recall important events in his career, his office address, or the names of some of his closest aides. Investigative reporters Wallace Matthews and Jack Newfield were deep into an investigation of misfeasance by New York's boxing regulators, most of who were juiced into their positions by political connections. King had wrangled tax concessions before putting the fight in New York. In return, cronies of Governor George Pataki hijacked 67 ringside passes.

The sanctioning bodies jointly mandated a rematch. Although Pataki promised swift reforms, it was a virtual certainty that the rematch would go to Las Vegas. Under the stewardship of Marc Ratner, the Nevada commission had acquired the reputation of being a very clean operation. Scandals in other jurisdictions heightened this perception. When Ratner made it known that only Nevada officials would be considered if the rematch landed in his bailiwick, his stricture was applauded. The abstract Las Vegas Boxing Judge had once been the butt of jokes, but this was far back in the rear-view mirror.

It was speculated that the rematch would be a tough sell. Lennox Lewis stayed out of the public eye between fights and lacked the charisma of Mike Tyson, begetting comparisons with Larry Holmes, who failed to capture the imagination of a society still enthralled with Muhammad Ali. It was hypothesized that the bad decision — blatant skullduggery in the minds of most people — was the last straw for fight fans who could tolerate only so much before turning away from the sport in disgust.

Those holding this opinion were naïve. The big stink was great publicity for the do-over, having the added advantage of blotting out the details of a dull fight marred by excessive clinching. The sequel at the Thomas and Mack on November 13, 1999, was an enormous attraction. Gross receipts averaged $985 per customer in ticket sales alone, producing a record gate of $16,860,000.

The general feeling among betting men was that the match would be a carbon of the first meeting, with the judges giving Lewis the benefit of the doubt in the close rounds. This was a prescient opinion. Holyfield was busier than in the first fray and earned a draw in the estimation of many ringsiders, but the judges unanimously favored Lewis, an 11/5 favorite, giving him the decision by margins of six, four, and two points. The verdict was deemed fair because it rectified an injustice and produced a stand-alone champion. If not for Lennox Lewis, an entire century would have passed without a universally recognized British heavyweight champion. Lewis beat the deadline by one year and 48 days. And in England, it made no difference that he felt a stronger emotional tie to his ancestral homeland of Jamaica than to the country of his birth.

Those expecting that the title would remain unified were hopelessly optimistic. The winner of the fight was contractually bound to fight John Ruiz, a King-controlled fighter who had been maneuvered to the top of the WBA ratings. When Lewis opted to fight Michael Grant instead, King successfully sued to have the WBA title vacated. The ruling was perplexing as Grant, undefeated in 31 fights, was judged to be a far more worthy opponent. He carried 250 pounds on a six-foot-seven frame and was considered the prototype of the next generation of heavyweights.

Lewis blew away Grant in two rounds, disposed of Francois Botha in the same fashion in his next bout in London, and then met David Tua at Mandalay Bay.

A stocky, 245-pound New Zealander born in Western Samoa, Tua had flattened John Ruiz in 19 seconds and was considered the hardest puncher in the division, but Lewis, using his 14-inch reach advantage, stayed out of harm's way and won an easy decision in such a disappointing bout that many patrons walked out before the start of the final round. The affable Tua had excellent rapport with sportswriters, many of whom felt bamboozled by his hollow effort and retaliated by writing about him in unkind terms. The fight did not redound well to Lewis either. None of the Las Vegas hotels were willing to put up a site fee for his next test against Hasim Rahman. It would go to the Carnival City Casino on the outskirts of Johannesburg, where scarcely 5,000 turned out to see it at the HBO-dictated local start time of 5:30 in the morning.

Born and raised in a rough section of Baltimore, Rahman had only two losses in 36 fights. In matches with David Tua and Oleg Maskaev, he was winning on the scorecards before running into trouble. However, he was so lightly regarded that the first pricemaker to post a line on the fight made Lewis a 20/1 favorite. The odds declined to 9/1 amid reports that Lewis wasn't taking the match seriously.

Rahman arrived in Johannesburg a full month before the fight to get better acclimated to the high altitude. He made a favorable impression with the locals, who felt snubbed when Lewis delayed his arrival to finish filming a cameo in the remake of the movie *Ocean's Eleven*. Lewis dismissed Rahman as "a piece of meat that I will play with," but with only 12 days of preparation he was indeed ill prepared, tipping the scales at a career-high 253 pounds.

With blood trickling into his left eye from an accidental butt, Rahman landed a sharp right hand in the fifth stanza that caused Lewis to back into the ropes. He came off the ropes smiling with his hands held low and Rahman knocked him flat on his back for the 10-count with a massive right hand to the jaw.

Don King swooped in on Rahman immediately, prying him away from his promoter Cedric Kushner with an offer that included a $500,000 signing bonus paid in cash. There was talk that Rahman would next fight the pampered Danish boxer Brian Nielsen, but his first defense would be a rematch with Lennox Lewis at Mandalay Bay. The promotional tour for the November 17, 2001, event included a stop at an ESPN-leased TV studio in Anaheim, California, where the obligatory exchange of insults escalated into a fracas that exceeded the bounds of the script. Rahman got the best of it, landing on top of Lewis when a table collapsed.

At Mandalay Bay, Lewis opened a 7/2 favorite. The odds were incongruent with the opinions expressed by a panel of 33 sportswriters. Although the tab was 17–16 for Lewis, the near-universal sentiment of those favoring him was that he would recapture his belts by decision in a dull fight. Conversely only one of the pro–Rahman scribes envisioned Lewis lasting the distance. Rahman had rattled Lewis in their studio scuffle, which several reporters construed as establishing an important psychological advantage.

In tip-top shape and completely focused, Lewis executed his game plan flawlessly, dictating the tempo with crisp jabs. In Round 4, he unleashed a sweeping right hand that thundered flush on Rahman's cheekbone. Spread-eagled on the mat, Rahman struggled to rise but fell back as the referee completed the count. Adding insult to injury, Lewis told reporters that the Baltimorean would be remembered as another Buster Douglas. But the reporters, with very few exceptions, were still reticent to lionize the man hailed by ring announcers as Lennox the Lion.

Emanuel Steward's work with Lennox Lewis cemented his stature as the sport's preeminent trainer. Steward (shown here around 2000) later worked with the Klitschko brothers. The Kronk Gym, where he got his start, was shuttered in 2007.

The mark against him was that he had no career-defining triumph, taken to mean a masterful performance against a foe with a lofty reputation. Riddick Bowe would have provided that yardstick had they met when Bowe was at the top of his game. The match flamed out when Bowe junked his WBC belt and then Bowe flamed out after winning his rubber match with Holyfield. He retired in 1997 after a second poor effort against the obstreperously unruly Andrew Golota. But Mike Tyson was still a viable opponent, especially from a revenue standpoint.

Tyson had taken his act to soccer stadiums in Manchester and Glasgow and then to Copenhagen following a stateside appearance at the Palace in Auburn Hills, Michigan.

The Manchester promotion was put in limbo when protesters called on the authorities to enforce the haphazardly applied law that denied ex-felons entrance to England, but the Home Office denied the petition and the excursion was otherwise without incident. Tyson pulverized 35-year-old British champion Julius Francis, knocking him to the canvas five times before the referee stopped the bout in the second round. The Copenhagen junket was likewise free of controversy. Tyson disposed of Brian Nielsen in six lopsided rounds. Despite a 62–1 record, the 36-year-old Dane was badly overmatched.

The middle bouts were suffused with the usual Tyson weirdness. Tyson stayed in London before heading to Glasgow for his bout with Lou Savarese. At London's Grosvenor Hotel, he had a row with promoter Frank Warren, whom he reportedly attacked when Warren came to his room to collect $690,000 for jewelry that Tyson had purchased on credit. The matter was finally laid to rest in Tyson's dressing room in Glasgow, where Tyson reportedly surrendered $3 million from his purse to escape legal trouble. He then dispatched Savarese in 38 seconds. That was the official time, although Tyson prolonged the program by continuing to throw punches after the fight was waived off. A deflected blow dropped referee John Coyle to his knees.

Warsaw-born Andrew Golota, dubbed the "Foul Pole" by boxing writer Michael Katz, bailed out after two rounds at Auburn Hills and was showered with garbage as he left the ring. His apologists rationalized his behavior as an anxiety attack, and criticism of him was muted by reports that he suffered a concussion, a fractured cheekbone, and a herniated disc during the brief battle. Tyson was sorely aggravated that the contest was another bummer through no fault of his own. Sympathy for him deadened when he tested positive for marijuana.

Lewis vs. Tyson was positioned for the MGM Grand on April 6, 2002. The match would be historic from a business standpoint, marking the first joint venture between rivals HBO and Showtime, the cable TV arms of media giants AOL Time Warner and Viacom. The formal announcement came at the Hudson Theatre in midtown Manhattan.

The contract for the fight contained a record number of clauses. In the event of the bout being terminated by a flagrant foul, the culprit would forfeit three million dollars, the money added to the purse of the sufferer. But while seemingly every precaution was taken to nip any lawyerly hocus-pocus, no one thought to beef up security at the Hudson Theatre. The oversight was baffling, as scuffles at pre-fight press confabs were becoming endemic. The previous week, there had been an incident between Oscar De La Hoya and Fernando Vargas, and before that a squabble between Marco Antonio Barrera and Erik Morales. Tyson had called out Lewis after his fight with Lou Savarese in Glasgow, threatening to rip out his heart and eat his children (he had none). Common sense dictated some sort of buffer zone.

All hell broke loose when a member of Lewis's entourage shoved Tyson as Tyson moved toward Lewis with a menacing look for the photo-op face-off. In a flash, bodies were rolling on the stage. Jose Sulaiman, age 71, was bowled over, suffering a concussion when his head hit a table. Although not immediately apparent, Lewis suffered a deep puncture wound to his left thigh where Tyson bit him. When Tyson was pulled off Lewis, he got into a screaming match with a man in the audience shouting for a straightjacket. The news conference was aborted without ever getting started.

The following Tuesday, the Nevada Boxing Commission held its monthly meeting. Among the items on the docket was Tyson's application to have his license restored. This was considered a mere formality until the eruption.

The feeling outside Nevada was that the application would be approved, but there was scant chance of this happening. Bob Arum's unsolicited take spoke to the hot-button issue in Las Vegas: a proposal by the National Energy Commission to use a nearby mountain range for a nuclear waste dump. Arum postulated that letting the fight go forward would paint Nevadans as greedy, hurting the cause of those fighting to keep nuclear waste out of the state. Complicating matters for Iron Mike, a police spokesperson announced that a search of Tyson's home had uncovered evidence corroborating the testimony of two rape victims. The charges were eventually dropped, but the lurid details were released to the press. The *Review-Journal* summarized the allegations leveled at Tyson in a front-page story.[3]

Tyson's application was denied, forcing a delay while promoters scrambled to find a new venue. The haven would be Memphis, where a spokesman for the Convention and Visitors Bureau gushed that the promotion was "an excellent vehicle for boosting tourism awareness." The MGM Grand replaced the fight with a Paul McCartney concert, an event with negligible economic spillover for rival casinos that planned to show the fight on closed circuit screens.

On the island of Maui, where Tyson had opened a training camp, parts of two days were set aside for meetings with a select group of writers and broadcasters. These sessions produced rich material for the thesis that Tyson was incurably demented. The most widely regurgitated of his remarks was directed at broadcasters: "I wish that you guys had children ... so I could stomp on their testicles, so you can feel my pain."

These quotes hit the papers concurrent with the release of data documenting Tyson's boundless capacity for profligate spending. It was revealed that during the four years following his release from prison, he spent more than six million dollars on automobiles and motorcycles alone. One of his acquisitions was a Rolls Royce, whereabouts unknown. Most of the other vehicles, 17 in all, were gifts to lap dancers identified only by their first names. A larger sum, $7,362,331, went to legal fees, accounting fees, and lawsuit settlements.

Tyson, the consummate "chalk," had never dressed as an underdog. However, few eyebrows were raised when Lewis was installed a 9/4 favorite. Although he was ten months older than Tyson, the 36-year-old Brit was perceived to have youth on his side. Tyson was no longer seen as a primordial force. The scuttlebutt from the Las Vegas gym where he trained was that he slowed down conspicuously after sparring just a few rounds. His fellow boxers attributed this to a sudden change in metabolism caused by sweating anti-depressant medication out of his system.

With Tyson, a disqualification was a distinct possibility. Most of the top bookmakers in cyberspace posted odds on this happenstance, as did some of the betting chains in the U.K., a development without precedent. The William Hill chain was forced to chop the odds on a disqualification from 6/1 to 4/1.

Several days after tickets went on sale, the Memphis promotional group announced that all 19,185 seats (priced from $100 to $2400) were sold. The truth was far different. Steeply discounted tickets flooded the market in the days preceding the event, producing a turnstile count of 15,327. The fight itself was noncompetitive. Lewis lost the first round on the scorecards, but was always in command. He drew first, second, and third blood and closed the show with an overhand right in Round 8. Lewis had a point deducted for holding, but otherwise the match was contested cleanly.

Tyson's failure to make a competitive showing was less surprising than his conduct after the bout. He was humble and contrite and had only kind words for Lennox Lewis. He seemed relieved that the circus was over. In his comportment, there were ghosts of Jack Johnson following his bout with Jess Willard: "Perhaps now they will leave me alone."

# CHAPTER 26

# The Wise Old Owl

Lennox Lewis fought once more before announcing his retirement. On June 21, 2003, he defeated Vitali Klitschko at the L.A. Staples Center. It was a difficult fight for Lewis, who had only twelve days to formulate a game plan after his original opponent Kirk Johnson withdrew with an injury. He weathered several rough patches before the bout was halted after six frames because of a terrible cut over Klitschko's left eye. Lewis left the scene with his detractors harping that he was nothing special, but it was plain to all but the most hopelessly myopic that he would come to be numbered among the elites.

Mike Tyson had little choice but to keep on fighting. Eight months after his loss to Lewis, he returned to Memphis, where he knocked out Clifford Etienne in 49 seconds. It was noted that Tyson had now knocked out six opponents inside of one minute, but his performance attracted less notice than his new tattoo. Tyson described the large engraving that swirled around his left eye as an "African tribal thing."

Tyson let 14 months elapse before his next outing. During this period of idleness, he spent considerable time in the company of accountants and bankruptcy lawyers. Each new revelation about his financial mess contained a fresh jaw-dropper. Could it really be true that Tyson had once spent $2 million on a bathtub for Robin Givens?

In documents presented to the bankruptcy court, Tyson's debts were pegged at $38 million. Chief among his 246 creditors was the IRS, owed $19.4 million, and ex-spouse Monica Turner, owed nearly $9 million in back alimony and child support for their two children.[1] According to reports in the *London Evening Standard* and the *New York Sun*, Tyson's situation had deteriorated to the point that he was reduced to sleeping in homeless shelters. Things were hardly this dismal, but Tyson had lost all of the homes he had once owned, one of which was said to be the largest single-family residence in Connecticut. He was now bedding down in a friend's home, a two-bedroom abode in a modest neighborhood on the outskirts of Phoenix.

Tyson's attorneys drew up a plan that called for him to fight seven times over the next three years. Because his situation would be moderated by a $14 million legal settlement from Don King, this was presented to the court as the worst-case scenario. If things went as hoped, Tyson would be debt-free in fewer fights.

Tyson's first announced opponent on his road to solvency was Kevin McBride. Hailing from Clones, Ireland, McBride fought out of Brockton, Massachusetts, under the tutelage of

Goody Petronelli. Standing six-foot-six and tipping the scales at about 270 pounds, McBride had a decent record (31–4–1), but each of his defeats had come inside the distance. Among his conquerors was a retired fighter who ended his career on a 1–17 skid. Slow as molasses, the so-called Clones Colossus seemingly posed no threat to Tyson, regardless of how badly Tyson had declined. But negotiations broke down and Shelly Finkel substituted Danny Williams.

A 31-year-old Brit of Jamaican lineage, Williams (31–3) was a massive man, carrying 265 pounds on a six-foot-three frame. He was light on his feet and had quick hands, but his defense was suspect and his psyche was said to be fragile.

Tyson came out smoking and it looked for a moment that Williams was doomed to go out in Round 1. However, Tyson's punches lost steam and the Brit began to land some telling punches of his own. In Round 4, a barrage of unanswered punches knocked Tyson against the ropes where he slumped to the canvas. The expression on his face as the referee tolled ten was that of a man more weary than stupefied.

It came out that Tyson had twisted his left knee in the second minute of the bout. An MRI revealed a ligament tear of such complexity that the surgeon expressed amazement that Tyson was able to continue for three more rounds. His effort was seen in a new light as valiant.

Tyson's supporters blistered Finkel for being penny-wise and pound-foolish. When Tyson was deemed ready to fight again, Finkel matched him with McBride. "I'm going to gut him like a fish," Tyson told reporters, but when the sloppy, foul-filled scrum was over, McBride's hand was raised in victory and Tyson's tattered reputation was scarred beyond repair. At the post-fight press conference, Tyson conceded that his heart was no longer in the game and announced his retirement.

If this was indeed Tyson's final fight, it was a fittingly sad closeout to a career marked by primal unruliness. In Round 6, the final round of the fight, Tyson nearly wrenched McBride's arm out of its socket and had two points deducted from his score for a head butt that opened a gash over McBride's eye. The round ended with Tyson on the canvas, the result of a shove that sent him sprawling against the ropes. Slow to get up, Tyson walked back to his corner on dead legs and told his handlers that he was finished. As for McBride, he didn't get much mileage out of his triumph. Two fights later, he was emphatically defeated by unsung Mike Mollo. Carrying 278 pounds on his flabby frame, the Clones Colossus was blasted out in the second round.

With Lennox Lewis having left the stage, the heavyweight division had no magnets. Moreover, the titlists and top contenders were getting long in the tooth and there were no hot prospects in the pipeline. Don King's November 13, 2004, show at Madison Square Garden was symptomatic of the times. None of the competitors in the four main heavyweight bouts were younger than 32 years of age. Their average age was 35 years and seven months. The promotion generated only 270,000 PPV buys.

As the heavyweight division was suffering another down cycle, Bernard Hopkins was cementing his reputation as one of the greatest middleweights of all time and finally commanding purses commensurate with his faithfully fine-tuned skill. Hopkins' fight with Oscar de la Hoya at the MGM Grand on September 18, 2004, was far and away the most profitable promotion of the year.

If Bernard Hopkins were a fictional character, his saga would be dismissed as a cliché. While boxing is lauded as a character-building tonic for young hoods, cases as dramatic as Hopkins are mostly imaginational.

As a teenager in Philadelphia, Hopkins survived three stabbings, the first of which was nearly fatal. At age 17, a third arrest for armed robbery drew an 18-year prison sentence. Released after four years and eight months, he found work scrubbing pots and pans, a job from which he was fired for failing to disclose his status as an ex-felon on his employment application.

Hopkins lost his first pro fight. Carrying 177 pounds on his six-foot-one frame, he was out-pointed by a fellow novice who never advanced beyond the four-round stage. Four years later, trimmed down to 159 pounds, he won a crossroads fight with Wayne Powell. Scheduled for 12 rounds, the bout was over in 21 seconds.

On May 22, 1993, at Washington's RFK Stadium, Hopkins came up short in his first stab at the middleweight title, losing a unanimous decision to Roy Jones, Jr. Two years later, he won the IBF version of the title with a seventh-round stoppage of Ecuador's Segundo Mercado.

Deep into his career, Hopkins was still known mostly for his gimmicky ring entrance. Dubbed "The Executioner," he entered the ring wearing a leather mask and carrying an axe, accompanied by shirtless bodybuilders in matching Halloween costumes. While this act made him more generally known, it slowed an appreciation of his talent.

Hopkins successfully defended his IBF title twelve times and then out-pointed WBC counterpart Keith Holmes in the first of back-to-back unification matches. A month later, Felix Trinidad seized the third remaining piece of the middleweight title, destroying William Joppy while elevating his ledger to 40–0.

Hopkins vs. Trinidad would rank among the most important fights ever staged at Madison Square Garden. The middleweight division had not had an undisputed champion since Marvin Hagler. With 13 successful title defenses, Hopkins was only one win removed from tying the middleweight record set by Carlos Monzon.

Hopkins, now 36 years old, was theoretically in very deep water. Trinidad had roughly the same amount of experience despite being eight years younger and had participated in more title fights against stiffer competition. While Trinidad had only one fight under his belt at 160 pounds, he had the frame to carry the weight and was in excellent form. Considering the make-up of the crowd, Hopkins might as well have been fighting in San Juan. At a pre-fight press confab, he had heightened his villainy by grabbing a Puerto Rican flag from Trinidad's clutches and throwing it on the ground. Video replays of the incident showed Don King giving Hopkins his cue.

A 3/1 underdog, the supremely confident Hopkins upset the odds with a shockingly dominating performance. Trinidad landed some powerful punches, but Hopkins answered every hard blow with swift combinations. Late in the bout, Hopkins was still fresh and shifted into the role of the stalker. In the final round, he put the exclamation point on his brilliantly executed battle plan with a snapping right hook that brought the contest to a finish. Fighting out of a city known for producing tough middleweights, Hopkins became the first fighter actually born in Philadelphia to become universally recognized as a world middleweight champion.

Hopkins had three more fights under Don King's aegis before inking a two-fight deal with Bob Arum. During his end days with King, the word on Hopkins was that he was too petulantly independent for his own good. Big money fights with bigger men were there for the taking, but Hopkins had no interest in moving up in weight, a seemingly foolish disposition for a man of his advancing years. But when Hopkins hooked up with Arum, lining up a rich payday with Oscar De La Hoya, his obstinacy came to be seen as the mark of a wise old owl.

Reporters found Hopkins interesting because he was a blue-collar fighter without a posse (shades of Hagler), and was at the opposite pole of Mike Tyson when it came to managing his money. A conversation with him might meander into a discussion of which national retailers offered the best deals on household staples. He couldn't fathom why a man would buy a Rolex when his Timex kept the same time. He didn't aspire to be a rich man, he said, but rather a wealthy man because wealth stays in a family for generations. This was not the kind of talk that one expected from an ex-convict whose body was scarred with knife wounds.

Employing a strategy that he had used many times before, Arum put Hopkins and De La Hoya on the same bill in appetite-whetters. Hopkins out-pointed Robert Allen with little difficulty, but Oscar very nearly came a cropper to Felix Sturm, a fighter of Polish extraction who fought out of Germany, carrying the banner of Hamburg's flowering Universum Gym stable.

## Catching Up with Oscar De La Hoya

De La Hoya rebounded from his setback to Felix Trinidad with a seventh-round stoppage of Derrell Coley. Oscar was more of a fighter than a boxer in this bout, pressing the action and sapping Coley's will with hurtful body punches. This was one of his best performances, but the fight didn't attract much mention in major dailies because no title was at stake.

Oscar returned to Los Angeles for his next fight, his first ring appearance in the city of his birth in nearly six years. His match with area rival Shane Mosley for the 147-pound title vacated by Felix Trinidad — the first boxing event at the Staples Center — drew 20,774.

De La Hoya and Mosley were old acquaintances. They had fought once before as preteen amateurs. Mosely, older by 17 months, was awarded the decision. A three-time national amateur champion, "Sugar Shane" was 34–0 as a pro and had stopped 23 of his last 24 opponents. He was the total package, but yet thought to be in over his head because he had fought almost exclusively as a lightweight. Oscar, two inches taller, was the proven commodity at 147 pounds and the general feeling was that he would use his greater strength to take command in the late rounds.

As Oscar entered the ring, music from his new CD was piped over the loudspeakers. His budding career as a recording artist would be numbered among the outside distractions that kept him from rising to the occasion. Mosley had the best of it in the late rounds and won a narrow decision. The last round of the suspenseful fight was especially spirited, but yet it would be suggested that Oscar was losing his passion for boxing because other interests had become larger priorities.

Bob Arum felt that De La Hoya's style had become too robotic. He put the blame on Roberto Alcazar, who had been coaching Oscar since his amateur days. Alacazar's authority had been repeatedly undermined. Legendary Mexican trainer Jesus Rivero and Emanuel Steward had each taken control of Oscar's training regimen for a few fights, but Alcazar, a close family friend, had remained part of the team and was always the loudest voice in the corner. Now, at Arum's behest, he was cut adrift, yielding his post to Floyd Mayweather.

Mayweather wasn't a big-name trainer, but he was highly respected by his colleagues. His masterwork was his estranged son of the same name. An undefeated fighter then competing at 130 pounds, Little Floyd was a marvel. Mayweather's big regret was that he wasn't around to share the moments when his son scored his biggest amateur wins. He was in prison on a cocaine-trafficking conviction.

It redounded well to the outspoken Mayweather when Oscar overpowered former light-weight titlist Arturo Gatti in his next outing. Using his right hand effectively, Oscar landed 62 percent of his punches, the highest ratio of his career. Gatti's eyes were swollen nearly shut when his handlers tossed in the towel in the fifth round. This victory would take on a brighter tint down the road when Gatti came to be more firmly stamped as a stouthearted warrior, but the New Jersey-based Gatti, a fighter of Italian extraction from Montreal, was out of his element fighting a man as skilled as De La Hoya at 147 pounds and wasn't accorded much chance of making a strong showing.

Oscar was far less impressive in his next outing while easily out-pointing Madrid's Javier Castillejo. While the bout was largely a bore, Oscar emerged with the Spaniard's 154-pound belt, elevating his legend by winning titles in five weight classes. The bout drew a reported 380,000 PPV buys, not a big number but impressive considering that De La Hoya was a 20/1 favorite and that the promotion went head-to-head with a Showtime telecast featuring ultra-talented 140-pound champion Kotsya Tszyu.

The win over Castillejo set up a match between Oscar and Fernando Vargas. A fighter who had traveled the same California amateur circuit as De La Hoya, Vargas had been point-ing toward this match since the very onset of his pro career, stirring the pot with trash talk that belittled Oscar's fighting heart. Vargas's resentment was genuine. It stemmed from the fact that Oscar had never extended him the courtesy of wishing him well when he went off to compete in important amateur tournaments. Although born in the United States and raised in a less hardscrabble district of East Los Angeles, Vargas avouched that he was innately more Mexican.

Turning pro at age 19, Vargas ran off a skein of 16 knockouts en route to winning a piece of the 154-pound title in a dominating performance against well-regarded Raul Marquez. He lost the belt in a vicious fight with Felix Trinidad, but recaptured it after Trinidad moved up to fight as a middleweight. A well-muscled, heavy-handed fighter, Vargas had a swagger that contrasted sharply with De La Hoya's executive boardroom treble. An estimated 3000 fight-goers showed up for the weigh-in, at which "Ferocious" Fernando drew the loudest ovation.

Although he was only 24 years old and coming off two solid outings, Vargas was con-sidered damaged goods in some quarters because he had absorbed massive punishment in his bout with Trinidad. The smart money was on De La Hoya, a 12/5 favorite, but it was easy to visualize the strong-willed Vargas gritting out the upset.

Vargas had several strong rounds, but Oscar kept his composure. The turning point came with five seconds remaining in Round 10 when Oscar stunned Vargas with a devastating left hook. Vargas was still in a fog when he came off his stool for Round 11 and Oscar pounced on him, knocking him down and then pinning him on the ropes with a flurry of punches that forced the referee to stop the fight. The Mandalay Bay event, billed as "Bad Blood," was a big moneymaker, ranking second only to De La Hoya's fight with Trinidad in PPV receipts for a non-heavyweight fight. More than any bout before it, it demonstrated that a bout between two fighters of Mexican descent could be molded into an event with national appeal.

After a tune-up fight with shopworn Yory Boy Campas, Oscar renewed his rivalry with Shane Mosley. On paper, the rematch had less pull than the first meeting because Mosley's reputation had taken a tumble with back-to-back losses to former amateur nemesis Vernon Forrest. However, Oscar was a bigger star than ever within the Latino community. His debut album had been nominated for a Grammy in the Latin Pop category. His company Golden Boy Enterprises, a fight promotion firm, was becoming a force in the industry, begetting sto-ries about him in business publications. His recent marriage to sultry Puerto Rican singer

Millie Corretjer had fired up the paparazzi. Young women still swooned at his public appearances, notwithstanding the wedding band on his ring finger. De La Hoya-Mosley II, at the MGM Grand on September 13, 2003, was a bonanza for ticket-scalpers.

A 2/1 underdog, Mosley had the upper hand again, at least in the eyes of the judges. The HBO commentators saw it differently, as did Arum, who bawled that something was fishy, but the majority of ringside reporters thought the judges got it right. While the decision was roundly lambasted in Web forums, the controversy died quickly as sportswriters rallied to the defense of the officials whose integrity Arum called into question.

Oscar got the benefit of the doubt in his contest with Sturm. Doughy around the midsection in his maiden trip at 160 pounds, De La Hoya landed fewer punches than his lightly regarded adversary, but won by a 2-point margin on each of the scorecards. The sentiment that Oscar had too many irons in the fire now became the prevailing wisdom. The general feeling was that De La Hoya had scant chance to defeat Hopkins unless the longtime middleweight ruler — approaching his 40th birthday — got old overnight. Unbeaten in more than a decade, Hopkins had appended four more wins to his ledger since his celebrated victory over Felix Trinidad and would be making his 19th title defense.

In one survey of boxing writers, 40 of 54 favored Hopkins. Twenty-one opined that he would win inside the distance, whereas all of those favoring De La Hoya, a first-time underdog, envisioned the bout going to the scorecards. Nonetheless, Las Vegas bet-takers wrote substantially more bets on Oscar, shortening the odds from 12/5 to 9/5 and even lower at properties with small limits. This was foreseeable.

Both were tentative in the early rounds, but Hopkins gradually took command. Near the midpoint of Round 9, he landed a left hook to the liver that sent De La Hoya to the canvas grimacing in pain. Oscar was on his knees, pounding the canvas in frustration, as the referee completed his count. The famously frugal Hopkins commemorated his victory by purchasing a Rolex on wheels — a Bentley. His next bout — a successful title defense against Howard Eastman — was a Golden Boy Enterprises promotion.

# CHAPTER 27

# Atomic Salsa

Ten weeks after his bout with Bernard Hopkins, De La Hoya was ringside at the MGM Grand for the rubber match between Marco Antonio Barrera and Erik Morales. Oscar now promoted Barrera. The 15-year veteran from Mexico City was the shining jewel of Golden Boy Enterprises' growing stable.

Although a year younger than his new promoter, Barrera was an established 12-round fighter before Oscar turned pro. While it was common for a Mexican fighter to turn pro before his sixteenth birthday, Barrera's case was unusual as he came from a middle-class home. His father owned a company that manufactured background sets for movies and TV commercials. Barrera planned to be a lawyer if his boxing career fizzled out and completed a few of the required classes.

Barrera's original style of fighting invited comparisons to Julio Cesar Chavez. He was a high-pressure fighter who wore down his opponents with withering body punches. There were other similarities too. Conversant in English, Barrera was too much the perfectionist to address a formal gathering in his second tongue. He required an interpreter, as did Chavez, who late in his career was more fluent in English than he let on.

Barrera won his first 43 fights. His most talked-about conquest was a 12th-round stoppage of former Olympic gold medalist Kennedy McKinney. Their 1996 fray at the L.A. Forum — the inaugural show of the HBO series *Boxing After Dark* — was such a rip-snorter that it was considered a shoo-in for Fight of the Year, but a late entry, Holyfield-Tyson I, filched the prize.

Back-to-back losses to Junior Jones sent Barrera back to the drawing board and he emerged a more flexible boxer. He was still by nature a stalker, but now somewhat more elusive and more of a counterpuncher.

After advancing his record to 49–2, Barrera stepped into the ring with the Tijuana-bred Morales, a fighter rated a cut above him. Undefeated in 35 fights, he was taller than Barrera and threw crisper punches. His ledger was studded with a knockout of Junior Jones and he could fairly be called the linear "world bantamweight champion of Mexico," even if he was a few pounds too heavy for this accreditation. Carlos Zarate had been knocked into retirement by Daniel Zaragoza, who in turn was knocked into retirement by Morales, knotting young Erik with revered bantamweight champions in the division with the longest line of Mexican world-beaters.

The first fight in the Barrera-Morales trilogy, staged at Mandalay Bay on February 19, 2000, was thrilling from start to finish. Barrera landed the harder shots and seemingly clinched the victory with a flash knockdown of Morales in the final round, but Morales retained his 122-pound title on a split decision.

A 7/2 underdog in the first meeting, Barrera was a 7/4 favorite when he caught up with Morales 28 months later. While Morales had beefed up his record to 41–0, he had looked rather ordinary in wresting the WBC featherweight title from Guty Espadas Jr. and was again lackluster in a successful title defense against unheralded In-Jin Chi. Meanwhile, Barrera had put on a clinic while out-pointing British sensation Naseem Hamed and had looked super-sharp while hammering Enrique Sanchez into submission in six lopsided rounds. There was also the reasonable expectation that the judges would give Berrera the benefit of the doubt in the closely contested rounds, atoning for the unpopular verdict in the prequel. The Lewis-Holyfield rematch was referenced as a manifestation of this "make-up syndrome."

Barrera-Morales II had fewer toe-to-toe exchanges, but was another entertaining fight laced with drama. Both were credited with landing 34 percent of their punches, the first deadlock in CompuBox history. Morales landed more power punches, but those landed by Berrera did more damage. In an informal tally of 15 ringside scribes, seven scored the bout a draw. Rarely was a fight ever more even, but the judges knocked Morales from the ranks of the unbeaten, awarding Barrera a unanimous decision.

There were more surprises preceding the inevitable third meeting. The cool-headed manner in which Barrera handled the treacherous southpaw Naseem Hamed made him a heavy favorite when he was paired against Manny Pacquiao at the Alamodome. But the relentless Pacquiao, a budding superstar in the Phillipines, roughed him up, knocking him to the canvas twice en route to an 11th-round stoppage. Barrera's showing forced the conclusion that all the hard fights had finally taken their toll. In his next bout, Barrera shellacked former bantamweight titlist Paulie Ayala in the same fashion that Pacquiao had shellacked him, but this performance failed to dispel the notion that he was slipping. Erik Morales scored six wins between his second and third encounters with Morales, most impressively a third-round stoppage of Guty Espadas Jr.

Barrera was uncharacteristically unassertive in the weeks leading up the rubber match. It would be contested at 130 pounds and Barrera conceded that the higher weight was probably an advantage for his taller opponent. Before the second meeting, he had shown his dislike for his countryman with a racial slur — Morales had an obvious Indian strain in his bloodline — but Barrera refused to reprise the insult to hype the third meeting. Because Morales's belt was at risk, he got to choose the gloves. Barrera cried foul and threatened to pull out of the match when the brand of gloves that Morales selected didn't properly fit the contour of his hand.

In boxing as in poker, a man's armament is often foretold by his "tells." Barrera was sending off signals that suggested he would not be at his best. Late action boosted Morales from a 2/1 to a 16/5 favorite.

Once the bell sounded, Barrera's adrenaline kicked in. Barrera-Morales I was the 2002 Fight of the Year; the 2004 rubber match was even better. Barrera won the epic battle by a majority decision.

The three-fight series most closely mimicked the Olivares-Castillo trilogy, but there were instructive dissimilarities beyond the fact that the scene had shifted from Los Angeles to Las Vegas. The first meeting between Ruben Olivares and "Chucho" Castillo did not bubble into appreciably more profitable sequels. By contrast, the second Barrera-Morales

Marco Antonio Barrera and Erik Morales embellished the legacy of Mexican fighters with their great trilogy or fights in 2000, 2002 and 2004. Both also had memorable bouts with Filipino stalwart Manny Pacquaio. Photograph taken in 2002 or 2004. *Michael Grecco HBO/PPV provided courtesy of Lee Samuels.*

fight produced substantially more revenue than the first and the rubber match did even better.

The contracts for Barrera-Morales I stipulated that each would receive $200,000. The guarantees for the second and third meetings, PPV telecasts, reportedly escalated from $1.5 million to $2.1 million. These sums were paltry when measured against the purses commanded by the likes of Mike Tyson and Oscar De La Hoya, but were a big leap forward for lower-weight fighters from Mexico.

The inflation was concordant with America's most conspicuous demographic trend — the astounding growth of the Mexican population. Many of the biggest gains were in cities and regions where few Mexicans had previously resided. The dispersion opened new vistas for Mexican fighters, but the fighters themselves deserve part of the credit. There was a kernel of truth in the stereotype that Mexican fighters in general fought more fiercely than their non–Mexican brethren, making them an easier commodity to sell.

North American boxing below the middleweight level had become increasingly dependent on the burgeoning Hispanic market. This suggested that the sport was becoming more marginalized, but Mexicans were moving up the economic ladder in increasing numbers. More had the freedom and money to indulge in the Las Vegas experience at an upscale hotel. None of the three Barrera-Morales fights was staged on a Mexican holiday weekend. The coupling, although still advantageous, was becoming superfluous.

# CHAPTER 28

# The "X" Factor

On August 12, 2000, the Paris Hotel in Las Vegas hosted a card featuring a match between Evander Holyfield and John Ruiz. The first undercard bout was a heavyweight affair between Richie Melito, Jr. and Thomas Williams. Melito upped his record to 26–1 with a first-round knockout. Williams almost landed in the lap of a ringside judge after going down from what appeared to be a clean punch to the chin.

The fight was less than two hours old when Charles Jay — writing from New Jersey — posted an article on his "Total Action" Web site telling his readers that the fight was fixed. One could have guessed as much when the order of bouts was shuffled and the fight went off an hour before the bulk of the crowd had filtered into the arena. There were very few witnesses to the alleged swindle, but among them were FBI agents on stakeout.

When things shook out, Williams, his manager Robert Mitchell, and booking agent Robert Mittleman were charged with various counts of sports bribery. Mittleman, who cooperated with the authorities, was sentenced to six months' home detention, fined two thousand dollars, and ordered to perform 250 hours of community service. Mitchell, a father of three school-age children who operated in the boxing backwater of Irmo, South Carolina, drew a much harsher penalty. He was sentenced to serve 37 months in prison.

Some of America's early boxing writers would have dismissed the episode with mordant humor. Westbrook Pegler acknowledged that he enjoyed fake fights: "They are intrinsically entertaining and have the added virtue of allowing spectators to experience the catharsis of moral indignation." When Damon Runyon went to have his appendix removed, he went to a hospital situated a stone's throw from Madison Square Garden: "It is said that on fight nights the medics never go to the expense of anesthetics," he wrote. "They merely open the windows and the odors of some of the fights creep in and chloroform the patients."

Addressing the jury, the federal prosecutor in the trial of Robert Mitchell said: "Mr. Mitchell represents everything that is wrong with boxing as a sport, because does he view it as a sport? No, he views it as a business."[1] Indeed, it is a business and tricksters were thick in all eras, perhaps most active in the nascent bare-knuckle phase. Pierce Egan used the letter "X" to denote a fixed fight. Occasionally he saw fit to double the dosage. "XX" was Egan's shorthand for a double-cross.

There hasn't been much written about the fairgrounds boxing scene, but the history of boxing from a business perspective cannot be assayed without reference to it. Although its history is deeply rooted, a convenient starting point is the period between the two world wars, when the fairgrounds scene in Great Britain was especially robust.

In common with other midway attractions, the boxing booth had an eye-catching façade. The frontispiece was a gaily painted mural that depicted legendary prizefighters in standard fighting poses. An opening in the center allowed for a platform, a stage for the fighters and the spieler who introduced them. The spieler aggrandized each of the fighters as the champion of a particular county or region. After attracting a crowd, the spieler would throw down the gauntlet, offering a cash prize to anyone who could prove himself equal or superior to the booth fighter nearest his weight. A challenge would be accommodated if certain stipulations were met — the volunteer could not be too young, too old, or inebriated — but often there was no volunteer, and regardless a shill was preferable.

The local toughs that answered the siren of the spieler were usually back-alley brawlers that stood little chance with a professional fighter. Moreover, even if a challenger had an aptitude for boxing, it was doubtful that he had the stamina to provide much more than a dollop of artful milling. The ability to fight more than a few rounds at an unrelentingly fast clip is a feat beyond the pale of the average Joe, even a Joe who appears to be in the pink of condition. A one-sided match was not good business because it could not be milked for more money. Then too, an outsider was more likely to vent his frustration by fighting dirty, increasing the risk of an injury, not to mention a riot. Precautions were always taken to diminish the chance of a bad happenstance. The booth operator made certain that his man had all the little edges, like harder gloves. But yet there were always inherent risks to fighting an unknown.

When a man from the audience threw his hat in the ring, this was merely the beginning. The people standing about had to be animated into paying to see the affray, which was held behind a partition or perhaps in a tent. Typically the spieler would initially turn down the challenger, saying something to the effect that he could not in good conscience permit a boy to tackle a man's job. If the challenger were a shill — a plant in the audience — he had a ready-formed counter-slur. The exchange of insults would escalate into a shouting match with eurhythmic posturing, salting the illusion of a grudge fight. The ritualistic war of words has endured. The fairgrounds boxing booth would disappear, but not the "psychology" associated with it.

Booth fighters in England came to call a faked fight a "gee." The best booth fighters became so adept at pulling their punches that booth fights were invariably more crowd-pleasing than genuine competitions at established boxing halls. When an outsider was allowed to test his mettle, it was common to offer him the option of a geeing or playing it straight, the overture made in private as he was being outfitted in his gear. The incentive for choosing the former was guaranteed compensation, a flat fee perhaps, or more conventionally half the "nobbins" that would be collected at the conclusion of the bout. A shill normally started the collection, throwing a conspicuously large bill into the hat that was passed among the crowd. This too was good psychology, a prod to "over-tipping." In the best-case scenario, the "gee" would be executed so adroitly that the spectators would cry out for a rematch. The sequel would be scheduled for a longer distance, with the price of admission jacked up accordingly.

The July 15, 1886, match between Jim Dillon and Duncan McDonald, contested under Queensberry rules on the stage of a Salt Lake City opera house, was a very slick gee in the mind of the *Salt Lake City Tribune* reporter assigned to cover the event, but yet the crowd was so thoroughly entertained that the referee was exhorted to let the fight continue after it had run its six-round course. Some of the spectators proposed to start a pool to subscribe a fight to the finish, but the fighters left the ring before the idea took flight.

The reporter noted that only Dillon had a representative in the box office when the receipts were tallied. He found it odd that while both men were limp as dishrags at the final bell, they appeared fresh as daisies ten minutes later. He also found it peculiar that while McDonald had the best of the milling, he did not protest when the referee declared the bout a draw. "It might have been a hippodrome," he told his readers.

McDonald, billed as the champion of Montana, was fairly well known. Dillon, introduced as the champion of California, was a complete unknown. This would have been true even if he had competed under his real name — James J. Corbett. Young Jim hadn't yet engaged in his attention-getting fights with Joe Choynski. Decades later, sleuths would uncover the subterfuge and find other "lost bouts" for him and many of his contemporaries.

Fourteen years after his Salt Lake City booking, the now internationally famous Corbett participated in a fight so roundly condemned as fraudulent that it came to be erroneously credited with begetting anti-boxing legislation in New York. Let's look at that fight and some others that raised a big stink, taking them in chronological order.

## Fitzsimmons-Sharkey (December 2, 1896)

Born in Ireland, Sailor Tom Sharkey came to the fore in Honolulu while serving in the United States Navy. A square-jawed and square-shouldered man who carried 180 pounds on a five-foot-eight frame, Sharkey looked every inch a fighting man, especially after he coated his chest with a tattoo of a battle schooner. A hard puncher, he was unbeaten in 24 fights with 20 stoppages when he was matched against Fitzsimmons at Mechanics Pavilion.[2]

Promoter Jim Coffroth billed the fight for the world heavyweight championship, a designation somewhat justified as Corbett hadn't defended his title in almost three years. Fitzsimmons, fresh off his fast demolition of Peter Maher, was a consensus 3/1 favorite in the final hours of betting when a late surge of Sharkey money dropped the odds to 3/2.

The event became a larger topic of discussion when it sparked a protest by suffragettes riled that the event was restricted to men. They succeeded in getting the ban overturned. A larger controversy erupted when it became known that the referee would be Wyatt Earp, who was then residing in San Francisco while managing a stable of racehorses. Earp had never refereed a fight of national importance. Coffroth picked him after both camps rejected other choices, exercising a clause in the Articles of Agreement that gave him the power to make this decision.

Earp entered the ring with a conspicuous bulge beneath his frock coat, an ill-concealed Colt .45. Police chief Charles Whitman, seated at ringside, burst into the ring and demanded the weapon, which Earp surrendered without protest. This matter resolved, the fight commenced and seven rounds passed without incident. The contest was basically even at this point, although Fitzsimmons had a strong fifth round, during which he opened a cut over Sharkey's left eye.

Two minutes into Round 8, Fitz connected with a left to Sharkey's chin followed by right aimed at the pit of the stomach. Sharkey crumpled to the canvas, moaning and clutching his groin. Earp called time-out, conferred briefly with both sets of cornermen, and then, with Sharkey still down, scampered out of the ring without any indication that he was disqualifying Fitzsimmons for a low blow. "The information became general by a slow trickling process," wrote *San Francisco Examiner* scribe Edward H. Hamilton, "passing from mouth to mouth and tier to tier so that by the time the full significance of the situation had reached the throng, Earp was gone."

The offending punch was only visible to those seated in one section of the arena, and even they could not agree on whether it landed low. The unsatisfactory ending could have easily triggered a riot, but the multitude filed out in an orderly fashion. This owed to several factors. There was a large sprinkling of women in attendance. Their presence was a deterrent to rowdyism. Most of the betting was on the rounds proposition, six or seven rounds depending on the bet-taker, a wager that wasn't affected by Earp's queer behavior. Noting that fortunes were undoubtedly lost, reporter Hamilton doffed his hat to those that had wagered on Fitzsimmons for accepting their fate "with Christian fortitude and gentlemanly forbearance."

Charles M. Shortridge, the publisher the *San Francisco Call,* wasn't about to accept the fate of his wager with a stiff upper lip. Shortridge accused the managing editor of the *Examiner* of arranging Earp's selection as part of a betting conspiracy. In the ensuing weeks, Shortridge dug up plenty of dirt about Earp to keep the cauldron bubbling. He alleged that Earp had once attempted to rig a horse race and that he had conspired in his role as a referee to rig the outcome of a prizefight in Ogden, Utah. Readers were also told that Earp was pals with three bunko artists arrested for cheating a farmer in a gold brick swindle.

A panel appointed by the mayor to review the fight uncovered other information that cast more doubt on Earp's integrity. It was revealed that the racehorses he claimed to own were only leased and that he was $2,121 in debt to a loan company. The panel was also reliably informed that his common-law wife was a degenerate horseplayer and that her jewelry was frequently in hock.

Testifying before the panel, Earp said, "If I had any leanings they would have been toward Fitzsimmons, for I know that [my best friend] Bat Masterson, who is in Denver tonight, had every dollar he could raise on Fitzsimmons." As for the Colt .45, Earp offered two explanations. He said that he always wore a gun as a precaution in the event of a chance encounter with someone he had sent to prison and that he thought it prudent to carry it because he had come to the arena directly from the racetrack and was holding a large sum of cash. The panel ultimately decided that there was insufficient evidence that the fight was fixed, but Earp was fined $50 for carrying a concealed weapon.

With respect to his public persona, Earp rebounded nicely from this discomfiture. The first books about him ignored or downplayed the Sharkey-Fitzsimmons episode, focusing on the younger Earp and his escapades as a lawman. This was true of the most influential of these works, a 1931 book by Stuart Lake that was serialized in the *Saturday Evening Post.* But in the last quadrant of the twentieth century, the Earp legend would come under attack by revisionist historians who would persuasively argue that Wyatt was hardly the paladin that he was portrayed to be in Lake's hagiography and the slew of movies based on it. The Earp that emerges in this literature is boastful, henpecked, deceitful, and corrupt, more fodder for the supposition, now rarely challenged, that he was in cahoots with gamblers who needed Sharkey to win.[3]

## Corbett-McCoy (August 30, 1900)

Kid McCoy was one of the most famous boxers of his day. A colorful character with a signature punch — the corkscrew punch — McCoy won the middleweight title in 1897 and went on defeat several top heavyweight contenders. A Broadway playboy, McCoy attracted attention outside the ring with his stormy love affairs. His tempestuous union with actress

Julia Woodruff Crosselmire, whom he married and divorced three times, was fodder for the scandal sheets.

When the Corbett-McCoy fight came to fruition, boxing in New York was literally on its heels, damned as a cesspool of corruption. Both McCoy and Corbett had contributed to the cynicism by participating in fights that left a bad odor. Corbett's 1898 match with Tom Sharkey — his first fight after losing the heavyweight title — ended in chaos when Corbett's second entered the ring to protest a foul. A melee ensued, Corbett was disqualified, and all bets were called off. McCoy's rock-'em, sock-'em affair with Joe Choyski in January of 1900 was even more malodorous. In the second round, McCoy was down four times and almost out when the timekeeper hit the gong, clipping the round short by 40 seconds. In the next frame, Choynski was disabled by an apparently intentional low blow. A near-riot ensued when the referee awarded the fight to McCoy.

Scheduled for 25 rounds, Corbett vs. McCoy was the third fight card in Madison Square Garden in four days. Three days prior, Barbados Joe Walcott had been jeered out of the building after quitting on his stool after 11 frames in a bout with Tommy West. Walcott claimed an arm injury, but the general feeling was that he had gone in the tank. Against this backdrop, it became more firmly fixed in the public mind that Corbett vs. McCoy would be a fraud. The most prevalent rumor had McCoy taking his bath in the fifth round, ultimately the very round in which Corbett knocked him out.

Both fighters insisted that the bout was on the level, but reporters got a different story when they interviewed the fighters' wives. Mrs. Corbett dropped a bombshell when she told a *New York World* correspondent that the fix was arranged in her living room. Mrs. McCoy added fuel to the fire by saying that her husband was a pathological liar and had revealed to her many of his ring deceptions.

Mrs. Corbett's accusations were damning, although the alleged hoax would be largely forgotten when Corbett's reputation was re-whitened by the alabaster of nostalgia. But her testimony was of dubious validity because of her agitated mental state. When she was interviewed, her husband was somewhere in the Atlantic Ocean on a ship bound for Europe, sharing a compartment with vaudeville singer Marguerite Cornille. Mrs. Corbett filed for divorce while her husband was at sea, coincidentally on the very same day that Julia McCoy filed for divorce from her husband, charging the "Kid" with infidelity and, in a separate deposition, swearing out a warrant for his arrest on grounds that he had stolen some of her jewelry. (Both couples would reconcile.)

News accounts of the fight do not substantiate the allegations. The ringside reporter for the *New York Times* wrote that the fight was "as ferocious an encounter as ever has taken place in this city" and declared that it was a clean knockout. W.W. Naughton described the knockout blow as a "wicked punch" but subsequently hinted in his 1902 book, *Kings of the Queensberry Realm*, that he might have been duped. The odds favoring Corbett escalated from 9/5 to 3/1 in the weeks preceding the fight, but the betting was extremely light. The shift in the odds was understandable as McCoy, a physical fitness addict, was uncharacteristically undertrained. The weights were not announced, but when McCoy disrobed it was plain that he was too fleshy.

The burst of boxing activity in New York during the final week of August of 1900 owed to the imminent shutdown. The Horton Law that countenanced boxing had been repealed. A harsher law would take effect on September 1. Corbett vs. McCoy was conceptualized as something of a farewell party for Empire State boxing. Pitting two clever ring tacticians, the match figured to be a cerebral competition, not a slugfest, and while slugfests were more crowd-pleasing, the promoters were hoping that this particular fight would play out as an exhibit of ring artistry. What they got instead was a violent altercation between two fighters who threw caution to the wind (perhaps in rebuttal to scurrilous rumors) and a devastating autopsy woven from the avowals of spouses with axes to grind.

## Gans-McGovern (December 11, 1900)

Staged at Tattersall's, an equestrian theatre built by British investors for the 1893 Chicago World's Fair, the fight between Joe Gans and Terrible Terry McGovern was fairly touted as the most important match in Chicago fight history. It acquired this tint despite being restricted by local law to six rounds. Although there was some question about whether the police would let it continue if it became too violent, out-of-town sportsmen descended on Chicago in droves.

The first fighter of the Queensberry era to win a title fight by knockout in the opening round (his victim Pedlar "Box o' Tricks" Palmer was touted by his English countrymen as a peerless defensive fighter), McGovern was the reigning featherweight champion. A terrific hitter, he was unbeaten in his last 38 fights, but he was only 20 years of age and judged to be in over his head against the stronger and more experienced Gans. The Articles of Agreement stipulated that McGovern would be declared the winner if he lasted the distance, and the contest was framed this way for betting purposes. One could also wager on whether McGovern would win by knockout.

On the day of the fight, the odds on McGovern's winning by knockout sank from 2/1 against to even money. According to the *Chicago Record*, "there was a hurried effort to hedge by colored porters and others who had wagered on Gans." The *Chicago Tribune* reported that thousands of dollars were being sent from Chicago to betting commissioners in other cities to place on McGovern.

With the scent of larceny so strong, Gans was under a microscope. The scent became a fetid odor when McGovern blew right through him. In barely five minutes of actual fighting, Gans was on the deck six times. None of the punches that knocked him off his pins — not even the punch that felled him for the 10-count — appeared to have been delivered with great force.

George Siler, the third man in the ring, concurred with the universal opinion that the fight was a palpable hippodrome. "If Gans was trying last night," he wrote in the *Chicago Tribune*, "then I don't know much about the game." Gans signed a sworn affidavit that he gave his best, but the overriding sentiment was that he went into the tank at the bidding of his manager Al Herford, who resorted to an occasional scam as a way of compensating for the fact that he wasn't able to get his fighter purses commensurate with his ability. In the court of public opinion, Terry McGovern was absolved of any complicity.

Of all the important fights that were reportedly fixed with the foreknowledge of one of the principals, this one offers the least grist for a contrarian. No circumstantial evidence is more persuasive than "unnatural money," and plenty of it showed in this instance. However, Gans didn't look right when he entered the ring — his appearance was described as wan — and it's hardly far-fetched to think that he may have been drugged. In the days before the fight, he was spied shooting craps in the predawn hours in Chicago's notorious Levee district. The district's most fabled character, bartender Mickey Finn, was a knockout artist of a different stripe. The chloral hydrate solution that he used to put his customers to sleep before robbing them came to be called a Mickey Finn. By 1900, Finn was gone from the Levee district, but his spirit lived on.

For some time after this tempest, no new boxing licenses were issued in Chicago.

# Johnson-Willard (April 5, 1915)

Jack Johnson was gracious in defeat. "I think it will be a long time before they beat Willard," he told a ringside correspondent for the *Philadelphia Tribune*. "He is too tall and hits too hard for the rest of them. He is far cleverer than I had any idea of. Youth had to assert itself, I guess, and I will take my defeat like a man."

Within a few months, the Mann Act fugitive was singing a different tune, saying he laid down in return for a $30,000 bonus and a promise that he would get off light when he had his day in court. Johnson said he knew that promoters Jack Curley and Harry Frazee might be lying about greasing the skids for an early parole, but that it was plain to him that he would be treated more leniently if he disposed of his title before returning to the United States to face the music. White America was bound to be less vindictive if he bore the stamp of a has-been.

According to Johnson's version of events, his bonus would be forthcoming after Curley shut down the box office. Curley would signal him when he had the money in hand, he in turn would relay the news by semaphore to his wife Lucille, seated at ringside, she would go get the money, return to her seat, and then indicate to her husband by a nod of her head that the promoters had fulfilled their end of the bargain. This libretto was expected to play out at the conclusion of the tenth round.

When the gong rang for Round 11, recollected Johnson, Curley was nowhere in sight. Johnson said it now dawned on him that he was being double-crossed, but he elected to give Curley more time on the chance that the delay resulted from an unforeseen problem. In the nineteenth round, he could no longer curb his impatience and came out of his shell, hammering Willard with a series of sharp body blows. This roused Curley to stop procrastinating, but six more frames elapsed before Johnson was fully satisfied that he was going to get the money promised him. After the twenty-fifth round, he gestured to his wife to complete her appointed rendezvous. As she was being escorted down the aisle, he allowed Willard to tap him on the jaw and flopped to the canvas.

There were indeed queer goings-on in Johnson's corner, as affirmed by Damon Runyon's widely disseminated ringside report. Johnson beckoned Frazee to his corner before the start of the twenty-second round. After conversing with the champion, Frazee trundled off, disappearing in the crowd. Curley turned up in Johnson's corner before the start of the knockout round. Curley then went to gather up Mrs. Johnson. He was escorting her out of the arena as the bout reached its climax. According to Runyon, the first words that the glassy-eyed Johnson spoke after being counted out were, "Now they will leave me alone." Johnson directed this remark to his trainer Tom Flanagan.

Flanagan refuted Johnson's testimony, saying that Johnson quit when he came to realize that he was running out of gas and that he signaled his wife to leave so that she would not witness his disintegration.

Johnson stuck tight to his story after his confession hit the papers. Whether one chose to believe it rested largely on whether one considered him a more credible witness than Curley, who never sued Johnson for defamation of character while branding him a bald-faced liar. Curley's long-running verbal battle with Johnson would come to overshadow his other accomplishments, diminishing his legacy as an extraordinary promoter who made a large impression on American popular culture.

The man who took the name Jack Curley was born Jacques Armand Schuel to Alsatian immigrants in San Francisco. At age seventeen, he ran off to Chicago, stowing away on a freight train to visit the World's Fair, where he found employment on the midway in a shooting gallery. When the fair ended, he latched on with the *Chicago Inter-Ocean*, earning recognition as a boy wonder when he finagled an exclusive jailhouse interview with Eugene V. Debs, the famous socialist incarcerated for agitating a national railroad strike.

In common with many promoters of his time, Curley honed his entrepreneurial skills in mining and railroad camps. He first became involved with Jack Johnson in Colorado and later manufactured a title fight for Johnson in Las Vegas, New Mexico. After hunkering down in New York City, he established himself as a promoter of great versatility. Curley arranged lecture tours for suffragette Emmaline Pankhurst and promoted concerts for the Vatican Choir. Among his many clients was Annette Kellerman, the "Million Dollar Mermaid" from Australia, recognized as the mother of synchronized swimming. Kellerman's innovative one-piece bathing suit, scandalous for her time, became a standard fashion accessory across much of the world. Jack Curley would be credited with inventing it.

Curley would also be credited with reinventing the sport of wrestling, substituting acrobatics and theatrics for scientific techniques to reach a wider audience. The transition was well under way when Curley arrived on the scene, but he was instrumental in making the sport more outlandish, introducing masked marvels and tag-team matches, among other novelties, while exerting tremendous sway as the baron of the so-called New York Wrestling Trust, which shunted wrestlers about the country, employing the business model of a burlesque wheel.

Curley was indispensable to Tex Rickard when Rickard was promoting the Dempsey-Carpentier fight. Fluent in French, Curley became a foster parent to Carpentier, sequestering the boxer on his Long Island estate, where he trained inside a compound patrolled by state troopers. Stealth was deemed necessary because reporters were liable to harp on Carpentier's frail physique if permitted free access to his workouts. There were many parallels between the Dempsey-Carpentier promotion and the match between wrestlers George Hackenschmidt and Frank Gotch at Chicago's Comiskey Park in 1911. In both instances, a European cloaked as a worldly sophisticate was pitted against an unrefined but superior American. Hackenschmidt, the Russian Lion, trained for the bout in secret to hide the fact that he had an injured knee, and Gotch was purportedly pressured to carry him so that patrons would not feel cheated. A Jack Curley promotion, this match set an attendance record for a wrestling show that lasted for 28 years.

Curley died of a heart attack in 1937 at age 61. He would come to be regarded as a relatively minor boxing character, sometimes confused with Jack Hurley, a fight manager from the Northwest, or Herman Salzman, a handyman at Stillman's Gym who was named Jack Curley by the denizens of that establishment, an inside joke lost on many young reporters. It is somewhat ironic that Harry Frazee, the junior partner in the Havana prizefight, surpassed Curley in name recognition. A successful producer of stage shows, Frazee purchased the Boston Red Sox in 1917 and two years later, strapped for cash, sold his star player Babe Ruth to the rival Yankees, afflicting four generations of Red Sox fans with the "Curse of the Bambino."

On June 13, 1935, Curley appeared before the New York Supreme Court to contest a motion filed by a former spouse. His ex-wife's attorney asked him whether the wrestling matches he promoted were on the level. Replied Curley: "I've never promoted a wrestling, boxing or tennis match that was not absolutely honest." But this audacious assertion didn't tip the debate in Johnson's favor because he had the larger reputation as an inveterate liar. While it's doubtful that any athlete ever led a more harum-scarum life, Johnson, well versed in the folkways of the circus, couldn't resist embellishing his adventures with wildly implausible anecdotes. His 1927 autobiography, actual author unknown, was clearly inspired by Jules Verne's great novel, *Around the World in 80 Days*.

The strongest argument that the fight was fixed comes not from attestations to this effect, but from the weight of history. Black heavyweight champions of later vintage would test the fixed-fight hypothesis, repeatedly deflating a slew of heavily hyped Jess Willard facsimiles.

Nonetheless, the scenario outlined by Johnson is hard to swallow because his wife figured so prominently in the sequence of events. In 1915, reporters were still noting the presence of women at prizefights because this was deemed an item of sociological importance. Even in famously libertine New Orleans, professional boxing shows were off-limits to women, a ban eventually lifted in 1920. A provocatively attractive woman, scandalously married to a famous (and infamous) man of color, Lucille Cameron Johnson was the most conspicuous person in the audience, the more so after her husband commanded the ushers to evict a female scribe from the ringside press section before he let the bout commence. Mrs. Johnson could not stray from her seat without attracting attention. It makes no sense that she would be conscripted into a covert operation.

Covert or not, it would be nearly impossible to fix an internationally important prizefight without big gamblers getting wind of it and causing an upheaval in the marketplace. While the odds favoring Johnson would be nicked down, this was foreseeable in hindsight — money invariably shows on Caucasian underdogs in important mixed-race bouts. Big Jess was the sentimental favorite in Havana, where descendents of European settlers outnumbered their darker-skinned brethren. In his final public workout, Johnson looked extremely slow sparring with Sam McVea, a development that undoubtedly had an impact on the betting, which was reportedly very light, even on-site where parimutuel wagers returned $4.40 for each two dollars wagered on Willard.

San Francisco bookmaker Tom Corbett estimated that barely $15,000 was wagered in his city, a pittance compared to the money bet on Johnson's fight with Jim Jeffries barely five years earlier. Johnson closed a 5/3 favorite in Corbett's book, down from an opening posting of 2/1, a common vacillation. "Surely if it had been arranged for Johnson to win," said Corbett, "the money would have poured into San Francisco with commissions on Willard. As it was, we had Johnson money at all times." Sunny Jim Coffroth was numbered among the losers. A man privy to strong inside information, Coffroth was satisfied that the contest was on the up-and-up.

On April 4, 1915, the leading paper in New Orleans ran a curious sidebar to its story of the next day's battle: "Dominick Tortorich, New Orleans boxing promoter, Saturday received a commission of $2500 from Harry H. Frazee, backer of the Johnson-Willard fight at Havana, to bet on Willard if he could get it down at 2 to 1. Tortorich was unable to place the commission."[4]

If Harry Frazee knew that the fight was fixed, why was it so important for him to get the best odds?

## Jake LaMotta-Blackjack Billy Fox (November 14, 1947)

This infamous fight had many threads in common with the Gans-McGovern fight. Whispers of an "arrangement" became so loud that some reporters felt duty-bound to share the scuttlebutt with their readers. The late action was all one way, forcing the bookies to take the fight off the board. The charade — if it was that — was done so maladroitly that the authorities were compelled to take punitive action.

The buyer-beware forewarnings did not discourage ticket sales. The bout between La-Motta (64–11–3) and Fox (49–1, 49 knockouts) drew 18,340, one of the top turnouts ever for a non-title fight at Madison Square Garden.

Blackjack Billy Fox was a rare specimen of African American fighter. Managed by Blinky Palermo, he was brought along as gingerly as any Great White Hope. He began his career with a record-setting 43-fight knockout skein and stopped six more opponents after losing to lightheavyweight champion Gus Lesnevich. Blackjack Billy was favored to defeat Lesnevich — the odds in his favor rose as high as 4/1— but Lesnevich took him to school en route to a 10th-round stoppage.

LaMotta, the so-called Bronx Bull, was battle-tested. He had twice defeated Jimmy Edgar, an outstanding fighter from Detroit whose career was cut short by an eye injury, and he had fought 52 rounds with Sugar Ray Robinson, ending Robinson's 40-fight winning streak in their second meeting. A more noteworthy aspect of his career was that he had never been knocked down. Mindful that they had been so wrong in assessing Fox's chances against Lesnevich, the oddsmakers opened the husky Italian an 8/5 favorite. Betting was light until the day before the fight, when there was an avalanche of Fox money.

In the opening round, it looked as if the "sure thing boys" had been suckered. Banging left hooks to the body at close quarters in his patented style, LaMotta won the round handily. But from that point until the fight was waived off in the fourth round, LaMotta fought passively with his back to the ropes, letting Fox flail away at him without retaliation save for a few half-hearted flurries.

LaMotta attributed his poor showing to a spleen injury suffered in training, producing a letter from his personal physician attesting to the impairment. After fining him one thousand dollars for concealing the injury, the New York State Athletic Commission remanded the case to District Attorney Frank Hogan for further review. Hogan found no hard evidence that the fight was fixed.

Thirteen years later, LaMotta sang a different tune while testifying under oath in a chamber of the United States Senate. In his revised version of events, he was "play-acting" when he foxed the referee into stopping the contest. He said he tanked the fight in return for a promise that he would get a crack at the middleweight title.

Although he had denied wrongdoing in earlier depositions, LaMotta's statements in Washington came to be consecrated as the testament of authenticity. But with LaMotta, one never knew when he was being truthful, and his reputation for insubordination was inconsistent with the presumption that he would ratchet up his veracity for a more august caucus of interrogators. His about-face, he conceded flippantly, was made possible by the statute of limitations. He was beyond the pale of New York authorities that might want to indict him for perjury.

Testifying before the Senate, LaMotta acknowledged play-acting on other occasions. He said he had carried Cecil Hudson in their 1947 bout in Chicago but inadvertently overdid it, with the result that he lost the decision. The LaMotta-Hudson fight, which directly preceded LaMotta's match with Billy Fox, was a very crowd-pleasing mill. It's strange that Jake play-acted so skillfully in the one and so unskillfully in the other. While LaMotta eventually got his crack at the title, 19 months elapsed before it came to pass, by which time he had nine more bouts under his belt.

In his original version of events, LaMotta asserted that Fox hit him with a punch in the spleen late in the first round that left him with a clammy feeling he could not shake off. But he made no mention of it in his 1970 as-told-to autobiography, saying that Fox's best punches couldn't dent a bowl of yogurt.

It would have been interesting to get Blackjack Billy's take on the matter. An unassuming young man with a soft, schoolboy appearance that belied his menacing nickname, Fox must have shown great promise early in his career, notwithstanding his callow efforts against Gus Lesnevich, who pitched him straight to the scrap heap with a first-round stoppage in their second encounter. While Fox's whereabouts were made known during the Senate hearings, there was no sentiment for drawing him into the investigation. After quitting the fight game, Fox made ends meet as a bowling alley pinsetter while drifting in and out of homeless shelters. At the time of the Senate hearings, he was the ward of a Long Island mental hospital.

Anecdotes about ring scandals enliven books about boxing. Hack historians have recklessly twisted facts to make these anecdotes more entertaining. To take one example, it would be written that Wyatt Earp brandished his revolver in the ring to save his hide from a lynch mob. Even the respected chronicler Rex Lardner swallowed this balderdash, or at least saw no reason to spoil a good yarn.

Dishonest fights come in many different hues. Lumping then together makes as much sense as conveying information about the prevalence of crime without distinguishing between felonies and misdemeanors. A rigged fight for the purpose of a betting coup doesn't belong in the same category with a fight between an up-and-comer and a professional loser, yoked with the understanding that the professional loser will stay in character and perform his role in the established manner.

Crooked fights are common cargo in the steerage compartment of the boxing boat, but far less prevalent in the upper suites. The view from here is that the outcomes of the five fights examined in this chapter were probably *not* prearranged — at least not by those directly involved in the promotions. By the very nature of boxing, queer fights are inevitable.

# CHAPTER 29

# Shifting Sands

During the early years of the twenty-first century, there were two developments certain to engage the next generation of boxing historians. The heavyweight division acquired a new tint as boxers from the former Soviet Union came to rule the roosts. The sport faced a new threat from the encroachment of mixed martial arts, in particular the alloy called Ultimate Fighting. In the minds of some observers, the sharp surge of interest in this less bridled form of man-to-man combat meant that boxing required a makeover — both in its rulebook and its business model — to remain commercially viable.

During a brief period in 2006, the most valued heavyweight belts belonged to Wladimir Klitschko (Ukraine), Oleg Maskaev (Kazakstan), Nikolay Valuev (Russia), and Serguei Liakhovich (Belarus). The stranglehold was broken by a refurbished Brooklynite, Shannon Briggs, who won Liakhovich's belt with a dramatic Round 12 stoppage, but another Eastern bloc fighter hopped on the merry-go-round several months later when Rusian Chagaev (Uzbekistan) out-pointed Valuev in Stuttgart. Extolled the eighth wonder of the world by Don King, Valuev had the distinction of being the first 7-footer to become a world title claimant. He had a Marciano-like 46–0 record until Chagaev — 12 inches shorter and 99 pounds lighter — exposed him as a fighter more in the mold of Primo Carnera.

Chagaev, a southpaw with a solid amateur background, was considered part of the second wave of Soviet heavyweights. The cast included Sultan Ibragimov (Russia), who recomposed the all-Soviet upper crust by outhustling the listless Briggs in Briggs's first title defense.

In the United States, this development was interpreted as the symptom of a manpower shortage created by the dispersion of athletically skillful big men into football and basketball. The so-called arms race in college revenue sports created unprecedented opportunities for athletes from disadvantaged backgrounds. It was generally understood that Soviet bloc fighters received better nourishment at the amateur level. They were channeled into boxing at an earlier age and tended to stay in amateur programs longer. However, this explanation also fed into the conceit that America still produced the best heavyweights. Their ranks were thinned by outside forces.

In 2006, the only Eastern bloc fighter with any marquee value outside Europe was Klitschko. However, casual fans were prone to confuse him with his brother Vitali, who had a short run as the WBC titlist before taking his leave to recuperate from mounting injuries of the sort associated with football players.

The confusion was understandable. Although Vitali, born in 1971, was older by nearly five years, the siblings looked almost like twins. They had launched their pro careers concurrently, debuting on a card in Hamburg. With their careers running on parallel tracks, each had stumbles that advanced the other by comparison. Wladimir (the German spelling of Volodmyr, his birth name) was more fluid and seemingly less prone to cut, but Vitali had a sturdier chin and fewer problems with stamina.

Outside the ring, the brothers were highly unconventional. The sons of an Air Force colonel, both held doctorate degrees in sports science and were conversant in four languages. Their hobbies ran from playing chess to piloting helicopters. At home in Ukraine, the land of their forefathers, they attended high-level cabinet meetings and contributed money and muscle to restoration projects. They were credited with strengthening bonds between Ukraine and Germany, an important trading partner.

A fitness book they co-authored in German reportedly had an initial printing of 500,000 copies, a measure of their great popularity in this part of the world. However, the Klitschkos were slow to gain adherents in the U.S., a by-product of their European-ness. Their defeats — a combined five as this book went to press — resonated louder than their victories because their defeats were more congruent with the soiled reputation of European heavyweights. But both were excellent boxers who lost bouts they were handily winning because of physical breakdowns that could be rationalized as tough luck.

In his last fight before going on the shelf, Vitali Klitschko advanced his ledger to 35–2 with a dominating performance against Danny Williams. The man that defeated Mike Tyson was no factor in a bout halted in the eighth round. The fight at Mandalay Bay reportedly drew only 120,000 PPV buys, a dismal figure for a match packaged as a heavyweight title fight. Not quite eight weeks later, an Ultimate Fighting Championship (UFC) event at the same venue drew a larger and lustier crowd that swelled the arena before the first bell of the first preliminary bout. The show was an advance sellout.

The first promotion under the UFC label was held in 1993 in Denver. Other early shows were staged in North Carolina, Oklahoma, Wyoming, and Alabama — states without regulatory oversight. In 2001, second-generation Las Vegas casino moguls Frank Fertitta III and his brother Lorenzo Fertitta acquired the company. The driving force behind the takeover was Lorenzo's childhood friend Dana White. Installed as the president of Zuffa LLC, the parent company, White quickly became recognized as the most powerful man in mixed martial arts. He solidified his power in 2007 when Zuffa acquired Pride, a rival organization based in Japan.

Flavored with the disciplines of boxing, judo, jiu-jitsu, and freestyle wrestling, so-called Ultimate Fights were originally billed as no-holds-barred. Even before the Zuffa takeover, steps were taken to temper the sport's rogue image. The rulebook was expanded, weight divisions were created, and matches were restricted to a predetermined length (five 5-minute rounds for championship bouts).

The *Los Angeles Times* sent a reporter to cover the UFC show staged on November 23, 2002, at the MGM Grand. The significance, as Kevin Iole noted, was that this marked the first time that an important paper sent a reporter to cover a mixed martial arts competition held outside its circulation area.[1]

Despite a steadily growing constituency, the UFC was hemorrhaging money until *The Ultimate Fighter* reality series debuted on the fledgling Spike cable network in January of 2005. The program was a hit that drew higher ratings than basketball and baseball games aired in the same time slot. Most viewers were males in the 18-to-34-year-old age bracket, a coveted demographic.

A dramatic spike in gate receipts and ancillary revenue was credited to the TV show and its spin-offs. A UFC card on August 17, 2005, at the MGM Grand drew 14,562, a North American record (quickly broken) for an event of this kind. On December 30, 2006, a UFC promotion at this venue generated $5,397,300 in ticket sales and became the first mixed martial arts event to attract more than one million PPV buys. Chuck Liddell defeated Jacob "Tito" Ortiz in the featured bout. A subsequent UFC show in Columbus, Ohio, broke the Ohio box office record for an indoor event, topping a concert by the Rolling Stones.

Was the mixed martial arts phenomenon simply a fad? Or were the Fertitta brothers and cohort Dana White the modern day equivalents of John Graham Chambers and John Sholto Douglas, fomenting a sea change destined to alter the landscape of commercial man-to-man fighting? The May 5, 2007, match between Oscar De La Hoya and Floyd Mayweather was contested against the backdrop of this burning question. There was no doubt that this particular fight would be a huge moneymaker (the first-day sale guaranteed a record live gate), but would it bubble into more megafights or would it be remembered as the last hurrah? Even in the best of times, there were those postulating that boxing was on the ropes. This opinion was now a louder drumbeat and skeptics with insights born from a deeper knowledge of boxing history weren't so quick to dismiss the notion as shortsighted.

Hailing from Grand Rapids, Michigan, Floyd Mayweather Jr. was known as Floyd Sinclair until the age of 12 when he assumed the last name of his biological father (his parents never married; Little Floyd was raised largely by his paternal grandmother). A child prodigy who mimicked a boxer while still in the crib, he won three National Golden Gloves titles. At the 1996 Olympiad, he was forced to settle for a bronze medal after losing a hotly disputed decision to his Bulgarian opponent. In his fifth pro fight, he appeared on a show in Grand Rapids with his uncles, Roger and Jeff, whose careers were winding down. As expected, it was a clean sweep for the Mayweathers, all of whom were then based in Las Vegas.

Roger Mayweather was Floyd's chief trainer through his first 14 pro fights. Roger passed the reins to his older brother when Floyd Sr. was released from prison. However, Floyd had a rocky relationship with his father that splintered when he hired James Prince as his manager. The founder and CEO of Rap-a-Lot Records, Prince was identified with gangsta rap music. The elder Mayweather, persona non grata in Floyd's inner circle, then hooked up with Oscar De La Hoya.

Floyd seized a share of the 130-pound title in his 18th pro fight with an eighth-round stoppage of "Chicanito" Hernandez. Thoroughly outclassed, Hernandez retired with a 38–2–1 record. During the course of nine title defenses, he had a noteworthy match with undefeated (33–0) Diego Corrales. Although anorexically thin, Corrales had a harder punch and was noted for fighting with more fire in his belly. The fight shaped up as a doozy, but in a breathtakingly brilliant performance, Mayweather, a 13/10 favorite, was dominant from the opening gong. He had Corrales on the deck five times. The final knockdown, in Round 10, prompted Corrales's corner to toss in the towel.

Two fights later, Mayweather wrested a share of the 135-pound title from Mexicali's Jose Luis Castillo. This was a difficult fight for him. The swarming Castillo landed more punches but failed to impress the judges. The unanimous decision in Floyd's favor drew catcalls from the largely Hispanic crowd.

Mayweather was somewhat busier in the rematch, fairly winning a close decision in a dull fight. Three fights later, competing at 140 pounds, he routed DeMarcus Corley in Atlantic City, scoring two knockdowns en route to a lopsided decision. Floyd's name had figured prominently on pound-for-pound lists since his demolition of Corrales. With this victory, he was widely hailed as *numero uno,* surpassing Roy Jones Jr., who had fallen from grace seven days earlier, suffering a shocking knockout at the hands of Antonio Tarver. This was the first defeat for the 35-year-old Jones, other than a fluke loss by disqualification that he had quickly avenged.

Floyd solidified his stature as the most talented fighter on the planet with victories over Arturo Gatti, Zab Judah, and Carlos Baldomir, a late-blooming Argentine who was recognized as the linear welterweight champion. Fighting before a hostile crowd in Atlantic City, he demolished Gatti more thoroughly than he had demolished Corrales. Landing five- and six-punch combinations with laser-like accuracy, he beat Gatti into submission in six one-sided frames. Against Baldomir at Mandalay Bay, he won every round on two scorecards. However, the fight was monotonous and there was a streaming toward the exits before the final bell.

Seemingly effortless wins had become a Mayweather trademark. This was something of a curse. For all the accolades showered on Roy Jones, Jr., he never became a big draw. He was a ring artisan, but he wasn't a ring personality. Mayweather would have likely suffered the same fate if he hadn't chosen the nickname "Pretty Boy" and commanded attention with his fulsome behavior.

Twenty-two fights into his pro career, he was offered a 6-fight deal with HBO worth $12.5 million. He turned it down, calling the offer "slave wages." His pre-fight trash talking sometimes crossed the line. With Diego Corrales facing a court date for spousal abuse (he

served 14 months), Floyd dedicated their fight to battered women. He then attracted notoriety for incidents of a similar nature. In 2004, he received a suspended one-year sentence and was ordered to undergo impulse-control counseling after a skirmish with two women at a Las Vegas nightclub. The following year, he was charged with domestic abuse after a disturbance in his Bentley. He was acquitted after his accuser, the mother of three of his children, recanted her testimony.

To promote the De La Hoya-Mayweather fight, HBO created a reality series consisting of four half-hour segments. Viewers got a closer look at the indecorous Mayweather clan. (Roger Mayweather was once again Floyd's lead trainer, a position he reassumed after serving a 6-month jail sentence for slugging the grandmother of one of his children.) Absent from the infomercial was Jeff Mayweather, with whom young Floyd was long estranged. A cat of a different stripe than his brothers, Jeff had a degree in graphic arts from Western Michigan University. In his spare time, he composed thoughtful, well-written articles for a boxing Web site.

Floyd "Pretty Boy" Mayweather circa 2004. *Top Rank file photograph*

The contrast between Floyd and Oscar

was especially sharp in their approach to money. For Mayweather, a big wad of cash was something to flaunt when he wasn't spending it or betting on sporting events. At the final press conference, he wore a $500,000 watch and two other pieces of jewelry reportedly worth another half million. For De La Hoya, money was primarily a tool for making more money. With his partners, he was growing Golden Boy Enterprises into a diversified company with real estate holdings that included a 12-story office building in downtown Los Angeles.

Oscar was no angel and Floyd was too smart to whiten his image with a middle-class veneer. The match between the best fighter and the most popular fighter was made more captivating by the interplay of hero vs. villain.

Oscar had rebounded from his loss to Bernard Hopkins with a blastout of Ricardo Mayorga, a free-swinging Nicaraguan who owned a piece of the 154-pound title. A full year had elapsed since that match. At age 34, the Golden Boy was effectively semiretired. It was widely assumed that he had lost his hunger for boxing and was now in it only for the money. With Floyd Mayweather Sr. relegated to the sidelines after a productive 8-fight run as his trainer (retaining his services would have been creepy), De La Hoya was seemingly more vulnerable to making a bad showing. The elder Mayweather's replacement, Freddie Roach, was a respected name, but basically a hired hand whose role for this fight was less that of a trainer than a camp coordinator.

While young Floyd was no stranger to pricey late-night haunts, he was most at home in the gym and never slacked off in his workouts. However, there were concerns that he was moving up in weight too quickly. He carried 139 pounds for Arturo Gatti. For this fight, he would need to bulk up. (He weighed in at 150 pounds, four pounds less than Oscar.) He was also prone to develop sore hands during a fight, diminishing his punching power.

The leading oddsmaking concern in Nevada opened Mayweather a 12/5 favorite. Predictably, many more wagers were written on De La Hoya. The consensus closing line in Nevada was 9/5. Most of the large wagers were on Mayweather, but Las Vegas saw very little of this money. The times had changed and the leading bookmaking establishments were "online stores" headquartered in places like Costa Rica and Curacao.

In conformance with the expectation of the majority of knowledgeable fans, the fight went the full distance with Mayweather grabbing the decision. One of the judges dissented and the verdict was greeted with a shower of boos, but virtually all the ringside scribes thought that the outcome was just.

Viewed as a form of entertainment, the bout drew mixed reviews. While Oscar slowed down in the late rounds, he was never deterred from pressing the action. The best flurry of toe-to-toe activity came in the waning seconds and the crowd responded with a standing ovation. However, the next day there was an outpouring of negativity from Web bloggers complaining they didn't get enough bang for their $54.95 PPV buck. A common grievance was that the contest, although suspenseful, played out as a sparring exhibition.

A Golden Boy Enterprises promotion, the fight harvested more money than any fight before it. Playing to an expanded PPV universe, it drew 2.1 million buys. De La Hoya's swag before taxes was pegged at $45 million. Mayweather reportedly stood to earn a shade under $25 million. This was a bitter pill for Bob Arum, who had shrewdly promoted both fighters only to see them fly the coop. With neither Arum nor Don King sharing in the proceeds, the event seemed to signify a changing of the guard.

Born a year apart, Arum and King were now in their mid–70s. However, neither had yet showed signs of slowing down. Five weeks after the big shebang, Arum promoted a card on the eve of New York's annual Puerto Rican Day Parade that filled Madison Square Garden to the rafters. With the crowd in his corner, welterweight titlist Miguel Cotto kept his unbeaten streak alive with an impressive 11th-round stoppage of spirited Zab Judah.

Of all the names bandied about as a choice opponent for Floyd Mayweather, Cotto's name bumped to the top of the list. There were holes in his defense, but he was stronger than Mayweather and seemingly a legitimate threat to the reigning pound-for-pound king. More importantly, he had an avid following, albeit largely localized to the Caribbean and older cities in the Northeast.

A fight between Mayweather and Cotto wasn't likely to set any PPV records, but if staged in New York it had the potential to sell out Yankee Stadium, turning back the clock to the glory days of boxing in the Big Apple. There were numerous impediments to making the match, plus the possibility that intervening developments would waste away the sheen, but the shiver of anticipation was a sign that boxing as a spectator sport, despite ongoing ills, was far from comatose. The situation called to mind Mark Twain's famous quote upon reading his premature obituary: "The reports of my death are greatly exaggerated."

# Chapter Notes

## Chapter 1

1. Writing about the Johnson-Jeffries fight of 1910, Finis Farr drew an excellent portrait of a Fancy man: "...an amateur or semi-professional gambler and therefore a student of form and odds; and, more generally, a man of wide and easy views, tolerant, willing to live and let live; most probably something of a dandy according to his means and background" (Finis Farr, *Black Champion: The Life and Times of Jack Johnson*, pp. 98–99).

2. In badger-baiting, a fox terrier was placed in a tunnel that led into a wire cage housing a badger. The two instinctively locked horns and fought to the death. The outcome could not be determined in advance, making it ideal for betting. In bear-baiting, a bear was tethered to a post, taunted, and set upon by bulldogs bred to accentuate their fighting instinct. Bets were placed on which dog would die first or survive the longest. These grotesqueries were outlawed by the Cruelty to Animals Act of 1835.

## Chapter 2

1. In England, many prizefights were likewise held on Tuesdays. With the sport under siege, fights were pushed into remote places, thereby forcing many fightgoers to spend an entire day just getting to the battleground. This ruled out Mondays because abolitionists would have been roused to a higher state of indignation to see a fight caravan leaving London on the Christian day of worship.

2. *Spirit of the Times*, September 17, 1842, pp. 339–346.

3. Elliott J. Gorn, *The Manly Art*, p. 141.

4. Sullivan was sincere when he boasted that he never engaged in a dishonest bout, but by that he meant that he never acted in consort with gamblers to affect an outcome. In fights on vaudeville stages, his opponent was customarily a member of his troupe, although he occasionally drew a volunteer, invariably an impetuous lad who developed a bad case of stage

fright the moment John L. threw a punch with bad intentions.

5. Edward Van Every, *Muldoon: The Solid Man of Sport*, p. 186.

6. Van Every, *op. cit.*, p. 193.

## Chapter 3

1. An eighth-generation Marquess of Queensberry, John Sholto Douglas was descended from a long line of sporting eccentrics. He was an excellent foxhunter, as was his brother Lord Francis Douglas, who died climbing the Matterhorn. The boxing rules that bore his titular name became his great legacy, but late in his life his name conjured up another image in his native country, that of a cantankerous moral avenger. This owed to his vendetta against the flamboyant Oscar Wilde, who carried on an open affair with the Marquess's son, Lord Alfred "Bosie" Douglas. At times Douglas's crusade took on a comical dimension, as when he appeared at a theater where Wilde was performing and showered the stage with rotten turnips. The Marquess achieved a measure of satisfaction when Wilde was sentenced to prison for "gross indecency."

2. Padded gloves served a cosmetic purpose. A downside from a safety aspect is that more boxers became headhunters. While hard evidence is lacking, boxers of the Queensberry realm were likely more susceptible to developing pugilistic dementia than were bare-knuckle battlers.

3. Douglas Sutherland, *The Yellow Earl*, p. 29.

4. Gerald Walter (with Patsy Hagate), *White Ties and Fisticuffs*, pp. 60–63.

## Chapter 4

1. At the height of his celebrity, Corbett appeared in numerous minor league regulation games as a guest first baseman. Joe Corbett, his youngest brother, was a 24-game winner for the 1897 Baltimore Orioles.

## Chapter 5

1. Ringside correspondent Billy Coffey may have spun more than a little fiction into his story. Reminiscing about his days with the *Enterprise*, Mark Twain recollected that mundane feats and calamities took on a larger dimension on days "when the public needed matters of thrilling interest for breakfast."

2. Few fighters deteriorated as quickly as Maher, who came to be remembered, if remembered at all, as a fighter who finished his bouts in a horizontal position. He suffered 14 more knockouts before his career was done, five in the opening round.

3. *Daily Territorial Enterprise*, February 2, 1897, p. 1.

4. *New Haven Register*, March 8, 1897, p. 6 (cited in Charles Musser, *The Emergence of Cinema: The American Screen to 1907*, p. 195).

5. Alf Doten, *The Journals of Alf Doten 1849–1903*, vol. 3, p. 1946.

6. Barton W. Currie, "Prize-Fights as Mine-Boomers," *Harper's Weekly*, August 22, 1908, p. 25.

7. After leaving politics, Dickerson landed a cushy job as a prison inspector. After being removed from this post, he ran into some trouble. In 1921, he was fined one thousand dollars by a federal judge in Los Angeles for the crime of transporting a fight film across state lines. The contraband was a copy of the Dempsey-Carpentier fight. ("Nevada Ex-Governor in New Enterprise," *Las Vegas Age*, Sept. 10, 1921, p. 1.)

8. *Butte Daily Miner*, June 7, 1923, p. 13.

## Chapter 6

1. *New York Times*, September 22, 1896.

2. "A Warning Cry for our Troops on the Border," *Literary Digest*, July 29, 1916, pp. 254–55.

## Chapter 7

1. It doesn't sit right that the odds would be this high as Dempsey had knocked out a slew of opponents in the opening round, including such reputable men as Fred Fulton and Carl Morris, neither of whom survived the opening minute. The seemingly sturdy Willard, the heavier man by almost 60 pounds, was a consensus 5/4 favorite on the morning of the fight.

2. Davenport's article was reprinted under the title "Moonlight Sonata" in *Sports Extra*, an anthology edited by Stanley Frank (A.S. Barnes and Company, 1944, pp. 61–72). In the April 1953 issue of *The Ring*, Ted Carroll reported that Firpo had 28,000 head of cattle grazing on 64,000 acres.

3. The cover story of the January 13, 1964, issue of *Sports Illustrated* was excerpted from Kearns's soon-to-be-released biography. The gist of the piece was Kearns's confession that he had loaded Dempsey's gloves with plaster of Paris for his bout with Jess Willard. The allegation was preposterous. A fighter with hardened plaster in his gloves could not land a powerful punch without breaking most of the bones in his hand. Dempsey sued for libel. His attorney reached an out-of-court settlement with Time Incorporated, the parent company of *S.I.* When the book was finally published, the offending portion was deleted.

4. *San Francisco Chronicle*, September 22, 1926, p. 4H.

5. In his 1999 biography of Dempsey, *A Flame of Pure Fire*, Roger Kahn reopened the debate about whether Barry performed his duties honestly. After analyzing newsreel tapes, Kahn deduced that Barry was crooked (p. 422), a conclusion born of a troubling inconsistency. In the round following the "long count" round, Tunney caught Dempsey off balance and put him on the mat with a lightning-quick combination. Barry began his count without commanding Tunney to a neutral corner. Because Dempsey was up in a flash, this went largely unnoticed. Dave Barry died in 1936 at age 47 after a lingering illness. At the time of his death, he was under investigation for allegedly embezzling $54,473 from the Amalgamated Trust and Savings Bank of Chicago (*New York Times,* Aug. 27, 1936, p. 21).

## Chapter 8

1. J.C. Reid, *Bucks and Bruisers: Pierce Egan and Regency England*, p. 91.

2. *Boxiana* is a treasure trove for students of underworld slang. Slang terms that may have first appeared in print in a piece by Egan include *filly* (young woman), *lush* (inebriate), and *dead beat* (defaulter). While these words had staying power, Egan's vernacularizing hastened the obscuration of his body of work. It was inevitable that much of the jargon would disappear and, when it did, *Boxiana* became freighted with too many strange words.

*Life in London*, also a compendium of previously published stories, had longer legs and a greater impact on British popular culture. "Tom and Jerrying" became a popular expression, denoting a rowdy night on the town. Taverns that sold cheap ale were sometimes referred to as jerry-shops. The libation called a Tom and Jerry was once a popular Christmastime cocktail. In more modern times, Tom and Jerry were reborn as a cat and mouse team in a popular animated children's cartoon series.

3. Jack DeMattos, *Masterson & Roosevelt*, p. 49.

## Chapter 9

1. John Harding (with Jack Berg), *Jack Kid Berg*, p. 27.

2. Heywood Broun, "The Orthodox Champion," reprinted in W.C. Heinz (ed.), *The Fireside Book of Boxing*, pp. 52–53.

3. An excerpt of Conway's article appears in Ruby Goldstein's memoir *The Third Man in the Ring* (p. 60). It was common in Conway's day to identify big winners and big losers. The practice faded as gamblers became more discreet in the face of heightened IRS scrutiny.

4. Ben Sharav, "Jackie 'Kid' Berg," May 1990, p. 48.

5. On April 18, 1947, Leonard refereed the fights at St. Nicholas Arena. In the second minute of the walk-out bout, he toppled to the floor dead from a sudden heart attack. At its next meeting, the boxing commission passed a rule requiring the attendance of an extra referee at future shows. During the early years of the

century, it was common to name a back-up referee for important fights. This ensured that the fight would continue in the event that the ref was injured with an accidental punch.

6. In adding the extra syllable, wisecracking reporters imbued Levinsky with the qualities of the George "Kingfish" Stevens character of the hit radio show *Amos and Andy*. Like his quixotic radio counterpart, Levinsky became known as the master of the malaprop. On April 28, 1964, shortly after the ring death of Benny "Kid" Paret, NBC aired a documentary called "The Last Round." Levinsky was shown peddling neckties in Miami Beach. His face, his walk, and his slurred speech spoke to the barbarity of boxing.

7. *The Ring*, May 1934, p. 13.

8. *The Ring*, May 1940, p. 45.

9. *New York Times*, Nov. 22, 1945, p. 48. The story about Bummy's murder began on the front page.

## Chapter 10

1. The NCAA decertified boxing in 1960 after Charlie Mohr suffered a fatal brain hemorrhage in a bout at the University of Wisconsin fieldhouse. The defending NCAA middleweight champion, Mohr represented the University of Wisconsin, a perennial power that won six national titles. Other schools that developed strong programs were San Jose State, Idaho State, and Idaho. A popular sport on many campuses during its heyday, especially in Olympic years, intercollegiate boxing was in decline when it was reduced to a club (non-scholarship) sport.

2. Eleven days after out-pointing lightheavyweight champion Maxie Rosenbloom, Stribling suffered fatal injuries in a motorcycle crash. Record-keepers would credit him with 128 knockouts, a record eventually broken by Archie Moore (131). However, Moore also recorded several curious knockouts. Late in his career, he stopped Professor Roy Shire and Mike DiBiase on cuts. Shire and DiBiase were popular grunt-and-groan wrestlers.

3. Paul Gallico, *Farewell to Sport*, p. 58.

4. Five fighters born in Italy preceded Carnera as internationally recognized champions. They were known by their aliases — Frankie Conley, Johnny Dundee, Joe Dundee (no relation), Bushy Graham, and Young Corbett III.

## Chapter 11

1. There are different versions of the Molineaux saga. Depending on one's source, Molineaux (Molyneaux?) was born in northern Virginia or South Carolina and had his dock fights in Norfolk or New York City. However, all of these versions follow the same general outline.

It's interesting that Molineaux turned up in England in the same year as the tragic Sarah Baartman, a sensation known on the fair circuit as the Hottentot Venus. Discovered by a ship's doctor in Capetown, South Africa, Baartman had unusually large buttocks and genitals and was put on display as a medical curiosity. When the novelty wore off, she was exhibited in France, where she died in 1818, her death attributed to alcoholism and syphilis.

The conventional wisdom is that fights between slaves were extremely brutal. The noted filmmaker John Singleton opined that the exploitation of black college athletes has its genesis in slave fights where "[slave owners] would put black men in pits and make 'em fight each other to the death" (Lonnie White, "Q & A with John Singleton," *Los Angeles Times*, February 5, 1995, p. C5).

This impression is inconsistent with the only reference to slave fights in a first-person narrative by a runaway slave. Recalling his days in servitude on a Kentucky plantation, abolitionist Henry Bibb recalled that slave holders encouraged boxing, wrestling, and head-butting contests among their chatel on Sundays, but that "if they are likely to hurt each other very bad, their masters would rap them with their walking canes, and make them stop." (*Narrative of the Life and Adventures of Henry Bibb, An American Slave*. New York: Negro Universities Press, 1969, p. 23. This book was originally published in 1850.)

In researching an article about Tom Molineaux that ran in the Negro history journal *Phylon* (December 1951, pp. 329–336), Paul Magriel was surprised to find only two references to him in American newspapers of the period. He surmised that this reflected an editorial conspiracy. On Internet Web sites, however, there are references to Molineaux as America's first spots celebrity.

2. For a broader overview of Jackson's career and a closer look at Jackson the man, see David K. Wiggins' "Peter Jackson and the Elusive Heavyweight Championship: A Black Athlete's Struggle Against the Late Nineteenth-Century Color-Line," *Journal of Sports History*, Summer 1985, pp. 143–168.

3. It's rather ironic that a district redeveloped to memorialize Jack London is a tourist attraction in Oakland, incubus of the Black Panther movement and a city that once boasted the longest uninterrupted run of black mayors of any major city in America. The most translated novelist of his generation, London was an unabashed white supremacist whose views were a queer amalgam of socialism and social Darwinism.

4. *Boxing*, February 19, 1910, p. 588.

5. A.J. Leibling authored the definitive profile of Tim Mara. See *The New Yorker*, September 18, 1937, pp. 25–29.

6. It's doubtful that any fighter acquired such an adhesive nickname so late into his career. Damon Runyon is credited with affixing Braddock with the sobriquet "Cinderella Man," but Mike Jacobs' publicist Francis Albertanti, a holdover from Tex Rickard's PR department, was quick to seize on it and may have thought of it first.

7. "Wendell Smith's Sports Beat," *Pittsburgh Courier*, July 19, 1952.

## Chapter 12

1. W.C. Heinz, "Brockton's Boy," *Cosmopolitan*, June 1954, p. 64.

2. *Ibid.*

3. Of the four black heavyweights in Woroner's fantasy tournament, only Joe Louis advanced as far as the semifinal round. Jack Johnson (out-pointed by Max Baer) and Jersey Joe Walcott (TKOed by Jim Jeffries)

were eliminated in the opening round. Cassius Clay out-pointed Max Schmeling and then lost his quarter-final match on points to Jeffries.

## Chapter 13

1. Writing the Roy Harris profile was good practice for Joe David Brown, who subsequently penned the novel that begat the movie *Paper Moon*. Tatum O'Neal won an Oscar for her portrayal of a tomboy traveling the back roads of the South with her newly appointed guardian, a grifter tacitly understood to be her biological father.

2. *Los Angeles Times,* August 17, 1958, section III, p. 4.

3. Eight fights into his pro career, Patterson married a 16-year-old girl. Two children were born from the union, which was officially dissolved in June of 1956 as Patterson was preparing for his first fight with Hurricane Jackson. The story of Patterson's marriage and divorce first appeared in a scandal magazine. Boxing writers were kept in the dark for fear that this would taint Patterson's wholesome image. Decades later, Cus D'Amato would be accused of burying dirt about Mike Tyson so as not to smudge the portrait of Tyson that he was crafting.

## Chapter 14

1. "Legion Fight Card Entertains Big Crowd, *Las Vegas Age,* September 25, 1926, p. 1.

2. John F. Cahlan, "Punts, Pokes, Putouts," *Las Vegas Review-Journal,* August 22, 1942, p. 7. Managed by Eddie Mead in his fighting days, Lynch had taken control of Armstrong after Mead's sudden death on May 25, 1942. As indicated in the record books, this fight was not in Las Vegas per se, but in Pittman. Expunged from the map when it was annexed by the Las Vegas border town of Henderson, Pittman was originally a Hooverville — an auto and tent camp for people seeking work at the dam — and then company housing for workers at a big magnesium plant.

## Chapter 15

1. Hank Greenspun, "Where I Stand," *Las Vegas Sun,* April 11, 1955, p. 1.

## Chapter 16

1. Howard Cosell, *Like It Is,* p. 288.

2. Many people got the wrong impression when reading that Louis was employed as a greeter, his unofficial title. The word conveyed the image of a uniformed valet who welcomes guests as they check in. To the contrary, Louis dressed casually, had no set hours, and when he was summoned to "schmooze," it was often to a golf course. On the links, Louis was a wonderful companion, known for his drop-dead one-liners.

His funeral was held in a large tent on the Caesars Palace parking lot. Frank Sinatra and Sammy Davis, Jr., were among those paying tribute in a service cli-

maxed by a stirring eulogy delivered by a young preacher named Jesse Jackson. Sinatra, Muhammad Ali, and Larry Holmes were among the pallbearers. Louis was buried with full military honors at Arlington National Cemetery.

3. Liston was a 3/1 favorite over Martin, a former sparring partner who worked as an assemblyman in a Philadelphia locomotive plant. Trailing on the scorecards, Martin brought the fight to a close in the ninth frame with a wicked combination. Liston needed a second shot of smelling salts to regain consciousness. The upset ruined a proposed match between Sonny and Joe Frazier. Martin suffered a detached retina during the fight and never fought again.

## Chapter 17

1. The World Boxing Association (WBA) sprouted from the National Boxing Association of the United States, an organization formed in 1921. Delegates from 15 states attended the constitutional convention. Representatives from New York were present, but did not participate in the voting process. The New York Commission was unwilling to subordinate its authority.

2. Ali-Liston II went to Maine after being kicked out of Las Vegas and Boston. Nevada governor Grant Sawyer prohibited the fight from taking place in his jurisdiction, heeding the plea of boxing commissioner Art Lurie, who was spooked by rumors of a fix. Liston succumbed to a phantom punch in the opening round of his second fight with Ali, but the general feeling was that the fight was on the level.

3. *The Ring,* September 23, 1963, p. 11.

4. Pacheco shared his dire warnings with reporters from many dailies. This quotation is from the Las Vegas weekly tabloid *Sports Form,* July 5, 1980, p. 12.

5. On August 20, 1981, four months before his swan song fight, Ali was licensed to fight in Richland County, South Carolina. At a crowded news conference in the Carolina Coliseum in the state capital of Columbia, Ali announced that he planned to fight Gerry Cooney for the world heavyweight title at this venue. Ali was confident that Cooney would win his forthcoming match with Larry Holmes.

## Chapter 18

1. Caesars Palace opened in 1966 with 680 rooms. During the property's heyday as the Mecca of boxing, the majority stockholders were the Perlman brothers, Clifford and Stuart, who built their fortune from the seed of a Miami Beach hot dog stand. Executives Harry Wald, a former Nevada Army National Guard brigadier general, and Bob Halloran, a former Miami sportscaster, played significant roles in bringing the big fights to Caesars Palace. Subsequent management teams under new ownerships were less committed to sports promotions. The property currently has 3349 rooms in five towers and is the flagship of the Harrah's casino chain.

2. Royce Feour, "Leonard-Hagler Investigation Reveals No Wrongdoing," *Review-Journal,* May 30, 1987, p. 2C. For a good profile of Billy Baxter see John Underwood, "Look Up and He's Got Your Money," *Sports Illustrated,* May 28, 1984, pp. 81–94.

# Chapter 19

1. William Nack, "Ready To Soar His Way to the Very Top," *Sports Illustrated,* Jan. 6, 1986, pp. 22–27.
2. *The Ring,* Sept. 1961, p. 28.
3. A four-time New York City Golden Gloves Champion, Mitch "Blood" Green had a second fight with Tyson that attracted considerably more news coverage. On August 23, 1988, shortly before dawn, they clashed on the street in front of a Harlem clothing store. Tyson dominated the impromptu fracas, but suffered a broken hand.
4. The author interviewed Mackie Shilstone for this book. For more about the relationship between Shilstone and Spinks see Pat Putnam, "A Champ With Strange Ideas," *Sports Illustrated,* October 7, 1985, pp. 44–46.
5. During her marriage to Tyson, it was widely rumored that Givens had an affair with Donald Trump. In 1997, she married her Yugoslavian tennis instructor. The marriage was quickly dissolved. Two years later, she had a son with tennis pro Murphy Jensen.
6. Stephen Nover, "Big Bets Don't Faze Mirage's Vaccaro," *Review-Journal,* January 23, 1994, p. 4E. Vaccaro, a longtime friend of the author, conveyed other figures to other reporters (see Royce Feour, "Douglas Victory over Tyson voted Biggest Upset in Boxing History," *Review-Journal,* February 13, 2000, p. 11C). The largest of the three wagers reported to Nover, sized to win $3650 after breakage, was curious, to say the least. While the betting line was indeed volatile, it often "moved on air" as Vaccaro played with the number as an antidote to boredom, creating the illusion of wagering activity.

# Chapter 21

1. Lore has it that William Holden gave Aragon his nickname. Holden starred in the movie version of *Golden Boy,* the 1936 play by Clifford Odets. In Odets' mawkish play, the central character is an angst-ridden violinist-turned-prizefighter. After watching Aragon in action, Holden purportedly said: "this fellow here is the real golden boy."
2. Quoted in Ross Newhan's column, *Los Angeles Times,* December 7, 1968, Section III, p. 5.

# Chapter 22

1. A larger crowd, reportedly 135,132, attended an August 16, 1941, show at Milwaukee's Juneau Park. However, there was an extenuating circumstance — the event was free! The bleachers, reserved for delegates to a visiting Eagles convention, seated only 13,000. Jack Dempsey refereed the main event, a non-title affair between middleweight champ Tony Zale and badly outclassed Billy Prior.

# Chapter 23

1. Dershowitz alleged that Tyson's accuser was motivated by financial gain. *Boxing Illustrated,* October 1992, pp. 20–23.

2. Reported in the *Review-Journal,* August 24, 1995, p. 1D.
3. *Review-Journal,* August 31, 1995, p. 9B.
4. *Review-Journal,* August 23, 1995, p. 1B
5. Miller reprised his stunt at a soccer match in England and later landed his home-built craft on the roof of Buckingham Palace, which got him banned from England for life. In March of 2003, hunters found his remains under a tree in a remote area of Valdez, Alaska. Reportedly despondent over medical bills from two heart surgeries, he had been reported missing six months earlier. The death of "Fan Man" was ruled a suicide by hanging.

# Chapter 24

1. Chuck DiRocco, "Insiders: 'Boxer Broke His Nose Before Fight?'" *Gaming Today,* September 16, 1995, p. 3.

# Chapter 25

1. Ali's letter to McCain, released to the Associated Press, contained a plug for the boxing reform bill that McCain named in Ali's honor. "Professional boxers have for too long been the target of unscrupulous managers and promoters," Ali wrote. "As witnessed, the three sanctioning organizations that award the title belts have joined the list of abusers" (*Review-Journal,* March 25, 1999, p. C8). Who actually wrote this letter, and whether it expressed Ali's true feelings, will likely never be known.
2. *Review-Journal,* March 15, 1999, p. 2C.
3. J.M. Kalil, "Police Report Details on Tyson Case," *Review-Journal,* February 23, 2002, pp. 1, 6. If the charges had not been dropped, Tyson would have been charged with 10 counts of sexual assault. The unnamed accusers were identified as a 19-year-old college student from a small town in Michigan and a 23-year-old topless dancer. During a search of Tyson's home, police confiscated videotapes of him having sex with numerous women.

# Chapter 26

1. Mark Schlabach, "The Punch Line? A Knockout Debt," *Washington Post,* July 24, 2004, pp. D1–3. In this article, Schlabach noted that while Tyson had set up separate trust accounts for his five children (three born out of wedlock), he had only recently set aside some money for himself, depositing $5000 in a money-market account.

# Chapter 28

1. "Fight Fixer Handed Prison Term," *Review-Journal,* February 23, 2005, p. 1.
2. A block-long entertainment palace consuming more square feet than any building in the city, Mechanics Pavilion was destroyed by fire on the day of the great San Francisco earthquake. In its final hours before evacuation, the facility served as a hospital and morgue. A

smaller edifice built after the earthquake took the name Mechanics Pavilion, but this structure was too small for major fights and boxing in and around San Francisco became largely an outdoor sport.

3. In his 1998 book *Reinventing Wyatt Earp*, Allen Barra asserts that the revisionists overcorrected in their zeal to set the record straight, manufacturing a new Earp as counterfeit as the gilt-edged Earp of romanticized Western folklore. Regarding the Sharkey-Fitzsimmons brouhaha, Barra opined that it was unlikely that a crooked referee would wait until the eighth round to invent a phantom punch. He noted that referees versed in the new Queensberry rules were in short supply and faulted the anti-Earp brigade for implying that this was an isolated instance of puzzling behavior by a boxing referee. He might have added that the dip in the wagering odds would nowadays be considered a mundane fluctuation.

4. *New Orleans Item*, April 14, 1915, p. 8.

## Chapter 29

1. Kevin Iole, "UFC Continues Fight for Public Acceptance," *Review-Journal*, November 17, 2002, p. 6C. Iole penned the first in-depth newspaper article on the evolution of mixed martial arts into America's fastest-growing spectator sport. Titled "Fresh Blood," it ran in the *Review-Journal* on August 20, 2006 (pp. 1–4J). See also Ron Kantowski, "Fighting to the Top, Q + A: Lorenzo Fertitta and Dana White," *Las Vegas Sun*, April 21, 2007, p. 6.

# Bibliography

Astor, Gerald. ...And a Credit to his Race. New York: E.P. Dutton, 1974.

Barra, Allen. Inventing Wyatt Earp: His Life and Many Legends. New York: Carroll and Graf, 1998.

Barton, George A. My Lifetime in Sports. Minneapolis: The Olympic Press, 1957.

Batchelor, Denzil. British Boxing. London: Collins, 1968.

Beadle, Bill. Boxing's Mister President. Dagenham, Essex: Wat Tyler Books, 1997.

Bell, Frank. Gladiators of the Glittering Gulches. Helena, MT: Western Horizons Books, 1985.

Bell, Leslie. Bella of Blackfriars. London: Odhams Press, 1961.

Berger, Phil. Blood Season: Tyson and the World of Boxing. New York: William Morrow, 1989.

Birley, Derek. Sport and the Making of Great Britain. Manchester: Manchester University Press, 1993.

Bodner, Allen. When Boxing Was a Jewish Sport. Westport, CT: Praeger, 1997.

Bogdan, Robert. Freak Show. Chicago: University of Chicago Press, 1988.

Bok, Richard. Joe Louis: The Great Black Hope. Dallas: Taylor Publishing Company, 1996.

Brady, William A. Showman. New York: E.P. Dutton & Co., 1937.

Brailsford, Dennis. Bareknuckles: A Social History of Prizefighting. Cambridge: Lutterworth Press, 1988.

Brenner, Teddy (as told to Barney Nagler). Only the Ring Was Square. Englewood Cliffs, NJ: Prentice-Hall, 1981.

Brier, Warren J. The Frightful Punishment: Con Orem and Montana's Great Glove Fights of the 1860s. Missoula: University of Montana Press, 1969.

Brown, Warren. Win, Lose, or Draw. New York: G.P. Putnam's Sons, 1947.

Cantwell, Robert. The Real McCoy. Princeton, NJ: Auerback Publishers, 1971.

Carpenter, Harry. Boxing: An Illustrated History. New York: Crescent Books, 1982.

Cavanaugh, Jack. Tunney: Boxing's Brainiest Champ and His Upset of the Great Jack Dempsey. New York: Random House, 2006.

Century, Douglas. Barney Ross. New York: Schocken Books, 2006.

Chadwick, Bruce. When the Game Was Black and White: The Illustrated History of Baseball's Negro Leagues. New York: Abbeville Press, 1992.

Chidsey, Donald Barr. John the Great. Garden City, NY: Doubleday, 1942.

Clapson, Mark. A Bit of a Flutter: Popular Gambling and English Society. Manchester: Manchester University Press, 1992.

Cochran, Charles B. Showman Looks On. London: J.M. Dent & Sons Ltd., 1945.

Cohane, Tim. Bypaths of Glory: A Sportswriter Looks Back. New York: Harper and Row, 1963.

Cohen, Mickey. In My Own Words. Englewood Cliffs, NJ: Prentice-Hall, 1975.

Collins, Nigel. Boxing Babylon. New York: Citadel Press, 1990.

Conrad, Harold. Dear Muffo: 35 Years in the Fast Lane. New York: Stein and Day, 1982.

Cosell, Howard. Like It Is. Chicago: Playboy Press, 1974.

Croft-Cooke, Rupert. Bosie: Lord Alfred Douglas, His Friends and Enemies. Indianapolis: Bobbs-Merrill, 1963.

Dahlberg, Tim. Fight Town. Las Vegas: Stephens Press, 2004.

Daniel, Daniel M. The Jacobs Story. New York: The Ring Book Shop, Inc., 1950.

Davies, Richard O. Sports in American Life: A History. Malden, Massachusetts: Blackwell Publishing, 2007.

Deighty, Guy. Noble and Manly: The History of the National Sporting Club. London: Hutchinson, 1956.

DeLisa, Michael C. *Cinderella Man: The James J. Braddock Story*. Preston, England: Milo Books, 2005.

DeMattos, Jack. *Masterson and Roosevelt*. College Station, TX: Creative Publishing Company, 1984.

_____. *The Earp Decision*. College Station, TX: Creative Publishing Company, 1989.

Dennet, Andrea Stulman. *Weird and Wonderful: The Dime Museum in America*. New York: New York University Press, 1997.

Doten, Alf. *The Journals of Alfred Doten 1849–1903*. Edited by Walter Van Tilburg Clark. Reno: University of Nevada Press, 1973.

Duff, Mickey (with Bob Mee). *Twenty and Out*. London: Collins Willow, 1999.

Dunphy, Don. *Don Dunphy at Ringside*. New York: Henry Holt and Company, 1988.

Durso, Joseph. *Madison Square Garden: 100 Years of History*. New York: Simon and Schuster, 1979.

Edwards, Billy. *Legendary Boxers of the Golden Age*. Secaucus, NJ: Chartwell Books, 1990 (originally published by the Pugilistic Publishing Company of London and Philadelphia under the title *The Pugilistic Portrait Gallery*).

Egan, Pierce. *Boxiana; or, Sketches of Ancient and Modern Pugilism from the Days of the Renowned Broughton and Slack, to the Championship of Cribb*. An Elibron Classic originally published by George Virtue and by Ivy Lane, London, in 1830.

Erenberg, Lewis A. *The Greatest Fight of our Generation: Louis vs. Schmeling*. New York: Oxford University Press, 2006.

Evensen, Bruce J. *When Dempsey Fought Tunney: Heroes, Hokum, and Storytelling in the Jazz Age*. Knoxville: University of Tennessee Press, 1996.

Fair, James R. *Give Him to the Angels: The Story of Harry Greb*. New York: Smith and Durrell, 1946.

Farr, Finis. *Black Champion: The Life and Times of Jack Johnson*. New York: Charles Scribner's Sons, 1964.

Fields, Armond. *James J. Corbett: A Biography of the Heavyweight Boxing Champion and Popular Theatre Headliner*. Jefferson, NC: McFarland, 2001.

Fleischer, Nat. *Fifty Years at Ringside*. New York: Greenwood Press, 1969.

Ford, John. *Prizefighting: The Age of Regency Boximania*. Newton Abbot: David and Charles, 1971.

Fountain, Charles. *Sportswriter: The Life and Times of Grantland Rice*. New York: Oxford University Press, 1993.

Fowler, Gene. *Beau James: The Life & Times of Jimmy Walker*. New York: The Viking Press, 1949.

Fried, Ronald K. *Corner Men: Great Boxing Trainers*. New York: Four Walls Eight Windows, 1991.

Gallico, Paul. *Farewell to Sport*. New York: Alfred A. Knopf, 1938.

Goldstein, Ruby, and Frank Graham. *Third Man in the Ring*. New York: Funk and Wagnall, 1959.

Gorn, Elliott J. *The Manly Art: Bare-Knuckle Prizefighting in America*. Ithaca: Cornell University Press, 1986.

Graham, Frank Jr. *A Farewell to Heroes*. New York: The Viking Press, 1981.

Griffin, Marcus. *Wise Guy: James J. Johnston, a Rhapsody in Fistics*. New York: Vanguard Press, 1933.

Grombach, John V. *The Saga of the Fist: The 9,000 Year Story of Boxing in Text and Pictures*. Cranbury, NJ: A.S. Barnes and Company, 1977.

Hague, Jim. *Braddock: The Rise of the Cinderella Man*. New York: Chamberlain Bros., 2005.

Harding, John (with Jack Berg). *Jack Kid Berg*. London: Robson Books, 1987.

Heimer, Mel. *The Long Count*. New York: Atheneum, 1969.

Heinz, W.C., ed. *The Fireside Book of Boxing*. New York: Simon and Schuster, 1961.

_____. *Once They Heard the Cheers*. Garden City, NY: Doubleday, 1979.

Henderson, Eugene. *Box On*. London: The Sportsmans Book Club, 1959.

Hoffer, Richard. *A Savage Business: The Comeback and Comedown of Mike Tyson*. New York: Simon and Schuster, 1961.

Holloway, John B. *Josh and Satch*. Westport, CT: Meckler, 1991.

Horan, James David. *The Authentic Wild West*. New York: Crown Publishers, 1980.

Hoyt, Edwin P. *A Gentleman of Broadway: The Story of Damon Runyon*. New York: Little, Brown and Company: 1964.

Isenberg, Michael T. *John L. Sullivan and his America*. Urbana: University of Chicago Press, 1988.

Johnson, John. *Jack Johnson Is a Dandy: An Autobiography*. New York: Chelsea House, 1969 (reprint of Johnson's 1926 autobiography).

Johnston, Alexander. *Ten—And Out! The Complete Story of the Prize Ring in America*. New York: Ives Washburn, 1947.

Jones, Jimmy. *King of the Canebrakes*. Macon, GA: Southern Press, 1969.

Joselit, Jenna Weissman. *Our Gang: Jewish Crime and the New York Jewish Community, 1900–1940*. Bloomington: Indiana University Press, 1983.

Kahn, Roger. *A Flame of Pure Fire*. New York: Harcourt Brace & Company, 1999.

Kawakami, Tim. *Golden Boy: The Fame, Money, and Mystery of Oscar De La Hoya*. Kansas City, MO: Andrews McMeel, 1999.

Kram, Mark. *Ghosts of Manila*. New York: HarperCollins, 2001.

Lake, Stuart. *Wyatt Earp: Frontier Marshall*. New York: Houghton Mifflin Company, 1931.

LaMotta, Jake (with Joseph Carter and Peter Savage). *Raging Bull: My Story*. Englewood Cliffs, New Jersey: Prentice-Hall, 1970.

Lardner, John. *It Beats Working*. New York: J.B. Lippincott Company, 1947.

_____. *White Hopes and Other Tigers.* Philadelphia: J.B. Lippincott, 1991.

Lardner, Rex. *The Legendary Champions.* New York: American Heritage Press, 1972.

Legge, Harry. *A Penny a Punch.* Christchurch, Dorset: Curtis Publications, 1981.

Leibling, A.J. *The Sweet Science.* New York: The Viking Press, 1956.

Levine, Peter. *Ellis Island to Ebbets Field: Sport and the American Jewish Experience.* New York: Oxford University Press, 1992.

Littlewood, Thomas B. *Arch: A Promoter, Not a Poet.* Ames: Iowa State University Press, 1990.

London, Joan. *Jack London and His Times.* Seattle: University of Washington Press, 1968.

Margolick, David. *Beyond Glory: Joe Louis vs. Max Schmeling, and a World on the Brink.* New York: Alfred A. Knopf, 2005.

McCabe, James D., Jr. *New York by Gaslight.* New York: Arlington House, 1994.

McCallum, John (with Dumb Dan Morgan). *Dumb Dan.* New York: Tedson Publishing, 1953.

McCallum, John D. *The World Heavyweight Boxing Championship.* Radnor, PA: Chilton Book Company, 1974.

McIlvanney, Hugh. *McIlvanney on Boxing: An Anthology.* New York: Beaufort Books, 1982.

Mead, Chris. *Joe Louis: Black Hero in White America.* New York: Charles Scribner's Sons, 1985.

Mee, Bob. *Bare Fists: The History of Bare-Knuckle Prizefighting.* Woodstock, NY: Overlook Press, 2001.

Miletich, Leo N. *Dan Stuart's Fistic Carnival.* College Station: Texas A & M Press, 1994.

Moehring, Eugene P. *Resort City in the Sunbelt: Las Vegas 1930–1970.* Reno: University of Nevada Press, 1989.

Mosedale, John. *The Man Who Invented Broadway.* New York: Richard Marek Publishers, 1981.

Mullan, Harry. *The Ultimate Encyclopedia of Boxing.* London: Chartwell Books, 1996.

Musser, Charles. *The Emergence of Cinema: The American Screen to 1907.* New York: Charles Scribner's Sons, 1990.

Myler, Patrick. *The Fighting Irish.* Kerry, Ireland, and Dover, NH: Brandon Book Publishers, Ltd., 1987.

Nagler, Barney. *James Norris and the Decline of Boxing.* Indianapolis: The Bobbs-Merrill Company, 1964.

O'Connor, Richard. *Bat Masterson.* Garden City, New York: Doubleday, 1957.

Odd, Gilbert. *Encyclopedia of Boxing.* New York: Crescent Books, 1983.

Pilat, Oliver. *Pegler: Angry Man of the Press.* Boston: Beacon Press, 1963.

Pollack, Adam J. *John L. Sullivan: The Career of the First Gloved Heavyweight Champion.* Jefferson, NC: McFarland, 2006.

Rader, Benjamin G. *American Sports: From the Age of Folk Games to the Age of Televised Sports.* Upper Saddle River, NJ: Prentice Hall, 2004.

Radford, Peter. *The Celebrated Captain Barclay.* London: Headline Book Publishing, 2001.

Reid, J.C. *Bucks and Bruisers: Pierce Egan and Regency England.* London: Routledge and Kegan Paul, 1971.

Reiss, Steven A. *City Games: The Evolution of American Society and the Rise of Sports.* Urbana: University of Illinois Press, 1989.

Remnick, David. *King of the World: Muhammad Ali and the Rise of an American Hero.* New York: Random House, 1998.

Rice, George Graham. *My Adventures with Your Money.* Las Vegas: Nevada Publications, 1986 (originally published by R.C. Badger Publishing House of Boston in 1913).

Rice, Grantland. *The Tumult and the Shouting: My Life in Sport.* New York: A.S. Barnes and Company, 1954.

Roberts, Randy. *Jack Dempsey: The Manassa Mauler.* Baton Rouge: Louisiana State University Press, 1979.

_____. *Papa Jack—Jack Johnson and the Era of White Hopes.* New York: The Free Press, 1983.

Rose, Charlie. *Life's a Knockout.* London: Hutchinson's Library of Sports and Pastimes, 1953.

Ross, Barney, and Martin Abramson. *No Man Stands Alone.* Philadelphia: J.B. Lippincott, 1957.

Rothman, Hal. *Neon Metropolis: How Las Vegas Started the Twenty-First Century.* New York: Routledge, 2002.

Rozen, Wayne A. *America on the Ropes: A Pictorial History of the Johnson-Jeffries Fight.* Binghamton, NY: Casey Press, 2004.

Ruck, Bob. *Sandlot Seasons: Sport in Black Pittsburgh.* Urbana: University of Illinois Press, 1987.

Rudd, Irving, and Stan Fischler. *The Sporting Life.* New York: St. Martin's Press, 1990.

Sammons, Jeffrey T. *Beyond the Ring: The Role of Boxing in American Society.* Urbana: University of Illinois Press, 1988.

Samuels, Charles. *The Magnificent Rube: The Life and Gaudy Times of Tex Rickard.* New York: McGraw-Hill, 1957.

Sante, Luc. *Low Life: Lures and Snares of Old New York.* New York: Farrar Straus Giroux, 1991.

Sawyer, Tom. *The Noble Art: An Artistic and Literary Celebration of the Old English Prize-Ring.* London: Unwin Hyman Limited, 1989.

Scarne, John. *The Odds Against Me.* New York: Simon and Schuster, 1966.

Schulberg, Budd. *Sparring with Hemingway.* Chicago: Ivan R. Dee, 1995.

Schulian, John. *Writers' Fighters and Other Sweet Scientists.* Kansas City: Andrews and McMeel, 1983.

Skehan, Everett M. *Rocky Marciano.* London: Robson Books, 1983.

Snelling, O.F. *A Bedside Book of Boxing.* London: Pelham Books, 1972.

Solomons, Jack. *Jack Solomons Tells All.* London: Rich & Cowan, 1951.

Somers, Dale A. *The Rise of Sports in New Orleans 1850–1900.* Baton Rouge: Louisiana State University Press, 1972.

Sugar, Bert Randolph. *The 100 Greatest Boxers of All Time.* New York: Bonanza Books, 1984.

Sullivan, Russell. *Rocky Marciano: The Rock and His Times.* Urbana: University of Illinois Press, 2002.

Sutherland, Douglas. *The Yellow Earl.* New York: Coward-McCann, 1965.

Tosches, Nick. *The Devil and Sonny Liston.* Boston: Little, Brown and Company, 2000.

Toulmin, Vanessa. *A Fair Fight: An Illustrated Review of Boxing on the British Fairgrounds.* Oldham: World's Fair Publications, 1999.

Van Every, Edward. *Muldoon: The Solid Man of Sport.* New York: Frederick A. Stokes Company, 1928.

Walker, Mickey (with Joe Reichler). *The Toy Bulldog and His Times.* New York: Random House, 1961.

Walsh, George. *Gentleman Jimmy Walker.* New York: Praeger, 1974.

Walter, Gerald (with Patsy Hagate). *White Ties and Fisticuffs: The Story of Patsy Hagate, the Famous Boxing Announcer.* London: Hutchinson's, 1951.

Ward, Geoffrey C. *Unforgivable Blackness: The Rise and Fall of Jack Johnson.* New York: Alfred A. Knopf, 2004.

Watson, Margaret G. *Silver Theatre: Amusements of the Mining Frontier of Early Nevada.* Glendale, CA: The Arthur H. Clark Company, 1964.

Winick, Charles, and Paul M. Kinsie. *The Lively Commerce: Prostitution in the United States.* Chicago: Quadrangle Books, 1971.

Zanjani, Sally. *Goldfield: The Last Gold Rush on the Western Frontier.* Athens: Ohio University Press, 1992.

# Index

261